KT-230-024

A Day in the Life: Polar Animals

Emperor Penguin

Katie Marsico

WAKEFIELD LIBRARIES
30000010232813

www.raintreepublishers.co.uk
Visit our website to find out more information about Raintree books.

To order:
Phone 0845 6044371
Fax +44 (0) 1865 312263
Email myorders@raintreepublishers.co.uk

Customers from outside the UK please telephone +44 1865 312262

Raintree is an imprint of Capstone Global Library Limited, a company incorporated in England and Wales having its registered office at 7 Pilgrim Street, London, EC4V 6LB – Registered company number: 6695582

Text © Capstone Global Library Limited 2012
First published in hardback in 2012
First published in paperback in 2013
The moral rights of the proprietor have been asserted.

All rights reserved. No part of this publication may be reproduced in any form or by any means (including photocopying or storing it in any medium by electronic means and whether or not transiently or incidentally to some other use of this publication) without the written permission of the copyright owner, except in accordance with the provisions of the Copyright, Designs and Patents Act 1988 or under the terms of a licence issued by the Copyright Licensing Agency, Saffron House, 6–10 Kirby Street, London EC1N 8TS (www.cla.co.uk). Applications for the copyright owner's written permission should be addressed to the publisher.

Edited by Daniel Nunn, Rebecca Rissman, and Sian Smith
Designed by Joanna Hinton-Malivoire
Picture research by Hannah Taylor
Original illustrations © Capstone Global Library
Production by Victoria Fitzgerald
Originated by Capstone Global Library Ltd
Printed and bound in China by South China Printing Company Ltd

ISBN 978 1 406 22880 9 (hardback)
15 14 13 12 11
10 9 8 7 6 5 4 3 2 1

ISBN 978 1 406 22887 8 (paperback)
16 15 14 13 12
10 9 8 7 6 5 4 3 2 1

British Library Cataloguing in Publication Data

Marsico, Katie, 1980-
Emperor penguin. -- (A day in the life. Polar animals)
1. Emperor penguin--Juvenile literature.
I. Title II. Series
598.4'7-dc22

Acknowledgements

We would like to thank the following for permission to reproduce photographs: Corbis pp. 12 (Paul Nicklen), 14 (Ralph Lee Hopkins), 18 (Frans Lanting), 23d (Gerald & Buff Corsi/Visuals Unlimited Inc.); Getty Images pp. 9 (Minden Pictures/Pete Oxford), 13 (Nobert Wu); Photolibrary pp. 7, 23f (Picture Press/Thorsten Milse), 8, 23b (Superstock/ John Higdon), 10, 23a (All Canada Photos/ Wayne Lynch), 11 (Oxford Scientific/Doug Allan), 15 (Oxford Scientific/Oliver Kruger), 17 (Photononstop/Christian Simonet), 19 (Tsuneo Nakamura), 20 (Peter Arnold Images/Bruno P Zehnder), 22 (Oxford Scientific/Sue Flood); Shutterstock pp. 4 (© Bryan Lintott), 5, 16, 21, 23c (© Gentoo Multimedia Ltd.), 6, 23e (© Armin Rose).

Cover photograph of emperor penguins (Aptenodytes forsteri) near their nesting colony at Atka Bay, Weddell Sea, Antarctica reproduced with permission of Photolibrary (All Canada Photos/ Wayne Lynch). Back cover photographs reproduced with permission of Shutterstock: flipper (© Armin Rose), chick (© Gentoo Multimedia Ltd.).

The publisher would like to thank Michael Bright for his assistance in the preparation of this book.

Every effort has been made to contact copyright holders of material reproduced in this book. Any omissions will be rectified in subsequent printings if notice is given to the publisher.

Disclaimer

All the Internet addresses (URLs) given in this book were valid at the time of going to press. However, due to the dynamic nature of the Internet, some addresses may have changed or ceased to exist since publication. While the author and publishers regret any inconvenience this may cause readers, no responsibility for any such changes can be accepted by either the author or the publishers.

Contents

Some words are shown in bold, **like this**.
You can find them in the glossary on page 23.

What is an emperor penguin?

An emperor penguin is a large bird that lives in snowy areas.

Birds are feathered animals that have wings and lay eggs.

Emperor penguins cannot fly.

They have other ways of surviving in a world of snow and ice.

What do emperor penguins look like?

Emperor penguins are the largest type of penguin.

They are mainly black and white but have some yellow feathers.

These feathers are **waterproof** and keep the birds warm and dry.

Emperor penguins also have **webbed** feet and flippers to help them swim.

Where do emperor penguins live?

Emperor penguins live in **Antarctica**.

In Antarctica it is light all day and all night for part of the summer.

In Antarctica it is dark all day and all night for part of the winter.

Antarctica is the coldest and windiest place on Earth.

What do emperor penguins do in the day?

Emperor penguins are usually most **active** during the day.

They spend the day swimming and searching for food.

Emperor penguins are excellent swimmers and divers.

They dive underwater for about two to eight minutes, before going up for air.

What do emperor penguins eat?

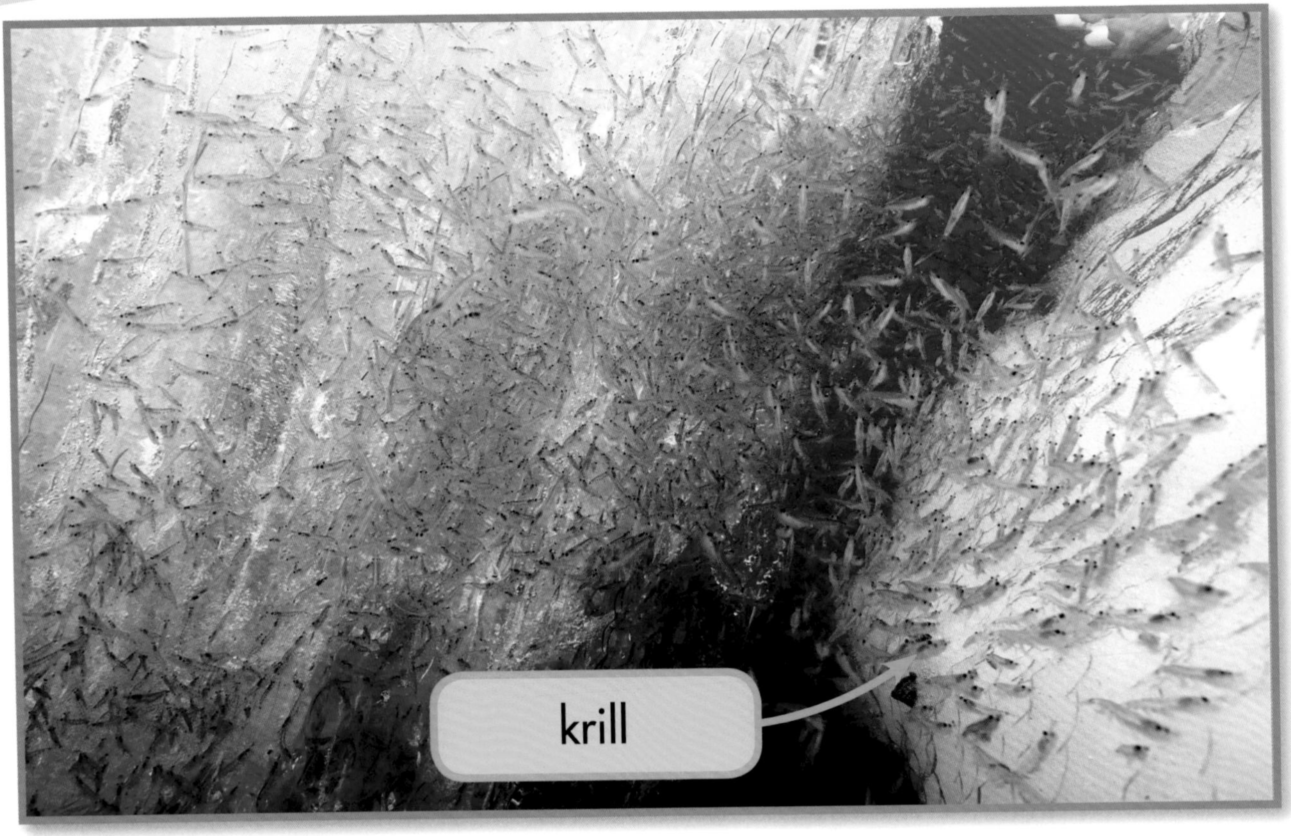

Emperor penguins use their beaks to catch fish.

They also eat squid and tiny animals called **krill**.

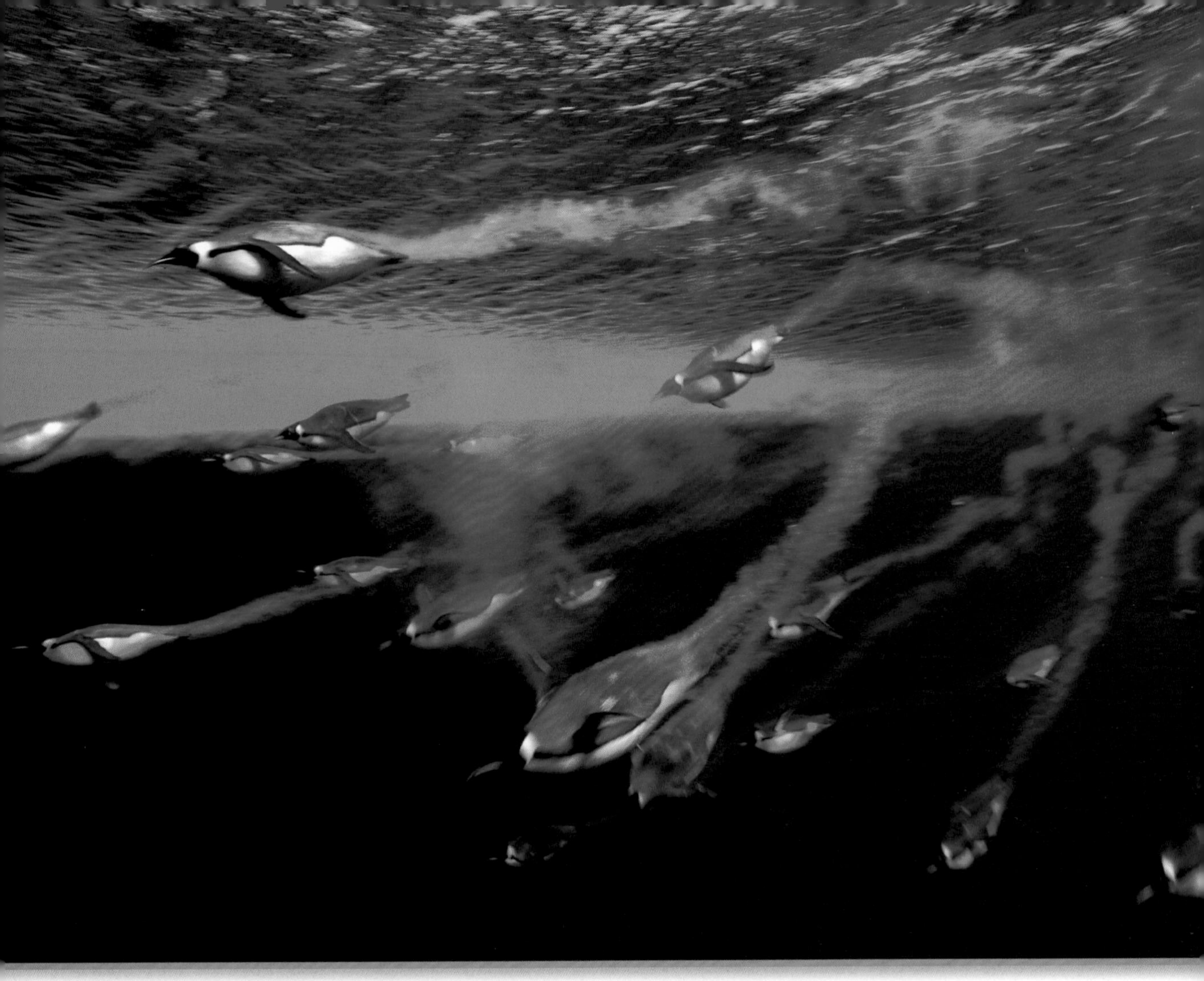

Emperor penguins swim far and dive deep into the ocean to find food.

They dive for food about 26 times every day.

What hunts emperor penguins?

Leopard seals and killer whales hunt emperor penguins.

These animals often sneak up on the penguins as they enter the water.

Emperor penguins also have enemies on the ice during daylight hours.

Sea birds like skuas and petrels eat eggs and baby penguins.

Do emperor penguins live in groups?

Emperor penguins live in groups called colonies.

There can be between a few hundred birds and tens of thousands of birds in a colony.

Emperor penguins travel long distances during the year.

They travel to different places to lay eggs and search for food.

What do emperor penguins do at night?

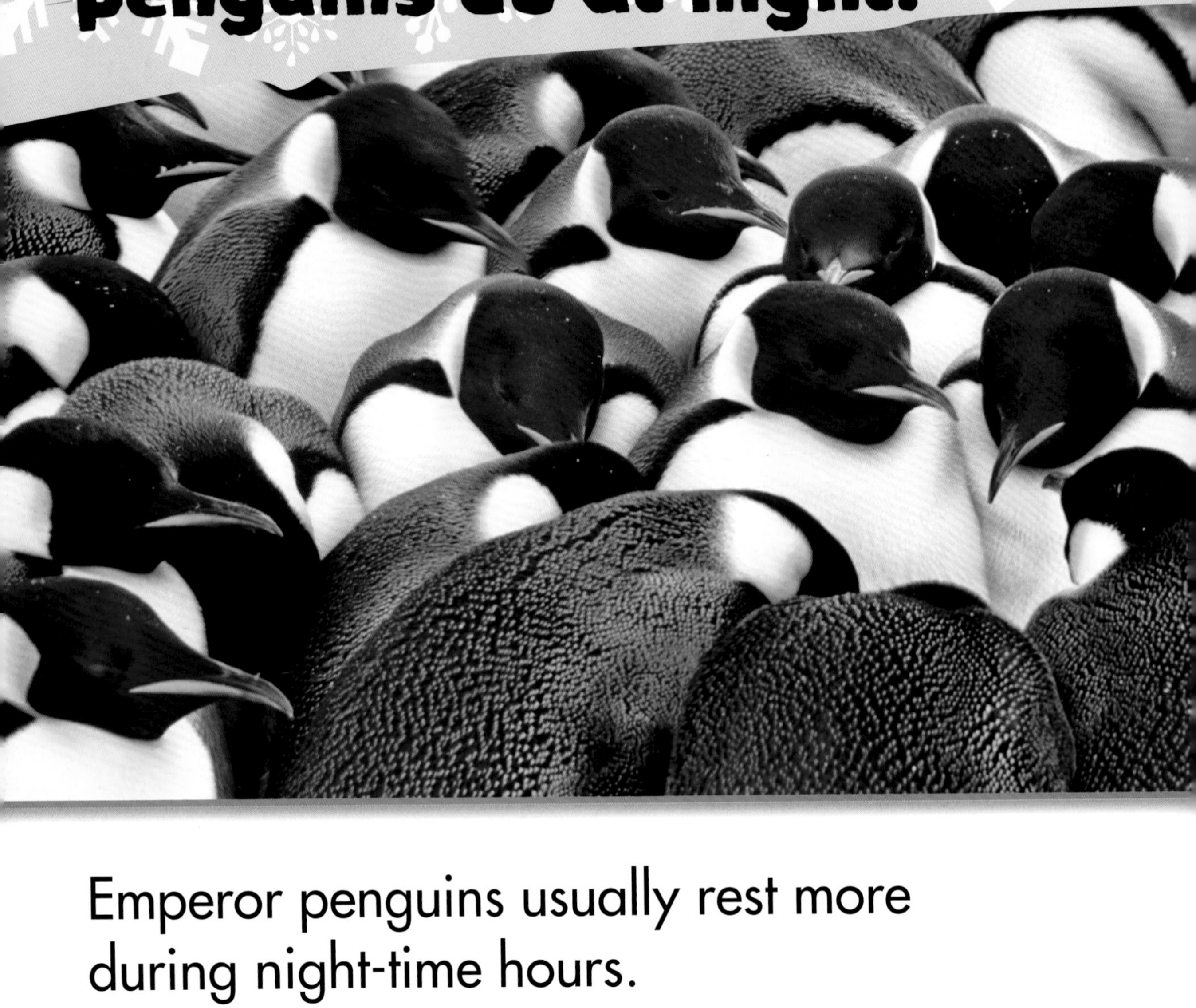

Emperor penguins usually rest more during night-time hours.

They keep warm by huddling together in groups.

Emperor penguins can sleep while they are standing up.

This keeps their bodies away from the cold ice.

What are baby emperor penguins like?

A mother emperor penguin lays one egg every year.

The father balances the egg on his feet. He keeps the egg warm until it hatches.

Both parents take turns caring for the fuzzy **chick** for about 150 days.

Then young emperor penguins leave their parents to explore the snowy world around them!

Emperor penguin body map

Glossary

active busy doing lots of things

Antarctica very cold continent located at the South Pole

chick baby emperor penguin

krill small shrimp-like animals

waterproof not allowing water to soak through

webbed having toes that are connected by a thin fold of skin

Find out more

Books

Arctic and Antarctic (Eye Wonder), Lorie Mack (DK Publishing, 2006)
Emperor Penguins of the Antarctic, Sara Miller (PowerKids Press, 2009)

Websites

www.kidskonnect.com/subject-index/13-animals/44-penguins.html
Find out interesting facts about penguins on this website.

www.kids.nationalgeographic.com/kids/animals/creaturefeature/emperor-penguin/
Watch a video on emperor penguins and learn all about them on the National Geographic website.

Index

CONTENTS

KT-466-484

AUTHOR'S NOTE

The central aims of this book are to encourage students to think through their own historical judgements and to organise their study of history effectively so that their efforts produce the best A or AS-level results of which they are capable. The vast majority of students work very hard at this subject; they know a great deal. Too often in examinations and assessed coursework this knowledge is not used to the best effect: it is not adapted directly enough to the questions which have been set. Student reading of textbooks does not seem to give enough clues on thinking in terms of historical problems which need to be argued about or commented upon. If this book has any virtue it is that it tries to provide these clues. So often students have worked so hard that they have not thought through the purpose of their study of history. It could well be sensible to work less and to think more about what you are doing. Do not use this book uncritically; the advice, and especially the proposed answers to typical A-level questions, are there to be thought about and to be challenged. You may enjoy history or its study may just be a necessary chore, but in either case you have everything to gain from using your time to the maximum effect.

I would like to thank the editors of this study series and Gordon Halliday of Maidstone for constant help and encouragement in the writing of this book. The cartoons which enliven Chapters 2 and 3 are the work of Jacqueline East, a gifted young book illustrator of Bristol. I have been helped greatly with specific problems by Hilary Crompton, Pam Moore, Ruth Powell and Dilwyn Porter, all of Worcester, and generally by my colleagues in the world of A-level history examining. My chief professional debt is to my colleagues in the History Division at Worcester College of Higher Education, who have created there an oasis of good humour, high professional competence and academic excellence. My main personal debt is to Susan, my wife, who had the good sense to grow fuchsias instead. Finally I must acknowledge the role of those who run the affairs of Worcestershire County Cricket Club, whose 'improvements' at the country's most attractive cricket ground ended my obsession with watching the game and so released the hours needed to write this piece.

NAMES AND ADDRESSES OF THE EXAM BOARDS

Associated Examining Board (AEB)
Stag Hill House
Guildford
Surrey GU2 5XJ

University of Cambridge Local Examinations Syndicate (UCLES)
Syndicate Buildings
1 Hills Road
Cambridge CB1 2EU

Northern Examinations and Assessment Board (NEAB)
Devas Street
Manchester M15 6EX

University of London Examinations and Assessment Council (ULEAC)
Stewart House
32 Russell Square
London WC1B 5DN

Northern Ireland Schools Examinations and Assessment Council (NISEAC)
Beechill House
42 Beechill Road
Belfast BT8 4RS

Oxford and Cambridge Schools Examination Board (OCSEB)
Purbeck House
Purbeck Road
Cambridge CB2 2PU

Oxford Delegacy of Local Examinations (ODLE)
Ewert Place
Summertown
Oxford OX2 7BZ

Scottish Examination Board (SEB)
Ironmills Road
Dalkeith
Midlothian EH22 1LE

Welsh Joint Education Committee (WJEC)
245 Western Avenue
Cardiff CF5 2YX

CHAPTER 1

HISTORY AT ADVANCED AND AS-LEVEL

HOW THIS BOOK IS ORGANISED

A-LEVEL SYLLABUS STRUCTURE

NEW APPROACHES TO THE SYLLABUS

INDEPENDENT CANDIDATES

GETTING STARTED

This book is based on the conviction that many good A- or AS-level history students do not gain the best grades of which they are capable and which their efforts deserve. the main reason for this is that such students are content to put their heads down, receive a weekly dose of historical knowledge, write up some notes, compile some essays and move on to final examinations, often without pausing to analyse what they are trying to do and how best to go about it. It is a strange way to spend two valuable years of your life.

Many students could well achieve better grades by doing less work, provided that they thought about what they were trying to do and devised an effective study strategy. This book tries to help bring this about. It is offered to those who enjoy the study of history for its own sake and to those who would much prefer to be doing something more interesting. Efficient methods of study will be to the advantage of both groups. The simple central idea is that efficient students are those who are actively critical in their approach to study: they find out the dimensions of the task at the outset, check that they have appropriate resources available, and think about the way they are using their study time.

The examiners' report on the 1990 history examinations run by the University of London Examinations and Assessment Council contained the following:

> 'The weaker candidates, as always, had difficulty in the essays in selecting and adapting the material they had learnt to the precise requirements of the question asked. So often a moment's reflection and a brief comment could have promoted a slab of narrative so that it became a worthwhile contribution to an argument. The best candidates are analytical; their less ambitious colleagues should at least try to lace their narratives with pertinent comment.'

Read this passage through again; it gives you the best possible clues as to how improving your study techniques could transform your history examination marks out of all recognition.

ESSENTIAL PRINCIPLES

HOW THIS BOOK IS ORGANISED

The next section of Chapter 1 tries to define the purpose and the scope of the A-level history syllabus. The last section of the chapter is only for those (independent) students who need advice on which examination board syllabus to take.

Chapter 2 contains the heart of the matter; it first proposes a series of ideas for effective reading and writing of history at A-level, including the writing of assessed course work and the handling of documentary material. It would be useful to read this part through before proceeding to the later chapters. The ideas are for you to adopt or to adapt; you may well devise more useful alternative ideas, which will be fine, just as long as you do not drop into the habit of being so busy working that you do not have time to think about and to improve your patterns and techniques of study.

"Improve your study techniques."

The second part of Chapter 2 is concerned with revision and examination techniques; it can be looked through at this stage or left until after your studies are under way. Do remember to read it through at some stage during your course!

CHAPTERS 3–26: THE TOPICS

Fig. 1.1 gives a broad indication of the topics and examination boards for which this book will be useful.

Fig. 1.1 Topics and courses

EXAMINATION BOARDS									
CHAPTER AND TOPIC	A-LEVEL								SCOTTISH HIGHER
	AEB	*C*	*NEAB*	*L*	*NI*	*O*	*O&C*	*WJEC*	*SEB*
3 The Industrial Revolution	√	√	√	√	√	√	√	√	√
4 Social reform 1830–1870	√	√	√	√	√	√	√	√	√
5 Political life 1830–1868	√	√	√	√	√	√	√	√	√
6 Gladstone and Liberalism	√	√	√	√	√	√	√	√	√
7 Disraeli and the Conservative Party	√	√	√	√	√	√	√	√	√
8 Politics and society 1900–1914	√	√	√	√	√	√	√	√	√
9 Inter-war politics 1918–1939	√	√	√	√	√	√	√	√	√
10 Politics and society 1939–1951	√	√	√	√	√	√	√	√	√
11 British History 1950–1993	√	√	√	√	√	√	√	√	√
12 Europe: the 1815 Settlement	√	√	√	√	√	√	√	√	√
13 French history 1815–1870	√	√	√	√	√	√	√	√	√
14 Russian history 1815–1914	√	√	√	√	√	√	√	√	√
15 The Eastern question	√	√	√	√	√	√	√	√	√
16 Italian unification	√	√	√	√	√	√	√	√	√
17 German unification	√	√	√	√	√	√	√	√	√
18 France: the Third Republic	√	√	√	√	√	√	√	√	√
19 Causes of the First World War	√	√	√	√	√	√	√	√	√
20 USSR 1917–1941	√	√	√	√	√	√	√	√	√
21 Mussolini and Italy	√	√	√	√	√	√	√	√	√
22 Germany 1918–1939	√	√	√	√	√	√	√	√	√
23 The USSR since 1945	√	√	√	√	√	√	√	√	√
24 The USA since 1945	√	√	√	√		√	√		
25 Communism in China	√	√		√		√			
26 Western Europe since 1945	√	√		√	√	√	√	√	√

"Study the topic chapters in any sequence you think best."

These chapters are centred on different topic areas in British, European and modern world history. They can be taken in any order as they fit best into your particular syllabus. Each chapter sets up an area of study, proposes how to get started, identifies essential issues, lists some useful outline information, offers examples of questions with outline answer plans or examples of full answers by students or tutors for you to consider.

"Be critical of the 'Tutor's Answers' which are provided."

All the material in these chapters should be approached critically. Above all the 'Tutor's Answers' are not to be seen as perfect answers: look for ways of improving them. All were written within roughly forty-five minutes and without the aid of books. By the end of your course you will almost certainly have more knowledge to offer than these attempts contain. They do however try to stick to the point of the question as set!

Each chapter contains suggestions for introductory and further reading, for this book is not intended as a substitute for the use of textbooks and other reading. It is essential that you bear this in mind; all that is offered here is the prospect of making that reading more purposeful and effective.

At the end of each chapter there are proposals for linked topic areas. Your reading and writing on one topic should open up other related themes and you should be constantly on the lookout for getting double value for your efforts in this way. Take these linked themes and think out how you could most efficiently get started on studying them and what their essential issues are likely to be. Then look up questions in these areas in past papers. In this way you will have your own series of brief outlines of topic areas to supplement the examples offered here. If one of your examination papers is itself based on a quite detailed, restricted area of study then your topics for study and revision will have to break this up into even smaller areas. The best guidance for structuring the material will be contained in recent past examination papers. The examination is not competitive so you could usefully work at some of these strategies with other students. Remember none of this is intended to make you devote more time to studying history (unless you want to): it is rather to show you how to employ your time more effectively and to get a better A-level grade than you might have done otherwise.

“Use past examination papers to form your study patterns.”

A-LEVEL SYLLABUS STRUCTURE

“Get to know your syllabus.”

Most students will have their history syllabus chosen for them by the staff of their school or college. If you are following a syllabus concerned with the period after 1800 you will almost certainly find useful examination and study ideas in many of the topic chapters in this book. To make the best use of them you need to know the title and contents of the history syllabus on which you will be examined. Ideally you should find this out at the beginning of your A-level history course. You will then be in a position to make the most effective use of your study and revision time. Do not settle for being doled out one piece of subject matter after another with no idea of the overall structure of the task ahead.

For independent students, who are investigating which examination board syllabus they should enter for, there is more information at the end of this short chapter. The addresses of the examination boards are given on page iv.

THE CONTENT OF THE SYLLABUS

Typically you will take two examination papers each of three hours, both of which are largely, but not entirely, made up of essay questions. In a great number of history syllabuses the normal pattern is to take one paper in British history and one in European history: the period studied is often not identical in the two papers. Where there is overlap look for the possibility of study for one paper giving you valuable background for the other.

With several examination boards the two papers include one outline paper, where you will be expected to study at least a century within the outline dates given, and a special topic paper with a much narrower focus in time and content. In social and economic history syllabuses foreign history is often omitted and the two papers on British history are frequently divided chronologically or by means of an outline and an in-depth paper. There are also a growing number of syllabuses in modern world history where British history plays a very small part.

The first rule is get to know what your syllabus requires from you. Almost certainly you will not attempt to cover it all now but at least you will know what *not* to spend your time on.

NEW APPROACHES TO THE SYLLABUS

We are, in the 1990s, seeing the development of a variety of new A-level history syllabuses.

AS-LEVEL

This is now well established. It is intended to be at the same standard as A-level but to cover only half the range of content. The Cambridge Examinations Syndicate and the

Oxford and Cambridge Board have joined with the Southern Universities Board, who no longer offer A-level history, to offer a combined AS-level syllabus. Their booklet is a good introduction to AS-level and costs only a few pence.

"AS-level history is far from an easy option."

The pressure to widen the range of subjects studied by students aged 16 to 19 may lead to the rapid development of AS but this is by no means certain. Most students who take an AS-level do so in a subject linked to their other A-levels and, at this stage, there is little evidence of, say scientists, taking AS-level history – to widen their studies, though this may come. One disadvantage to history as an AS subject is that its study involves a lot of reading and students taking AS seem agreed that their studies take up much more than half the time of their companions who are taking the full A-level. It is not an easy option.

NEW EXAMINATION STYLES

"A rapidly changing assessment picture."

These logically follow from the introduction of a wide range of assessment procedures at GCSE level. As well as the already established use of documentary questions from the period being studied (i.e. primary sources) there are likely to be questions which require interpretation of given extracts from works by historians and, most radical of all, the use of coursework for a substantial part of the grade assessment. The new Syllabus E of the London Board examined for the first time in 1992, the recently introduced Individual Study of the Oxford and Cambridge Board and the History (Alternative–673) of the Associated Examining Board are examples of these new developments. The Cambridge Advanced Level History Project entitled *People, Power and Politics* is the most tightly structured of the new breed of examinations; started in 1985 it is still only at project stage in 1992. The Scottish Examination Board's Certificate of Sixth Form Studies also has a well established tradition of assessing coursework.

One feature of the new style syllabuses will be the opportunity to write about the aims and the techniques of historians and about their sources of evidence or to undertake a local history study. These matters are considered again in Chapter Two.

DOCUMENTARY QUESTIONS

Such questions are now a compulsory part of all examination board syllabuses. The style of questions asked varies much more than is the case with essay questions. All the boards give some indication of the topics on which they will, in each syllabus, be free to set document questions but some boards give much more specific information than do others. This affects the type of questions that are then set on the documents. The more information you are given in advance about the documents the more the questions are likely to expect full background knowledge to be available to support the answers. At the other extreme almost all of the marks could well be available for an intelligent study of the documents alone.

"Practice in using documents is essential."

You cannot avoid documentary questions so you must practise the techniques that they require well in advance of the examination. In order to understand what will be required from you, use only the past papers of the board for which you are entered.

If the decision on which syllabus to take is out of your hands you can now move on to the next chapter which examines the most effective techniques of study and revision.

INDEPENDENT CANDIDATES

If you are one of that rare breed, the totally independent candidate free to search for the ideal paper before you embark on your A- or AS-level studies, then a whiff of commonsense might be in order before you spend too much time and money pursuing your ideal.

There is no such thing as an easy period to study or an easy board to be examined by. All boards are seeking the same range of skills to be on display and the comparability of their standards is constantly scrutinised by the Schools Examination and Assessment Council. Some of the larger boards offer as many as thirty to forty different papers: it would be pointless to try to give their flavour here. If you have no strong preference as to which period you study then it would be commonsense to take a period available through local evening classes; in this case you should take the examination papers that the rest of the group are entered for and your search is over, only the study remains!

"There are no easy examination boards."

Fig. 1.2 An ideal syllabus may be difficult to find!

Even if you do not join an evening class it would be sensible to take the papers of a board which has a local examinations centre and a telephone call to your nearest Further Education College, to the secretary of a local school with a sixth form or the Local Education Office, could be the most direct route. Then contact the relevant board and ask them for their arrangements for private candidates.

> Consult your local board.

The pattern of examinations (though not the purpose or the techniques employed) in history examinations in Scotland is sufficiently distinctive to merit a first contact with the Scottish Examination Board to find out about both the Higher Grade and the Certificate in Sixth Year Studies arrangements. In Northern Ireland and Wales it would also be sensible first to contact the respective local board. See the addresses on page iv.

Although the Joint Matriculation Board is the most strongly represented in the north of England, the other English boards do have examination centres in the region. Elsewhere in England pursue the four remaining boards in any order and ask about both their arrangements for private candidates and about your own interests. The London board has special examination halls for private candidates in central London.

Those who wish to study a particular topic and no other will have to dig a little deeper. Try the main branch of your local library to see whether it holds copies of A-level syllabuses but do not be surprise if it does not have the full range, or indeed any. You then have to approach the examination boards in turn. Try to ask a specific question which can be answered by letter, for the full syllabus booklet might well cost you several pounds. Experience suggests that the boards are so busy that several days may pass before you receive a reply. There is no evidence that sending a stamped addressed envelope helps much.

All the English boards offer papers in the main stream of British and European political history from 1800 and either options, or complete syllabuses, purely on social and economic history. The Welsh and the Northern Ireland boards add to these, questions on Welsh and Irish history respectively, though neither offers the range of special options available elsewhere. In compensation both of these examination boards seem to be particularly helpful towards private inquirers.

> Make sure that your copy of the syllabus is up to date.

When you have decided through which board to study and be examined make sure that you have an up-to-date syllabus applicable to the year in which you will take the examination. Spend the necessary money at this point and read the details carefully.

CHAPTER 2

STUDYING HISTORY

GETTING STARTED

A **Health Warning** before you start studying: history is very hard work. To establish the basis for dealing with historical issues you have to be prepared to read extensively. Before you can have bright ideas about the past you have to acquire at least a minimum knowledge of what happened. But history at A-level is mainly about problems and to do well you will need to consider alternative explanations of what occurred and why. The general consensus is that the only way to do this effectively is through reading and reflecting on the ideas of established historians.

All this reading is very time-consuming. If you do not enjoy reading and cannot see yourself settling down to a two year stint where reading to a purpose plays a substantial part in your life, then look for other options. The burdens, and the need for thought, are of course all the greater for those many students whose other subject choices make similar demands.

The good news is that reading history can be interesting and occasionally utterly absorbing. Indeed it can become habit forming. It cannot be avoided.

ESSENTIAL PRINCIPLES

THE PURPOSE OF ADVANCED AND AS-LEVEL HISTORY

The general purpose of historians is to find out as much of the truth about past events as is possible. To this end they develop skills in finding evidence about the past, assessing its significance and structuring it to develop an interpretation of the topic studied. Many books have been written to explain what constitutes good practice in all these endeavours and these characteristic study techniques lead to history often being referred to as a 'discipline'.

The intention in using the study of history as a means of education, usually of the unprotected young, is to introduce students to the techniques and practices of the professional historian on the assumption that it will be good for them.

HISTORICAL SKILLS

"Historical skills can be valuable."

At the end of your course in A-level history you will probably be the best person to judge the effectiveness of historical study in promoting skills and understanding which can be of use in the wider world. Those with a vested interest in encouraging students to study history rather than another subject argue that the study of history develops skills in finding information, in recognising the relevance of such information to the task in hand, in sorting and structuring information logically and in interpreting its significance. On this basis emerges an ability to construct an analysis or a case and then go on to substantiate and to defend it.

These are precisely the skills that are in demand in a sophisticated economy. The Historical Association, a well known pressure group on behalf of the history industry, produces elaborate diagrams of the vast range of job opportunities historical study opens up.

Some historians also hold it to be self-evident that the intelligent study of history provides valuable perspectives on living and working in society. None now argue, on nineteenth century lines, that it is an ideal training for solving the world's problems. This torch was long ago passed on to the geographers and the sociologists who in turn strive to drop it before their fingers are too badly burned.

The purpose of most students at your level is simply to gain as good a grade as possible at A-level and then to cash out the more problematic advantages of a historical education at a later date. There is much to be said for such broad-minded cynicism. It has the great merit of avoiding commitment too early in life to narrowly professional or temporarily fashionable courses of study which, when the tide of fashion recedes, leave one stranded on the beach.

STARTING THE COURSE

THE SYLLABUS

"Be clear what is in your syllabus."

Find out the scope of the syllabus which you are to follow. Do not settle for receiving chunks of historical information, week by week, without knowing the size of the task ahead. The start and end dates of the period of study are essential but so is information on whether all of social, political and economic history is included and what balance is struck between them. The details will be lost on you at this stage but, for example, does the title British History include foreign policy or not? When the paper covers a wide span of time find out which parts of the syllabus your class will be concentrating on for examination purposes. Forget the rest.

THE EXAMINATION

At the start look at a recent examination paper. Consider the range of the questions on offer, the division of the paper into sections, the existence of compulsory questions. Check that the syllabus and examination structure will be the same by the time you have to take it.

You should now have some idea of the size and nature of the task ahead, so set aside thoughts of examinations for a time, and get on with studying some history.

STARTING TO STUDY

> Obtain a simple overview of the period to be studied.

Get an overview

Usually A- and AS-level study means a start on a new historical period. An overview, before the detailed essay tasks begin, will be helpful to many students but it needs to be easily and quickly assimilated. An elementary text book account prepared perhaps for younger students should give you what you need and should be skimmed through rather than totally absorbed. Jotting down a few dates and names across the period covered will give you an initial framework for later study. The blinkered vision of the student, who only in the second year of his course realised that there were two world wars in the first half of the twentieth century, is not helpful to one's prospects.

Organise your notes

The organisation of notes, from class-work and from reading, also requires some early thought and decision. Your arrangements can be reviewed but preferably not too often. See the section that follows for some ideas.

Organise your study space

Some thought should be given to study space. Few students have ideal study facilities made available to them and many of us would probably fall asleep in them too frequently if we had. Making the most efficient use of what is available does, however, make a lot of sense. Where are you going to do most of your work and where and how are you going to store your books and your notes? Do not move valuable notes around more than you have to but do consider having more than one place where you can work. Moving to a new location for half an hour can be a powerful antidote to boredom.

READING HISTORY

> Make full use of your local public library.

BOOKS

Find out what books will be made available to you as class textbooks. Check on whether school or college library resources will be useful for essay writing. Then check on possible alternatives in your local Public Library. You do not need access to the very latest scholarly works but your efforts do deserve to be supported by a sustaining stock of relevant reading matter. If this is not evidently available at the outset then start to search it out.

Try, if you can, to make one or two purchases of paperback books. Do not hurry into this. First use textbook and library resources and look out for the best buys for your purpose over a period of time. The examinations are not competitive so there is much to be said for some joint purchasing on a modest scale. Fig. 2.1 is one example of a useful collection of sources for the study of modern European history.

CONSTRUCTING A RESOURCE BASE
EUROPEAN HISTORY IN THE 19TH AND 20TH CENTURIES

GENERAL READING

J B WATSON *Success in European History 1815–1941* (John Murray 1981) Packed with information on the course of events	A RAMM *Europe in the Nineteenth Century, 1789–1905* *Europe in the Twentieth Century, 1905–1970* (both Longman 1984) A goldmine of ideas and valuable comments. Less useful for factual information on the course of events	A WOOD *Europe 1815–1960* (Longman 2nd edition 1984) An admirable ability to summarise complex issues

NATIONAL HISTORIES

W CARR *A History of Germany 1815–1985* (Arnold 4th edition 1992)	A COBBAN *A History of Modern France: Volume 2 1799–1945* (Penguin 1961)	J N WESTWOOD *Endurance and Endeavour: Russian History 1812–1986* (Oxford U.P. 3rd edition, 1987)

TOPIC WORKS

J LOWE
The Concert of Europe: International Relations 1814–70
(Hodder & Stoughton 1990)

K RANDELL
1 *France: Monarchy, Republic and Empire 1814–70*
2 *France: The Third Republic 1870–1914*
(Arnold 1986)

A STILES
1 *The Unification of Italy 1815–1870*
2 *The Unification of Germany 1815–1890*
(Arnold 1986)

B WALLER
Bismarck
(Blackwell 1985)

B WILLIAMS
The Russian Revolution 1917–1921
(Blackwell 1987)

M LYNCH
Stalin and Khrushchev: The USSR, 1924–64
(Hodder & Stoughton 1990)

PERIODICALS

History Today (History Today Limited) monthly since 1951

Modern History Review (Philip Allan) published 4 times a year (began September 1989)

Fig. 2.1 Constructing a resource base

A few students carry round too many books. This perhaps enables them to feel good without actually doing any reading. Far more common is a sad poverty in the range of reading matter available. You may well have to fight to overcome this. Do so: you are committing two years to this enterprise and you deserve the best support possible. Get the advice of your tutors on resources; then organise yourself in the early stages of your course so that a wide range of reading can be made available and its use becomes a matter of habit. Anyone studying British history would, for example, find great value in having access for reference purposes to a copy of J P Kenyon's *A Dictionary of British History* published in 1981 by Secker & Warburg, and in 1988 by Sphere in paperback format.

HOW TO READ EFFICIENTLY

"Read to solve problems."

This is best done by making your reading about the historical past part of a problem solving exercise. You have an essay to submit next week. This defines an area of reading and provides criteria on what to look out for and to note. Do not expect all such reading to be enjoyable but when it isn't develop a pride in carrying it out as economically as possible. Look at a number of books but extract what is useful for your immediate purpose quite ruthlessly.

"Ask questions as you read"

When you are reading generally, pleasure, or at least a happy sense of developing skill, should be more evident. It will still be helpful to read within a problem-solving structure. Ask questions from your reading. Start with one question and go on to elaborate and add to it in the light of your reading. Do this on paper. You may finish reading without reaching a single answer but it is probable that you will have learned more about the subject from a page of scribbled questions than you realised at the time. Fig. 2.2 offers an example of asking questions on paper whilst reading.

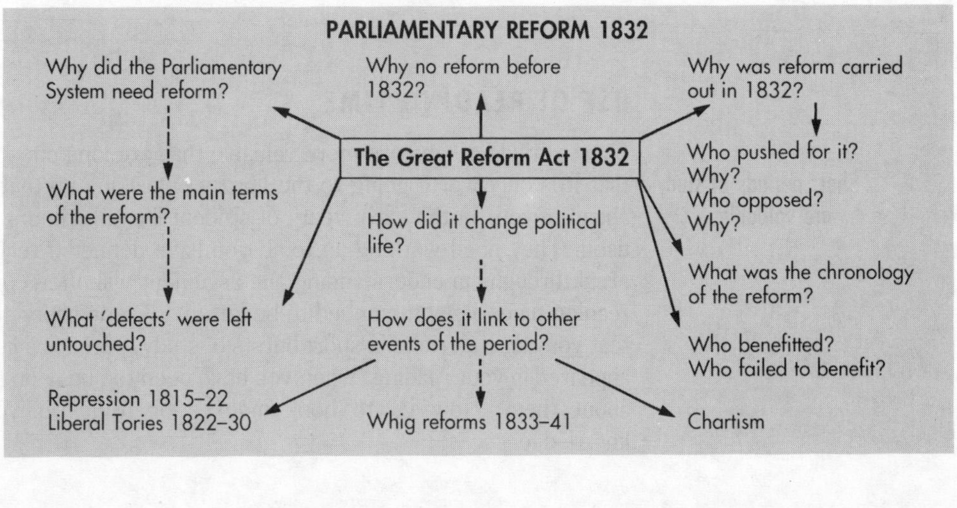
PARLIAMENTARY REFORM 1832
Why did the Parliamentary System need reform?
Why no reform before 1832?
Why was reform carried out in 1832?
The Great Reform Act 1832
Who pushed for it? Why? Who opposed? Why?
What were the main terms of the reform?
How did it change political life?
What was the chronology of the reform?
What 'defects' were left untouched?
How does it link to other events of the period?
Who benefitted? Who failed to benefit?
Repression 1815–22
Liberal Tories 1822–30
Whig reforms 1833–41
Chartism

Fig. 2.2 When reading, ask questions

Life is too full to spend long studying books on reading techniques but it is worth giving some thought from time to time to how to improve your own reading efficiency. The most important advice – **Read to a purpose** – has already been offered in the paragraph above. Some further ideas follow: if they do not work for you then forget them.

SPEED UP YOUR READING

Glance at the introduction of the book; look at the chapter headings; consult the index: use all these aids to reach matter relevant to your purpose as quickly as possible.

“Start by skimming through to find out what is there.”

It is not the speed of your eye but your ability to understand what you read that will determine your speed in reading. The key to faster reading is to recognise that not all the pages are of equal importance. Try the following approach: first skim the chapter that you have decided to read, note its length and one or two key words or phrases on each page. Then read the first paragraph slowly and from it try to identify the author's purpose; now read the last paragraphs in the chapter. If the introductory and the concluding comments seem relevant to what you are looking for go through the chapter more slowly.

Try still to avoid reading these intermediate pages all at the same speed; when the argument is important slow down, read it twice or more, but try to see where the writing is simply illustrating a point or is frankly irrelevant to what you want and then start skimming over the pages again. In the early stages you may miss important points but, in a world filled with far too many history books, the rewards of learning how to speed up your reading will, in the long run amply compensate for this.

Anyone who wishes to think about this more systematically could usefully turn to pages 58–62 of Manya & Eric De Leeuw's *Read Better, Read Faster* (Penguin) where stress is laid on the importance of motivation, interest, an intention to concentrate, reading actively and the use of existing knowledge in promoting fast effective reading. For historians a central part of 'reading actively' is to read for the purpose of solving problems so that all the time you are questioning what you are reading.

DIFFERENT TYPES OF READING

“Try not to read just textbooks.”

Textbooks are difficult to read because they are so densely packed with facts and ideas. It is valuable to read one textbook at the start of any topic but then other reading will be more valuable than a second textbook. Typically you might move from a textbook on nineteenth century Europe to a national history of Germany. Inevitably some topics in the syllabus will interest you more than will others so look out for specialist books in these areas of interest. You are more likely to make more use of them than you would books on subjects which are largely a chore to you.

Articles in history periodicals like *History Today* and the *Modern History Review* can often be particularly valuable at A-level. The author has to present ideas briefly, which is usually helpful, but do check the relevance of the article to your purpose at an early stage. In more learned periodicals it is not unknown for a grand title like 'The Crisis of Hitler's Reich' to come down to some minutiae on an episode in mid September, 1936 on which the writer has based a well-earned research degree. Skim the article first before you invest too much valuable time on it.

USE OF READING TIME

“Short periods of study are valuable.”

Short periods of time are more valuable than are long ones. Beware the tendency to think that it is only worth going to the library or picking up that book if you have a solid hour ahead of you. In the early years of student life solid hours of study are often inefficiently used. They need working up to. If you have defined a reading task for yourself then the breakthroughs in understanding and argument will often come in a much shorter space of reading time. They then need to be jotted down on paper. Keep a list of ten minute tasks that you can undertake in short bursts of study, perhaps a list of names of people who have appeared in your reading, when you have been too busy on the job in hand to find out more about them. Now go to book indexes or to an encyclopaedia and flesh out your knowledge.

NOTE TAKING AND MAKING

SYSTEMS OF NOTE TAKING

Preferences here are very personal. You need a system that you are happy with. Preferably it should also be efficient. One guide to studying history devotes twenty-five pages to notes. It might be better to read some history. Here are some pretty obvious tips.

Keep notes legible and attractive

Notes should not discourage you from returning to them. Organise them logically according to the progress of your studies so that they are easily accessible for revision purposes. Above all keep them safe. Carry around with you only those currently needed.

Fig. 2.3 Take good care of your notes!

Update your notes

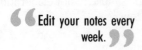

“Edit your notes every week.”

As with your reading it is important to have an active relationship with your notes. Read them through at the end of a lecture or at the end of the topic being studied. Try, at that stage to understand their content, tidy them up, do some underlining or add marginal headings. Occasionally try to write a coherent summary of what you are able to deduce from them on a specific issue.

Received notes

Dictated notes and large bundles of notes prepared and handed out by someone else are usually a waste of time. The latter have to be worked on, read through and underlined for significance and, if the former are to be anything other than a source of future frustration, they have to be thought about soon after the dreaded dictation has ceased.

Do not make too many notes

Try to note ideas rather than just facts. Make notes, or summaries of notes in diagrammatic form (see Fig. 2.4). Centre these on a problem.

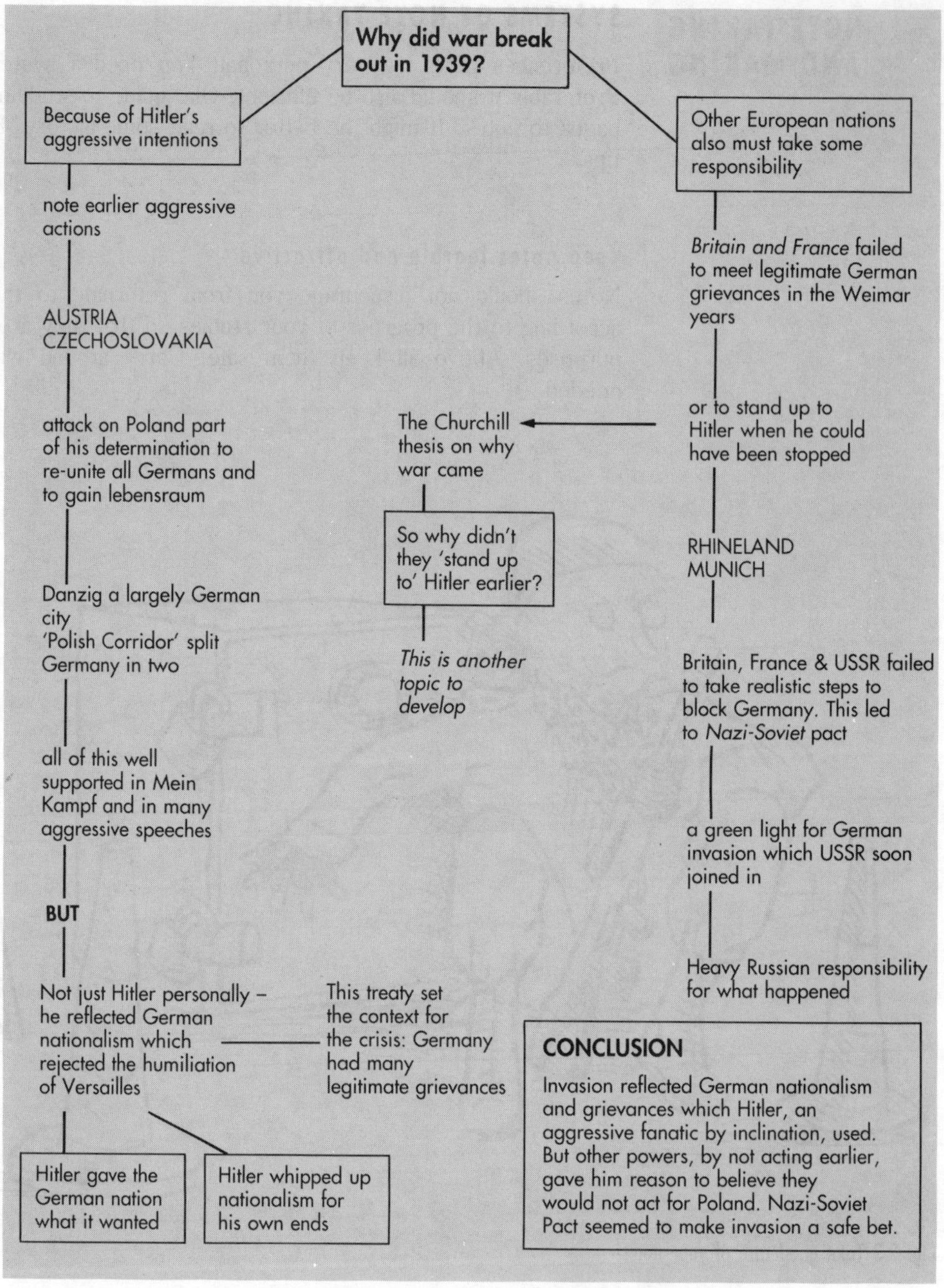

Fig. 2.4 Making note diagrams

At the end of your first term devote an hour to thinking through how you could make your notes (taking, making and keeping) more efficient. Aim for simplicity not elaboration. Then stick to the revised system for the remainder of your course.

WRITING HISTORY

THE NEED TO WRITE CLEARLY

Examiners and teachers of history are agreed that the ability to write well is a great asset for students of the subject. The central plank in the presentation of work at A-level is the history essay. Even in the now compulsory document questions many marks are earned from what are really miniature essays. Essays proper, in any event, still make up some three-quarters of the marks in the examination. New forms of assessment are being introduced by some examination boards but largely in experimental format and with a substantial porportion of the final marks arising still from writing in continuous prose.

> "The ability to write clearly is important . . ."

A few teachers may deplore this in-built bias in favour of the literate candidate and the new modes of assessment may usefully help redress the balance but most history teachers and examiners still believe that only through coherent use of language can valid historical judgements be made at this high level. A-level history is about sophistication in analysis and argument and these skills require sophistication in communication.

HOW TO WRITE EFFECTIVELY

Agreement on the need to be able to write effectively is, unfortunately, followed by diversity of opinion, or simply deep silence, on how this ability is best acquired. What agreement there is supports the view that regular doses of reading at the appropriate level are the best basis for competence in writing history. It might be possible to take this advice further but it is an area where fully satisfactory help will be difficult to find. Happy the student who writes well without realising it. The vast majority of us are less fortunate and have to struggle towards competence. That a distinguished publishing firm gave the contract to produce this manual to someone who feels he writes so badly should give all A-level students heart to persist in their own efforts to express their views coherently and simply. This, rather than perfection, is the goal.

Motivation

"... but practice and motivation can work wonders."

The most important single factor in improving your written style may well be motivation. If obtaining a loan from a favourite aunt depended on your skill with the pen then you might surprise yourself. Early in your course it is a good idea, when writing a coursework essay, to move towards a first draft of the bulk of it and then, after an interval go back and re-draft it in terms of style, vocabulary and spelling. The first sentence and the first paragraph will be the most difficult, and the least satisfactory, but if you await perfection at this point progress may be slow. Press on and double back later. It has been suggested that at the end of a writing session it is a good idea to stop in mid-paragraph, in the full flow of your ideas, as this provides a better starting point when you resume than if you face the obstacle of an entirely new start at the beginning of the day's work.

Write what you mean

Develop a pride in writing what you mean as effectively as you can and read through all your work to this end. Your progress may then be dramatic.

Three tips may help:

1. Do not let your sentences become so long that they lose impact; vary the length of sentences, for a short sentence can convey an important point very effectively.
2. Plan your essay by paragraphs with one major point of the argument to each. Writing coursework essays with attention to paragraph development will make this come naturally in examinations. This has one priceless advantage to the student: it discourages a drift into an endless narrative which unconsciously moves further and further from the judgements through which you intend to impress the examiner.
3. In coursework and, when time permits, in examination answers, read through what you have written. This is just for spelling, clarity of handwriting, correcting ambiguities or omitted words and not an occasion for massive re-drafting of paragraphs and arguments.

ENJOY ANSWERING THE QUESTION

"Practice to improve but do not become obsessed."

Finally – do not let worries about your writing get in the way of either the history or your own enjoyment in answering the question to the best of your ability. Examiners meet many scripts where candidates, once launched quite happily and confidently into a congenial topic, do not bother to consider rules of grammar or matters of style but who emerge with a good and thoroughly deserved mark.

VOCABULARY

"Resolve to extend your historical vocabulary."

Extending your vocabulary is important and may be largely an unconscious process. Few of us can remember when we first met a word or went on to use it for the first time in our own writing. Reading actively, searching for meaning in what you read as advocated above, is the most likely route to an extensive vocabulary. Historical explanations are rarely simple and so often require nuances of meaning which a limited range of language may well prevent. Inevitably examiners will be impressed by a student who can use the right vocabulary to develop ideas. A rich and interesting vocabulary is also more likely to keep examiners awake to the brilliance of your exposition.

1. Small group of people ruling a state
2. one-party state that regulates every relm of life
3. Body of persons vested with power to make + repeal laws
4. the branch of the central authority in a state concerned with the admin of justice
5. arbitrary or tyrannical authority or behaviour

HISTORICAL VOCABULARIES

Different branches of history have quite complex technical vocabularies of their own. It is not just a case of knowing meanings but also one of making such terms part of your own essay vocabulary. In political history how confident would you be in handling the following?

Parliament	Government	Executive	Legislature	Judiciary
Democracy	Oligarchy	Autocracy	Totalitarian	Despotism
Reactionary	Repressive	Liberalism	Nationalism	Anarchism

> Own and use a dictionary.

Social and economic history also employ their own terms, often drawn from the writings of sociologists and economists. You do not need to have studied economics or sociology for examination purposes to do well in economic or social history but, when in your reading you meet a term about whose meaning you are not entirely confident, do not slip hurriedly away. Get out your dictionary and then make it part of your own working vocabulary.

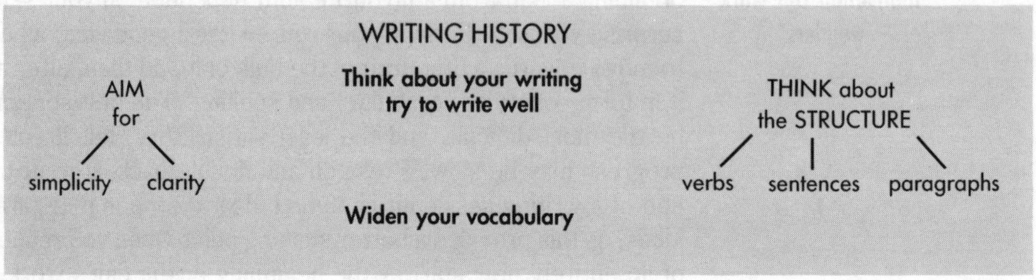
WRITING HISTORY
AIM for
simplicity
clarity
Think about your writing try to write well
Widen your vocabulary
THINK about the STRUCTURE
verbs
sentences
paragraphs

TYPES OF HISTORY QUESTION

Your coursework will make you familiar with the different types of history question. Here are some suggestions to help you approach writing your answers.

'Why' questions

'Why . . .' questions usually involve a straight exploration of causes and the great danger is to leave important causes out. They cry out for a concluding paragraph in which you either assess the relative importance of the causes you have listed and discussed, or link them together in an overall statement.

'Examine/assess' questions

'Examine . . .' or 'Assess . . .' questions usually relate to the effects of, say, a war, legislation, or, of some economic or social development: again avoid important omissions. Aim to provide a balanced verdict. Do not, for example, attribute all of Britain's post-war economic difficulties to the 1914–18 war. Acknowledge that longer term causes also operated. Do not let the form of the question lead you into a narrow answer.

'Discuss' questions

> Note the different types of history question.

'Discuss the view that . . . ' gives more scope but less of a lead in. Make sure that you stay relevant to the proposition to be discussed. If you are outlining some arguments or ideas that have now been discredited make clear as you go along that you know this, so that it is not such a shock to the reader when you later proceed to discard or ridicule these.

'How far/to what extent' questions

'How far . . .' and 'To what extent . . .' need the most thought. They are inviting you to challenge the explanation offered, to come up with other factors and to set these against those in the question. A sensible response is to take the explanation offered and discuss its merits before proposing other factors to be taken into account. Do not be afraid of this type of question for it often leads to an extended discussion of issues and this can be very rewarding. It is unwise to state 'this proposition is rubbish . . . ' and then to write exclusively about other factors. This leaves the suspicion that you are dodging the question set. First explore the proposition on offer and only then propose your own more valid argument.

'Compare' questions

'Compare . . .this with that' questions. Do not write two separate little essays, one on 'this' and one on 'that'. Make a statement about 'this' and follow it with one on 'that' and so on, keeping the comparisons you are making directly before the reader.

COURSEWORK ASSESSMENT ITEMS

“Coursework assessment is now much more common.”

ASSESSMENT AND GRADE

The assessment of items of coursework as one of the techniques for establishing A-level grades in history has become increasingly popular in recent years and is almost certain to play a more significant part in the A-level examination in the future. In no sense can it be regarded as an easing of the examination requirements but it may bring some reassurance to those who feel that they do not do themselves justice in the examination room.

EXAMPLES OF COURSEWORK ASSESSMENT

Personal study (AEB)

The AEB Personal Study is one example of the use of coursework assessment. The AEB have issued some very helpful notes of guidance for students and for any student undertaking this option under the AEB they are essential reading whilst students with other examination boards could well find them valuable. Amongst other advice they stress the need, in personal studies based on national and international history, to make sure from the start that you identify a problem that will enable you to make your own distinctive contribution and avoid merely copying out the interpretations of established historians. Equally you must be sure that local libraries have suitable resources for you to be able to develop your study at an appropriate level.

Local history research

If you plan to undertake a piece of local history research then you will first need to consult a guidebook on how to proceed: W G Hoskins, *Local History in England* published by Longman (3rd edition 1984) is both useful and generally available in libraries. Many town libraries have local history collections and the staff there could well become your most valuable allies.

The nature of history

The assessment of coursework can also give students the opportunity to do work on the nature of history or on the techniques of the historian. Again some preliminary guidance will be needed. There are countless books devoted to this end but not all of them are as clear or as brief as the A-level student might wish. Many have been written to guide students in higher education. If you are required to venture into this area then one useful book to dip into at an early stage would be John Tosh, *The Pursuit of History* published by Longman (1984), which includes a bibliography with commentary on other relevant works.

Syllabus E (London)

In 1992 the London Board offered a new, Syllabus E, Examination which is skills-based and aims to be a natural follow-on from the techniques of study deployed in the GCSE examination. The syllabus is assessed by a final examination, including documentary questions, (50%), coursework (30%) and an individual assignment (20%). Under the assessment arrangements, in addition to the personal study on the AEB pattern, there are four assessed coursework assignments devised and assessed by school and college staff with samples of the work moderated by the board's examiners.

History Individual Study (Project) Scheme (Cambridge)

The Cambridge Examinations Syndicate offers a History Individual Study (Project) Scheme where the assessment includes examiners interviewing candidates about their project work. They too have issued helpful notes of guidance to candidates.

COURSEWORK TIPS

Consult your tutors

“Obtain tutorial advice at an early stage.”

Perhaps the best advice that can be offered is to consult your tutors at the earliest possible stage and establish the rules under which your study has to be conducted: its length, its layout, the limits on subject matter, the proportion of the assessment which depends on it, its relation to your other work across the course, what is likely to be the best timetable for doing the work, the date on which it has to be handed in. Any student who embarks on such a project without a clear understanding, preferably in written form for later reference, of the terms under which he or she is operating shows scant respect for the importance of their own time and effort. The reward for those who do organise the work effectively could well be a fascinating and challenging opportunity.

With all types of coursework assessment you will need to make a prompt start on the assignments. With the aid of your tutors try to devise coursework topics that involve genuine historical problems or investigations. All the dangers of writing long descriptive pieces in examination essays are that much more acute when you have more time and a mass of information to work on. The coursework assignment, like the examination essay, is there to test your ability to argue and to analyse historically. The right title will focus you on this approach and will also help you resist the temptation to write at far too great a length.

“Coursework tests your ability to argue and analyse historically.”

General advice

- keep a note of all your sources of information
- organise your notes and other paperwork systematically and keep it all in a safe place
- seek advice early and often
- do not spend a disproportionately large amount of time on this work
- longer will not necessarily mean better but perhaps the opposite

Note the advice in Fig. 2.5, given by some students on the day they handed in their AEB personal studies.

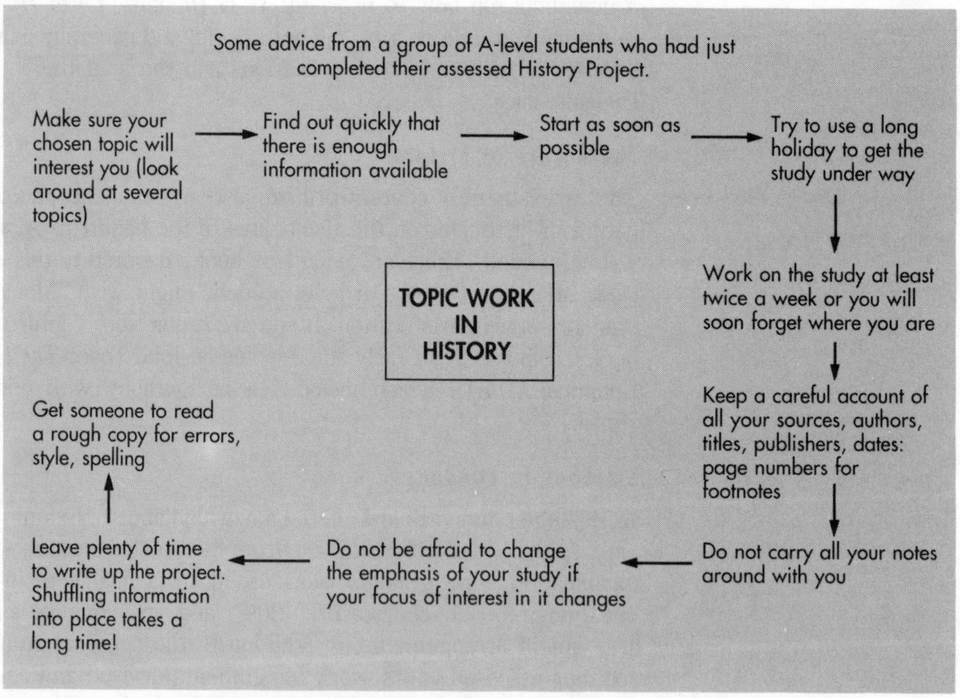
Some advice from a group of A-level students who had just completed their assessed History Project.
Make sure your chosen topic will interest you (look around at several topics)
Find out quickly that there is enough information available
Start as soon as possible
Try to use a long holiday to get the study under way
Work on the study at least twice a week or you will soon forget where you are
Keep a careful account of all your sources, authors, titles, publishers, dates: page numbers for footnotes
Do not carry all your notes around with you
Do not be afraid to change the emphasis of your study if your focus of interest in it changes
Leave plenty of time to write up the project. Shuffling information into place takes a long time!
Get someone to read a rough copy for errors, style, spelling
TOPIC WORK IN HISTORY

Fig. 2.5 Advice on topic work

REVISION

The approach to revision needs to be as active and self-aware as the approach to reading and to writing. It is an intensely personal activity and each student must find the revision pattern which suits him or her best. A sense of proportion will help: results will not improve through overwork leading to illness so take some exercise and do something enjoyable each day. It is equally true that worry will not help for you can do only one task at a time so do the most important one first and forget the great piles of work that remain to be started. Much will still not be done the day after the examination and doing it would probably have made not a jot of difference.

“You need your own revision plan.”

Here are some general precepts on how to revise, they may start you on the way but they are unlikely to do more.

- **Make a plan**
- **Make a timetable**
- **Make a start**

A REVISION PLAN

Drawing up a revision plan can be a useful first step in actually revising. Look through your notes and list the topic areas covered; compare this with the topics covered in past papers and prepare a possible list of priorities. Then set the topic areas in a diagram that shows links between them. Ask yourself if there is a prospect of revision in one area helping you in linked areas. Have a diagram of what needs to be done and, as you proceed with your revision, gradually edit it; identify both priorities and areas to be discarded.

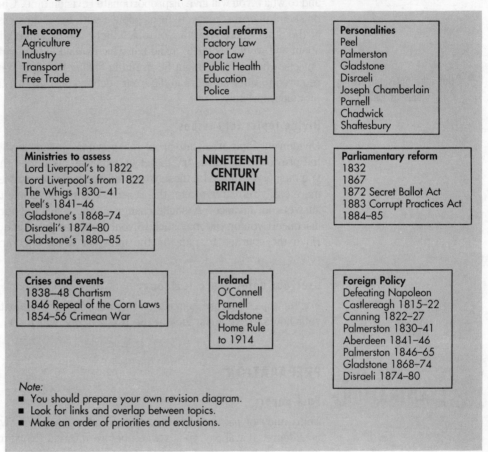

The economy
Agriculture
Industry
Transport
Free Trade

Social reforms
Factory Law
Poor Law
Public Health
Education
Police

Personalities
Peel
Palmerston
Gladstone
Disraeli
Joseph Chamberlain
Parnell
Chadwick
Shaftesbury

Ministries to assess
Lord Liverpool's to 1822
Lord Liverpool's from 1822
The Whigs 1830–41
Peel's 1841–46
Gladstone's 1868–74
Disraeli's 1874–80
Gladstone's 1880–85

NINETEENTH CENTURY BRITAIN

Parliamentary reform
1832
1867
1872 Secret Ballot Act
1883 Corrupt Practices Act
1884–85

Crises and events
1838–48 Chartism
1846 Repeal of the Corn Laws
1854–56 Crimean War

Ireland
O'Connell
Parnell
Gladstone
Home Rule
to 1914

Foreign Policy
Defeating Napoleon
Castlereagh 1815–22
Canning 1822–27
Palmerston 1830–41
Aberdeen 1841–46
Palmerston 1846–65
Gladstone 1868–74
Disraeli 1874–80

Note:
- You should prepare your own revision diagram.
- Look for links and overlap between topics.
- Make an order of priorities and exclusions.

Fig. 2.6 Constructing a revision topic list

A REVISION TIMETABLE

"Draw up a revision timetable as well."

Link the revision plan to a revision timetable. This, obviously, will have to be part of a wider plan embracing all your subject revision commitments. For a summer examination, a timetable reaching forward from the end of the spring term through to the examination date is probably appropriate. You might make a wall-chart from it and mark off your progress. Ensure that your plan for the vacation guarantees you one or more breaks of a few days during which you will forget all academic work. Having this to look forward to will keep you going before and the break itself will do wonders for your subsequent work rate. This theory does of course rely on a prompt resumption of work on the day appointed; make this the first day of the summer term so that the fateful decision is out of your hands.

Leave the final two weeks before the examination clear for reviewing what you consider to be the most important issues which you would like to come up on the examination paper.

One important qualification remains: if none of this advice appears to work in your case then ignore it. Study techniques can be improved by adapting sensible advice to your purposes but that should really have come earlier in the course. As the examination approaches have the self-confidence to follow the strategy that seems to work best for you. If you have developed sensible study patterns on the basis of active questioning of the topics studied you are unlikely to go far wrong. Better this than an unrealistic master plan which becomes such a daunting burden that energy and purpose are both sapped.

Note: However many plans and timetables you are tempted to make and to discard, **do make an early start on the actual revision.**

MAKE A START

Organise your revision topics

> Bank on some topics coming up.

Work through the topic areas according to the logic of your plan, as tested by scrutiny of recent past papers, and in accordance with your timetable. Logic may well suggest that to cover every topic would be a waste of effort so discard judiciously, erring on the side of caution. With those topics you retain there is virtue in having some that you are banking on and to which you will give disproportionate revision time. Check that those you are banking on seem, over the years, to be as popular with the examiners as they are with you. Equally at the other end of your list of topics there can be some which you are not too confident about and would prefer to avoid but which would extend your range if things do not work out elsewhere. They might be useful in finding that fourth essay question. When you are required to offer answers in different sections of a paper remember to allot your revision time appropriately.

> But take out some saving bets as well.

Divide topics into issues

Divide your topic areas into problems or issues. Just as in your first study of these topics in the previous five terms try to set up explanations rather than memorise facts. The facts you memorise should be those which form part of your problem solving. They will be all the more easily remembered for this reason. It is not advisable to prepare answers or parts of answers in advance. A slight change in the expected form of the question may well disconcert you or you may stick to your prepared piece in quite the wrong circumstances. Have the courage to take on the question when it comes to you in the examination room.

Use your notes and a textbook

For the topics you are banking on to appear in the examination do not rely exclusively on your notes. Take a last look at the textbook for which you have the highest regard.

THE EXAMINATION

PREPARATION

Past papers

Your study of past papers, as urged in previous pages, will be the best boost to your confidence. It will pay you, a week before the real thing, to sit in an empty room with a recent paper in front of you and, taking ten minutes, think out the questions you would attempt and in which order. Try to have a look at the exam room before you have to take your first paper; it can help you settle more quickly on the big day.

Examination instructions

Those previous papers will have made you familiar with the examination instructions:

> Note the examination instructions.

- The number of questions.
- How many from each section?
- Compulsory questions.

Fig. 2.7 Keeping calm

Make totally sure that you understand and follow these instructions to the letter. You cannot compensate for not doing a required question by doing too many elsewhere.

First look through the paper. Remind yourself of its layout and of the instructions on questions. Skim through the questions and mark possibilities. In the very unlikely event that something seems to be wrong then raise your hand and bring the problem to the attention of the invigilator immediately. You can lose nothing by being wrong but gain a great deal in confidence by being re-assured.

More likely it will all seem familiar and the years of study and the months of revision can now begin to pay off. Remember to keep calm.

Identify possible questions

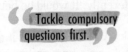

"Tackle compulsory questions first."

Proceed coolly through the possible questions and mark down those which you are likely to do. Check whether there are good questions in all the sections of the paper that you have to attempt. Select your likely second question before you start on your first; this will help your confidence. It is probably best to tackle any compulsory question first. In history examinations this is almost certainly the 'document' or 'extract' question or questions. These are usually best answered before any essay questions. They require careful attention to the details in the documents and so need a fresh mind. Getting them out of the way first also means that they will not break up the flow of essay writing.

Time

The most important thing now is to use the time rationally. Be aware of the starting time and mark down the ideal finishing time for each question. Try to stick close to this, giving each question a fair share of the time available. Be particularly careful not to spend longer than the due time on the document questions.

Complete the paper

"You must attempt all the required questions."

The most wasteful thing to do is to fail to answer the questions which the examination instruction requires from you but the second most wasteful thing is to leave too little time to provide an adequate answer to the final question by spending too long on earlier ones.

Remember:

- It is far easier to score up to 10 marks out of 25 on the last question than to improve an earlier answer from 12 to 15 by writing at greater length.
- By writing at length in earlier questions you are probably falling into the trap of merely describing what happened instead of dealing with the problem posed. In this event you are throwing marks away here as well.
- If, despite all this good advice, you find yourself in trouble on the last question then do all you can to open it up quickly. You need, from it, those easily obtained first few marks. Essay plans are difficult to give credit to, especially if they are just a list of facts to be used. Two paragraphs of connected prose, offering argument relevant to the problem, might just save your bacon or 5 marks out of the 25.

It is better to get the timing right and make the last question count for every mark you can squeeze out of it.

Fig. 2.8 Use your time rationally

ESSAY QUESTIONS

The different types of history essay questions set in examinations were identified on page 14 of this chapter. Go back to that section now and remind yourself of these.

Read the question

Read the question through carefully. Make sure it reads as your first impression led you to believe. Get it wrong now and your answer will be wrong all the way through. Just because you have revised the results of the Parliamentary Reform Act of 1832 does not mean that you can use that material to answer a question clearly on the defects of the pre-1832 political system. A question on the development of nuclear power cannot be answered by an analysis of the nuclear deterrent. *You must answer the question set.* Do not delude yourself as to its meaning just because you want it to read differently. It would be better to look for another question to answer.

“Never write out the question.”

Keep the question in front of you on the examination desk. A quick glance at it as the essay develops may well keep you on the right track but do not waste time writing out the title or the question itself at the top of your script.

Examination essay plans

These are a matter of taste but should in any case be kept brief. Note the structure of your argument, preferably by paragraphs rather than by jotting down factual information. Use your own shorthand. Before you start on the essay, take five minutes to think about the argument you are going to use: note a few key words which will remind you of it as you proceed. It is the thinking which will clear your head for the challenge of writing the essay; the notes are as much an aid to thinking as to memory. Long essay plans followed by an unfinished brief final essay with 'ran out of time' scrawled at the end tend to make cynics out of the most kindly of examiners.

“Use the topic chapters to practice making essay plans.”

Study the questions in the topic chapters in this book and practise drawing up brief but useful plans. In each chapter some of the questions are provided with suggested plans but these may not suit you. Try to form your own plan before looking at those provided and then compare it to the one provided. Do not be too modest for your plan may well offer the more effective approach. In the examination room your plans should be much more cryptic than those offered here. Then get on with the essay which will actually earn you the marks!

Writing examination essays

Read again the section of this chapter on writing history. Then in the examination remember:

- **Write in paragraphs** – it helps planning and avoids narrative
- **No casual English** – your historical skills deserve the best
- **A brief introduction** – indicate your line of argument
- **Never** – just describe what happened
- **Be relevant** – there is a problem posed before you: answer it
- **Come to a general conclusion**

The advantage of using the opening paragraph to outline your approach is that the later paragraphs can take each point in turn. For most of us this is easier than turning the essay into a mystery story with all revealed in the last lines. Resolve never to start an answer with: 'Before answering this question it is necessary to describe/explain what happened'. That is the way to an endless and an unrewarding narrative.

Example of an opening paragraph

Question: Why did the Bolsheviks come to power in Russia in 1917?

Opening:

“An effective opening paragraph.”

> The Bolsheviks' coming to power owed much to the fact that Russia faced imminent defeat in war and that both the country's economy and social structure were close to collapse. They were also considerably assisted by the impotence and the mistakes of Kerensky's Provisional Government in the face of these

```
catastrophes. Above all, however, they came to power through the
schemes and plots of a small, ruthless and brilliantly led group of
political extremists who exploited Russia's and Kerensky's
difficulties for their own ends. In no sense was their position the
result of an irresistible mass rising on their behalf.
```

This has opened up some four themes for further development. These can be developed in turn but with the bulk of the discussion being devoted to the point mainly emphasised here, namely the coup of the political extremists.

At the start of each subsequent paragraph think 'am I still being relevant' and 'am I still arguing/commenting/discussing or am I lapsing into merely describing and narrating what happened'?

In your final conclusion do not just repeat points made earlier. If you have offered several ideas earlier then try now to link them together, or suggest which is the fundamental point amongst them, or indicate that there is more to the question than its wording suggests. Keep it brief. The weakest endings come to descriptive essays where all the relevant comments are reserved for the concluding lines. Even this is preferable to no comments at all.

DOCUMENT/EXTRACT QUESTIONS

You will not do these well unless you have made yourself familiar with them during the A-level course. You also need practice in timed conditions, simulating the examination, before the real thing comes along. As this type of question varies greatly between the examination boards, these notes can offer only a starting point for an effective approach. Six of the topic chapters have examples of the different styles of document question being set by the various examination boards but, if you are to do yourself justice, you really do have to seek out, study and practice on the past papers set by 'your' board.

Use your time carefully

“Note the marks available . . .”

“. . . and use your time accordingly.”

Tailor the time you spend on any sub-question to the mark tariff on offer against the question. With only 1 or 2 marks available then a single sentence or even a one word answer might well be all that is needed. Even the best rewarded sub-question will have a maximum of about 7 or 8 marks. You do not have time to write an essay in the attempt to earn them. Keep within your overall time limit and even for these more valuable sub-questions settle for an answer covering little more than one side of paper. If you have a lot to say make every word count. You will probably still have essays to write before the paper is completed!

Read the documents

“Pay close attention to what is in the documents.”

Read the documents provided thoroughly. Nearly all the questions will want deductions and/or evidence from the documents so do not write general essays that make no use of the evidence provided for you.

Attributions of documents

Note the attribution of the document – a speech, a memoir extract written after the event, a diary, a newspaper account. Think if the origin of the document opens up the possibility of bias or propaganda or other opportunities for relevant comment. You may be able to bring this into the answer to some of the questions. Indeed you could be asked a specific question on these lines. Many students find difficulty commenting on the value and limitations of a document in the light of the source from which it came. This is nearly always because they have had no advance practice in the necessary skills.

Language and tone

Some papers ask you to comment on the language and tone of the documents. Practise this too. Many candidates lose marks at this point by ignoring the instruction and writing about the historical content instead of the language and tone. Looking at the attribution of the document may give you a vital clue. An obvious example could be a politician in a public speech arousing the emotions of his audience by employing loaded words and images. Think through his likely motive and assess how he employs language to achieve his ends.

Types of question

'How far . . .' and 'To what extent . . .' questions arising from documents can be a problem. Usually this form of question is an invitation either to consider in what way the document(s) is/(are) inadequate and/or to suggest other sources to supplement it.

Questions which invite you, in at least one sub-question, to make use of your own knowledge, vary in frequency from board to board. This will often depend on how much information candidates have been given as to the documents to be set. Even here you may also be asked to use the documentary evidence provided and, in this case, the examiners may well be reserving some of the marks for comments arising from the documents and some for your own knowledge. So provide both.

Bias

Many candidates, well-schooled in answering document questions develop a deep pessimism, even to the level of 'Unfortunately this is an eyewitness account and therefore likely to be biased.' Do try to see why a historian might value a source, might even dance for joy at finding it, before you go on to show why it might nevertheless have to be treated with caution.

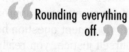

> "Whenever possible relate your comments to what is in the documents."

There is not much value in merely stating that a document is, or may be, biased. The examiner will expect this comment to be explained and illustrated by reference to the specific document referred to in the question. Remember that bias in documents can itself sometimes be revealing.

ENDING THE EXAMINATION

> "Rounding everything off."

The ideal candidate will have budgeted for ten minutes in which to read through the exam script. Few of us are so well-organised. One last deep breath and, if there is time to spare, a final dash through your paper.

First go to the document questions and attempt to fill any gaps you have left. The advantage of this is that second thoughts can quickly be added in this area. Then read through your essay answers or, if too little time remains, look just at their conclusions to see if there is anything you would now wish to add. If too much time remains by all means edit your script and add any second thoughts. Do, however, try not to destroy it by scribbling in amendments at too many points. If you delete anything then the examiners will ignore it. They are unlikely to deduct marks already earned because some error has subsequently crept in, so it is probably better at this final juncture to leave well alone.

CHAPTER 3

THE INDUSTRIAL REVOLUTION

TERMS AND CHRONOLOGY

LONG TERM BASIS

ECONOMIC CHANGES 1760–1830

THEORIES OF ECONOMIC ACCELERATION

FACTORS PROMOTING CHANGE

SOCIAL CONSEQUENCES

POLITICAL CONSEQUENCES

POSITION IN 1830

USEFUL INFORMATION

GETTING STARTED

This is a vast study topic and its treatment here will be most suitable for students intending to answer questions on it as part of a general outline paper. Students of more specialist economic and social history option papers should find that what follows provides a useful series of signposts to developing detailed revision topics of their own. A survey of recent past papers will soon give you a realistic idea of the detail required in the questions you will face. Then plan study and revision topics accordingly.

You need to establish a *chronology of economic change:* start with the conventional dates 1760 to 1830 but later be prepared to consider whether economic and social history can be divided so neatly into packages. What spills over the edges may be a most interesting field of study. Find out what sort of a country Britain was around 1760. Thirty minutes with a middle-school text book, supplemented if possible by any one of the numerous collections of economic sketch maps on this period, could give you a series of helpful jottings. It was a country blessed by political and social stability and the reasons for this are important. The nature of its government system, the rule of law, the aristocratic constitution allied to relatively free social mobility are all significant. You will later be looking for non-economic reasons for economic growth so a general social and political framework will be helpful but should be quickly acquired. A mental picture of what sort of a country Britain was in 1760 will greatly strengthen your judgements of cause and consequence which are likely to dominate essays. Population, the size of towns and the appearance of the countryside, the character of industries, farming practices, the occupations of the people, how people and goods moved about the country, all sound mundane but will give you a solid start.

In almost all respects the way of life and its physical setting was totally different from that of the second half of the nineteenth century. Little may have changed in the previous hundred years but now the forces unleashed by economic acceleration were about to transform both the appearance of the country and the lives of the people.

ESSENTIAL PRINCIPLES

TERMS AND CHRONOLOGY

"The validity of the term 'Industrial Revolution'."

Some historians question the validity of the term 'Industrial Revolution', seeing a gradual non-revolutionary advance of workshop techniques and practices over a wide span of time as being a more characteristic form of economic development even in this period. The really revolutionary changes, it has been suggested, were those in commerce and finance in the late seventeenth and early eighteenth centuries: later advances in manufacturing techniques are then more easily explained. The opposite tendency is to dramatise the 'Industrial Revolution' as a watershed in economic and therefore in social history: a process leading to Britain becoming the 'First Industrial Nation'.

No-one imagines that the economic acceleration started or ended in a specific year. The acceleration did however occur, its characteristics, causes and consequences have been much studied and for present purposes need to be understood. 'Industrial Revolution' is a useful shorthand term for these events, no more.

LONG TERM BASIS

ECONOMIC FACTORS

The Industrial Revolution occurred in an already *advanced economy*: you must be able to illustrate this. Look at the 'Useful Information' section of this chapter to see some of the evidence you could use to establish this point. This information can be used to point to the existence of extensive internal trade in industrial and agrarian products, a sophisticated market economy promoting large-scale agricultural improvements, developing transport and financial facilities, rapid growth in international trade; all this well before 1760.

One way of looking at the various factors would be to say that Britain before 1760 had the potential for industrialisation. The importance of the period just before 1760 was that certain pre-conditions, or prerequisites, which were necessary before an industrial revolution could take place, were satisfied. Many economic historians now see Britain in the mid-eighteenth century as '**proto-industrial**', i.e. an economy which had the potential to undergo industrialisation. Note that not all proto-industrial economies industrialise: it is simply a potential which is not always fulfilled and sometimes disappears.

NON-ECONOMIC FACTORS

"Non-economic factors are an essential part of any explanation."

Britain's advanced economy was only one aspect of a rapidly developing society. Explanations of economic growth have long ago outstripped purely economic explanations. It is no longer fashionable to explain economic advance simply in terms of Protestant freedoms and the Protestant work ethic or to base it on a Whig interpretation of the unique blessings conferred by a parliamentary Constitution and the rule of law, but it would be advantageous for students treating this study area in a special topic examination to be able to indicate why these once-fashionable interpretations are not now accepted uncritically.

In any event political stability and the real, if limited, social mobility had great importance in encouraging wealth creation, investment and general agrarian and industrial progress, all of which have a long history before 1760. Developments in science and in education also played a part in all this. The exclusion of those who were not members of the Church of England from public life may have been partly responsible for the great numbers of nonconformists, like the Quakers and the Unitarians, who became prominent in economic development but do not exaggerate this issue for there were many Anglican businessmen also.

In short the type of society which existed in Britain in the eighteenth century has to feature prominently in any full explanation of why an industrial revolution occurred here. It would pay dividends for you to organise the points you would use to demonstrate this.

ECONOMIC CHANGES 1760–1830

NATURE OF THE ECONOMIC CHANGES

It is often the case that essay questions in this area can be answered without specific reference to the actual detail of industrial change but enough solid knowledge to illustrate argument could transform an answer. Do not fall into the trap of memorising lots of detail of change which will only lead to long descriptive accounts. In particular examination revision should be rigorously structured in terms of *problems*, *explanations* and *issues*.

“Information must be organised to support argument.”

At least understand in outline what happened in agriculture, in the cotton industry (and later developments in woollen textiles), in the iron and coal industries, in transport, in steam power. Useful revision techniques could include a doodled diagram on how changes in one industry affected other areas of the economy or a sketch map exercise to think through how the changes from 1760 had, by 1830, altered the economic geography of the country. It will be very important that your knowledge is available in a form that can quickly be adapted to supporting argument and ideas; there is little value in merely learning off lists and dates of developments. You will not have time to use them in any examination and, at worst, they may encourage you to write long narrative accounts which forget the point of the question as set.

THEORIES OF ECONOMIC ACCELERATION

This is the popular area for examination questions. You need to be aware that a great number of explanations for the economic acceleration have been advanced. Names of and quotations from historians matter a lot less than your ability to offer commonsense informed comments of your own on the causes of the economic acceleration.

STAGES OF GROWTH

“Rostow's explanation.”

The name of W W Rostow is worth noting for his ideas on stages of growth leading to a take-off point for industrialisation which could happen quite suddenly with just one sector leading the way and drawing other parts of the economy along. In his explanation the dramatic changes in the techniques and organisation of the cotton spinning industry in the 1780s are seen to provide this thrust. Study of other industries appears to suggest that a model could be constructed in which creeping changes on many fronts are more characteristic of what happened to the British economy. Remember that all explanations are weakened by the absence of many relevant and easily comparable statistics: economic historians would love to quantify changes, be ready to say why they find it so difficult to do so and how this increases the chances of dispute amongst them.

Single factor explanations

Be wary of single factor explanations. Explanations of economic change will usually require consideration of a number of factors and, above all, an ability to write perceptively about the interaction between them.

FACTORS PROMOTING CHANGE

LONG TERM FACTORS AND THEIR INTERACTION

Tackle this in two parts; first list the long-term factors which created the mid-eighteenth century take-off point, then think through how the changes occurring in the conventional 1760–1830 period of the Industrial Revolution reacted on each other to promote further change. (If appropriate to your syllabus this can be continued through for the 1830–1870 period so that you are ready to answer questions on how mid-nineteenth century Britain finally became a mature urban industrial state.)

Prepare a list

Preparing and refining your list of factors will be an essential revision process far more valuable than revising notes or memorising knowledge for its own sake. So draw up your own list, though it should probably include most of the following:

- The role of invention and technical innovation (what is the difference?).
- The natural resources and wealth available in the country, the sources of capital for investment.
- The availability of labour and skilled labour.
- Demand for goods; home and overseas (i.e. the growth of markets and of domestic and international trade).
- The impact of improvements in transport transforming local markets into a national market, and in opening up natural resources for exploitation.
- Population changes; growth of population, reasons for its occurring, the migration of labour, occupationally and geographically.

- The prospect of profit leading to enterprise and the emergence of a political philosophy (laissez-faire) which was anxious to maximise this.
- The social and political conditions promoting some or all of the above.

The list should be added to, sub-divided, and interactions noted. You then need to be able to support your ideas with specific information. Fig. 3.1 offers an outline version of the proposed exercise.

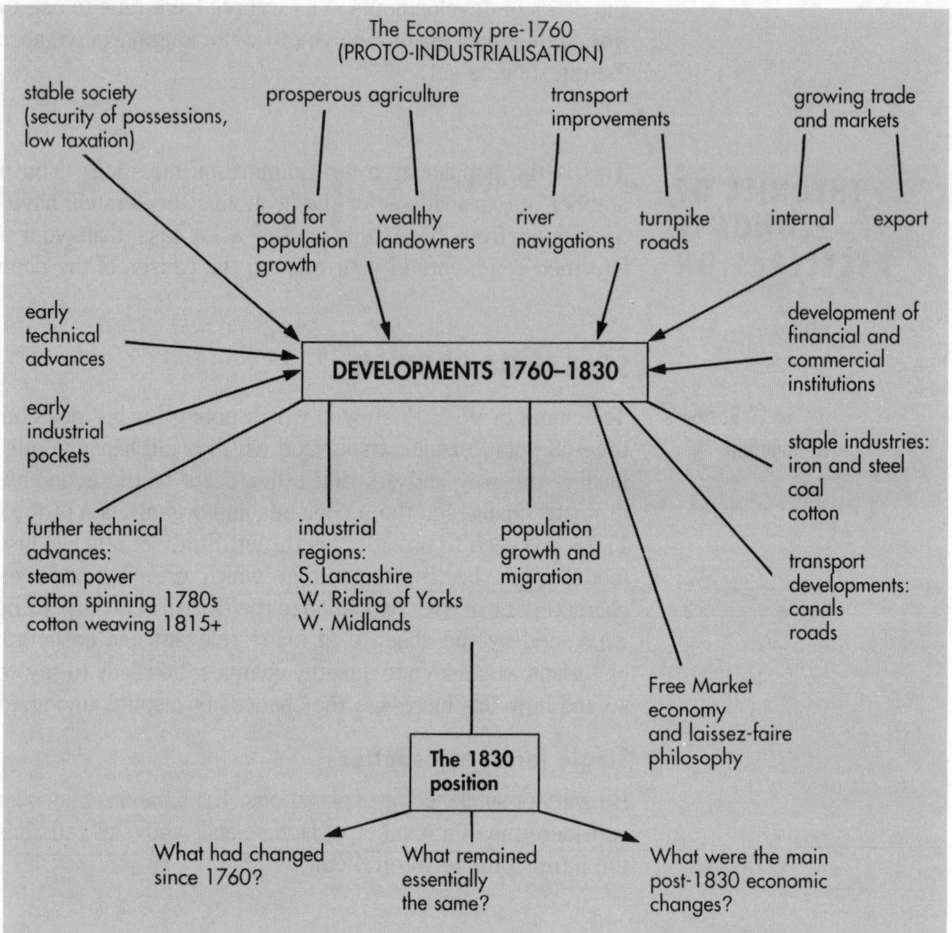

Fig. 3.1 The Industrial Revolution: a simplified revision diagram

SOCIAL CONSEQUENCES

This topic provides an ideal introduction to the study of nineteenth century social history. The 'Outline Answers' to Questions 2 and 4 on pages 30 and 31 and the 'Student Answer' to Question 2 on page 32 touch on different aspects of it.

The debate

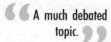

"A much debated topic."

The social impact of the economic changes has been extensively debated by historians. There has been a great debate over what happened to the working-class standard of living in the early nineteenth century. Social historians have tended to be pessimistic pointing to low wages, and to appalling living and working conditions as evidence. Economic historians have often taken a more optimistic view, pointing to the continuing rise in population as part of their case that standards were not deteriorating. A shortage of relevant statistics has bedevilled and prolonged the debate. Most A-level textbooks explore the controversy which has in any event moved on from argument over the material standard of living to one about the quality of life. Here those who take a pessimistic view emphasise the horrors, often using the evidence in the Reports of Parliamentary Committees of enquiry into contemporary social problems which became common in the 1830s and 1840s. Those historians who take a brighter view stress the higher wages in industry and the freedoms, economic and social, of town, as opposed to village life. The debate may well keep historians in work for decades more. *Adopt a commonsense approach.*

Prepare your own analysis

Unless past papers suggest that an ability to comment on the interpretations of leading historians is needed avoid working-up lists of names to be dropped at suitable moments.

Instead draw up a list of the main features of working-class life and be ready to comment briefly on each one to support both the pessimistic and the optimistic view. Have a series of opinions of your own but illustrate them coolly; this is not the time for political conviction and rhetoric to take over from clear analysis directly relevant to the question as set. You are not a hanging judge. If, commendably, you become angry at what you have read then step back and work out a defence for whoever appears to be the oppressors and exploiters. This will teach you much about the need to study the past for its own sake and on its own terms. It will also help make you a more effective advocate for the causes you still wish to promote. If you are impressed by Marxist analysis in terms of class exploitation and struggle and 'reforms' as intended to control the 'lower orders', then spend some time, in advance of any examination, thinking through your argument. There are many half-baked references to Marxist analysis which do neither their originator nor the candidate justice.

“Marxist analysis.”

Note that a more diversified economy led to a more complex stratification of society. The number of middle-class occupations increased sharply. In the 1840s Disraeli wrote of the 'Two Nations – the rich and the poor': it was a gross distortion of the economic and social realities of the time. Unless you come to terms with the growing numbers, wealth and influence of the middle classes (think about the plural here) then much of the social and political history of Victorian Britain will remain a mystery to you.

POLITICAL CONSEQUENCES

Population and economic growth put strains upon the aristocratic constitution, largely unchanged since the seventeenth century. The build up of pressure for political change, and the resistance to it, is best illustrated in the period 1815 to 1822 or with the rise of Chartism in the 1840s. The most significant political adjustment of the period was the Great Reform Act of 1832 (see Chapter 5) which makes much more sense when set in the context of the demographic, economic and social changes of the previous fifty years. But beware of oversimplification here. Working-class political movements were not simply a reflection of industrialisation and its problems. Other factors, like the influence of revolutionary ideas from France or America, were important.

“Political crises and political accommodation.”

POSITION IN 1830

A survey at this point can serve a number of purposes. Consider each of the areas of the economy in turn and be prepared to state in what ways and to what extent they have changed over the previous half century or so. Be aware that in each area that the change was almost certainly not total or final. The first public railway opened in 1830 and a new period of dramatic economic development opened.

At that date, despite the great enclosure of open fields with its attendant social changes, agricultural techniques were little changed and still almost totally unmechanised. Numerous trades, for example boot and shoe manufacture, were still handicraft industries; in the greatly expanded pottery industry steam power played almost no part in manufacture; even more remarkably there were still some three hundred thousand handloom weavers struggling to survive; Birmingham was a city of small workshops; the lives of hundreds of thousands of mainly female domestic servants were unchanged by all that had occurred. Much of this was to survive for many more decades, nicely illustrating the point that, as the Industrial Revolution had no specific start so it had no clear end. *History is about continuity as well as change:* you must be ready to assess and to illustrate both.

“There is no end date for the Industrial Revolution.”

USEFUL INFORMATION

In this topic area it is dangerously easy to accumulate a vast amount of factual information, assembled into far too many notes. The facts you choose to note need to be put into useful categories where they will be able to give substance to the arguments you are developing in order to answer the question set. They are not, in themselves useful. At the revision stage, if not earlier, draw up some lists of information that you could use to answer questions on different topics. Often the information can in itself be comparatively trivial except as illustrating an argument; local examples are often valuable. You will, in any event only have space enough to make very brief use of them. Fig. 3.2 is a simple example of such a list.

“Do not accumulate information for its own sake.”

Information to support an analysis of the sophistication of the British economy well before 1760

1 Many improvements in agrarian techniques even in the 17th century, experiments with new grasses, turnips as a field crop, new crop rotations. Application of new ideas advanced in early 18th century. Large scale market in agricultural products based on London demand created much trade and traffic. Growing agrarian prosperity created, by early 18th century, a wealthy class of landowners many of whom invested in other economic activities e.g. the Duke of Bridgewater in coal mines and canals.

2 Northumberland coalfield goes back to pre-1600: by 1750, 3000 small ships plying North Sea to bring coal mainly to London. Newcastle was a prosperous port with a large merchant class.

3 Great development of provincial ports in early 18th century: Bristol and Liverpool moving from local trade with their hinterlands to become trans-ocean ports involved in very profitable trade in slaves and tropical products. Importance of the coastal trade for passengers and goods. The 18th century was one when small provincial ports flourished.

4 Existence of industrial pockets in early decades of 18th century e.g. tin mining in Cornwall, iron at Coalbrookdale, brewing at Burton on Trent, Defoe's 1720s description of the sophisticated structure of the woollen industry and its markets and trade routes in the West Riding of Yorkshire. The Wedgwoods were already wealthy potters by 1750, living in the 'Big House' in Burslem, which was by then an industrial town with a population of over 5000.

5 Note also the late 17th century emergence of London financial institutions, insurance at Lloyds, the Stock Exchange, and the emergence of country banks in the provinces in the early 18th century.

6 The first Acts of Parliament to establish road improvements by setting up Turnpike Trusts date from the reign of Charles II (1660–1685), the River Navigation Acts from 1700 to 1750, especially of the River Severn opening up the Midlands to water-borne transport of goods.

7 Technical advances had a long history e.g. steam pump pre-1700, one of the key improvements in it, by Newcomen, came into use in 1712. In 1709 Darby used coal instead of charcoal in the smelting of iron. Water power was being used to drive textile machinery at Lombe's silk mill at Derby as early as 1720.

Figure. 3.2 List of information

Making such a list, and it could be much extended, will remind you of interesting details related to the topic which would bring substance to any essay.

Other lists could be made on the 1760–1830 period:

- industrial developments, (not just a list of inventions though!)
- the impact of the application of steam power in the economy
- transport developments and their effect on the economy; agricultural improvements
- the growth in trade and in population.

Note: Remember you need this information to inform and to illustrate your answers and not just to use in descriptive form. This should help you to decide how many lists and how much information will be of use.

EXAMINATION QUESTIONS

Q1 Was agricultural development a necessary precondition for the industrial revolution? (Cambridge 1989)

Q2 Discuss the economic and social consequences, in the period between 1780 and 1830, of the rise in population. (Cambridge 1989)

Q3 Examine the importance of overseas trade to the economic expansion of eighteenth-century Britain. (AEB 1988)

Q4 'The living standards of British workers improved rapidly in the period 1780 to 1850.' How far would you agree with this view? (NEAB 1989)

Q5 Document Question – Britain and the Industrial Revolution (Oxford & Cambridge 1989)

You are advised to spend one hour on this section.

1 You must answer this question. Read passages (a) to (c) and answer questions (i) to (iv) which follow.

a) Were we required to characterise this age of ours by any single epithet, we should be tempted to call it, not an Heroical, Devotional, Philosophical, or Moral Age, but, above all others, the Mechanical Age. It is the Age of Machinery, in every outward and inward sense of that word; the age which, with its whole undivided might, forwards, teaches and practises the great art of adapting means to ends. Nothing is now done directly, or by hand; all is by rule and calculated contrivance. For the simplest operation, some helps and accompaniments, some cunning abbreviating process is in readiness. Our old modes of exertion are all discredited, and thrown aside . . . What changes, too, this addition of power is introducing into the Social System; how wealth has more and more increased, and at the same time gathered itself more and more into masses, strangely altering the old relations, and increasing the distance between rich and poor . . .

(From: Thomas Carlyle, *Signs of the times*, 1829)

b) On coming out of the workhouse in March 1856 I secured my first job. It consisted of scaring crows from the fields of a farmer close to the house. I was then six years of age, and I was paid 1s. for a seven-day week . . . Having to work long hours, I had to be up very early in the morning, soon after sunrise, and remain in the fields until after sunset. One day, being completely worn out, I unfortunately fell asleep. Equally unfortunately for me the crows were hungry, and they came on to the field and began to pick the corn. Soon after the farmer arrived on the scene and caught me asleep, and for this crime at six years of age he gave me a severe thrashing, and deducted 2d. from my wage at the end of the week...In 1856, I entered upon my first harvest. During the wheat-cutting I made bonds for the binders. There were no reaping machines in those days, the corn all having to be cut by the scythe. Women were engaged to tie up the corn, and the little boys made bonds with which to tie the corn.

(From: George Edwards, *From crow-scaring to Westminster*, 1922)

c) . . . woollen yarn . . . is spun into a much feebler, looser, and less twisted thread, than other kinds of yarn. But this feebleness of the yarn constitutes a principal difficulty in applying the power-loom to the woollen manufacture . . . The weaving of woollen cloth by hand is a man's work, whereas the weaving of cotton, linen, or silk cloth by hand was a woman's or child's work. Hence the hand-loom weaver in the woollen manufacture has never been reduced to the miserable wages paid to the same class of operatives in other manufactures, and hence he maintains a more equal competition with the steam-loom. It is to this cause that we must principally ascribe *the continued existence of the system of domestic manufacture in the woollen trade*; and to the same cause we must ascribe the slower advances made in the woollen than in those manufactures *where all the processes can be more advantageously carried on in factories, by one vast system of machinery, under a single eye, and by the power of great capital.*

(From: Edward Baines, *Account of the woollen manufacture of England*, 1858)

i) Explain what is meant by, or is being referred to, in the following:
Passage (a) line 5 'the great art of adapting means to ends'. *(2)*
Passage (a) lines 9–10 'the Social System'. *(2)*
Passage (c) line 9 'the system of domestic manufacture'. *(2)*

ii) With reference to two of these passages examine the difficulties faced by historians using them because of their origins and sense of purpose. (7)

iii) Does the evidence in passages (b) and (c) undermine the argument put forward in passage (a)? Give your reasons. (5)

iv) Using your wider knowledge, how do passages (b) and (c) help us to understand the impact of the industrial revolution on family work and income? (7)

(*Total 25 marks*)

Recommended Time Scheme: total time for question = 60 minutes
time for reading = 15 minutes
time for (i) = 10 minutes
time for (ii) = 12.5 minutes
time for (iii) = 10 minutes
time for (iv) = 12.5 minutes

OUTLINE ANSWERS

Question 1

Argue that it was necessary and give reasons, for example:

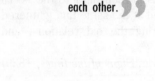

“Industry and agriculture did not exist independently of each other.”

- necessary if a non-agrarian labour force was to be fed
- necessary to rapid population growth which stimulated the industrial revolution
- led to agrarian prosperity which provided capital for non-agrarian developments; landowners were important as entrepreneurs, especially in the development of the coal industry and canals
- much industry linked to agriculture – woollens, brewing
- provided a market for industrial products
- provided an incentive for transport improvements which also encouraged larger scale industry
- provided commercial and trading base for later industry

Conclusion: to realise importance reflect on how impossible industrialisation would have been in a subsistence peasant economy.

Question 2

Remember to remain in period stated.

Suggest *population size* circa 1780 at around nine million and quote 1831 census figure for Britain of 16.4 million. Quote 1801 figure at 10.8 million.

Economic consequences:

- led to growth of home demand for products of industry so stimulating industrial innovation (give examples)
- growth of towns especially London a stimulus to agrarian improvements (give examples) to internal trade and therefore communications improvements (give examples)
- increased population provided a ready labour force for more intensive agriculture and for the rapidly developing industrial pockets

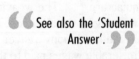

“See also the ‘Student Answer’.”

Social consequences:

- over-populated villages so poor relief rose
- concern about led to 1834 Poor Law Amendment Act
- surplus population emigrating to nearby towns
- town growth providing labour force for industrial growth
- living conditions and mortality in the rapidly developing towns

Conclusion: population growth, by increasing the size of the home market was a key stimulus to economic acceleration, the social problems it also created had not begun to be tackled by 1830.

Note: Now compare this outline with the ‘Student Answer’ to the same question, see p. 32.

Question 3

- Indicate the main markets and trading routes in 18th century including main overseas trading ports i.e., London, Bristol, Glasgow, Liverpool.
- Show how *any one* grew and affected the economy of its hinterland e.g. Liverpool, and the development of the South Lancashire cotton industry and its associated inland transport structure.
- Overseas trade not the only factor but an important one: a port like Liverpool first developed as a local port for its own hinterland and this remained important to it.
- Use triangular trade to illustrate how trade produced wealth for investment in estates (agriculture) and commerce.
- Emphasise European markets as a major stimulus to economy e.g. the textile industry, importance of the colonial entrepot trade to commercial expansion.
- Overseas trade encouraged the growth of the City of London which developed as a centre for banking, insurance and brokerage services e.g. Lloyds.
- Argue that the most convincing explanation of the Industrial Revolution is that it was demand led through market growth but finally acknowledge that home market developments may well have been more important, indicate why.

Question 4

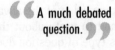

"A much debated question."

- Much historical debate about working-class standards of living:
  - some pessimistic, e.g. views of the Webbs
  - some economic historians more optimistic, give names if known, e.g. Hartwell.
- A key argument of the economic optimist would be that the continued growth of population argues against any serious decline in standards. Even the most optimistic would be chary of accepting this claim unreservedly.
- Problem complicated by:
  - lack of statistical evidence (develop this)
  - by absence of a clear definition of British workers.
- Different groups had varying fortunes; discuss for:
  - agricultural workers (enclosures, poor relief)
  - hand workers in industry
  - new skilled workers.
- Fortunes also varied at different times:
  - wars against France, post 1815 depression
  - 1820s trade recovery.
- Much depends on the period studied, the nearer you come to 1850 the more optimistic can be the view taken.

Conclusion: no certainty that this statement is true for large portions of the working class prior to 1850.

Question 5

"The documents must be closely read."

Your syllabus will have given you reasonably precise information on the range of topics on which the examiners will be entitled to set document questions. Working out how you deal with this example, before you look at the Tutor's comments that follow, would make you think about the topic and give you practice in reading documents; it would therefore be a very useful piece of general revision. Do not spend the time suggested at the end of the question in producing a full answer unless you are entered for the Cambridge Examinations Syndicate papers. Document questions vary sufficiently between the examining boards to make it essential for you to look at past papers from the board for which you are entered.

Tutor's comments on document question

This question is taken from an AS-level paper. The board concerned is anxious for it to be made clear that these comments are not treated as a model answer to the question but simply as the author's personal approach. This is equally the case with all the answers proposed in this and other chapters.

i) These need one sentence each in reply:
   - Using machinery to produce goods (it is given in the lines above)

– Society, relations between the classes (it is given in the lines immediately after the reference)
– The references above make it quite clear 'The weaving of cloth by hand'

ii) This is very difficult and documents (b) and (c) seem the best choice.
With (b) the date needs a reference, it is personal reminiscence deliberately recalling his poor childhood long ago. Memory may have failed, he may well be drawing a moral (the attribution of the document encourages this possibility, he is an MP).
With (c) we have a history from someone who appears to favour the capitalist system and the advance of factory production and mechanisation and in a sense, despite the date this is not strictly a primary source of evidence. We are seeing the industry through the historian's eyes. In particular his claims about the wages and conditions of the handloom weavers must be treated cautiously for he is clearly not one of them.

iii) This looks to be more straightforward. The key is to establish the argument in (a) and one sentence gives it 'Our old modes of exertion are all discredited.' There is then lots, in two different industries twenty plus years later, to challenge this claim. Note there are only 5 marks available so do not write for too long.

iv) You must relate your own knowledge to the documents but (b) would enable you to use your knowledge of child labour, the labour intensive nature of agriculture with its relative lack of machinery, still relatively untouched by the Industrial Revolution. Document (c) provides an opportunity to use your own knowledge of the advance of factory production in the different branches of textiles and to write about the long survival of domestic manufacture. How well you do in this type of question does to a large extent depend on how much reading you have done in the past. Do not however fall into the trap of forgetting to relate your answer as required to the passages provided.

"You must relate your own knowledge to the documents given."

A STUDENT'S ANSWER TO QUESTION 2

"Why is Ireland then forgotten?"

"Some useful comments on rural Britain."

A growing awareness that population was rising at an unprecedented rate led in 1801 to the first population census which suggested a population, excluding Ireland, of around ten millions. By the 1831 census this had risen to about 17 millions. This essay will discuss the economic and the social consequences of this rise first in the country and then in the towns.

In the country areas the population growth provided an increasing labour force for the development of agriculture. The new enclosed farms often needed more labour for there were few labour saving inventions in farming in this period. This was particularly important during the Napoleonic wars. Of course the growing population also provided an expanding market for this farm produce and acted as an incentive to increase production and in this way it stimulated the agricultural revolution. Eventually the continuing growth of rural population outstripped the farming industry's need for labour particularly in the slack winter months when there was a growing unemployment problem. This led to all sorts of problems with poor relief with the cost rising sharply and more and more labourers relying on hand outs in the winter. The cost of poor relief rose sharply and there was increased discontent among ratepayers that they were having to subsidise the farmers' workforce. People began to be afraid that the labourers were becoming demoralised and losing the will to work and right at the end of this period there was a lot of rural violence and rioting. The other consequence of the rise in rural population and the surplus workers in the country was that agricultural wages declined giving labourers even less incentive to find work rather than live off poor relief. The more ambitious farm labourers especially the young started to emigrate to find work in the towns.

In the industrial areas the economic consequence of population growth was to provide industry with the labour force necessary for it to expand. This occurred partly as a result of natural increase of the urban population and partly as a result of immigration of the surplus population of the villages. This urban growth created a demand for more food and encouraged improvements in agriculture and in transport to satisfy it. The canal system which developed in this period was as important for farmers as it was for industry. The people in the towns needed vast quantities of cheap housing at minimum rents and this in turn led to the growth of slums with terrible sanitary problems and a high mortality rate. Nothing was done about these problems until long after 1830. The rising birth rate meant that there were great numbers of children available to work in the new factories. The main industries for child labour were cotton and woollens situated in Lancashire and Yorkshire but children were also employed in the metal work industries of Birmingham and underground in the mining industry. For the first time many children were being employed outside the family and there were no laws to protect them from long hours of work and bad treatment by the factory owners.

“Is this really relevant?”

“Economic and social information muddled together unhelpfully.”

Other social problems caused by the rising population of the towns included a growing problem of crime and violence such as that at Peterloo when a demonstration in favour of political reform had to be broken up by troops.

EXAMINER COMMENT

This is at first sight a quite brief, simple and ill-organised essay but in fact it contains a large number of relevant comments. It needs more solid information to illustrate the major points e.g. the total population according to the 1831 census and the numbers in 1831 in one or two of the towns. The paragraph on the country is the best organised part. The sections on the economy and on the society of the towns are thoroughly muddled so that a great number of sensible points lose their impact. A paragraph on the economic consequences and then one on the social consequences would have worked wonders. The essay then fails to establish the importance of population growth in stimulating demand for cheap industrial products and its importance therefore in encouraging industrial innovation.

This is an essay many of us could see ways of improving and it would be a useful exercise to try this (start by looking back to the ‘Outline Answer’ on page 30). Note though that this candidate has offered an impressive array of ideas and that this would almost certainly secure a pass mark and with just a little more information and thought it could soon have been into the C/B grade.

USEFUL SOURCES OF INFORMATION

General reading

P Gregg, *A Social and Economic History of Britain 1760–1980* (8th Edition) Nelson 1984; a textbook with a long and distinguished pedigree.

P Hudson, *The Industrial Revolution,* Hodder & Stoughton

P Mathias, *The First Industrial Nation, 1700–1914* (2nd edition) Methuen 1983; detailed and comprehensive.

T May, *An Economic and Social History of Britain 1760–1970* Longman 1987; more social than economic.

Further reading

J Langton & R J Morris (eds), *The Atlas of Industrialising Britain 1780–1914* Methuen 1986

C More, *The Industrial Age: Economy and Society in Britain 1750–1985* Longman 1989

Linked topic areas

There are many topics in eighteenth and nineteenth century British history whose study will benefit directly from an awareness of the main features of the economic history of the 1760–1830 period. These include:

- The domestic policies, in peace and war, of Pitt the Younger
- Lord Liverpool and repression, 1812–1822
- The Liberal Tories, 1822–1830
- The Whig Reforms 1830–1841
- The economic policies of Sir Robert Peel
- Chartism
- The Anti-Corn Law League
- Victorian social problems and social reforms
- The British economy, 1830–1900

CHAPTER 4

SOCIAL REFORM 1830–1870

GETTING STARTED

Any analysis of social problems and social reforms must be set in the economic and political context of the time. The best social history embraces economics and politics.

You will need to understand the effects on British society of the industrial changes of the late eighteenth and early nineteenth centuries with the emergence of heavily industrialised pockets in such areas as South Lancashire, the West Riding of Yorkshire and the West Midlands. The industrial growth continued throughout the nineteenth century and the ability to illustrate it briefly might provide the context for your essays on social reform. Information is readily available and for this purpose you probably only need a few illustrative items: in 1787 there were 41 cotton factories in Lancashire and 119 in all England; in 1835 there were 683 such factories in Lancashire and 1,071 in all England and by this date over 120,000 people, divided almost evenly between the sexes, worked in the Lancashire factories. This pocket of Britain had become urban and industrial in less than sixty years. It was in new settings like this that the most pressing of the social problems arose. The other factor which contributed to the emergence of the world's first urban industrial nation was the dramatic growth of population. This had begun in the eighteenth century and continued through the nineteenth. A larger and larger proportion of these people lived in towns which were a product both of natural increase and immigration from the surrounding countryside. Even if your syllabus only starts in 1830 it would be advisable at this stage to look through Chapter 3.

The most important political reform of the century was the passing of the Parliamentary Reform Act of 1832. This reformed the aristocratic constitution and gave a measure of representation and some political influence to middle class males. Almost any attempt to deal with the social problems of the day involved legislation passing through Parliament. Typically a concerned pressure group secured the support of sympathetic MPs who persuaded the House of Commons to set up a Parliamentary Committee of Enquiry into the matter. The Committee's Report would be debated and used to promote a Bill, which, after three 'readings' (i.e. debates and perhaps votes), and probably scrutiny in committee, in both Commons and Lords, it would receive the Royal Assent and become an Act. The opportunities for the measure to fail or to be modified were numerous. Do not fall into the trap of assuming or implying in your answer that the passing of an Act solved the problem. Some Acts were defective, many more were ineffectively enforced. Chapter 5 will give you valuable political background on ministries and politicians.

ESSENTIAL PRINCIPLES

OBSTACLES TO REFORM

Too little attention can be devoted to the obstacles to reform; ignorance, lack of money, vested interests, and, most of all, the general political climate of the period. Britain in the mid-nineteenth century has been described as a laissez-faire state. An attempted definition of the term follows. You need to consider it and be in a position to consider its implications for reforms of all types. Laissez-faire philosophy is associated with such ideas as minimal government, or 'good government is cheap government', with self-help, and with the idea of the free workings of the labour market alongside all other aspects of the economy.

LAISSEZ-FAIRE

This term expresses the principle of non-interference by government with the actions of individuals. It has been particularly used with reference to trading and industrial matters but can be applied to social issues. It comes from the French – 'let people do as they think best'. From the early nineteenth century the principle was applied to remove regulation of trade and industry, including duties on foreign trade. This had been largely achieved by the mid-century, by which time the pressures for social reforms were just beginning to lead to more active government in those spheres. Even in the period 1850 to 1870 Britain was never totally a laissez-faire state but certainly no state before or since has been subject to less government interference with the individual.

SOCIAL PROBLEMS OF THE PERIOD

THEIR NATURE, EXTENT AND GRAVITY

To make sense of this complex topic area you will need, for study and revision purposes, to look at the various areas of social concern separately. The depth of your study will depend on the scope of the syllabus and the type of questions in past papers. Study of these will show that they give you no scope to do well simply by describing the horrors of the time.

Structuring your ideas

For study purposes make a list of headings which need following up, for example:

- **Poverty**
- **Working conditions**
- **Living conditions**
- **Education provision**
- **Law and order**

"You must organise your 'facts' into coherent patterns."

Notes under these headings may break the overall topic area down into manageable sections but you should go beyond this and write a brief continuous narrative, on each area, explaining what the problem was at the start of the period being studied. You are not going to try and memorise this for future use but, in social history, it is especially important that the mass of information is set in a framework of ideas around which you can organise your written work. Social history essays can swiftly decline into mere description but the essay title, as much as in economic or political history, will be posing a problem. Writing coherent summaries of your ideas, rather than leaving the results of your reading simply in note form, will be a great help in adapting often quite diffuse historical information into a relevantly structured answer.

Note: You are here practising techniques of writing and structuring ideas, not trying to memorise prepared sections of an answer. Such attempts rarely work effectively.

Viewpoints

Working as suggested on the above topics will soon indicate that the nature of each problem depends on the viewpoint taken. A destitute person's version of the problem of poverty may well differ greatly from that of the well-to-do ratepayer. Make a virtue of this and, as you proceed through study of these topics try to note the various points from which contemporaries could view them.

Evidence

"Make brief use of contemporary evidence to make a point."

When you need to show your understanding of any of these areas at greater length then an awareness of some of the evidence from the time will be more valuable than repetition of textbook generalities. For maximum effect it will have to be brief; it does not need learning by heart and putting in quotation marks. There is an enormous amount of evidence available for this topic area; be in a position to exploit it in examinations without letting it swamp either your study time or your essays. An example might help make the point:

> In the years 1837 to 1842, when reliable mortality statistics first became available, almost 600 of every thousand babies born in the heavy industrial town of Wolverhampton died before their fifth birthday.

This can be briefly stated but, appropriately used, it can bring to life a range of generalisations. Do not arm yourself with scores of such illustrations: many an essay dealing with Public Health problems has failed to re-surface from an unnecessarily long and vivid account of sanitary horrors.

Note: In essays make your use of contemporary social evidence both brief and relevant to the problem you are answering. If in doubt leave it out.

Overall picture

By the time you have produced brief written statements on each of the topics it will be clear that the way they have been divided up may have helped you to study them but that, in practice, they are all closely linked together. Make a study virtue of this and write a continuous statement on these connections; think about causes and effects. What overall picture can you begin to assemble of, for example, the problems of working-class life at this time? You could well be assembling the basis of an answer to a range of more general questions on the period.

"Make an overall pattern from the separate social themes."

ORIGINS OF THE SOCIAL REFORM MOVEMENTS

The origins and growth of pressure for reform have been much debated by historians and are, probably for this very reason, a popular source of examination questions! Here more than anywhere else in this topic it is important to reflect on the nature of the syllabus for which you are entered and to peruse past question papers. The depth of interpretation needed for success will vary widely between special option papers and outline British nineteenth century history papers. The advice here attempts a middle path.

Humanitarian impulses

The place of humanitarian impulses in promoting reform, and their links in turn with religious movements, are one strand to explore. The work of Shaftesbury and Wilberforce, at least, needs setting in context alongside the motives of other individuals, like Sadler and Oastler.

Jeremy Bentham

The historical debate has centred around the influence of the writing of Jeremy Bentham and his followers, most notably the work of Edwin Chadwick with Poor Law and Public Health reform (see the 'Tutor's Answer' on page 42). Again you need to have a clear opinion of their impact.

Oliver MacDonagh

One historian, Oliver MacDonagh, has promoted the idea of the very passing of legislation as leading to the development of an administrative machine whose work in turn brings about pressure for further reforms. The role of ideas is, in this explanation, very limited: if you decide on the contrary that Bentham's views were powerful promoters of social reform then be ready to explain precisely how you think this came about. Avoid a long commentary on the ideas which fails to explain how they brought about reform.

Prepare to debate

It is essential that you are ready to debate the relative importance of the various reform impulses. In preparing for this bear the following in mind:

- Whilst humanitarianism may be more important than Benthamism in some spheres (reform of factory or mining conditions, or the abolition of slavery in the British Empire, perhaps) the balance you wish to strike in others may well be very different (perhaps in poor law or sanitary reform).

- Prepare then a revision note on each of the great social problems of the day and be ready, from your reading to offer an opinion of what, *in each case*, brought about reform.
- Draw up an outline time chart of the chronology of social reforms in different fields. Be ready then to draw connections between one area and another.
- Often the case for reform is apparently so overwhelming and yet so little is enacted or enforced. Try to establish why this was so.
- Identify and assess the relative importance of the obstacles to reform, for this is a field where candidates often lack knowledge and produce only flimsy accounts.

"Think about the obstacles to reform."

PATTERN OF REFORM

This is in particular a matter of chronology and of periods of reform.

The Liberal Tories

You need, for example to have an opinion on how much had been achieved by the Liberal Tories before 1830; was their work mere administrative tinkering or had a new reforming era already dawned? A key feature of your assessment here is likely to rest on how far you think they had, by 1830, recognised and tackled the problems of law and order which faced British society. A judgement on the early achievements is bound to affect your assessment of the significance of later reforms.

The Whig reforms

The Whig social reforms of the 1830s were both fundamental and wide-ranging but you need to be ready to assess their significance in their respective fields. Note the apparent loss of impetus in social reform in the 1840s and the late enactment, in 1848, of the first general Public Health Act. Later legislation seems less dramatic, more a case of extending powers and rearranging administration until there is another great outburst of reforming activity in Gladstone's 1868–1874 and Disraeli's 1874–1880 ministries (see Chapters 6 and 7).

The Mid-Victorian achievement

An informed general view of how far, by 1870/1875, the Victorians had succeeded in meeting the worst of the social problems that they had inherited, could be of much value.

1870–1914

"And, if appropriate, have an end of century comment ready."

Be ready in outline papers covering the period beyond 1870 to make the basis of your assessment 1900 or 1914. A few minutes with an outline textbook will give an adequate extension of the range of knowledge that you will need. The longer period of time is often invoked by examiners when they ask questions on the continuing problem of poverty. This involves the work of Charles Booth and Seebohm Rowntree and leads on to the Liberal reforms of the 1906–1914 period (see Chapter 8).

ASSESSING THE ACHIEVEMENT

In concrete terms this is more difficult to do than one might assume.

Legislation is important, especially set against its virtual absence in the early century. In this sense much had been achieved but do not fall into the elementary trap of assuming that passing laws means that a problem had been solved, for there were many difficulties in enforcing legislation. A balanced and informal general assessment is needed in each of the major areas.

In **Public Health** for example one could point to a battery of Acts which had extended the powers under the 1848 Public Health Act and to the fact that by 1871 there were around 700 Local Boards of Health on the 1848 pattern in England and Wales: their powers and their responsibilities, and their limitations could form part of an evaluation. The continued growth of towns, the advance of drainage and piped water, together with the vast reservoirs, as well as mortality statistics and population figures, are all part of the picture. A different approach would be to consider how little had been done to improve the urban environment generally, and working class housing in particular, with Joseph Chamberlain's pioneering work in Birmingham only starting. It was to be the end of the century before the worst of the early slums were removed and adult mortality rates fell only slowly.

In another field **poverty** continued to exist on a grand scale and the work of Booth and Rowntree is a powerful illustration of the fact.

> Those obstacles again.

An **overview** of the reform achievement, with some corroborative evidence and commentary is needed. In weighing the achievement bear in mind the difficulties in the way of improvement, the fact that the early Victorians had had no precedents to guide them in that they were the first industrial urban nation, and above all, that as population continued to grow this was not a static situation. There was a lack of knowledge of what to do for the best (the most energetic and far-sighted sanitary reformer in nineteenth century Britain, Edwin Chadwick, created tragedy in London when, to restrict the outbreak of cholera which was killing hundreds he flushed the cholera germ from the sewers into the Thames and killed thousands). In the field of Public Health for example there was a lack of money for capital projects, a lack of engineering and medical knowledge, no local adminstrative framework to administer any programme of improvement and, perhaps above all no political will to accept responsibility for meeting the problems facing urban societies in particular.

Your **assessment** of what was achieved by the reformers will be more effective if it takes account of this context. Note also the contents of the next section of this chapter.

ACCEPTED SCOPE OF GOVERNMENT ACTIVITY

This issue was touched upon in the 'Getting Started' section of this chapter but it is so central to any assessment of the process of reform that you need to remind yourself of its significance in relation to all the social topics you have studied and revised since then.

The art of the possible

> There were limited expectations of what the government should be doing.

This section of these notes is 'the art of the possible' because in all these matters it is important in arriving at any judgement to appreciate the philosophical obstacles to improvement, as well as the practical ones already referred to above. The expectations placed upon Government in the mid-nineteenth century were minimal, namely defence against foreign enemies and the maintenance of law and order at home, both please at minimal cost. A nation with a Government revenue, in the 1860s, of circa £70 million could not have been expected to do much of social significance after half of that revenue had been used to pay the interest on the National Debt. Good government was cheap government. The central social principle was 'self-help'. Such ideas were the bedrock of social policy and it is profoundly unhistorical to ignore them in judging the reforming activity of the period.

Laissez-faire

You need to understand the meaning of terms such as laissez-faire (see the 'Getting Started' section). Be able to discuss the effect of the general belief that free competition worked for the best and would be disturbed to everyone's peril, and how this affected the activities of government and society in facing, or ignoring, the social problems of the day. The most advanced public thinkers of the time believed that the chief function of Government, after defence and law and order, was the removal of obstacles to the free operation of the economics of the market. The demand for a more positive, active role by the State in social matters takes us outside the period.

Changing expectations

> But this began to change by the end of the century.

The changes in philosophy and expectations after 1870 provide one of the most fascinating political and social themes of the last quarter of the century. The mid-century, though, is often described as a period of laissez-faire; you need to be able to discuss this term, its origins in the writings of the Classical economists, its advocates, its effect on Government activity and, above all, the legitimacy of the term as applied to mid-nineteenth century government and society. Was the period 1850 to 1875 in fact the age of laissez-faire? The validity of the term laissez-faire to British society in the mid-nineteenth century has provoked intense debate amongst historians. It is a debate in which you need to be involved. Alternatively the period is sometimes described as one of 'minimalist government' and it would be well-worthwhile to understand what this means and what the implications are for government reforming activity.

USEFUL INFORMATION

1801	First population census: population of England, Scotland and Wales around 11 million – 33% in towns of over 2,500 people (1831 census population of the countries was over 16 million with 43% in towns over 2,500 people; 1851 total 21 million and 54%; 1871 total 26 million and 65%; 1901 total 37 million and 78%.) In 1801 only one town had over 100,000 inhabitants; in 1831 there were 7; 1851:10; 1871:17; 1901:33.
1812–1827	Lord Liverpool Prime Minister
1815	End of Napoleonic War
1815–1822	Period of economic hardship and political repression
1822–1830	**Period of the Liberal Tory Reforms:** prisons, capital offences, moves towards free trade, repeal of the Test Act, Catholic Emancipation Act, formation of the Metropolitan Police Force.
1830–1841	**Period of Whig Reforms**
1830	General Election: formation of Whig Government under Lord Grey.
1832	Parliamentary Reform Act (see Chapter 5).
1833	**Abolition of Slavery** in the British Empire, culmination of the life's work of the leading humanitarian, William Wilberforce.
	First government **Education grant** (£20,000) to church schools.
	Poor Law Amendment Act: milestone in administration of poor relief. Set up the Poor Law Commission to supervise relief. Edwin Chadwick its Secretary. Organised the parishes into Poor Law Unions with local elected Guardians to administer relief. Central principle of less eligibility established, to operate through ending outdoor relief and setting up a workhouse system.
1834–1841	Lord Melbourne Prime Minister
1835	**Municipal Reform Act:** created a national pattern of borough government through Councils largely elected by ratepayers.
1836	**Compulsory Registration of Births, Marriages and Deaths.**
1841–1846	**Conservative Ministry of Sir Robert Peel**
1842	**Mines Act:** no women, or boys under 9, underground.
	Chadwick's 'Report on the Sanitary Condition of the Labouring Population' published.
1844–1845	Reports of the Royal Commission on the Health of Towns published.
1848	**Public Health Act:** Established a General Board of Health to supervise the workings of Local Boards of Health. Localities could request that these be established but in areas of high mortality they could also be imposed.
1866	Sanitary Act.
1870	**Education Act:** first schools paid for from rates with local School Boards elected by ratepayers to run them. This extension of education provision had been held up by rivalry between the Churches. Provided elementary education only.
1872 & 1875	**Public Health Acts:** The latter was a measure codifying earlier Acts and remained the basis of the sanitary code until after the First World War.

EXAMINATION QUESTIONS

Q1 Consider the influences working for and against factory and mines reform in the period before 1850, and indicate the extent of such reforms. (AEB 1988)

Q2 Why had the Poor Law become a matter for concern by 1834, and how far was the Poor Law Amendment Act an improvement on the previous situation? (London 1990)

Q3 'The importance of the Public Health Act of 1848 has not been exaggerated.' Discuss this view. (JMB 1989)

Q4 To what extent and for what reasons did the application of the New Poor Law fail to conform to the original principles laid down in 1834? (Oxford 1989)

Q5 Was Edwin Chadwick more of a hindrance than a help to the public health movement in the years up to 1858? (London 1990)

OUTLINE ANSWERS

Question 1

Influences for – humanitarianism, work of individuals, Shaftesbury, Sadler, Parliamentary Committees and Royal Commissions giving publicity (illustrate this from the reports) Benthamism, build up of legislation, work of inspectors.

Influences against – vested interests notably employers, ideas of laissez-faire, cost, lack of working class commitment and in any case no political power, lethargy and ignorance of those with political power.

Indicate extent – list Acts and indicate limitations of terms but also limited number of inspectors and their problems (e.g. age of children); indifference of some magistrates. Stress that passing an Act did not solve a problem. Probably it was more important as a precedent for future reforming activity than for the practical consequences in the period covered by this question.

Question 2

See the 'Student's Answer' on page 43.

Question 3

"The 1848 Public Health Act was an administrative milestone."

- Refer to attention given by historians to the Act. Try to cite briefly two or three authors who have written on it.
- Refer at greater length to great public attention and debate it received at the time of its passage, mention the emphasis placed on it in the work of Edwin Chadwick.
- Stress on Act not exaggerated: explain why – foundation of sanitary reform, ineffective local government powers before (indicate briefly) replaced by national system of Local Boards of Health, indicate their powers and future achievement (give examples of sanitary improvement but keep it brief).
- Basis of later legislation tackling whole range of public health issues, give important examples especially 1875 Public Health Act.
- Refer to pattern of central supervision which also survived, for the 1854 death of the General Board of Health is misleading and reforms went on.

Conclusion: it was the first basic step towards the possibility of a civilised life in urban Britain and the basis of the sanitary achievement of the rest of the century.

Question 4

"The 1834 Poor Law Act provided a national pattern for poor relief."

- Establish principles of 1834, refer to Royal Commission and Act – deterrence, less eligibility, end of outdoor relief, discourage demoralisation of the poorer classes, keep costs down, workhouse test for relief, close central supervision.
- Forgotten principle is that it was accepted by the Act that *something* had to be done for the totally destitute.
- Much of the new system of poor relief was shaped by these principles, building of workhouses, harsh conditions, almost certainly discouraged many from seeking relief and so held costs down and promoted rugged independence.
- Pattern of national provision emerged and was closely supervised.
- Pattern of poor relief into twentieth century dominated by the principles laid down in 1834 and by the vision of the workhouse which was their central feature.
- Judgements on failures to conform must bear the above in mind.
- Chief failures in urban areas; outdoor relief went on, explain why: single purpose workhouses for each category of pauper, which was central to deterrence principle, were not built because of cost.
- Opposition in the North delayed but did not block implementation.

Conclusion: failures to conform interesting in detail but of less significance than remarkable uniformity imposed.

A TUTOR'S ANSWER TO QUESTION 5

Chadwick's contribution to the public health movement prior to 1848 was central to achieving the Public Health Act passed in that year. As that Act was the first major piece of sanitary legislation and the cornerstone of the sanitary code until 1875 it is difficult to see much merit in the judgement implied in this question. After 1848 his role was certainly more controversial but even then the final answer to the question would be a firm 'no'.

Awareness of the sorry state of urban public health developed slowly and legislation came later than in other fields. Both the Whigs before 1841 and Peel's Conservatives after 1841 failed to take action. Pressure groups only emerged in the late 1830s and the 1840s long after poor law reform and factory reform were exercising Parliament. Chadwick's role in building up an awareness of the extent and the gravity of the urban public health problem was crucial in securing the tardy legislation in this field and his 'Report on the Sanitary Condition of the Labouring Population of Great Britain' was a key document in this process. It alone played a large part in encouraging the formation of the most effective pressure group in this area namely the Health of Towns Association. He produced the evidence that expectation of life in the great cities was on occasion half that for similar groups in rural areas, at birth a Manchester labourer's child could expect on average to live 17 years, a Rutland farm labourer's child 38 years and almost 60% of children born in Manchester would die before their fifth birthday.

> Chadwick – the key propagandist and educator.

It was Chadwick who, from his privileged position as Secretary of the Poor Law Commission, provided this sort of ammunition for the sanitary cause and who made the moral case palatable to the influential middle class by linking the statistics on sickness and death to the high cost of providing poor relief. Chadwick established the scale of the problem at a time when it was being ignored by those with political influence.

By using statistics as the basis for the sanitary campaign Chadwick demonstrated that the problem was essentially linked to the urban environment. His first report was followed by his 'Report on the Practice of Internment in Towns', again making use of statistics as the basis of his message especially in relation to overcrowding in urban working class districts.

It cannot be argued that Chadwick was pressing at an already open door for the prevailing mood was one of indifference based on ignorance. The cholera epidemic of 1831 had produced local flurries of activity but the health committees then set up were only temporary and most of the sanitary legislation was at this time ineffective and was applied only through local Acts. The reform of municipal government carried out in 1835 had provided no powers in the sanitary field and a massive effort was needed to build up pressure to persuade a Parliament, with far more interesting things to pursue than national sanitary legislation, that action was essential. Chadwick's Reports were crucial to that campaign and in the years to 1848 he continued to be a relentless propagandist for the sanitary cause in letters, reports, debates and in organising evidence to the Royal Commission on the health of towns.

> He also had a programme for sanitary action.

In this period he went on to answer the problems he had done so much to identify by working out a sanitary code on which reform should be based. Reform, he argued, would have to be comprehensive taking in drainage, sewage, street paving and water supply, to be run by one comprehensive authority for each natural region of drainage and financed by mortgages on the rates. He went beyond this into the details of drainage and into methods of enforcement of the sanitary code. His was the vision which inspired the 1848 Act though some of his proposals were not adopted. He was so energetic and so brilliant a propagandist that the efforts of others in the field have been neglected but his importance at this time is scarcely open to challenge.

After 1848 his role is more open to question. The reform had aroused much opposition as a measure of centralisation and the General Board of Health had many enemies who grew in number as the Act was applied to more and more towns through the establishment of local boards of health. It was also something of a football in the game of Westminster party politics. Chadwick unfortunately was not good at playing political games, his energy in controversial causes had made him many enemies. He did not suffer fools gladly, was convinced of the rightness of his own opinions and had a sharp tongue. Amongst others he made enemies of the engineering profession (by his ruthless insistence on the use of small-bore drains), of the Parish Guardians and the magistrates of London over measures to deal with the cholera, of great numbers of ratepayers everywhere once the costs of sanitary improvement became clear. The working class who stood to benefit most from Chadwick's work were apathetic, voiceless and voteless. The Board's and Chadwick's

> But he found it easy to make enemies.

most powerful enemies were in Parliament; they resented his earlier role with the powerful Poor Law Commission, saw his present powers and proposals as an assault on English liberties and harnessed an assortment of local grievances to force his resignation in 1854. The Board itself survived him for only another four years. All this might suggest that there is substance in the charge which heads this essay but this is not, in fact the full story. The work done until 1858 by the General Board, did not end but was shared out amongst other government agencies, the number of Local Boards of Health continued to grow to over 700 and the 1848 Act was followed by major Public Health and Sanitary Acts in 1866, 1872 and 1875. The momentum of sanitary reform survived Chadwick's fall and legislating for public health became part of the normal business of government. The difficulties of the 1848–1854 period should not be allowed to detract from acknowledgement of the fact that this transformation from the 1830s was largely the result of Chadwick's efforts as administrator, educator and propagandist.

"The key figure in the sanitary movement."

A STUDENT'S ANSWER TO QUESTION 2

In 1832 the enfranchisement of the economically strong middle class occurred, a factor which was crucial in the reform of the old Speenhamland System (1795). The first reward that the working class received after their struggles to win the vote in 1832 was the Poor Law Amendment Act, an Act which was despised throughout the land. Certainly the increasing political influence of the middle class was the main reason why the Poor Law had become a matter for concern, as following the Victorian principles of thrift and laissez-faire the middle class strove to cut down the cost of the expensive Speenhamland System. It is certainly true that the System cost ratepayers a great deal of money, a cost which accelerated during the Napoleonic wars. The Speenhamland System paid out money depending on the number of children and the price of bread so with the advent of the Napoleonic wars it was impossible to import foreign grain, a factor which raised the cost of poor relief. The expense of the Poor Law therefore was a major factor why it became a matter for concern, not only amongst the middle, but also amongst the upper classes who had to pay rates.

"It wasn't all Speenhamland; you need to elaborate."

It was also noted that the Swing Riots which occurred at the beginning of the 1830s happened in areas where poor law payments were highest, a correlation which those in power were quick to seize upon in an atmosphere of European revolution.

"Good!"

Another reason why the Poor Law became a matter for concern was that the highly moral Victorians believed that the Poor Law System led the poor to a life of 'indolence and vice' (Gregg) making them 'immoral, thriftless, insolent and lazy'. Immoral because poor relief increased with the number of children one had, thriftless because one could not usually claim relief until one's savings had been exhausted, insolent because it was believed people expected relief and lazy because there was no incentive to work. These ideas had always been sounded but the enfranchisement of the middle class added another voice to these fears.

"A coherent analysis."

Another reason for concern was the increased awareness by ratepayers of local corruption in the administration of the poor relief.

"This needs elaborating."

The result of this concern was the 1834 Poor Law Amendment Act. Under the Act outdoor relief was abolished and less eligibility introduced where, to dissuade people from claiming relief, conditions were made less eligible than that of the lowest paid labourer. Also, a Poor Law Commission was set up to supervise expenditure and administration.

As to whether the Poor Law Amendment Act was an improvement or not, this depended very much on who you were. Certainly the middle

"Moves on to part 2 of the essay."

and the upper classes were very pleased as the cost of paying poor relief fell dramatically thus saving them money. The Commission too was said to be an improvement as it was less open to corruption and kept a check on local relief administration.

For the working class however, the new system was far from an improvement and the Act was bitterly resented. No distinction was made between the different types of poor, unlike the old system, and the Act blamed the poor for their situation without making any attempt to find out why so many were poor. Most men expected to have to receive poor relief at some time in their lives, not necessarily through any fault of their own but often through trade fluctuation or bad climatic conditions. Now the poor were made to feel ashamed of their situation, a situation which they could not rectify. The safety net of the Old Poor Law had been removed.

“Another effective paragraph.”

Certainly the sheer numbers of the poor who needed to claim relief meant that it was impossible to stop outdoor relief altogether as there were insufficient places in the workhouses to accommodate the poor so in this respect the Amendment Act did not bring about as clear an improvement as had been hoped when the Act was framed.

“Is this entirely logical?”

Despite its short-sightedness and ignorance to the true situation however, the Act changing the distribution of Poor Relief did last until the twentieth century so, although it had many faults, it could be said that if it was not an improvement it would not have lasted so long. For the poor in 1834 however, the situation was far from improved when many were placed still deeper into poverty.

EXAMINER COMMENT

This essay is quite fluently written and contains a range of relevant ideas which would ensure it a mark comfortably above the pass level. It needs rather more sustained analysis to move into the higher mark grades. The early references suggest that the pre-1834 system is all Speenhamland which was not the case and you need to be more fully informed on this than this candidate was. The best passages are those on what contemporaries saw as the defects of the pre-1834 system. The references to the middle classes and the vote may be over-emphasised but they show a candidate who is not afraid of ideas and prepared to use them.

How would you improve this attempt?

USEFUL SOURCES OF INFORMATION

General reading

F Bedarida, *A Social History of England 1851–1975*, Methuen 1979

P Gregg, *A Social and Economic History of Britain 1760–1980* (8th edition), Nelson 1984; a favourite of long-standing.

T May, *An Economic and Social History of Britain 1760–1970*, Longman 1987; mainly social history.

Further reading

E J Evans, *The Forging of the Modern State: early industrial Britain 1783–1870*, Longman 1980; very stimulating for its ideas and with much factual material to back them.

D Fraser, *The Evolution of the British Welfare State* (2nd edition), Macmillan 1984.

U Henriques, *Before the Welfare State*, Longman 1979; probably the most logically organised, and therefore the most valuable, of all the works listed here. It will be of most use to those taking an option paper on this topic.

E Hopkins, *A Social History of the English Working Classes 1815–1945*, Arnold 1979.

M E Rose, *The Relief of Poverty 1834–1914*, Macmillan 1972.

Of the above authors Evans, Fraser and Rose have been particularly noteworthy in the publication of important works on nineteenth century social history. Option Paper candidates may well find it of great value to follow up their other publications, perhaps through the Public Library. Most of the books listed here have bibliographies which will assist in this.

Linked topic areas

- Social consequences of the Industrial Revolution
- Political reforms and reform movements (Chartists & Anti-Corn Law League) 1815–1867 (see Chapter 5)
- The British economy in the 19th century
- The decline of laissez-faire philosophy in the late 19th century and the early 20th century moves to collectivism
- The Liberal Reforms, 1906–1914 (see Chapter 8)

CHAPTER 5

POLITICAL LIFE 1830–1868

GETTING STARTED

A good start could be made by reminding yourself of the fundamental economic and social changes which happened in Britain in the first half of the nineteenth century, for these dictated many of the political developments of the period through into the twentieth century. Read the 'Essential Principles' sections of Chapters 3 and 4. Then try to get a bird's eye view of the major political events of the 1830–1870 period from a simple textbook published for younger students. Do not memorise these but prepare an outline framework into which you can fit your ideas as your studies proceed. Remind yourself of the workings of the British Constitution: the powers of Commons, Lords (with a veto on legislation until 1911) and Crown, of the stages through which Bills passed to become law and the evolution in the period of political parties.

In terms of political ideas the events and the rallying cries of the French Revolution of 1789 onwards cast a long shadow which in Britain owed much to the writings of Tom Paine. The Revolution was a spur to Radical demands for political reform but had a more ambiguous effect on conservative thought. It drove some Conservatives to reaction, a dreadful warning on how minor reform could lead to destruction, and others to the notion that a similar outcome could best be avoided in Britain by timely concessions on a modest scale. The other important set of political ideas in this period concerned the notion of laissez-faire, of minimum government activity and financial stringency being desirable ends in themselves. A definition of the term is offered on page 36 in Chapter 4.

The 1815–1830 period is here regarded as an introduction to later events but in some syllabuses it will be an important topic area in its own right and so making your own list of the essential principles within it will be valuable revision practice. The distress and discontent after 1815 and the repressive policies of Lord Liverpool are a common source of questions. An assessment of whether matters changed fundamentally after 1822 with the Liberal Tories, or whether their work was largely tinkering around the edges of real problems, will give a balance to your study of the period to 1830. Treated purely as an introduction to later politics it is useful to be able to give examples of popular political demands from 1815 (quoting Peterloo as an example) and to be able to explain how and why the passing of Catholic Emancipation in 1829 had such dramatic effects for the Tory party.

ESSENTIAL PRINCIPLES

1832 PARLIAMENTARY REFORM ACT

"A common examination topic."

The reasons for this Act, how it was passed and its effects make up one of the most common examination topics in nineteenth century politics. The many defects which existed in the pre-1832 Parlimentary system became increasingly anomalous in a period of rapid economic acceleration, social change and population growth. Do not just learn a list of defects: be able to use them to explain why there was growing pressure for reform. The aristocratic constitution began to seem an anachronism in an emerging urban industrial society. Political radicalism had many sources and, despite repression, advanced rapidly after 1815. From 1822 disquiet grew within the Parliamentary system, not least because of the cost of elections, whilst the ability of the Tory government to resist the reform demands was fatally undermined by, first, Catholic Emancipation and then the results of the 1830 election.

"What were the motives of the Whigs?"

The period from the Election to the Reform Bill becoming law deserves close study. Be ready to explain how and why the Bill was passed. The motives of the Whigs in introducing a Reform Bill, whether to preserve aristocratic power or to accommodate the demands of the radicals, and the roles of Russell, Grey, Wellington, Peel, the Crown, and pressure outside Parliament, in securing the passage of the Bill, are all important.

The move to reform 1830–1832

1830 July	Death of George IV, accession of William IV, who was more prepared to tolerate reform and to be flexible if necessary, removed one obstacle.
1830 Nov	Lord Grey became Prime Minister.
1831 March	First Reform Bill introduced into Commons by Lord John Russell, greeted with outrage as far too radical. Defeated in Committee.
1831 April	General Election, demanded by Grey, amidst much popular reforming excitement.
1831 June	Second Reform Bill passed Commons.
1831 Oct	Bill defeated in Lords. Reform riots in Bristol and other towns.
1831 Dec	Third Reform Bill introduced.
1832 May	Lords amended Third Reform Bill. William IV, reluctant to create enough Whig Peers to carry the Bill through the Lords, asked Wellington, Tory leader, to form a government but he was unable to do so. William then indicated he would agree to create the peers and Grey, who had resigned on the issue, returned.
1832 June	Threat deterred enough Peers from opposition and Third Reform Bill was passed.

The participants

Lord Grey: Whig Prime Minister, from an ancient Whig family. He had a record of supporting reform since the 1790s. Believed in a moderate reform to secure political stability.

Lord Melbourne: Whig member of the Cabinet, moderate reformer.

Palmerston: had left Tories because he was in favour of Parliamentary Reform. Foreign Secretary, sat in the Commons as an Irish Peer.

Lord John Russell: also from old Whig family, enthusiastic reformer, chairman of Cabinet committee which drew up the Whig reform proposals seen by many MPs as very radical. His work ensured that there was an overall reform and not just tinkering with a few rotten boroughs.

Lord Brougham: became Lord Chancellor, wanted sweeping reform. Unpopular in the Cabinet.

Duke of Wellington: Tory Prime Minister 1828–1830, determined opponent of any measure of reform. In 1829 recognised the need for Catholic emancipation and reluctantly carried it, this split the Tory Party which lost the 1830 election.

Sir Robert Peel: leading Tory in Commons, fought reform, but after passage of Act accepted he had to work within the new system.

“Another common examination topic.”

The outline terms of the Reform Act form the basis for another common series of examination questions evaluating how fully the Act met the demands of radicals, what defects of the aristocratic constitution survived despite the Act, and for considering both the shrill hostility of its opponents and the deep disappointment of, particularly the working class, political radicals with the outcome. How satisfied were the Whigs entitled to be that the Act fulfilled their aims in introducing the Bill?

The main terms of the Great Reform Act of 1832

1 **Voting qualifications** (note Act throughout specified ‘adult males’)
a) *In county seats:* (previously only £2 freeholders could vote)
Owners of freehold land worth £2 per year:
Copyholders of land worth £10 per year: Leaseholders and tenants of land worth £50 per year. (This was introduced in debate in the Lords – the Chandos Amendment – to increase the influence of landlords in county seats by pressure on their tenants)
b) *In borough seats:* (previously no national qualification)
Owners and occupiers of property worth £10 per year. Pre-1832 voters who did not qualify kept their vote but no new voters under the old qualifications

2 **Changes in the distribution of seats**
- 56 boroughs lost both MPs, 30 lost one of the two.
22 new parliamentary boroughs gained two MPs, 19 gained one.
- Larger counties gained seats (pre-1832 all but Yorkshire had two MPs), with Yorkshire having six, 26 more having four, 7 having three and 6 keeping two.
- 5 new seats for Wales: 2 borough, 3 county.

3 **Separate Act for Scotland**
a) *In counties:* all owners of property worth £10 a year, £10 long leaseholders and £50 tenants could vote.
b) *In boroughs:* the £10 occupier qualification applied.
Scottish counties retained their previous 30 seats and the boroughs increased theirs from 15 to 23.

4 **For Ireland**
a) *In counties:* £10 property owners (this had existed since Catholic Emancipation in 1829) and £10 leaseholders could vote.
b) *In boroughs:* the main qualification was the £10 occupier.
County seats remained at 64 and borough seats increased from 35 to 39 plus a second seat for the University of Dublin.

RESULTS OF THE REFORM ACT

The Reform Act created the frame for political life until 1867. It was of course not a complete reform of all the earlier defects. The geographic redistribution of seats in favour of the Midlands and the North did not fully reflect the population balance and too many small boroughs, where the influence of individuals was strong, retained their representation. There was no secret ballot so that pressure could still be put on voters, nor was this seen as unreasonable. The ‘Outline Answer’ to Question 1 is relevant here.

It is a fallacy to see the Act as giving political power to the middle classes but, in increasing the electorate from around 435,000 to perhaps 700,000, it did bring many people of modest wealth and property within the political system; it was certainly a grievous disappointment to working class radicals, giving the vote to less than one adult male in five. Arguably the Act’s main importance was as a precedent for further reform. When you are studying political episodes after 1832 occasionally pause to reflect on what they tell you about the Act’s impact, for example:

- The abolition of slavery in the British Empire, in 1833, probably owes much to the 1832 Reform Act for the subsequent election had weakened the power of the West Indian plantation lobby and strengthened the representation of middle-class urban religious influences in the Commons.

- The Act required qualified persons to register for the vote and a Register of Voters had to be compiled for each constituency. Compiling these registers gave a boost to party organisation in the constituencies, especially in Boroughs and so marked a stage in the emergence of political parties in the country. In rural areas deference to your social superiors was still usually the main influence on how you voted.

SUCCESS OF THE ACT

Repeal of the Corn Laws in 1846 (see page 51) was possible without a prolonged controversy between urban and rural Britain because the 1832 Act had been based on recognition that the new urban interests had to be given due political representation. That this potentially grave crisis passed with relatively little turmoil is arguably the best tribute to the value of the Reform Act. The other is that further amendment did not occur, despite rapidly changing circumstances, for 35 years.

WHIG REFORMS

1833–1841

"A 'Decade of Reform'?"

In a special option paper each of the major reforms of these years, their origins, passage and impact could in its own right be the subject of an examination question. In outline papers the overall reforming achievement of the Whig governments of Grey and Melbourne needs assessing and in this enough will have to be known about the individual reforms to provide illustration and substantiation of the judgements made. The main measures are listed in the 'Useful Information' section of this chapter but their impact is also considered in Chapter 4 and in deciding what was the contribution of this 'Decade of Reform' to the modernisation of British Society it would be helpful to use the material and comments there. This is particularly true of the Factory Act of 1833, the Poor Law Amendment Act of 1834 and the Municipal Reform Act of 1835, which are the three most important measures to be considered. A government which provided for the world's first urban industrial nation:

- the first grant to provide education
- the first inspectors of factories
- a radically new scheme for relief of the poor
- a national pattern of town government
- the first requirement to register births marriages and deaths

is entitled to a serious and informed assessment of its achievements, and all this in addition to parliamentary reform. There was also a series of measures which rationalised the administration of the property of the Church of England and placed its finances on a more sensible basis.

As the decade proceeded the Whigs lost their reforming impetus. Lord Melbourne, one of Britain's most engaging Prime Ministers, was no natural reformer. The Tories recovered their nerve as they realised that the 1832 Reform Act was not going to lead to attacks on other parts of the Constitution and as their electoral fortunes revived. The Whigs found increasing difficulty with finances and after the 1837 election were content simply to be there. The notion that the Reform Act would destroy the Tories and lead automatically to long periods of Whig government was not borne out in practice.

PEEL AND THE CONSERVATIVES

1830–1846

"Tory recovery."

"Did Peel modernise the Tories?"

The other important theme in the 1830s is the revival of Tory/Conservative fortunes from the debacle of the 1830 election and of the failure of their resistance to the 1832 Reform Act to victory in the 1841 General Election. Peel's contribution to this has to be assessed as have the changes he brought to the tactics and the philosophy of 'Conservatism'; his Tamworth Manifesto usually forms the central piece of evidence in such assessment. It has been suggested that his success in modernising the party can be exaggerated and that his later difficulties over aid to the Catholic college at Maynooth in Ireland and more seriously over repealing the Corn Laws reveal how little reform of old Tory prejudices in favour of

Protestantism and landowners there had been. You should try to include comment of this sort in any overall assessment of his work.

The Tamworth Manifesto

The document deserves reading in full but the central argument is:-

'But the Reform Bill, it is said, constitutes a new era, and it is the duty of a Minister to declare explicitly – first, whether he will maintain the Bill itself, secondly whether he will act on the spirit in which it was conceived.

With respect to the Reform Bill itself, I will repeat now the declaration I made when I entered the House of Commons as a Member of the Reform Parliament – that I consider the Reform Bill a final and irrevocable settlement of a great Constitutional question – a settlement which no friend to the peace and welfare of this country would attempt to disturb, either by direct or insidious means.

Then, as the spirit of the Reform Bill, and the willingness to adopt and enforce it as a rule of government: if, by adopting the spirit of the Reform Bill, it be meant that we are to live in a perpertual vortex of agitation; that public men can only support themselves in public estimation by adopting every popular impression of the day, – by promising the instant redress of anything which anybody may call an abuse – by abandoning altogether that great aid of government – more powerful than either law or reason – the respect for ancient rights, and the deference to prescriptive authority; if this be the spirit of the Reform Bill, I will not undertake to adopt it. But if the spirit of the Reform Bill implies merely a careful review of institutions, civil and ecclesiastical, undertaken in a friendly temper, combining, with the firm maintenance of established rights, the correction of proved abuses and the redress of real grievances, – in that case, I can for myself and colleagues undertake to act in such a spirit and with such intentions.'

Fig. 5.1 The Tamworth Manifesto

A full examination of Peel's political achievement must also review his career between 1812 and 1830; from 1812 to 1818 he was Secretary for Ireland and from 1822 to 1827 and 1828 to 1830 Home Secretary (where he was involved in criminal law and prison reform, the establishment of the Metropolitan Police and passing of Catholic Emancipation, this much against his personal inclinations and through which he antagonised many of his own party).

PEEL'S MINISTRY 1841–1846

The main themes of Peel's Ministry of 1841–1846 are economic and the relative absence of social reforms requires explanation as do Peel's renewed difficulties with Catholicism, this time in Ireland. The Budgets of 1842 and 1845 were within the wider context of the growing importance of Free Trade ideas. The last months of the period were taken up by Peel's increasingly missionary zeal in repealing the Corn Laws and this must be set in the frame of his economic policy generally and needs to include reference to the part played by Gladstone.

“A national rather than a party leader?”

The charge is made, in the titles of examination questions at least, that Peel neglected the interests of his party over Catholic Emancipation, the Maynooth Grant and, of course, Corn Law Repeal. A common examination question invites discussion of the claim that he was more zealous in defence of national interests than in looking after the prospects of his party – a great statesman but not a great Party leader. Certainly he was aloof from the ranks of Tory MPs, despite the great affection in which his Cabinet colleagues held him, and this undoubtedly contributed to the party split of 1846. Peel's contribution to the Conservative Party is compared to that of Disraeli in the 'Tutor's Answer' in Chapter 7.

Revision exercise

A useful revision exercise would be to prepare a list of topics about which you will need to be able to comment with reference to what they tell you about Peel or what Peel did about them. There is no virtue in memorising this for it is the comments you are able to make around it and relate to a range of examination questions about Peel that will make it valuable. The A-level examination is not a competition so a joint group exercise, first identifying the important issues and then thinking of the comments about Peel that they give rise to, might well be appropriate.

REPEAL OF THE CORN LAWS

The Corn Laws of 1815, protecting the farming interest, were seen as increasingly anachronistic in a country where commercial and industrial wealth were growing in importance. The removal, in Peel's Budgets of 1842 and 1845, of many other duties on trade made their continued protection of agriculture seem all the more an offence to the middle-class trading interest.

THE ANTI-CORN LAW LEAGUE

The campaign of the Anti-Corn Law League, led by Cobden and Bright sought to bring pressure for repeal on the government by registering supporters of repeal as electors in a number of winnable urban county constituencies. Their tactics reveal much about the workings of the post-1832 political system but opinions differ as to their significance in bringing about repeal. It seems unlikely that Peel would have welcomed the prospect of having in 1847 to fight a general election as head of the party proposing to retain a tax on food. Be ready to evaluate the achievement of the Anti-Corn Law League in the light of other factors bringing about repeal. Look up the careers of Cobden and Bright.

PEEL AND REPEAL

"Peel's motives for repeal."

The appalling tragedy of famine in Ireland and Peel's own passionate conversion to repeal, whatever his reasons, should also be considered. Peel was perhaps intellectually convinced by the case for repeal but would have been happier, as leader of the party of the landed interest, to let others carry it out. It has however been argued that he had become so convinced of the rightness of repeal that he decided to use the excuse of the Irish famine to push it through regardless of party interests.

Exam answers

"The political results were more important than the economic."

You should try to indicate these conflicting interpretations in any appropriate answer. The course of the repeal conflict from the foundation of the Anti-Corn Law League in 1839 to repeal in 1846, and the consequences of repeal, far more dramatic for Westminster politics, especially the Conservative Party, than for British agriculture, form an easily organised and frequently posed examination topic.

Note: British farming enjoyed a period of prosperity in the 25 years after its protection had been removed: there was no immediate abundance of duty-free foreign corn to flood the British market and rising population and living standards generally ensured a steady rise in demand for food.

CHARTISM

This, by far the most successful working-class political movement of the nineteenth century, it is a topic of wide-ranging importance and the 'Student's Answer' at the end of this chapter discusses why so many working people became Chartists.

ORIGINS OF CHARTISM

"The origins of working-class radicalism."

The origins, as a reaction to the Parliamentary Reform Act and the Poor Law Amendment Act, and linked generally to economic distress, have to be gauged and the significance of the political proposals understood. Remember that they were not just conjured up but stem from the radical political tradition going back to such events as Peterloo and to men like Tom Paine. Unlike the Anti-Corn Law League, Chartism was an attempt to put pressure on the political system from the outside. This was a much more difficult thing to do. The tactics employed, first by mass petitions to Parliament followed by the Sacred Month or general strike, the growing frustration and the deepening divisions over how to proceed are all important. Central was the issue of violence as a weapon to be employed if all else failed; argument over this amongst the Chartists was never resolved and contributed largely to the deepening divisions in their ranks.

FAILURE OF CHARTISM

The reasons for the failure of Chartism are frequently asked for by examiners. Above all the relative importance of these should be evaluated for an undifferentiated list will be of limited value. The strength of the obstacles ranged against the Chartists is often forgotten in such explanations but is as much part of the answer as any discussion of Chartist weaknesses.

The People's Charter

- Adult manhood suffrage
- Secret ballot
- Annual elections
- Abolition of the property qualifications for MPs
- Payments of MPs
- Equal electoral districts

The Chartists

William Lovett & Francis Place: From the London Working Men's Association, responsible for drawing up the Charter.

Thomas Attwood MP: From the Birmingham Political Union, presented the first Chartist petition to the Commons; a banker with a programme for currency reform.

Feargus O'Connor: Ran the extreme radical paper *The Northern Star* from Leeds.

Note: Material on the Chartists can often be adapted to quite different essays on many aspects of the lives of the working class and should be studied with this possibility in mind.

POLITICAL FLUIDITY

Effects of 1846 crisis

This was a consequence of the political crisis of 1846, arising especially from the split in Peel's Conservative Party which had been the chief political result of the Repeal of the Corn Laws. Why the political fluidity continued for so long needs a wider assessment, including a look at the idiosyncratic role played at crucial points by the two great Whig leaders, *Palmerston* and *Russell* and at the abrupt end of the Anti-Corn Law League and the later loss of political support by its one-time leaders *Cobden* and *Bright*, in which their opposition to the Crimean War was of crucial importance. The refusal of Peel to give a lead to his distinguished ex-Conservative supporters, and their dwindling influence and numbers after his death, left the Peelites as a group who were too able to ignore but too few to form their own administration. In the 1850s the focus narrows from them to their most distinguished member, Gladstone, and where he was to find his political future.

Quest for stability

The Conservative Party under Disraeli even after it had, in 1852, abandoned protectionist policies, was unable to gain enough Commons support to provide stability. It remains necessary, starting with the ideas briefly sketched above, to examine why the anti-Conservative groups proved unable to work together to achieve that end. Arguably the most hopeful attempt, led by the Peelite Aberdeen, foundered on the many rocks thrown up by the Crimean War. The confusion began to abate with Gladstone's decision, in 1859, to join Palmerston's Government, which can be seen as opening a more stable period. There was nothing inevitable about this for he had, only a year earlier, given serious thought to the suggestion that he took office under the Conservative Lord Derby.

> "Gladstone joined with the Whigs."

ROLE OF THE WHIGS

1830–1868

This is a less popular topic with examiners than others referred to here. It is however worth some thought for much of the necessary information and many of the ideas needed to handle it will already have been met under other headings. From the high days of 1830 to 1832 the Whigs declined to electoral defeat in 1841. (See Whig Reforms on page 49). Thereafter their importance centres on the careers of *Palmerston* and *Russell* through to the 1860s; it is a series of personal judgements which are needed rather than an opinion on a political party, though after 1846 stable government was virtually impossible without Whig involvement. Questions often involve explanations of why the Whigs took so long in dying and on their contribution to the rise of the Liberal Party.

GLADSTONIAN LIBERALISM

BEGINNINGS – THE 1860S

"The sinews of the Liberal Party."

This topic can be studied in its own right or, more briefly, as a prelude to work on Gladstone and the Liberals at a later stage, especially the 1868–1874 Liberal Government. It is partly a study of social and economic developments, urban and industrial growth, developing middle-class wealth, an expanding Press, especially in the provinces, and the growing self-confidence of Nonconformist congregations. The other aspect is to evaluate the contribution of *Bright* and of *Gladstone* in their articulation of the demands of this new Britain. Too many candidates forget Bright.

GLADSTONE'S IMPORTANCE

The movement of Gladstone from a reactionary young Tory in the 1830s to his emergence as leader of the new Liberal Party in the 1868 Election deserves special attention: key points in this personal progress came in 1846 and 1859; try to establish how. His importance depended less, at this stage of his career, on his popular appeal than on his pre-eminent reputation as a finance minister and an outstanding Commons speaker. Gladstonian finance, in the 1850s and the 1860s, is a topic in its own right and can be linked to questions on laissez-faire and the role of government generally, telling a lot about the character of the later, fully-fledged, Liberal Party. It is a theme which is more fully developed in Chapter 6.

THE CONSERVATIVES

1846–1868

Survival and impotence

Often this topic is approached as an assessment of the early *Disraeli*, which would also require study of his, fairly limited, political career prior to 1846 (see Chapter 7). The dilemma the Conservatives were in after 1846 is illustrated by their three short-lived minority administrations. The achievement of both *Derby* and Disraeli in preserving the party for better times in the 1870s needs recognition.

Possible questions

Examiners often set Disraeli's contribution to the Conservative Party against that of Peel, whom he of course had destroyed in 1846. Such comparison is a logical extension of a specialised study of Conservatism under Peel and a valuable introduction to Disraeli's political actions in 1867 and indeed to his later career as Prime Minister. An essay comparing the contribution of the two men is presented in Chapter 7.

1867 PARLIAMENTARY REFORM ACT

There were in the 1850s and 1860s half-hearted attempts within Parliament at proposing another reform of the Parliamentary system and popular pressure groups emerged in the 1860s.

Popular pressure or party rivalry

"A product of party rivalry."

A key issue is to what extent popular pressure was instrumental in bringing about the 1867 reform. Opinions have, in the past, differed sharply on this. Today those who see the shape of the reform as a product of bitter party and personal rivalry and debate in the Commons appear to be in the majority. A few spectacular popular incidents, notably rioting in Hyde Park, are seen to have been of minor importance. First the Liberal Bill was defeated and then the Conservative Bill was made sharply more radical before it became law. Like the earlier struggle for the 1832 Reform Act, this episode deserves close study of the detailed interpretations of events. Thereafter it is only commonsense to know the main terms of the legislation, for the 1867 Act altered the pattern of party politics in the constituencies, extending greatly the trends to greater party activity first noted as a result of the 1832 Reform Act. It set the political frame for the next seventeen years, a period which was to be of crucial importance in the development of British party politics.

General questions

The same range of material is often useful in general questions on Gladstone and Disraeli, especially the latter, whose motives in pursuing reform in 1867 form a major feature of any assessment of his political career overall.

The main terms of the 1867 Reform Act

1 Franchise
  a) *In boroughs:* granted to all ratepaying householders (cf. 1832 £10 householders); an amendment making all occupiers responsible for their own rates, which doubled the number who would gain the vote, was accepted by Disraeli rather than lose the measure. Borough franchise also went to £10 lodgers.
  b) *In counties:* franchise given to £12 leaseholders (cf. 1832 £50)
  These clauses doubled the electorate from just over 1 million and gave substantial numbers of working men in towns the vote for the first time. County changes were nowhere near so radical, new voters were middle-class.

2 Seats redistributed:
- 45 taken from boroughs with less than 10,000 population
- 25 went to larger counties
- 15 went to new boroughs
- 4 cities got a third MP
- London University obtained one MP

FOREIGN POLICY

1830–1870

This topic involves an assessment of the work of *Palmerston* and of his Conservative counterpart *Aberdeen*. Note, in the 'Useful Information' section below, how they spanned the years and the incidents with which they were involved. A map of Europe from 1815 will help greatly (see page 126).

Exam questions

"Questions on Palmerston's foreign policy are common."

Questions on Palmerston are very common but do not neglect Aberdeen for sometimes an evaluation of policy across the period is asked for and knowledge of his distinctive contribution then becomes essential. Many of the incidents are colourful and therefore easily remembered. You are likely to be asked to explain the motives (the principles) which lay behind policy and how effective the policies were from a British point of view. A lot happened in foreign affairs in these years so that examiners frequently ask for examination of a specified part of the period:

- 1830–1841
- 1830–1846
- 1846–1865

Be ready for this. Each year, in this topic, a few candidates disregard the stated boundaries and so totally waste a proportion of their efforts.

USEFUL INFORMATION

(See also the 'Useful Information' section in Chapter 4.)

1830	Accession of William IV. General Election; formation of Whig Ministry under Lord Grey.
1830–1832	Struggle to pass the Parliamentary Reform Bill
1832	Parliamentary Reform Act (The Great Reform Act)
1833	Slavery abolished, grant to church schools, Factory Act
1834	Poor Law Amendment Act
1834–1835	Peel's First Ministry and Tamworth Manifesto
1835–1841	**Lord Melbourne Prime Minister**
1835	Municipal Reform Act
1836	Registration of Births etc. Tithe Commutation Act

1837	Accession of Victoria (reigned to 1901)
	General Election; signs of Conservative recovery.
	Whig Government loses momentum
1838	People's Charter drawn up
1839	First Chartist petition to Parliament
	Foundation of Anti-Corn Law League
	Bedchamber Crisis prevented Peel forming a government.
1841	General Election: formation of Conservative Government.
1841–1846	**Peel's Second Ministry**
1842	'Free Trade' Budget (income tax resumed)
	Mines Act
	Second Chartist petition to Parliament
1844	Bank Charter Act, Railways Act, Maynooth Grant controversy.
1845	Second 'Free Trade' Budget
1846	Repeal of the Corn Laws; opposition led by Disraeli
	Peel resigned
1846–1852	Russell's Whig Ministry
1852	**Derby's first minority Conservative Ministry**
1852–1855	Aberdeen's Whig–Peelite Coalition Ministry
1855–1858	Palmerston's Whig Ministry
1858–1859	**Derby's second minority Conservative Ministry** (Reform Bill not carried)
1859–1865	**Palmerston's Whig Ministry**
	Gladstone Chancellor of the Exchequer, his Free Trade Budgets.
1865–1866	Russell's Whig Ministry: failure of Reform Bill
1866–1868	**Derby's third minority Conservative Ministry**
1867	Second Parliamentary Reform Act
1868	General Election; Liberal victory
1868–1874	**Gladstone's First Ministry**

Foreign affairs 1830–1870

1830–1841	**Palmerston Foreign Secretary**
1830–1831	Belgian Independence
1833	Treaty of Unkiar Skelessi (see Chapter 15)
1834	Portuguese and Spanish Pretenders
1839–1842	The Opium War
1841	The Straits Convention
1841–1846	**Aberdeen Foreign Secretary:** his work to improve relations with France and the United States.
1846–1851	**Palmerston Foreign Secretary**
1846	Breach with France over Spanish Marriages
1848	Revolutions in Europe
1850	Don Pacifico Affair
1851	Palmerston forced to resign over his recognition of Napoleon III.
1854–1856	The Crimean War (see Chapter 15)
1855–1865	**For almost all this period Palmerston as Prime Minister was the chief influence on British Foreign Policy**
1856	The Arrow incident and bombardment of Canton
1857	The Indian Mutiny
1859–1860	Key events of Italian Unification
1861–1865	American Civil War: the Trent and the Alabama affairs
1863	Polish Revolt: Palmerston unable to assist
1864	Schleswig–Holstein affair. Palmerston unable to fulfill threat to help Danes against Prussia
1865	**Death of Palmerston**
1866	Prussians defeated Austrian Empire
1870	Prussians defeated France. The setting-up of the German Empire created a totally new balance of forces in continental Europe. Britain no longer so able to influence the course of events.

EXAMINATION QUESTIONS

Q1 'When the dust had settled down, Tories might have asked themselves what they had been afraid of, Radicals what they had been fighting for.' Discuss this view of the results of the Reform Act of 1832. (AEB 1988)

Q2 Why had the Whig Party, which carried through parliamentary reform in 1832, become so unpopular by 1841? (Oxford 1989)

Q3 'The reforms of Peel's ministry (1841–1846) were more constructive than those passed by the Whigs between 1830 and 1841.' Discuss. (Welsh 1989)

Q4 Why did many working people become Chartists? (NEAB 1989)

Q5 Document question 'The Parliamentary Reform Act 1832' (London 1990)

Study Documents 1, 2 and 3 below and then answer questions (*a*) to (*f*) which follow:

Document 1

They had taken the population returns for 1821, and they proposed that every borough which appeared by that return to contain less than 2000 inhabitants in 1821 should lose the right of sending members to Parliament (Loud cheering and laughter which lasted for some minutes). This would utterly disenfranchise 60 boroughs. (Cheers and laughter). But they did not stop here (renewed cheers and laughter) – They proposed that 47 boroughs which contained less than 4000 inhabitants, should be deprived of the right of sending one member to Parliament (Cheers and laughter) . . .

To get rid of these complicated and vexed questions of right of voting, it was highly desirable that the franchise should be vested in real householders and respectable citizens . . . What they proposed then was this – namely that inhabitants of houses paying rates to the amount of £10 a year . . . should have a vote . . . in cities and towns.

(Speech of Lord John Russell in the House of Commons, as reported in *'The Times'*, 2 March 1831)

Document 2

Lay not the flattering unction to your souls that the Whig Bill of Reform will do you any good, except it prove ancillary to Universal Suffrage. The Bill was never intended to do you one particle of good. The object of the promoters was not to change that 'glorious constitution' which has entailed upon you so much misery, but to make it immortal . . . They (the Whigs) know that the old system could not last and desiring to establish another as like it as possible and also to keep their places, they framed the Bill, in the hope of drawing to the feudal aristocrats and yeomanry of counties a large re-inforcement of the middle class. The Bill was in effect, an invitation to the Shopocrats of the enfranchised towns to join the Whigocrats of the country and make common cause with them in keeping down the people and thereby to quell the rising spirit of democracy in England.

(Editorial in *'The Poor Man's Guardian'*, in the form of an address to a forthcoming working-class meeting in Birmingham, 27 October 1832)

Document 3

With respect to the Reform Bill itself, I will repeat now the declaration I made when I entered the House of Commons as a member of the Reformed Parliament – that I consider the Reform Bill a final and irrevocable settlement of a great Constitutional question – a settlement which no friend of the peace and welfare of this country would attempt to disturb, either by direct or by insidious means.

(Address of Sir Robert Peel to the Electors of the Borough of Tamworth, January 1835)

a) In the context of these Documents, explain what is meant by:
   i) 'The population returns for 1821' (line 1);
   ii) 'Universal Suffrage' (line 15); and
   iii) 'a great Constitutional question' (lines 27–28). (*3*)

b) Identify the two broad areas of reform proposed by Russell in Document 1. (*2*)

c) Why might Russell decribe the 'right of voting' as 'complicated and vexed' (line 9)? How might his proposals improve that situation? (*4*)

d) What, in the view of *'The Poor Man's Guardian'* (Document 2), was the Whigs' intention in promoting parliamentary reform? How does the language of the document indicate the newspaper's attitude towards those intentions? (*6*)

e) Examine the reasons given by Peel in Document 3 for his change of attitude towards parliamentary reform. (*4*)

f) On the evidence of these documents, would the writer of Document 2 feel greater hostility towards the author of Document 1 or the author of Document 3 with respect to parliamentary reform? Explain your answer. (*6*)

(*Total 25 marks*)

OUTLINE ANSWERS

Question 1

Indicate Tory fears of sweeping reform briefly and then indicate limitations of the terms of the Act: e.g. many small boroughs survived, only one adult male in 5 had the vote, landlord influence still dominated county seats. Even more important it did not lead to other sweeping reforms, position of Lords, Church and Crown was secure.

Radicals, whose stirring of popular excitement at key moments had helped to secure the passing of the Act, had many grounds for disappointment: e.g. no secret ballot, no votes for working class. Whigs clearly saw it as the final reform, not as a first step. Legislation after the Act was as repressive to the working class as that before, especially the hated Poor Law.

Much truth in the comment for contemporaries could hardly see its importance as an eventual precedent for further reforms.

Question 2

Introduction: the issue is electoral unpopularity as measured in 1837 and 1841 election results. Popularity with non-voters is unmeasurable. Unpopularity with opponents irrelevant.

Post-1832: electoral position unreal, Tory party demoralised, numbers of seats, Whig belief their opponents destroyed.

Gradual recovery: seats reverted to old loyalties amongst a still narrow electorate where traditional pressures still effective. Peel's new image for the Tories saved them and attracted new voters (Tamworth Manifesto). Much of answer derives from revived Tory morale and appeal.

Whig 'mistakes': helped to varying degrees, discuss effect of Poor Law, suspected of attacking Church of England's position, did little on tariffs and trade to help the new middle-class voters, lost support of disillusioned radicals and, under Melbourne ran out of reforming steam.

Financial mismanagement: possibly most important Whig 'mistake'.

Question 3

Introduction: all depends on definition of 'constructive': define as effective in meeting the country's real needs (keep it brief). Argue these changed so simple comparisons unhelpful.

1830–1841: needs were for constitutional and institutional reforms: Whigs did a great deal, refer to impact of 1832 Parliamentary Reform, Poor Law, Municipal Reform, Birth etc. registration. Also tackled long standing social abuses to some extent, brief assessment of Factory, Education, Slavery measures. Agree not all perfect.

1841–46: great issues were economic and Peel did much to meet the challenge; budgets, Corn Laws, Railways, Banking. Basis of future prosperity and social stability? – perhaps but there were other reasons why this came about, he does not deserve all the credit. He did nothing much on pressing social issues, working conditions (except Mines Act) or especially on Public Health.

"Different emphasis of Whig and Conservative reforms."

Conclusion: constructive in different fields. Great Whig achievement was to make Parliamentary constitution adaptable to changing circumstances. Great Peel achievement was to herald in era of Free Trade which survived to 20th century. Record of both on strictly social issues less impressive but the Whigs' poor law and borough government legislation was of pre-eminent importance for the future and on balance make for a rejection of the claim in the essay title.

Note: vast question so be careful not to get involved in describing measures, simply illustrate impact of major ones.

Question 4

See the 'Student's Answer' below.

Question 5

Document question: *The Parliamentary Reform Act, 1832* (London 1990).

Tutor's comments on document question

It is urged that you work out your own answers before reading on.

a) Need very brief answers for example:
   i) the census
   ii) one man one vote
   iii) the reform of Parliament

b) Equally brief – reform of constituencies and reform of franchise.

c) No national pattern in Borough constituencies (this rests on your own knowledge) but Russell's proposals would create one – £10 ratepayer (line 12).

d) For six marks some elaboration needed but the central points are that they know the system is collapsing and to safeguard their own position they are putting up a limited reform which will satisfy the middle class. Explain by reference to the document. The paper is clearly against this and the language shows it, 'One particle of good' is emphatic, 'glorious constitution' in inverted commas is ironic; 'Shopocrats' is contemptuous of the Whigs alleged allies. Can you see other examples?

e) Not much here but his view is based on the fact that re-opening the reform question will disrupt the peace of the kingdom. You need to refer to the great excitement in 1831–1832 as the likely basis for Peel's feeling. Common sense suggests that he was surely right.

f) Start by re-reading Document 2: the writer sees the Document 1 proposals as a Whig trick, he is clearly and directly hostile to the proposals. Document 3 comes later so we can only infer his likely attitude but he would surely object to the view that the Reform Bill could stand as a final settlement. This could be justified from comments in Document 2. He would not be unduly grateful that Peel did not propose to return to the unreformed system. Equally hostile to both? But it is your ability to 'Explain your answer' from the documents that will earn you the six marks. This question requires you to relate Document 2 to both of the other documents. It is a very good example of this type of question.

A STUDENT'S ANSWER TO QUESTION 4

The central aims of the Chartist movement were political and if implemented would have given political power to the working class of the country. Some Chartists, especially in the early stages of the movement joined to achieve this. The London artisans who formed the London Working Men's Association and the Birmingham craftsmen and self-employed of the Birmingham Political Union had largely political motives. Their leaders, Lovett, Place, Attwood were politically inspired. They sought to obtain what the terms of the Great Reform Act of 1832 had denied them, the vote by secret ballot, the opportunity to become MPs and to be paid for this and Parliaments accountable each year to the voters in elections. They were extreme democrats, some with links to political protest in the early years of the century. Chartism in places like London and Birmingham was supported by many quite well-off working people and their interests were often political.

“Political reasons.”

This essay however is concerned with the mass supporters of Chartism and their motives are not so clear. No simple answer is possible for, in the mass, Chartism was never a single coherent movement. There were many regional variations in its tactics and in what was sought. The other difficulty is that after the defeat of Chartism the mass of the Chartists left very little in the way of written evidence to help explain their motives and their actions. Conclusions can be made only with care. The political message of Chartism was an attractive one. It was simple to understand and, lacking totally any detail, it could be made to seem to offer a great deal. The Chartists had many fine orators who could sway vast open-air crowds to near frenzy. Feargus O'Connor, one of the most powerful was almost worshipped in the North of England and his reckless use of language and threats of violent doings aroused great passions amongst the great crowds who flocked to hear him speak.

“Chartism had many causes.”

But these listeners had come for many different good reasons which probably had in common the misery of their lives. The victims of the Industrial Revolution were attracted to Chartism because they thought that the political power its demands would secure could be used to ease their lot in life. For this reason many of the dwindling band of handloom weavers of the cotton and woollen industries became Chartists, driven by their economic misery. This claim is probably true for most of the support the Chartists received in the North of England.

“Economic causes of Chartism were very important.”

Chartism did well when the economy was doing badly and this supports the idea that many working people were Chartists for economic reasons. The late 1830s and 1842 were years of much Chartist agitation. They were also a time of bad harvests, food taxes and a trade depression affecting many industries. Add to this the appalling working and living conditions of the time and Chartism was likely to flourish. For this misery the authorities and the Whig Government could only offer, and this in the last resort, the help of the hated workhouse. Even before Chartism there had been massive protests in the North of England against the introduction of the Poor Law Amendment Act and it was only as Chartism began that workhouses began to appear in many Northern towns. Part of Chartism's appeal was that it took up the anti-poor law agitation. It also for some took the place of the fight for more control of working conditions which had been betrayed by the very limited terms of the 1833 Factory Act. Indeed the legislation of the so-called Whig reformers had brought misery rather than benefits to the working people and they had proved as repressive of working-class 'agitation' as Lord Liverpool at his worst.

“Some good points here.”

“Chartism was a reaction to the 1834 Poor Law.”

It is interesting that Chartist activity often 'coincided' with industrial unrest, the Rebecca Riots in South Wales, the Plug Plots in Lancashire and the Black Country and strikes in the Staffordshire Potteries were all closely linked to Chartist activity and were caused by the same economic hardship.

The misery which many working people had in common brought them together to hear the orators and to sign the petitions. It created a class solidarity which made it easier to stand up and protest. This beginning of class-consciousness is perhaps the main reason why so many working people became Chartists. It was not because they had any clear idea how the Charter was going to solve their problems but their common misery made them wish to believe Feargus O'Connor and his like when, writing in the mass-circulation Chartist paper *The Northern Star* or addressing a mass meeting, he made the wildest of promises to them.

"The beginnings of a common identity?"

The negative evidence, that when slightly more prosperous times came after 1848 then Chartism lost its mass appeal, supports this argument that the main single reason why so many people became Chartists was the economic misery of their lives.

"An effectively relevant essay."

Examiner comment

This is a good essay. It offers ideas rather than description and it avoids irrelevance by carefully not straying into such matters as why Chartism failed which is not the question set on this occasion. It needs a bit more specific illustration on all those diverse reasons why people became Chartists, even just a list would have given that excellent point much more support. With time available, and this is not a long answer, some slight elaboration on any one example of people who were Chartists, and why, would have brought the essay to life. (Why for example did those South Wales miners march from the valleys and seize control of Newport?)

USEFUL SOURCES OF INFORMATION

General reading

P Lane, *Success in British History 1760–1914*, John Murray 1978
R K Webb, *Modern England*, Allen & Unwin (2nd edition) 1980
A Wood, *Nineteenth Century Britain*, Longman (2nd edition) 1982

Further reading

M Bentley, *Politics without Democracy 1815–1914*, Fontana Paperbacks 1984
E J Evans, *Forging of the Modern State*, Longman 1983
E J Evans, *The Great Reform Act of 1832*, Methuen 1983: a succinct analysis of a major topic as part of a series intended specially for A-level students
N Gash, *Aristocracy and People: Britain 1815–1865*, Edward Arnold 1979

Linked topic areas

- Lord Liverpool's governments, 1812–1827; repression and reform
- Social conditions and reforms (see Chapter 4)
- European history, 1815–1870 (see Chapters 12 to 17)
- The careers of Disraeli and Gladstone (see Chapters 6 and 7)
- The nineteenth century British economy

CHAPTER 6

GLADSTONE AND LIBERALISM

GETTING STARTED

Gladstone was in the House of Commons from 1832 until 1894, except for one brief interval in 1846. He was the major British politician of the nineteenth century and it would be helpful to have enough personal background information on him to help in bringing his political life into focus. He came from a wealthy Liverpool merchant family, was educated at Eton and Oxford, obtaining a Parliamentary seat through the influence of the Duke of Newcastle and in his early years was an unbending Tory. Religion was of very great importance to him: he was an Anglican, strongly disapproving of the action of those friends who became Catholics but, in the 1860s, coming to terms with the political importance of Nonconformity. From the age of fourteen until just months before his death he kept a diary of his reading, letters and engagements: it reveals both his wide range of interests and his enormous energy in political and private life. Take an interest in him as a man and you will learn much about his politics. You will need to know enough about Victorian religion, and its significance in political issues to set him in context.

He became pre-eminent at Westminster as a financier: his destructive attack on Disraeli's 1852 Budget established him as the greatest Commons speaker of his day; his own Budget of 1853 and those in the 1860s made him indispensable to any non-Conservative Government with any pretensions to stability. His finances are forever associated with economy and low taxation. This precluded, at different times, any ambitious government policies involving great expenditure. These financial constraints were closely linked to the notion of minimalist government, an emphasis on individual self-help, free-trade between nations and the ideas of laissez-faire. Again you need to have sufficient grasp of such terms and their application to set Gladstonian government in this general frame of 'Victorian Values'. Such understanding will be useful in answering many other questions on Victorian society, linking up with the political and social reforms considered in Chapters 4 and 5 to provide a substantial body of historical subject matter from which you can reasonably hope to draw a range of examination questions.

Some features of the wider context are also worth bearing in mind: in 1868, when Gladstone became the first Liberal Prime Minister, Britain was already established as the first industrial urban nation, with a fully established rail network. Politics were increasingly urban and middle class. The navy provided effortless security from foreign enemies. The Empire spanned the globe but had, as yet, scarcely penetrated into the hinterland of Africa. In continental Europe, Italy was already largely unified and Germany about to become so, the Empire of Napoleon III was about to disappear and be replaced by the Third French Republic.

ESSENTIAL PRINCIPLES

FROM TORY TO LIBERAL LEADER

"Gladstone, an unbending Tory in his early days."

"Key turning points in 1846 and 1859."

1832–1868

Gladstone's 1830s credentials as a hardened Tory are easily illustrated, from his defence of his father's record as a slave plantation owner to his extreme views on the proper role of the Anglican Church in the State. The various stages of his move to liberalism need noting and the move itself should not be seen as some inevitable progression for it did not seem that way at the time. Practical politics in the 1840s under Peel dented his religious bigotry and offered him financial probity as the base for a new political philosophy. Corn Law Repeal in 1846 marked one turning point, breaking his ties with the Conservatives and perhaps establishing his lifelong dislike of Disraeli. Joining Palmerston's Whig Government in 1859, after seriously considering a Conservative offer in 1858, was another turning-point; it meant overcoming adverse feelings towards Palmerston with a common sympathy for Italy providing the bridge. Gladstone went on, in the 1860s, to make a mark as a public speaker and, further abandoning his high Anglicanism, cultivated the support of the leaders of the Nonconformist Churches. In all these moves there is a sense of a series of conversions convenient to an ambitious politician with a career drifting into a cul-de-sac which is at odds with his high moral tone on many issues. Here, as happened frequently later in his career, the questions about sincerity and humbug abound. The advanced age of the Whig leaders, Palmerston and Russell, and his own Parliamentary pre-eminence now made him the inevitable leader of any non-Conservative government.

Fig. 6.1 William Ewart Gladstone

FIRST MINISTRY

"Impotence in 1867."

1868–1874

Gladstone's relative impotence in 1866–1867 in the matter of Parliamentary Reform is often treated within the context of Disraeli's achievement and the episode is considered in Chapter 7. It brought home to Gladstone the need for any non-Conservative party to have a programme for change around which to rally party factions and the electorate.

1868 ELECTION AND IRELAND

"But an election triumph in 1868."

In the 1868 election Gladstone scored a great triumph by making Ireland the issue: again the moral crusade must be set against the party advantage and a judgement made on the great man's sincerity. For good and ill the Liberal Party was now the reforming party on the Irish Question and Gladstone's wisdom in bringing this about, for it was very much his personal cause, may be questioned. By this, and his equally abrupt public departure in 1885 on the question of giving Ireland Home Rule, he made the 'Irish Question' one on which politicians increasingly divided on Party lines and nothing could have been more calculated than this to prevent acceptable solutions.

THE REFORMS

"A great Reforming Ministry."

The 1868–1874 Ministry is regarded as one of the greatest reforming ministries of the century. The legislation needs to be listed (for a starting point see the 'Useful Information' section later in this chapter, though you will need to consult an adequate textbook as well), its details noted and comments on the impact rehearsed. The volume of legislation is partly accounted for by the fact that Palmerston had earlier acted as a block on most reforming ideas.

Establish some motives behind the reforms, for example:

- Providing greater equality of opportunity for the middle classes.
- Meeting pressures from new, post-1867, working class voters.
- Responding (at last) to the lessons of the Crimean War.
- The needs of industry and commerce for a skilled labour force.
- Discontent in Ireland.

The 'Outline Answer' to Question 2 on page 67 discusses a parallel theme.

LIMITATIONS OF THE REFORMS

Consider then the limitations of the reforms; they are often seen as institutional, sweeping away administrative inefficiences or tending to provide equalities of opportunity. They are not social, not sweeping and, costing very little, it is difficult to see that they could have a dramatic effect in meeting the more serious problems of the time. You need to develop an overall assessment of their impact.

Exam questions

Questions in this area are often tied to Gladstone personally so you also need, for each of the major reforms, to be able to discuss the part he played; aloof leader, driving force, useful standby in debates? For a full view be able to add the Irish religious and land legislation, where Gladstone's personal commitment was certainly important, and the one or two foreign policy matters of importance to any examination of the Ministry's record. Equally important is an awareness of the strains which the reform programme imposed upon the Liberals and their loss of impetus in the Ministry's last months leading to electoral defeat in 1874.

GLADSTONE AND THE LIBERAL PARTY

This heading includes a range of topics: some may stand as essay subjects in their own right but in most examination papers information and ideas can effectively be used in a variety of questions.

THE NATURE OF THE LIBERAL PARTY

"The Liberal electoral base."

This needs to be borne in mind, for it changed with time (e.g. when the Whigs, and then Chamberlain, left over the question of Home Rule for Ireland). In the later decades of the century even the urban constituency base altered and electoral strength moved to the Celtic fringes of the kingdom. The Nonconformist religious base usually remained more solid. It was thoughout a party of pressure groups and factions, likely to splinter. For reasons not always entirely clear it was seen as the party most likely to carry out reforms.

LIBERAL PHILOSOPHY

This is equally complex. You need to show you recognize that it could mean different things to different men at different times. But, within the bounds of a short essay, you need a working definition which you can use as the basis for whatever specific purpose the examiners pose; do this undogmatically but clearly.

"And the party principles."

It was the philosophy of:

- Free Trade
- economy
- financial probity
- administrative efficiency
- self help
- morality
- caution in foreign affairs
- anti-imperalism (usually)

One useful form of revision would be to list occasions which can illustrate each of these characteristics and also to think of occasions which show that they are not universally applicable. Look out for a working definition that you might adapt from your reading. (See the 'Outline Answer' to Question 3 on page 68.)

GLADSTONE AS PARTY LEADER

"Gladstone an aloof leader."

He was by modern standards a very odd party leader. But why should you judge him by modern standards? He saw himself as needing to be above party sections (this became a great problem even in his first ministry) and he stoutly refused to become involved in maintenance of the party machine. From this point it became very easy for him to develop a policy from his own moral convictions and impose it, with little consultation, on the party. This happened most notoriously over Irish Home Rule but also in foreign and imperial matters. One of the leading political historians writing about the period notes that, from 1874:

> 'It is of great importance for interpreting the course of Gladstone's subsequent career to remember that he now saw his duty as to nation, not to party.'
>
> (D A Hamer, *Liberal Politics in the Age of Gladstone and Rosebery*, page 63).

This could be the touchstone by which to judge his later career and its impact on the Liberal party.

RELATIONS WITH DISRAELI

"Gladstone and Disraeli were bitter rivals."

The bitterness of Gladstone's rivalry with Disraeli is difficult to explain but cannot be gainsaid so have some suggestions ready, for example:

- That it arose from Gladstone's fury at Disraeli's 1846 attack on his beloved Peel when he, Gladstone, was out of Parliament and unable to help;
- That it may well have played a crucial part in the outcome of the 1867 Parliamentary Reform Act or the Gladstone family's conviction that Disraeli turned Victoria against Gladstone.

The grounds of their disagreements are important and particularly concern their differing views on foreign and imperial policy, ranging from Afghanistan to Southern Africa and to the Balkans. They need mastering for they marked one of the most interesting periods of deep party conflict in British political history and one which is considered from Disraeli's view in Chapter 7.

THE PUBLIC FIGURE

"His importance in the development of national politics."

"Morality or humbug?"

Gladstone's early political career had, as MP for the small borough of Newark and then for Oxford University, been a sheltered one. In the 1860s he emerged as a compelling public orator addressing vast gatherings and as his career continued he became addicted to these occasions: they embraced and enlarged his strong moral convictions and arguably made him the first national party leader, the one who ended the domination of political life by local elites as, in the cause of Bulgarians and Armenians, and indeed the Irish, he toured the country by train and secured full publicity in the national and provincial press. After 'retiring' from politics in 1875 his public speaking tours of Midlothian in 1879 and 1880 provide the best example of the moral basis of his view of foreign policy;they also marked a new phase in national politics. This episode tells so much about political life at the time that it is well worth having it at your fingertips for examination purposes. Disraeli saw much of it as humbug but to the British public Gladstone became the 'People's William'. It all fitted conveniently with the Liberal Party's need to secure unity and electoral success by association with a great cause; Gladstone's readiness to use such causes for party advantage may explain Disraeli's distaste.

SECOND MINISTRY

1880–1885

This was an anti-climax. The Midlothian Campaign had roused the Liberals and Gladstone was pressed to become Prime Minister once more when, after the 1880 Election, they again became the largest Party in the Commons. It did not prove a happy decision.

Troubles came from divisions within the Liberals, from the Irish Nationalists in Parliament and Ireland in general, from Lord Randolph Churchill, the Bradlaugh affair and a number of colonial entanglements stretching from Egypt, the Sudan and the Transvaal to Afghanistan.

Positive achievements were few but included The Married Women's Property Act, the Corrupt Practices Act and, in 1884–1885, Parliamentary Reform. You should assess the achievement, set it against that of the First Ministry, and be able to discuss the problems, personal and political, which undermined the record of this ministry. It is a convenient point at which to note that people's expectations from government were beginning to change and that Gladstone's type of Liberalism was going to find it difficult to meet these new social expectations. This was to be one of the two important issues on which Gladstone and Joseph Chamberlain came to differ deeply. Why this should be so is one of the key issues to an understanding of Liberalism from this point until 1914. The developing context is considered in Chapter 8.

"Changing social expectations."

GLADSTONE AND IRELAND

This is a vast topic to study. If you are hoping to answer an examination question on it, then it would be commonsense, in an outline paper spanning the nineteenth century to understand also:

- The Act of Union, 1800.
- Catholic Emancipation, 1829.
- The Repeal of the Corn Laws, 1846.
- The Home Rule controversies of 1912.
- The foundation of the Irish Free State in 1921.

Familiarity with the contribution of such leading Irish figures as:

- Isaac Butt
- Charles Stewart Parnell
- John Redmond
- Eamonn de Valera

would easily be gained via the index of a standard textbook and would greatly help you in writing generally about Ireland.

Gladstone and Ireland is only one aspect of all this. To evaluate fully the work of each of his first two Ministries you need to understand how he tried to meet Irish grievances over religion and land and be able to comment on his limited success. Gladstone's later career, his third and fourth terms as Prime Minister, have Ireland at their heart. His solution of Home Rule split the Party and divided the nation; it perhaps explains why the general flow of Liberal reforms dried up (see the 'Tutor's Answer' to Question 1 later in this chapter for a development of this).

THE GRAND OLD MAN

Many questions on politics in this period involve an assessment of Gladstone's personal motives, intentions, achievements. It is well worthwhile, even at the revision stage of your course, to form a series of impressions of him as an individual:

"The most important political figure of the nineteenth century."

- his deep religious sense;
- the charges of hypocrisy and humbug;
- the widespread public adulation;
- relations with Peel, Disraeli and Victoria.

Even in mundane examination terms he will reward personal study more than any other figure of the century. Equally his public career illuminates a vast range of political and social issues. From his virtual creation of the Liberal Party in the 1860s to his Irish obsessions and his failure, at the end, to lead his Liberals towards the new social realities, his career provides an ideal vehicle to survey and bring to life British politics in the second half of the nineteenth century.

USEFUL INFORMATION

1832	Gladstone elected Tory MP
1832–1841	His rigid Tory record on social reform and religious issues.
1841–1846	Experience of political practicalities in Peel's ministry. (Vice-President and President of the Board of Trade: responsible for 1844 Railway Act: resigned over the Maynooth Grant but began to shed narrow Anglicanism: supported Corn Law Repeal).
1846–1860s	Emerged as leading Peelite; attacking Disraeli's 1852 budget and proposing his own 1853 budget established his reputation as Parliamentary speaker and financier.
1859	Joined Palmerston's Ministry.
1860s	His budgets established Gladstonian finance. He forged links with middle-class Nonconformists in the country. Years of the emergence of the Liberal Party. Gladstone the only heir at Westminster to the elderly Whig leaders.
1866–1867	Bested by Disraeli over Parliamentary Reform
1868	But Liberals won the General Election in which Gladstone stressed problems in Ireland.
1868–1874	**Prime Minister: very important record of reform**
1869	**Anglican Church in Ireland disestablished**
1870	**Irish Land Act:** evicted tenants had to be compensated for any improvement they had made, and paid damages for eviction unless this because rent not paid. Did *not* secure fair rents and secure tenure of the land.
1870	**Forster's Education Act:** this established rate-financed schools but increased religious bitterness and undermined some of the Nonconformist support for Gladstone by giving grants to Church schools.
	British neutrality in the Franco-Prussian War.
	Gladstone merely protested when Russia re-fortified its Black Sea bases contrary to terms of 1856 Treaty of Paris.
1871	**Cardwell's Army Reforms:** shorter terms of service, no flogging in peacetime, abolished purchase of commissions, Commander-in-Chief made subordinate to the War Office, reduced colonial garrisons and tied infantry regiments to British and Irish districts, extended artillery provision. All this at reduced expenditure.
	Civil Service Reform: use of competitive examinations.
	University Tests Act: this opened Oxford and Cambridge to non-Anglicans.
1871	**Trade Union Act:** this made unions legal so could protect funds.
1871	**Criminal Law Amendment Act:** this made picketing illegal.
1872	**Secret ballot introduced**
1872	**Licensing Act:** this antagonised the brewers and publicans and lost Liberals popular support; gave a powerful election weapon for the future to the Conservatives.
	Britain paid 15½ million dollars to USA in the Alabama arbitration.
1873	**Judicature Act:** this reformed the High Court system.
1874	Liberal election defeat
1875	**'Retired'**
1879–1880	**The Midlothian Campaign:** a highly effective series of speeches appealing to the electors' moral judgement of Disraeli's foreign and imperial 'adventures'.
1880–1885	**Prime Minister (Second Ministry):** ministry beset by many troubles at home, especially over Ireland, and overseas (Egypt, The Sudan, Afghanistan, Transvaal) and by divisions between the Whig and Radical wings of the party. Gladstone increasingly autocratic.
1880	The Mundella Act made elementary education compulsory.

1880	Irish Coercion Act
1881	Gladstone's Second Irish Land Act gave peasantry fixed tenure, fair rents and free sale of any unexpired lease.
1882	The Married Women's Property Act
1883	The Corrupt Practices Act limited election expenses.
1884	Third Parliamentary Reform Act made the *county* voting qualification the same as the *boroughs*; 2 million more voters.
1885	Redistribution Act established principle of single member constituencies.
1886	**Prime Minister (Third Ministry):** controversial conversion to Home Rule for Ireland split Party. (Hartington and the Whigs and Joseph Chamberlain and the Liberal Unionists left).
1886	Home Rule defeated in Commons
1892–1894	**Prime Minister (Fourth Ministry)**
1893	Lords defeated Home Rule
1894	Gladstone retired. Lord Rosebery became Prime Minister.
1898	**Gladstone died**

EXAMINATION QUESTIONS

Q1 Why had Gladstone failed to solve the Irish problem by 1894? (AEB 1989)

Q2 How consistent were the principles upon which the reforms passed under the Gladstone ministry of 1868–1874 were based? (London 1989)

Q3 How far did Gladstonian Liberalism represent a coherent political philosophy and programme? (Northern Ireland 1989)

Q4 'The reforms of Gladstone's first ministry were less radical in reality than they appeared to be.' How far do you agree? (London 1989)

Q5 Compare and contrast the imperial policies of Disraeli and Gladstone between 1874 and 1885. (Cambridge 1989)

OUTLINE ANSWERS

Question 1

See the 'Tutors Answer' below.

Question 2

First identify the *principles*:

- providing efficient government administration
- minimal government spending
- removal of anomalies standing in the way of equal opportunity and equal legal rights
- redressing proven grievances

"Gladstonian principles and consistency."

Consider how different reforms illustrate the *application of each principle*. Aim to refer briefly to the *range of reforms* and indicate the principle involved quickly.
Note: Do not fall into the trap of long descriptions of the reforms.

Consider the *question of consistency* in relation to some of the reforms, Irish reforms. University Test Acts indicate consistent following of redress of grievances. Education, army and Civil Service reforms bow to the principle of more equal opportunity and the last two also improved administrative efficiency, indicate how. Offer other examples only if time.

Conclusion: however consistent the pursuit of principle appears to have been it is only part of the story for many other pressures came into the reforms: e.g.:

- Education Act and Licensing Acts were attempts to reward Liberal Nonconformist supports

- Irish Acts were a price to be paid for using Irish grievances as an election rallying cry in 1868
- Trade Union Act an acknowledgement that many working-class males now had the vote.

Compromises had to be made too: e.g. money paid to Anglican schools to help education reforms to be passed. Most consistent following of principle was in what did not happen, for the principle of holding expenditure down to the minimum prevented any worthwhile measures of social reform.

Question 3

The Liberals certainly had a philosophy; list some of its features:

- minimal government expenditure
- self-reliance
- free market economics
- a morality in the conduct of foreign affairs
- the reform of proven abuses

"Liberal philosophy."

It was quite coherent with its basis in the religious morality of the time allied to the notion of each person's own responsibility for their own lives.

It is much less certain that they had a coherent programme in *domestic matters* which were more carried through in response to pressure groups or to Gladstone's own overwhelming convictions: give examples of this occurring in relation to the Acts passed (including how the Irish legislation was arrived at). The most coherent feature was keeping expenditure down.

In *foreign affairs* too, not always consistent; had to be pragmatic at times, e.g. in the Sudan, but there was again a consistent series of ideals evident in the Alabama case and in the desire to avoid conflict everywhere but there was not a programme which is scarcely possible in foreign policy.

Conclusion: the basis of the philosophy is clear: the difficulty arises with the idea of a programme. The best that can be said is that they had a programme of things they wanted to do in 1868 but that as that Ministry went on they lost their way and never found it again, increasingly just reacting to issues and opportunities as they arose.

Question 4

Disagree with question and argue the opposite. Discuss each major reform in turn with this in mind. For example:

"The reforms of the 1868–1874 Ministry."

- The Education Act: it appears small but really is a major step against laissez-faire ideas of the time.
- Administrative reforms: army, civil service, remove century old corruption and introduce new competitive criteria.
- Irish Reforms: Church and land very radical in terms of constitution and free use of private property, Land Act opened way for even more radical measures later.
- University and Trade Union legislation also opened up new era for these institutions despite apparent timidity.

Conclusion: in total, reforms fully justify the Ministry being given title of the greatest reforming ministry of the century. Has to be set against failures to reform of the Palmerston years.

Question 5

- Try to avoid just describing each policy. Make sure points of similarity and of difference are listed and commented on at end.
- Briefly indicate basis of Disraeli's policy 1874–1881; Suez Canal shares, Imperial Titles Act, Afghanistan, Zulus, Cyprus.
- Gladsone's charge that it was a 'forward policy'.
- Basis of Gladstone's policy, morality in international affairs, avoid adventures, keep costs and so taxes down. But in practice unable to extricate Britain from commitments, illustrate this in Sudan and South Africa.

"Foreign and imperial differences with Disraeli."

- Differences were deep and left a mark on the parties they led which affected their policies and their electoral fortunes up to the First World War.
- Remember until this period the Whig, Palmerston, had been the man who held the 'patriotic card': all this now changed in these years.

A TUTOR'S ANSWER TO QUESTION 1

The 'problem' has of course never been just an Irish one. The British dimension is as important as the Irish in any assessment of Gladstone's failure. It was British perceptions of Ireland, including Gladstone's own, that repeatedly got in the way of possible solutions.

"Until 1885 he strove to alleviate social and economic grievances."

The first stage in Gladstone's dealings with Ireland, from 1868 to 1885, involved his recognition of the justice of Irish land and religious grievances and his realisation that until these were alleviated there would not be peace in Ireland or between Irish and British politicians at Westminster. In this Gladstone's perception of the problem differed from that of his Conservative opponents for whom it was essentially a matter of maintaining law and order.

In two Land Acts, of 1870 and 1881, Gladstone sought to settle the land tenure grievances of the Irish peasantry. The 1870 Act reflected the importance of property rights to the Victorians and also the political strength of the Irish landowners. It failed because it was too timid, failing to provide either fair rents or safe land tenure. The 1881 Act, on the other hand, was for the time a radical measure, involving important protection of peasant tenure at the expense of the landlords. In the interval however Irish demands had become more extreme and a tradition of rural violence was firmly established. The opportunity for quietening Ireland by the just settlement of land grievances had been lost. Perhaps it had never existed.

Even the comparative success of Gladstone's religious legislation of 1869, disestablishing the Anglican Church in Ireland, which met many Irish Catholic aspirations could not hide the fact that unrest in Ireland was growing whilst at Westminster the Irish MPs were becoming a force to be reckoned with. By the 1880s despite all the energy and thought Gladstone had given to the Irish problem as he then saw it, namely the need to redress economic and social grievances, Ireland was becoming increasingly ungovernable from London. It was, despite Gladstone's efforts to date, essentially a political problem.

"From 1885 he promoted political solutions."

The second phase of Gladstone's Irish policy involved accepting the political solution of Home Rule with a Dublin Parliament, re-created to run Irish domestic affairs. Twice, in 1886 and in 1893, he introduced into the Westminster Parliament legislation to bring this into effect and twice his efforts were defeated.

Defeat in 1886 came about firstly because Gladstone's 'conversion' to Home Rule, in the heat of the 1885 Election campaign, had made the matter a major issue between the Conservative and Liberal Parties. Henceforth the Conservatives were to be obdurate opponents of Home Rule and in this way became the main, but not the only, cause of Gladstone's final failure. In 1886 the effect of the Home Rule proposal on the Liberal Party seemed more important. First the Whigs under Hartington and then, more importantly, the Liberal radicals under Joseph Chamberlain left Gladstone's Liberal Party to work with his Conservative opponents to block his Home Rule proposals. The secretive nature of his conversion, and its timing had had disastrous consequences for his own party and led to the defeat of the Home Rule Bill in the Commons.

"Home Rule for Ireland a party issue."

The real impact of its becoming an issue between the Parties became more clear in 1893 when Gladstone's second Home Rule Bill passed through the Commons but was resoundingly defeated by the massive Conservative majority in the Lords.

Some measure of responsibility for Gladstone's failure must rest with the political leadership of the Irish MPs at Westminster and in particular with Parnell. The general suspicion of Parnell amongst large sections of the British electorate and with British MPs helped to undermine the strength of Gladstone's Home Rule case. Many Liberal nonconformists had little instinctive sympathy for the Catholic Irish; they were further alienated by the growing violence in Ireland and by Irish atrocities in Britain: Parnell's final disgrace through the O'Shea divorce scandal weakened their resolve to follow Gladstone down the Home Rule road. A more ably led and therefore more politically effective Irish presence at Westminster might have greatly strengthened Gladstone's hand with his own Party and disabused the Conservatives of the notion that all Ireland needed was the touch of strong government. Instead Gladstone's apparent obsession with the Irish question left him increasingly isolated: this did not become crucial until 1893–1894 when his own

COLLEGE LEARNING CENTRE TYCOCH ROAD SWANSEA SA2 9EB

Cabinet made it clear that they were not prepared to provoke a constitutional crisis with the Lords over the issue. Gladstone therefore retired from politics.

Eventually Gladstone himself must, in part, be held responsible for his failure. His taking up the Irish cause in 1868 may well have been for Liberal electoral advantage; his 1885 conversion to Home Rule certainly smacked of this to opponents. He more than anyone, other than perhaps Parnell, must shoulder blame for making Home Rule perhaps the most divisive party political issue of the nineteenth century. His failure to take his party with him simply adds to his responsibility for the outcome.

> "Gladstone in part, at least, responsible for the failure."

None of this may have been of crucial importance however, for the 1880s was a period marked by growing imperial fervour and the idea that, the Imperial frontier should, for the first time, be rolled back, was not likely to be easily accepted (even the radical Bright declined to do so). Imperial sentiment in Britain was, in Gladstone's time, a more serious obstacle to Home Rule for Ireland than was the spectre of Ulster Protestant protest at its imposition, though it remains true that such protest was significantly underestimated throughout by Gladstone.

To conclude: first Gladstone was unable, to 1885, to de-politicise the Irish issue by the redress of Irish economic and religious grievances. He then found, in Home Rule, what seemed to him a political solution but failed, in singular contrast to other issues on which he had stood, to build up a moral or a political pressure sufficient to beat down his opponents inside his own and the Conservative party. In the end only the British Parliament could solve the 'Irish Problem' and Gladstone could never gain the support of its two Houses nor browbeat them into agreement with his policy. He could, aged 85 in 1894, only hand on to often reluctant successors his vision of a peaceful Ireland governing its own affairs. Only when they, a generation later, had circumvented the Lords' veto did Home Rule have a chance of success. Even then it proved to be an illusion: this does not however mean that it would not have served a generation earlier.

USEFUL SOURCES OF INFORMATION

General reading

M Bentley, *Politics without Democracy, 1815–1914*, Fontana 1984
P Lane, *Success in British History 1760–1914*, John Murray 1978
E J Feuchtwanger, *Democracy and Empire: Britain 1865–1914*, Arnold 1985
A Wood, *Nineteenth Century Britain*, Longman (2nd edition) 1982

Further reading

P Adelman, *Gladstone, Disraeli and Later Victorian Politics*, Longman (2nd edition) 1983
B H Abbott, *Gladstone and Disraeli*, Collins 1972
E J Feuchtwanger, *Gladstone* Macmillan (2nd edition) 1989
M Pugh, *The Making of Modern British Politics, 1867–1939*, Blackwell 1982

Linked topic areas

- British Foreign Policy in the nineteenth century
- Disraeli – his motives in domestic, imperial and foreign policy
  – his career and political achievement
  – the development of the 19th century Conservative party (see Chapter 7)
- Free Trade and laissez-faire
- Joseph Chamberlain
- Ireland, 1800–1922
- Parliamentary and Social Reform in Victorian England (for the period to 1870 see Chapters 4 and 5)
- The Liberal Party to 1914 (see Chapter 8)

CHAPTER 7

DISRAELI AND THE CONSERVATIVE PARTY

CAREER TO 1846

POLITICAL WILDERNESS 1846–1866

PARLIAMENTARY REFORM 1866–1867

IN OPPOSITION 1868–1874

SECOND MINISTRY 1874–1880

ACHIEVEMENT AND LEGACY

USEFUL INFORMATION

GETTING STARTED

The best starting point would be to remind yourself of the political issues of the period 1830 to 1870 raised in Chapter 5. Disraeli's early political career was acted out within the political system created by the Great Reform Act of 1832 which, in 1867, he was to take a major part in remodelling. To understand what he did in 1867 you have to know the basis of Parliamentary representation which had been set up 35 years before. Disraeli, entering Parliament in 1837, spent his early years as a Conservative backbencher, failing to gain office from 1841 to 1846, when Peel was leading his great ministry. The debt of the Conservative Party to both these men is often raised in examination questions, sometimes with an invitation to compare their achievements. The 'Tutor's Answer' later in this Chapter opens up this theme. As with the 1832 Reform Act it would be economical of time and effort if, in preparing for a question on Disraeli, you also revised the record of his distinguished predecessor. Disraeli's political career reached public prominence in 1846 with his bitter attacks on Peel over Corn Law Repeal and this adds a sharp touch to any comparisons that are to be made.

Disraeli's great rivalry was of course with Gladstone and, in a nineteenth century political history paper, a student who was not faced with a question on one or the other of these great men could feel badly treated. This is not to argue that you would then automatically choose to answer one of these questions but certainly to be ready for questions on either would widen your options greatly. So remind yourself also of the issues raised about Gladstone in Chapter 6.

Later in life Disraeli had a close working relationship with Queen Victoria and it would be worth looking up an encyclopedia or textbook entry on the Queen. He was also alleged to be a social reformer and this is often the subject of examination questions so be aware of what the main social problems of the mid-nineteenth century were in order that your judgements are securely based. Disraeli also developed a reputation as an imperialist and it would be useful to have available a map showing the great areas of the globe which in the nineteenth century were shaded in British imperial pink and in particular to note the location of Afghanistan and the Transvaal. In 1878 he reached eminence in perhaps the most serious international crisis to afflict Europe between 1870 and 1914 and a map of the Turkish Empire, with its neighbours at the time, might help to keep complex issues simple. The European setting is considered in Chapter 15.

ESSENTIAL PRINCIPLES

CAREER TO 1846

"Young England largely a romantic dream."

In 1841 Disraeli failed in his efforts to seek government office from Peel. He became the unlikely leader of the 'Young England' group of young Conservative aristocrats who opposed Peel with a romantic vision of aristocratic responsibility for the poor. Disraeli's two greatest novels, *Coningsby* and *Sybil*, pursued these ideals and were written at this time. Young England is only important as part of his opposition to Peel's businessmanlike approach to political affairs and because of Disraeli's later concern for social reform. It was based on a romantic vision of social responsibility rather than on a practical reforming programme. Disraeli's emergence as leader of the protectionist Tories who in 1846 opposed the repeal of the Corn Laws was only one part of the final drama of Peel's political career but it was of the greatest significance for Disraeli's own future. His Jewish ancestry, his novels, his strange appearance and mannerisms, made him an unlikely candidate for a leading role in Conservative politics. The brilliance of his attacks on Peel however marked him as the outstanding Commons speaker of the depleted post-1846 Conservative ranks. Unlike Young England his role in 1846 deserves close attention. It set the context for his own and Conservative Party fortunes for the next twenty years.

"Repeal of the Corn Laws set the political pattern for the next twenty years."

POLITICAL WILDERNESS 1846–1866

The period from 1846 to the 1860s was one of great *political fluidity* at Westminster. If you are studying Conservative fortunes in these years then you should also understand the roles of *Gladstone* and of the Whig leaders, *Palmerston* and *Russell* and be ready to explain why there was so much governmental instability. Both Chapters 5 and 6 will help in this. *Note:* A question on Disraeli alone is more likely to be focused on the period from 1866.

Chancellor of the Exchequer

"Chancellor on three occasions."

There were however three minority Conservative governments from 1846 to 1867 (see the 'Useful Information' section at the end of this chapter). Disraeli served as Chancellor of the Exchequer in each one but saw his 1852 budget savaged in debate by Gladstone. In 1859 he introduced a Parliamentary Reform Bill but it was defeated. This was an attempt to widen the appeal of the Party (which had for the same reason abandoned protectionism in 1852). Disraeli's achievement in these years is best summed up as enabling the Party to survive as a Parliamentary force, ready to act with determination in 1867 and to establish a long-lived government in 1874, when it could so easily have degenerated into an irrelevant protectionist rump. Remember to give Lord Derby, three times a minority Prime Minister, some credit for the outcome.

PARLIAMENTARY REFORM 1866–1867

The survival strategy paid off in 1866 with the Liberal split over Parliamentary reform which enabled the Conservatives to defeat their Bill and in consequence form the Government. The events of the next year, centring on the introduction and the passage through Parliament of the Conservative Reform Bill, is one of those episodes where study of the detail of what happened is essential. It can scarcely be done justice here. First remind yourself what had happened in the 1832 Reform Act, you may just get a question inviting comparison of some aspects of that measure and the provisions of the 1867 Reform Act (see Chapter 5).

"For 1867 you need to master the detail."

DISRAELI'S MOTIVATION

It seems likely that Disraeli was motivated by party advantage and by a dislike of Gladstone to a determination that he was going to carry, in any form, a Conservative reform. So, having in 1866 defeated a Liberal reform as too radical, he introduced his own proposals and saw them made more extreme in the course of the debates (remember that the Conservatives were a minority government) as his safeguards were stripped away and the Borough electorate with whom the measure was mainly concerned was enlarged far beyond his original intentions. All this was done largely to 'dish the Whigs'. It has been argued that the 1867 Reform Act was pushed through because of rioting in London, especially at a rally in Hyde Park. Be ready to comment on this but also be aware that most historians now see Reform as the result of party and personal rivalry at Westminster. This is a detailed episode for which the only advice must be master the detail, but be ready to adapt it to whatever question is set and do not in any circumstances be trapped into a long description of what happened.

OUTCOME OF REFORM

The outcome was that the electorate in the borough constituencies doubled and a large number of male heads of working-class households, living in boroughs, got the vote. The 'Useful Information' section at the end of this chapter has some more detail.

IN OPPOSITION 1868–1874

Following Lord Derby's retirement Disraeli was, from February to December 1868, Prime Minister. The outsider of 1837, rebuffed by Peel in 1841 had indeed 'climbed to the top of the greasy pole' of politics, albeit as the head of a minority government. Whatever had been Disraeli's aim in the 1867 Reform Act the General Election of 1868 produced a decisive Liberal victory. Until 1874 Disraeli was the leader of the Opposition launching effective attacks on Gladstone's foreign and Irish policies. Particularly to be noted however are two public speeches he made in 1872, one at Manchester and the second at the Crystal Palace. In these he presented the Conservatives as the patriotic party offering social welfare to the people and the preservation of the Empire. All this of course in contrast to the divisive dangerous Liberals. It was during the Crystal Palace speech that he memorably compared Gladstone's Front Bench to a range of exhausted volcanoes. Firm knowledge of what Disraeli said in these speeches, and an ability to relate it critically to what his government actually did from 1874, could be very valuable in an examination.

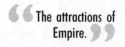

> "Two very important speeches."

SECOND MINISTRY 1874–1880

DOMESTIC AFFAIRS

In the 'Useful Information' section at the end of this chapter there is a long list of social reform measures passed in these years. You should know enough about the most important of them to be able to offer a sentence or two in comment on their significance. One of the most common questions to be asked about Disraeli is to what extent he was a social reformer. Despite the number of reforming measures it seems generally agreed that, set against the rallying speeches of 1872, Disraeli achieved little (see the 'Outline Answers' to Questions 2 and 4 below). The real credit should go to the Civil Service who promoted the measures and to the Home Secretary, RA Cross, whom it would be advisable to look up via a textbook index. Cross claimed that, when the Cabinet first met, Disraeli had no reform measures to suggest but rather relied on the other members of the Cabinet to make proposals. He cannot be given a large measure of credit for the reforms carried by his government. Perhaps age and ill-health explain his lack of personal involvement but it seems doubtful in any case whether the Tory Party (Disraeli much preferred this title to Peel's 'Conservative') would have accepted a large bundle of truly radical reforms, even to steal Gladstonian thunder.

> "Limited commitment to social reform."

IMPERIAL AND FOREIGN AFFAIRS

The other theme of the 1872 speeches had concerned the need to develop the Empire and in this Disraeli took a more active personal interest and again the major activity is listed below. His personal action in buying the Khedive of Egypt's Suez Canal shares with borrowed money is regularly cited as an example of his drive and flair. Certainly there was nothing similar under the heading of social reforms. Making Victoria Empress of India was also his personal initiative and helped to cement the warm relations which had developed between him and the Queen, whilst Gladstone's opposition to the idea had the opposite and, from Disraeli's point of view, equally happy effect on his relations with the Queen. The adventures in the *Transvaal, Zululand* and *Afghanistan* illustrate Disraeli's active imperial policy and its sometimes unhappy consequences.

> "The attractions of Empire."

The Eastern Question

The weakness of the Turkish Empire and the ambitions of Russia in the Balkans in 1878 threatened conflict in Europe (Chapter 15 has more information). Disraeli attended a Congress called in Berlin which proved to be a major triumph for him as he combined with the German Chancellor, Bismarck, to push the Russians back and to add Cyprus to the Empire, returning to claim that he brought 'peace with honour'. It was an international success of the sort that Gladstone, for all his foreign policy rhetoric, was never to gain. You need to be ready to comment on Disraeli's policies, actions and achievements in both imperial and foreign affairs, either alongside an analysis of his domestic achievement or, more likely, at essay length in their own right.

ACHIEVEMENT AND LEGACY

So Disraeli progressed from the romantic visions of Young England, via a major reform of the borough franchise, to create in two major speeches a new vision of the Tory Party and its appeal and to go on to be Prime Minister for six years. It is unlikely that he had any plan to make his party democratic (a bit of an anachronism at any time before 1918 in any case, for as many as 40% of even adult males did not have the vote until after that date) or to turn it into a party of social reform, where his record was fitful and disappointing. He was often a creature of impulse and lacking an evolved political philosophy, rather an opportunist and a pragmatist taking things as they came. In terms of personal and political depth he comes badly out of any comparison with Gladstone. The rivalry of the two men did much to establish the idea of the two-party system as the norm of British political life.

“The Conservative debt to Disraeli.”

Disraeli's legacy to the Conservative Party was an enduring one, not in turning it into a party allied to the common man or a party of social reform but in making it the party of imperialism and British greatness, perhaps the patriotic party, certainly the party you could rely on to look after British international interests. Do, of course, remember that until Disraeli it had been the Whig Palmerston who had claimed the national colours as his own. Even until late in the twentieth century Disraeli's vision of the Conservatives has been a great electoral asset to the party. One final legacy to the party was Disraeli's promotion of a radical overhaul of its administration, by his friend Gorst, which stretched from the Carlton Club at the top to the constituencies below and which was a significant strand in the development of political parties after the 1867 Reform Act. (Note the 'Tutor's Answer' to Question 1 below.)

USEFUL INFORMATION

1804	Benjamin Disraeli born: the son of a Spanish Jew and known author.
1817	Baptised as a Christian
1826	Publication of *Vivian Grey* which gave him entry to London society where he was well known for his expensive life and extravagant dress.
1837	Became an MP; his appearance and manner provoked laughter at his maiden speech.
1841	Failed to obtain office in Peel's Conservative Government Came to lead the Young England movement
1844	Wrote *Coningsby*
1845	Wrote *Sybil: or the Two Nations*
1846	Leading Commons opponent of Peel's repeal of the Corn Laws and, when the party split, came to lead the protectionist wing and helped to rebuild its fortunes
1852	**Minority Conservative Ministry with Lord Derby as Prime Minister** Disraeli Chancellor of the Exchequer for first of three times (1858 and 1866–1868 were the other occasions). Party at this point abandoned economic protectionism. Disraeli's role in bringing this about saved it from becoming a rump agrarian party.
1859	**Derby's second minority government** Disraeli promoted a Conservative Parliamentary Reform Bill which foundered.
1866	Led the successful opposition to Gladstone's Reform Bill joining with dissident Liberals under Robert Lowe to this end.
1866–1868	**Derby's third minority government**
1867	**Disraeli largely responsible for the Second Reform Act:** It extended the franchise to another 950,000 voters and so doubled the electorate. His motive was to respond to working class aspirations and to gain their vote for the Conservatives after too long in the political wilderness. The measure became more radical during the debate on it as Disraeli's safeguards were voted down. The most radical clause was the grant of the vote to every adult male ratepaying householder in the borough constituencies, to which was added an amendment abolishing the payment of rates by landlords, so that the number who were to receive the vote immediately doubled. Disraeli, determined to have a Conservative reform, persisted with the measure despite the radical changes.
1868	**Disraeli Prime Minister** Liberal election victory: (1868–1874 Gladstone Prime Minister).

1872	Speeches at Manchester and at the Crystal Palace advocating imperialism and social reform
1874–1880	**Disraeli Prime Minister**
1875	**Artisans' Dwellings Act**: this permitted councils to act against unhealthy houses encouraging slum clearance in larger towns.
	Public Health Act: this turned health measures since 1848 into a unified sanitary code compelling health action by councils. The work of civil servants, it was the basis of sanitary law until the 1930s.
	Factory Act: this consolidated earlier Acts; again civil service initiative.
	Sale of Food and Drugs Act: preventing adulteration.
	Merchant Shipping Act: on the initiative of Plimsoll, imposed a maximum load line.
	Climbing Boys Act: this made it illegal to send boys up chimneys.
	Conspiracy and Protection of Property Act: this permitted peaceful picketing.
	Employers and Workmen's Act: a breach of contract was no longer a criminal offence. This altered the law as laid down in Gladstone's Criminal Law Amendment Act of 1871.
1875	Purchase of Suez Canal shares gave Britain control of what became, in an age dominated by steamships, the main artery of traffic to the Empire in the East and across the Pacific.
1876	Victoria made Empress of India
	Disraeli made Earl of Beaconsfield
1877	Transvaal annexed to protect it from attack by the Zulu nation.
	War between Russia and the Turkish Empire.
1878	Treaty of San Stefano greatly increased Russian powers in the Balkans.
	Congress of Berlin: this was called by Bismarck. Key role of Disraeli in blocking Russian advances in the Balkans. Britain gained Cyprus. Established Disraeli's reputation as a European statesman.
	Afghan War: Disraeli sent an expeditionary force to support the king when the Russians seemed to be threatening the country.
1879	**Zulu War**: British defeated at Isandhlwana but victorious at Ulundi and Zululand annexed to Natal. Boers demanded restoration of Transvaal's independence.
1880	Conservative election defeat
1881	Disraeli died

EXAMINATION QUESTIONS

Q1 'Peel, not Disraeli, was the true founder of the British Conservative Party.' Discuss. (Northern Ireland 1988)

Q2 To what extent does Disraeli really deserve the titles 'Social Reformer' and 'Tory Democrat'? (Welsh 1989)

Q3 Examine Disraeli's political motives both for passing the Second Reform Act in 1867 and for the social reforms of his government of 1874–1880. (London 1989)

Q4 Was Gladstone or Disraeli the more effective in achieving social reform in the years 1868 to 1885? (London 1987)

OUTLINE ANSWERS

Question 1

See the 'Tutor's Answer' to Question 1 below.

Question 2

Neither title is merited by either what he achieved or by his motives.

“A Tory Democrat?”

Tory Democrat: 1859 Reform Bill was a measure for party advantage with little extension of franchise. In 1866 he wrecked Gladsone's reform in order to 'dish the Whigs' and combined with their most reactionary elements to do so. 1867 Reform Act was in some ways very radical, indicate this, but this again rose out of party conflict. Disraeli was determined to carry a Conservative reform and this, not any democratic notions, provided his motive – illustrate from the passage of the Act.

“A Social Reformer?”

Social Reformer: his claim here rests on his 1872 speeches, indicate what he said, and more dubiously on his Young England days. But his real motive in 1872 was to enhance the electoral appeal of the Tories against Gladstone. Examine social reforming record after he got into power in 1874; limited measures with Cross and the civil service, not Disraeli, the real inspiration. There was no programme of reforms to be enacted. Disraeli's true interest was imperialism which had also been prominent in the 1872 speeches.

Question 3

The thrust of the answer i.e. for party advantage and so to outbid Gladstone's Liberals, is offered in the preceding answer to Question 2. For 1867 it needs detailed illustration from the events of the passage of the Act and how Disraeli clung to the measure despite desertions from his own party and extreme amendments to his Bill forced on him by the hostile majority he faced in the Commons.

For the social legislation, his limited role also needs illustrating as in the preceding answer to Question 2 with the argument that by this stage there is little evidence of any sustained commitment to social reform and that the motives of others are of more significance for what was achieved from 1874 onwards.

Question 4

In this field the record of neither Prime Minister is particularly impressive. Both had non-social issues which interested them more.

“A comparison with Gladstone.”

Gladstone: Gladstone's reforms were largely institutional, administrative and political or related to his growing obsession with Ireland. Few purely social reforms in either the 1868–1874 or the 1880–1885 ministries. The 1870 Education Act had important social results but his motives were political to please his nonconformist supporters. Later he was against Joseph Chamberlain's ambitious and expensive reforming notions. More in favour of removing barriers to free competition and sweeping away inherited inefficiences, give examples:

- wished to keep government costs to a minimum
- believed in self-help
- these fatal obstacles to any real social reforms.

Disraeli: look at the social reforms of the 1874–1880 ministry, argue that they were individually limited in scope and did not constitute a programme of reform. The Trade Union legislation for example was largely a response to an effective campaign by the leaders of the 'New Model' Trade Unions. Disraeli was only involved in the promotion of any of the social legislation to a limited extent; foreign and imperial interests were closer to his heart. He never lived up to the promises of his 1872 speeches.

A TUTOR'S ANSWER TO QUESTION 1

“Characteristics of the Conservative Party.”

The Conservative Party in the late nineteenth and twentieth centuries has been characterised by a tradition of cautious reform and accommodation to political pressures in order to preserve the traditional institutions and social structures of the nation from revolutionary change. It has, at home, been the party of stability, seeking to attract support from as wide a range of voters as possible who could see that their own interests were best preserved by reforming proven abuses but resisting more sweeping radical demands for either political or 'social change. In regard to international affairs the Conservatives have been identified as, or promoted themselves as, the party of the national interest, once the party of the Empire but still today the patriotic party. Both Peel and Disraeli made important contributions to these foundations of the British Conservative Party but that of the latter it will be suggested was of the greater significance for the party's future.

“Peel's legacy to the Conservative Party.”

Peel was involved in the original reforming impulse of the Liberal Tories of the 1820s which led the party of repression from Peterloo and the Gag Acts to the reform of the criminal code and the prisons, to the formation of the Metropolitan Police and to Catholic Emancipation. It was again Peel who, after the 1832 Reform Act had been passed, took the lead in making his party accept its inevitability and, in the Tamworth Manifesto, provided a political philosophy of cautious reform of proven abuses which could attract the support of the widened electorate. His rewards appeared to come in the electoral successes of 1837 and 1841. In fact however, his success in transforming the outlook of what had traditionally been the party of the Anglican Church, the aristocratic and the landed interests, the party which instinctively resisted change, was limited.

When he attempted to take a small step to solve some of Ireland's problems by increasing an already established grant to the Catholic College at Maynooth, in the belief that an expanded and better educated priesthood would help make Ireland more easily governable, it produced a major crisis within the Conservative Party. He was again reviled as the man who in 1829 had granted Catholic emancipation and so betrayed the Church of England and in part undermined the constitution. This crisis was a forerunner of the far more serious split which developed over Peel's decision to repeal the Corn Laws. This measure was intended to help relieve famine distress in Ireland and also was made in response to a very effective campaign from the manufacturing and commercial interests who favoured free trade in all commodities. Peel had become convinced of the desirability of this measure but he was unable to lead the bulk of his party in that direction. His Cabinet colleagues were as convinced as he was of its necessity but the backbenchers, led by Disraeli and Bentinck, remained loyal to the traditions of the party's landed interests. They did not share Peel's faith in the new economics of Free Trade and this despite the fact that it was their government which had in the budgets of 1842 and 1845 taken giant steps towards it.

Peel in the crisis of Corn Law repeal seemed to lose interest in the fate of the Conservatives; he had never enjoyed close relations with its backbenchers, and became obsessed with carrying the measure with Whig support and at any cost to the party. After his subsequent defeat he drifted purposeless into the political backwaters. He would give no lead to those who continued to support him and, if he had any political commitment at all, it seemed to be to keeping the Whigs in office in order to guarantee that the Conservatives could not restore the Corn Laws. His efforts to modernise the party had in fact failed and he had finished by losing touch with its traditional supporters.

> Peel's achievement questioned.

> Disraeli the preserver of the Conservative Party?

Thanks to Peel the Conservative Party after 1846 could easily have drifted into the role of a rump agrarian party, continuing to control a declining number of rural constituencies but cut off from the increasingly important industrial interests and so with no prospect of again forming the government. This possibility was a real one until the election of 1874. It was the life's work of Disraeli, and arguably his greatest achievement, to avert this catastrophe.

With his budget of 1852 Disraeli removed the protectionist label from the party and in 1859, by introducing a conservative parliamentary reform bill, he removed the danger that the Conservatives would degenerate into a backwoods party. His persistence in carrying through the 1867 Reform Act brought no immediate electoral advantage to the party but its passage ensured that the Liberals under Gladstone would not have a monopoly on parliamentary reform and in the age of a wider electorate this was important.

In his speeches at Manchester and at the Crystal Palace in 1872 Disraeli offered a 'conservative identity', based on a programme of social reforms and imperial sentiment, which would appeal to that wider electorate. This was at the point where Gladstone and the Liberal Party were establishing their appeal on a national basis, removed from the local elites that had dominated parliamentary representation until this point. By establishing a 'conservative identity' Disraeli ensured that his party could compete with the emerging Liberal Party. It did not matter that the social reforms did not in practice measure up to the rhetoric. What mattered was that the Conservatives had avoided yet again the trap of becoming the party of resistance to reform and this was now to become a permanent feature of the party's appeal. It should be added that at this time also Disraeli played a significant role, alongside his friend Gorst, in modernising the Party organisation from the Carlton Club through to the constituencies and in this helped to fit it for post-1867 politics.

> The party of the national interest.

Perhaps Disraeli's most important legacy to the Party arose from his ill-thought out romantic imperial vision which he set against Gladstone's notions of international morality. The Conservatives became the party whom the electors felt could be trusted with the national interest. This was on several occasions to be of the utmost importance to their fortunes. It was the basis of their domination of political life from 1886 to 1906 when Gladstone divided the nation on the issue of Home Rule for Ireland. It left them, unlike their opponents, united during the Boer War and the First World War and made available to them the patriotic card which could be played in any crisis, real or fabricated. It left the Conservatives closer to the mood of popular patriotism than either the Liberal or later the Labour Party. This was Disraeli's real legacy to the Tory Party; the Churchill legend and, in lower key, even the Falklands War and the subsequent election victory of 1983 are merely confirmation of its importance.

“But does this verdict neglect Lord Derby's part?”

Peel's role, then, was important at the time but by 1846 he had failed to take the grassroot support of his party with him and had, almost wilfully, abandoned it to fate. It was almost entirely due to Disraeli that the Party survived to 1874 and then re-established itself as a party of government with a distinctive identity and a mass appeal.

USEFUL SOURCES OF INFORMATION

General reading

M Bentley, *Politics Without Democracy 1815–1914*, Fontana 1984
E J Feuchtwanger, *Democracy and Empire: Britain 1865–1914*, Arnold 1985
P Lane, *Success in British History 1760–1914*, John Murray 1978
M Pugh, *The Making of Modern British Politics 1867–1939*, Blackwell 1982
A Wood, *Nineteenth Century Britain: 1815–1914*, Longman (2nd edition) 1982

Further reading

B H Abbott, *Gladstone and Disraeli*, Collins 1972
P Adelman, *Gladstone, Disraeli and Later Victorian Politics*, Longman (2nd edition) 1983
R Blake, *Disraeli*, Methuen 1969: a long and detailed biography but one which should be dipped into by students with ambitions to do well for it is arguably the finest biography of a nineteenth century figure to be published in the last fifty years. Use it selectively.

Linked topic areas

- Peel and the Conservative Party (see Chapter 5)
- Gladstone and the Liberal Party (see Chapter 6)
- The Parliamentary Reform Act of 1867 (see Chapter 5)
- The British Empire in the late 19th century
- The Eastern Question (see Chapter 15)

CHAPTER 8

POLITICS AND SOCIETY 1900–1914

GETTING STARTED

Edward VII reigned from 1901 to 1911 but for study purposes the Edwardian period comes in practice to mean from 1900 to 1914. Within this period the themes you are studying – political, social or economic – will need setting against their late nineteenth century background. Before 1900 Britain's easy industrial supremacy had long been under threat, particularly from Germany and the United States whilst agriculture, faced with mounting grain and frozen meat imports was sunk into a long-term depression. Awareness of this darkening economic scene caused intense debate often linked to the ideas of *Social Darwinism* which saw societies as struggling, like animal species, to survive in competition with their fellows: to many Britain seemed, in this period, to be losing the struggle. This feeling was fortified by the knowledge that, in military terms Britain could no longer compete with the great conscript armies of the Continent, again especially with Germany. More serious was the growing realisation that the effortless naval supremacy of past decades was also under threat for the first time since Trafalgar. Painting much of Africa on the atlas in the pink of the British Empire, during the century's last two decades, was in many ways a hollow triumph achieved in the face of the new imperial ambitions of the Continental Powers. In reality the easy optimism of middle-class Victorian society about Britain's international position looked increasingly precarious.

At home too, Victorian values were being questioned. The late Victorians had to accept that, despite their belief in the redeeming power of self-help, they had failed to solve the problem of poverty in their society. Social surveys, by Booth and Rowntree, the growing weight of Trade Union and socialist political pressure, the widening of the franchise and the poor health of so many Boer War volunteers, all served to drive this point home. In consequence those mid-nineteenth century notions of minimal and cheap government, those unquestioned assumptions on which social provision had so often foundered, came increasingly to be questioned. A new mood of social expectation within British society came to coincide with the need for national efficiency in the international setting. This new mood is sometimes described as *'collectivist'* – meaning in this context the idea of society acting together to solve deep-seated social problems. In practice this meant the State having a duty to act to meet the problems. It stands in sharp contrast to the *laissez-faire* values of the earlier period and its emergence is essential background to the Liberal welfare reforms after 1906.

ESSENTIAL PRINCIPLES

The new context that existed both domestically and internationally at the turn of the century provided an imposing challenge for many traditional Victorian values, especially for those enshrined in Gladstonian liberalism. The Liberal Party had in 1891 adopted a reform programme, the '*Newcastle Programme*' which maintained their reputation as the party of reform but without committing them to an expensive package of social reforms. It was much more in the traditional spirit of Liberal administrative and constitutional changes. As the half-way house from Gladstonian Liberalism to Liberal welfarism it deserves reference.

LIBERAL DILEMMAS

"Liberal problems after Gladstone."

AFTER GLADSTONE

These are important as background to the great Liberal victory in the 1906 General Election. Lord Rosebery was Prime Minister, briefly, after Gladstone's 1894 resignation. Following his government's defeat in 1895, he was, in 1896, succeeded as Liberal leader by Campbell-Bannerman. During the Boer War further Liberal divisions became evident with Rosebery and the Liberal Imperialists supporting the Conservative Government's war policy whilst radical Liberals led by Lloyd George attacked it bitterly. Liberal fortunes were at a low ebb. A full analysis of why this was so involves reflecting on Gladstone's legacy, arising both from his failure to respond to demands for a progressive social reform policy and in responding too enthusiastically for many of his followers to the Irish question (for discussion of this see Chapter 6 and especially the 'Tutor's Answer' on p 69). His conversion to Home Rule had ensured Conservative domination of politics for the next twenty years.

Campbell-Bannerman

"Conservative policies helped re-unite the Liberals."

From the end of the century Conservative policies, the Education Act of 1902 and Joseph Chamberlain's campaign to convert the Conservatives to take up Tariff Reform, predictably united the Liberals in the defence of Nonconformity and of Free Trade. The factors bringing the Liberals once more together in time to secure election in 1906 and the role of Campbell-Bannerman in the process could be useful examination revision. Campbell-Bannerman became Liberal Leader in 1899 and deepened the divisions in the Party by opposing British tactics in the Boer War, particularly the use of concentration camps. When the Conservatives split over tariffs and Balfour resigned, Campbell-Bannerman formed a minority government in 1905. By this time he had healed the splits in his own party and went on to win the 1906 General Election.

1906 GENERAL ELECTION

LIBERAL GOVERNMENT

The sweeping Liberal victory in this election, with 377 seats (Conservatives 157, Irish 83, Labour 29) is the central political event of the period. It is seen as a watershed in British political life, ending a long period of Conservative political dominance and opening a road to new Liberal welfare politics. It has been described as 'One of the two great swings to the Left in twentieth century British politics'.

ANALYSIS OF THE LIBERAL VICTORY

"The 1906 election victory in many ways a negative one."

The factors behind the Liberal victory deserve cooler analysis than this might suggest. It was in many ways a negative election: one lost by the Conservatives through events in South Africa, unpopular education, trade union and above all tariff policies.

The Liberal victory rested on their new found unity: the full reasons for this deserve careful rehearsal. Be wary of accepting too easily the idea that the result constituted a great mandate for political and social change. This did not figure prominently in the election campaign and the impetus for reform seemed to emerge after the government had been formed, owing a lot to the individual members who made up one of the most remarkable Cabinets of the century.

The Liberal Government

Henry Campbell-Bannermann: Prime Minister 1905–1908, when he had to retire from ill-health. He died a few days later.
Herbert Asquith: Chancellor of the Exchequer 1905–1908; Prime Minister 1908–1916.
David Lloyd George: President of the Board of Trade to 1908; Chancellor of the Exchequer 1908–1915.
Winston Churchill: He had left the Conservatives in 1904 over tariffs: President of the Board of Trade 1908–1910; Home Secretary 1910–1911; First Lord of the Admiralty 1911–1915.
Edward Grey: Foreign Secretary 1905–1916; longest continuous holding of the office in British history.
Richard Haldane: Secretary for War 1905–1912.

The appointments date from 1905 because the Liberals had formed a minority government at the end of that year, prior to the General Election.

“Look up the record of these men.”

Note: In the case of all these men it would be valuable to prepare a brief assessment of their work. They may require individual treatment in examination questions and the same material could bring to life more general essays. Looking them up in encyclopedias or through the index of a textbook could be a very valuable form of revision, encouraging you to look at the period from a series of different viewpoints.

LIBERAL WELFARE REFORMS

“This is a very popular examination topic.”

The full programme is worth knowing in some detail (see the ‘Useful Information’ section later in this chapter) and its impact on the problems of the day assessing and also judging against the relative neglect of major social problems by the Liberal governments of Gladstone and more recently by the Conservatives. There is little or no value in just being able to recite the terms of the legislation. You need to be able to explain how and why this form of Liberal welfarism was different from Gladstonian Liberalism and this involves remembering the changing economic and social climate referred to in the ‘Getting Started’ section of this chapter. Then the impact of the reforms needs weighing against the size of the problems and the question, why more was not done, could well be asked.

Exam questions

Many examination questions invite you to discuss the reasons which inspired, or drove, the Liberals to these measures. This would involve some assessment of the roles of Lloyd George and Winston Churchill, the two ministers most committed to social reforms. The opinion that the Liberals were determined to outbid the new Labour Party or to block the Conservatives needs to be examined. You could look through the ‘Useful Information’ section and list those measures which you felt justify an argument that the Liberals were anxious either to attract working-class support or to hold the support of the Labour MPs.

“A Welfare State?”

Questions often also invite a consideration of whether these Liberal reforms amount to the emergence of a Welfare State: be ready with a definition of this which will structure your discussion. The Liberal reforms may all have been more important psychologically, or as a series of precedents, than in anything they did to improve the lives of many ordinary British citizens. If the *central point of a welfare state* is the idea of *comprehensive social services* and *social security provision* then the Liberal measures fall a long way short of this. But, set against Victorian ideas of self-help and the provisions of the nineteenth century poor law, they mark a gigantic step towards the later proposals of Beveridge, himself a Liberal, and the legislation of the 1945–1951 Labour Governments.

CONSTITUTIONAL CRISIS

1909–1911

This dramatic episode is quite popular as a source of examination questions; it provides the most common alternative to an assessment of the Liberal reforms.

Origins

It had its origins in the need for money to pay for the Navy’s new battleships and meet the costs of the welfare proposals, notably the new old age pensions. Lloyd George as Chancellor of the Exchequer in 1909 proposed new taxes which the House of Lords, contrary to all precedent with money Bills, rejected.

Crisis

"Perhaps the most serious political crisis since 1832."

This led straight into the crisis between the Liberal government with its Commons majority and the Lords with a massive Conservative majority and, of course, a veto on all legislation. It was arguably the most serious constitutional crisis since the fight over the 1832 Reform Act, involving both Houses of Parliament, the leaders of both political parties and first Edward VII and then his successor George V. Events took on their own momentum and you first need to master the narrative, including the chronology, of what happened, (some signposts are offered in the 'Useful Information' section). It is essential that this knowledge is later adapted to provide a direct answer to whatever examination question you face and is not narrated for its own sake.

Historical issues

Consider the historical issues which arise:

- Why, prior to this episode, were relations between the Liberal Party and the House of Lords so strained?
- Why did the Conservatives choose to reject the 1909 Budget and why did this develop into a major constitutional issue?

"Understand the issues."

- How grave was the constitutional crisis? Arguably the most serious since 1832 but how close was the nation to a breakdown in the Constitution and by what means was this averted?
- What were Lloyd George's motives: what can be learned from this crisis to help in an overall assessment of this major political figure?
- How did the ensuing Parliament Act alter the Constitution and, vastly more important, affect the practical working of everyday politics both immediately (the Irish Home Rule question) and in the long-term?

HOME RULE FOR IRELAND

(For an attempt to assess Gladstone's efforts to resolve the Irish question see the 'Tutor's Answer in Chapter 6). Anyone who has done some reading on nineteenth century Ireland is already well equipped to analyse the Liberal efforts to solve the problem from 1912 to 1914. For such students it would be sensible to take the study of Irish affairs through to the creation of the Irish Free State in 1921.

Threat to the state

Even if you have only limited acquaintance with Irish affairs it is important to be aware of what dangers the Liberals faced over Ireland and the fate of their proposed solution to Irish problems. From 1912 to 1914 the issue of granting Home Rule to Ireland posed a most serious threat to the stability of the British State. It seemed probable that there would be an armed rebellion against the Liberal proposals by the Ulster protestants and possible that the British Conservative Party would, in some shape or form, openly support them. You need to have enough information and ideas on the nature of the threat to be able to assess its gravity relative to other sources of political instability in the Edwardian period. Most historians regard it as the single most important threat to the State in this period.

THE LABOUR PARTY TO 1914

The groups, and the ideas, which in the late nineteenth century coalesced to bring about the formation of the Labour Party, have to be studied in their social and economic setting. The 1867 and 1884 extensions of the franchise form convenient starting points, if only as a reminder of how undemocratic many aspects of political life remained prior to 1918. The 1880s and 1890s saw a number of societies and publications committed to pressing for greater government action on social problems.

Socialism: societies and publications

1881 H M Hyndman founded the Social Democratic Federation, a small but influential propaganda organisation preaching socialist ideas.

1884 William Morris founded the Socialist League.

1884 The Fabian Society was founded which became the most important intellectual group promoting socialist ideas.
1890s The Clarion was a working-class paper urging social reform.
1890s Independent working-class candidates began to appear in elections following Keir Hardie's 1888 example in Glasgow. Hardie was elected in 1892.
1893 Hardie established the Independent Labour Party.

"A new collectivist mood emerged."

It was this development of ideas which may loosely be called socialist which provided the intellectual climate for a new, more collectivist, type of politics. The growing importance of the Trade Union movement, particularly the emergence of new unions for unskilled workers provided the framework within which the new party could be established. Why Gladstonian Liberalism failed to adapt sufficiently to meet new social aspirations is essential background to the 1900 decision by mainly the unskilled unions, the socialist societies and the co-operative societies to set up the Labour Representation Committee which by 1906 had become the Labour Party.

The Party's relations with the Liberals, its fortunes in the 1906 General Election, its growing independence of the Liberals, especially in 1910 when the Liberal insurance proposals required working people to pay insurance contributions, but its still uncertain electoral progress, take the story to 1914. Most British history syllabuses continue beyond 1914 and this topic is best studied in a longer perspective, taking in the associated reasons for the decline of the Liberal Party, through and beyond the First World War, to the Second Labour Government of 1929–1931 (see Chapter 9).

"Labour – worth following through to the 1920s for a question."

THE SUFFRAGETTES

"Women's history, a wider topic than just the vote."

The Suffragettes should ideally be studied as part of the wider movement for the emancipation of women to include the struggle for legal equality in property and divorce matters and for education and employment opportunities. Even within the narrower struggle for the vote it should be remembered that the Suffragettes were only the most colourful of the pressure groups fighting for the extension of the franchise to women. You can usefully prepare to offer both an assessment of why, in 1918, some women got the vote and also have ready a judgement on how serious an embarrassment pre-war Suffragette activities were for normal constitutional processes which you can use in general essays on the period. Do not assume that in doing this you have prepared yourself fully for more general questions on the emancipation of women or the role of women in history.

LABOUR UNREST

The last years before the First World War were a period marked by sharp industrial strife. You need to be able to comment on this as one aspect of the problems afflicting Edwardian society and to assess how serious a threat syndicalist ideas and labour unrest were to social and economic stability.

Syndicalism

Syndicalism was a French movement in origin, working for the transfer of the ownership of the means of production to the workers and using strikes to achieve this. Its importance in British labour history was not great and the chief causes of poor industrial relations in the last years of the period were the growing power of the big unions and economic stagnation. The real tests of Trade Union power were not to come until the 1920s.

Further study

Fuller study of these issues is best undertaken by studying the development of the Trade Union and Labour movements as topics in their own right. All students of the period should however understand the significance of the *Taff Vale Judgement* and the *Osborne Case* and the legislation enacted in each case to retrieve the position for these were important parts of the general record of the Liberal governments.

THE ROAD TO WAR

"You need to understand the European background."

Foreign policy does not appear in all syllabuses and even when it does it is worth checking on the frequency of actual examination questions. This is a big topic to come to terms with unless there is some prospect of examination reward. Conversely a parallel European history paper may have already helped to prepare the background. Do not, however, expect those who set papers to give you the opportunity to use the same material in both British and European papers.

The following are part of a complex but fascinating equation which will be fully understood only against its European background (see Chapter 19):

- The perception that Britain was under increasing threat from potential foreign enemies.
- The re-arming and reorganisation of the army and the navy, the growing militarism in society.
- The secretive conduct of foreign policy, the role of the leading personalities involved.
- The drift from isolation to Entente and virtual alliance.
- The precise way in which Britain entered the war in August 1914.

Five minutes looking at a map of pre-1914 Europe would be a good starting point but it is a topic which needs developing as the course proceeds and not one to open up in the last weeks of revision. The 'Document Question' below will provide one starting-point.

THE EDWARDIAN PERIOD

GENERAL FOCUS

The period ended abruptly with the outbreak of war and 1914 provides a very important point at which to carry out a general survey of the state of the British nation. Each of the topics studied in the nineteenth century context can be considered and the position in 1914 noted. The results could be invaluable in providing balanced conclusions to examination essays. The other advantage of preparing such a balance sheet is for those who go on to study the impact of the First World War on Britain. In many fields the origins of post-1918 trends are to be observed in the pre-war period and, where possible this should be pointed out. The most powerful example is with the wartime problems and the post-war demise of the Liberal Party where an eloquent but challenged thesis has been developed that the Party was already in a critical state of decline by the outbreak of war.

USEFUL INFORMATION

1899–1902	The Boer War
1901	Accession of Edward VII (died 1910).
	Taff Vale legal judgement awarded the Taff Vale Railway Company £23,000 civil damages against the Amalgamated Society of Railway Servants for loss of earnings from a strike. This reversed what had been the general perception of the law and was seen as an attack on Union power.
1902–1905	**Balfour's Conservative Ministry**
1902	Education Act annoyed Nonconformists because it provided aid from the rates to church schools, vast majority of which were Anglican or Catholic.
1905–1908	**Campbell Bannerman's Liberal Ministry**
1906	**Liberal victory in General Election**
	Trade Disputes Act: this put aside the Taff Vale decision and so protected unions from civil actions over damage from strikes.
	Workmen's Compensation Act: this ensured some compensation from employers for people injured at work.
	School Meals Act: this allowed rate money to be used to provide meals at school.
1907	**School medical inspections** were now introduced.
1908–1916	**Asquith Prime Minister**
1908	**Old Age Pensions Act**: for people over 70, they were non-contributory but were means tested.
1909	**Trade Boards Act**: this set up arrangements to supervise hours, conditions of work and wages, in industries where the Factory Acts did not apply.
	The People's Budget: this was introduced by Lloyd George to raise £16 million extra to pay for reforms and new battleships. Proposed higher rates of tax for higher incomes, death duties and a tax on increases in land values. Rejected by the House of Lords.
	Labour Exchanges Act: this was to assist the unemployed to find work.
	Osborne Judgement of the Law Lords decided that unions could not use their funds for political purposes. Hit at unions paying for working-class MPs.

1910 Jan **General Election**: Liberals lost overall majority (Liberals 275 seats, Conservatives 273). Liberal deal with Irish Nationalists in return for promise of Irish Home Rule and a way round any House of Lords veto on the measure.

May Parliament Bill introduced

May Death of Edward VII

1910–1936 **Reign of George V**. He called a Constitutional Conference to solve the differences between the political parties, met on 21 occasions over five months.

Dec **General Election**: some further Liberal losses (Liberals and Conservatives each had 272 seats).

Liberal government re-introduced the Parliament Bill which passed Commons and went to Lords. Enough Lords frightened by George V's promise to Asquith that he would, if necessary to break the deadlock, create Liberal Peers so that they abstained from voting.

1911 **Payment of MPs** introduced.

Parliament Act passed by Lords, 131–113, it received Royal Assent:

- Lords could delay Money Bills by only one month.
- Other Bills passed in three successive sessions by the Commons to become law even if rejected by the Lords which amounted to a delaying power of two years maximum.
- The maximum interval between General Elections was reduced from seven to five years.

National Insurance Act: this provided for contributions to obtain payment when sick and, in a few trades, in time of unemployment.

1912 Irish Home Rule Bill (passed Commons but delayed by Lords under terms of Parliament Act).

1913 Trade Union Act overturned the Osborne Judgement and so allowed unions to use their funds for political purposes.

1914 Aug **War** declared on Germany.

Irish Home Rule and Welsh Church Disestablishment (1914) legislation not to operate until after the war.

EXAMINATION QUESTIONS

Q1 Why did the Liberal governments of 1906–14 follow policies of social reform? (Cambridge 1989)

Q2 How radical, and how novel, were the social policies of the Liberal governments of 1905–1914? (London 1990)

Q3 Was the 'New Liberalism' of the years 1905–14 'merely an attempt to thwart the rise of the Labour Party?' (London 1990)

Q4 Assess Asquith's qualities and achievements as Prime Minister between 1908 and 1916. (Oxford 1989)

Q5 How far did the methods used by Suffragettes between 1906 and 1914 hinder rather than promote the aims of the movement? (NEAB 1989)

Q6 Document Question 'Great Britain and the European Powers, 1914' (NEAB 1989)

Read the extract below and then answer the questions which follow.

An Extract from the Statement by the Secretary of State for Foreign Affairs (Sir Edward Grey) to the House of Commons, 3 August 1914.

. . . And, Sir, there is the more serious consideration – becoming more serious every hour – there is the question of the neutrality of Belgium . . . I will read to the

House what took place last week on this subject. When mobilisation was beginning, I knew that this question must be a most important element in our policy – a most important subject for the House of Commons. I telegraphed at the same time in similar terms to both Paris and Berlin to say that it was essential for us to know whether the French and German Governments respectively were prepared to undertake an engagement to respect the neutrality of Belgium. These are the replies. I got from the French Government this reply:

'The French Government are resolved to respect the neutrality of Belgium, and it would only be in the event of some other Power violating that neutrality that France might find herself under the necessity, in order to assure the defence of her security, to act otherwise. This assurance has been given several times. The President of the Republic spoke of it to the King of the Belgians, and the French Minister at Brussels has spontaneously renewed the assurance to the Belgian Minister of Foreign Affairs today.'

From the German Government the reply was:

'The Secretary of State for Foreign Affairs could not possibly give an answer before consulting the Emperor and the Imperial Chancellor.'

Sir Edward Goschen, to whom I had said it was important to have an answer soon, said he hoped the answer would not be too long delayed. The German Minister for Foreign Affairs then gave Sir Edward Goschen to understand that he rather doubted whether they could answer at all, as any reply they might give could not fail, in the event of war, to have the undesirable effect of disclosing, to a certain extent, part of their plan of campaign . . .

There is but one way in which the Government could make certain at the present moment of keeping outside this war, and that would be that it should immediately issue a proclamation of unconditional neutrality. We cannot do that. We have made the commitment to France that I have read to the House which prevents us from doing that. We have got the consideration of Belgium which prevents us also from any unconditional neutrality, and without those conditions absolutely satisfied and satisfactory, we are bound not to shrink from proceeding to the use of all the forces in our power. If we did take that line by saying, 'We will have nothing whatever to do with this matter' under no conditions – the Belgian Treaty obligations, the possible position in the Mediterranean, with damage to British interests, and what may happen to France from our failure to support France – if we were to say that all those things mattered nothing, were as nothing, and to say we would stand aside, we should, I believe, sacrifice our respect and good name and reputation before the world, and should not escape the most serious and grave economic consequences . . .

a) Explain the meaning of the two phrases underlined. *(2)*
b) How does Sir Edward Grey, through the language and tone of his speech, seek to convey the seriousness of the situation? *(6)*
c) Why did Grey attach such importance to the question of Belgium in August 1914? *(8)*
d) What reasons for Britain's entry into the First World War were not stressed by Grey in this extract? *(9)*

(Total 25 marks)

OUTLINE ANSWERS

Question 1

See the 'Tutor's Answer' below.

Question 2

Deal with novel first and agree that against the traditions of Gladstonian liberalism and Victorian values like self-help or against the Poor Law provisions they were novel. But in other ways not entirely so; ideas of Joseph Chamberlain, of the socialist societies of the 1880s and even the Liberals' own Newcastle Programme had begun to pave the way. By end of the nineteenth century there was a collectivist mood growing (explain how and why) which paved the way for the Liberal measures.

Argue that in terms of changing peoples' lives – not all that radical, give examples. Argue that not comprehensive enough to be regarded as introducing some new welfare philosophy. They were useful tinkering with proven problems and also useful precedents for later measures but scarcely dented traditional Liberal philosophies of what government was about, which only came about when the country was fighting a total war after 1914.

Question 3

Briefly explain what New Liberalism was – collectivist ideas leading to social reforms, outline these very briefly to illustrate.

Most of essay discuss Liberal aims behind new policy, using specific examples of legislation to illustrate this:

- It was a logical development from traditional liberalism via the ideas of Joseph Chamberlain (explain).
- It was a natural if delayed response to the new social expectations arising from the spotlight on continuing poverty.
- It was a way of winning electoral support after a long period of Conservative domination.

Continuation of Liberal tradition as the party of reform but in a changed social context. Lloyd George and Churchill had real reforming idealism and fire. (Though Lloyd George's may have been more lukewarm at the end of the period.)

Only in small part to thwart the Labour Party who were not seen as the real enemy or as a real threat until after this period. Labour not doing all that well up to 1914.

Conclusion: cynicism lying behind the quotation is on this occasion unjustified. (*Note*: The 'Tutor's Answer' below has further comments relevant to this essay.)

Question 4

Separate the periods of peace and war for purposes of judging him.

Peace: To 1914 it is easy to underestimate his contribution to a record of remarkable legislation and in facing a great series of problems. He presided over a very talented Cabinet. Indicate the scope of all this and then suggest he was a very able Prime Minister in holding his team together and in overcoming in particular the crisis with the Lords and in keeping calm after 1912 faced with the Ulster threat. Reject the claim that the Liberals were in a state of decline in 1914. Argue that this was largely because of Asquith's skill in carrying so many reforms and meeting so many challenges.

War: War situation was different. Some things to his credit: he took most of the Party into the war with him, no easy task in view of Liberal traditions but in actually fighting the war he let too many things drift, give examples like conscription, though the role of Lloyd George and the Conservatives in undermining his position was not an honourable one. It has been said that he was too slow to act and that he drank too much. But his real weakness as a war leader was perhaps that he was too loyal in his support of his military leaders and too loyal to inconvenient Liberal principles. It thus became easy for ambitious men to strike him down.

Question 5

- Suffragette aims obvious, but state them anyway. Aim not achieved so temptation is to assume that nothing they did promoted their aim. In outline tactics are well known. Briefly give examples.

“Assessing the suffragettes.”

- Argue that some things were effective: early actions secured publicity that had not been achieved by the suffragists, it put the issue on the public agenda; hunger strikes, dignity and courage (give examples) won public sympathy.
- In other ways tactics not helpful, browbeating Liberal government which then could not afford to give in to violence (consider role of Asquith in this): offended notions of respectability and so lost support from both men and women.
- In other words it is a mixed verdict but that hides the important fact that as time went on tactics more extreme and so less effective, even in publicity terms. From 1911 getting nowhere, illustrate this. So perhaps much truth in statement overall but other tactics had done no better.

Tutor's comments on document question 6

This is offered both as an opportunity to practise documentary skills and as a focus for revision on why Britain went to war in 1914. Try to work out informal answers first and then go back to a textbook and see how to supplement your first answer. Sub-question (a) needs a dictionary at most and (b) requires close reading of the document to find enough clues to construct an answer. In (c) you must of course explain, from the document and from your own knowledge, why Belgium was important to Britain but you need also to add that for Grey any attack on Belgium would greatly help to unite the Liberals behind any declaration of war. With (d) you are dependent on your knowledge of the topic: first work out what is there, Belgian neutrality and the commitment to France. Then, from your reading on the topic construct an answer on the other reasons – fear of Germany upsetting the balance of power in Europe, its military might, the long rivalry in naval and colonial matters, the danger of future British isolation if it did not come into the war, obligations but not formal commitments to Russia, even anti-German feeling in the country? You will have to elaborate the points from the pre-war context for there does not seem to be a lot outside the document for the nine marks on offer.

A TUTOR'S ANSWER TO QUESTION 1

The Liberal social reforms of this period were the product of a new political climate which had been emerging since the last decades of the nineteenth century when a collectivist mood replaced the laissez-faire approach of Gladstonian Liberalism. But for this fundamental change there would have been no far-reaching social reform policies. In addition some policies had more specific causes: political calculation, the workings of pressure groups inside and outside the Liberal Party, the vision and energy of individual politicians and administrators.

“People were coming to expect more from the state.”

The changing climate of political expectation of the late nineteenth century had many causes. The work of Booth and Rowntree showed that charity and poor relief left one third of the people still trapped in poverty and the poor health of Boer War recruits dramatically underlined the potential dangers to the nation. Middle class intellectuals gave collectivism its new respectability, the Social Democratic Federation, the Socialist League, the Fabians were all part of this. At the same time the working class was becoming more organised, especially in the New Unions, and was voicing new social demands. More men had the vote, the first working class MPs had arrived, in 1900 the Trade Unions and sympathisers set up the Labour Representation Committee. The common call from these many sources was for greater action by the State in regard to social problems. The direct impact of these developments is well illustrated by the friendship and influence of the Webbs, leading collectivist intellectuals, with Winston Churchill, who emerged as a leading Liberal reformer.

“New Liberal thinking before 1906.”

Acceptance of the need for State-led social reform had established itself within the Liberal Party prior to the 1906 Election for example with Rosebery and the Liberal Imperialists influenced by the experiences of the Boer War. Without this ideological permeation there would have been no pattern of social reform. As it was those Liberal politicians who pressed for such reforms were in many instances pushing against a half-open door.

“But the Election was not won on a reform programme.”

Little of this can, however, be seen in the Liberal election campaign and it is difficult to view the Liberal triumph of 1906 as an overwhelming mandate for a programme of reform. The election result was largely a rejection of the Tory record and Tory tariff proposals. The most interesting reform proposal which was discussed during the election campaign, and which did become law, was to introduce Old Age Pensions on a non-contributory basis. It was a direct response to the effective case, presented by Booth and Rowntree, to the increased pressure upon the Poor Law system and to old fashioned humanitarianism. Proposals to change Trade Union Law were a pay-off for closer electoral arrangements with the infant Labour Representation Committee. Other reforms proposed in 1906, an Education Bill to counter the 1902 Act, a more restrictive licensing law, the Disestablishment of the Anglican Church in Wales (the only one to be enacted) were all debts which had to be paid to the Party's traditional Nonconformist conscience. They scarcely constitute a major reforming programme.

“Pressure from Labour had only a limited impact.”

By the end of 1908 the impetus had gone out of the Liberal victory. It is the recovery from this low point with the introduction of radical insurance proposals that is central to the Liberal reform record. Contrary to some opinion pressure from outside the Party appears to have played little part in bringing about this renewed Liberal energy. Some Liberals may well have seen the need to outbid socialism for the continued support of the working class electorate but the National Insurance Act of 1911 owed little or nothing to specific Trade Union or Labour Party pressure. The Labour Party indeed proved remarkably suspicious of the health and unemployment insurance proposals, as some Unions had earlier of Labour Exchanges. As the period advanced Labour, even as a pressure group on behalf of the working class, or more specifically the Unions, rather lost its way. Equally the long-established Friendly Societies proved a drag on, rather than a spur to, the extension of insurance provision.

It is difficult to avoid the conclusion that the National Insurance Act owed its existence mainly to the energy and commitment of a handful of leading Liberal politicians, notably to Lloyd George and to Churchill with an equally small group of radical and influential administrators notably Morant and Beveridge alongside them. The politicians saw it as a means of uniting the Party and getting it moving again and so dishing the Tories; for Lloyd George it may well have had useful links to his attack on the powers of the House of Lords. One should not be too cynical in all this for the contributory insurance proposals were far from being an automatic vote winner with the working class and were suspect for their generosity by the tax paying middle class. They may have been the cause of embarrassing by-election defeats. If Liberal reformers sought Party advantage in their proposals then it was not evident to someone as shrewd as Asquith that this would be the result. It seems likely that both Churchill and Lloyd George were genuinely moved by the plight of their poorer fellows.

The administrators had more pressing reasons to develop the insurance proposals for the system of poor relief was increasingly unable to cope with the demands placed upon it, as the Reports of the Royal Commission made uncomfortably clear. At a time when political power was still very narrowly based, a few leading figures were able to influence events and this happened in this case. Churchill and Lloyd George were fortunate to be swimming with the tide: they were also fortunate in the support given to their proposals by Asquith.

“A growing concern for national efficiency.”

Amongst other Liberal reforms some arose from a concern for national efficiency – school meals and school medical services are obvious examples. Others arose out of the perception that the Poor Relief system could not cope or that the prevailing levels of poverty were intolerable – Trade Boards for minimum wages and Labour Exchanges for labour mobility, and of course Old Age Pensions, come in here. The health and unemployment insurance proposals were, in some ways, different. Outside pressures did not bring them about so directly. They owe everything to the Liberal reforming tradition of the nineteenth century, updated by the New Liberalism of its last decade, imbibed by Lloyd George and Churchill and converted into practical proposals by their energy and vision and that of the leading administrators. With such reforms, perhaps too late, Liberalism had begun to grapple with the new social expectations of the wider nation.

“The Liberals at last facing up to a new world?”

USEFUL SOURCES OF INFORMATION

General reading

P Lane, *Success in British History 1760–1914*, John Murray 1978
A Wood, *Nineteenth Century Britain: 1815–1914*, Longman (2nd edition) 1982
R K Webb, *Modern England*, Allen & Unwin 1980

Further reading

M Bentley, *Politics without Democracy 1815–1914*, Fontana Paperback 1984
R C K Ensor, *England 1870–1914*, Oxford University Press 1936: a classic study, still in print and available in most public libraries, it remains the best reference book on the period. A paperback edition was published in 1986.
E J Feuchtwanger, *Democracy and Empire: Britain 1865–1914*, Arnold 1984
M Pugh, *The Making of Modern British Politics 1867–1939*, Blackwell 1982

Linked topic areas

- Gladstonian Liberalism (see Chapter 6)
- Irish Home Rule, 1885–1914 (see Chapter 6)
- Ireland, 1914–1922
- The British economy, 1870–1914

- The causes of the First World War (see Chapter 19)
- The effects of the First World War on Britain
- The rise of the Labour Party (see Chapter 9)
- Trade Union history
- The decline of the Liberal Party from 1914 (see Chapter 9)
- The emancipation of women

CHAPTER 9

INTER-WAR POLITICS 1918–1939

COALITION GOVERNMENT

ECLIPSE OF THE LIBERAL PARTY

LABOUR'S RECORD

CONSERVATIVE DOMINATION

THE GENERAL STRIKE

FORMATION OF THE NATIONAL GOVERNMENT

NATIONAL GOVERNMENTS

PROSPECTS FOR FASCISM

PERSONAL ASSESSMENTS

USEFUL INFORMATION

GETTING STARTED

You will need outline knowledge of both the problems faced and the reforms introduced by the Liberal governments between 1906 and 1914. The problems included Suffragette agitation, Labour unrest, a crisis with the House of Lords and the question of Home Rule for Ireland. These have been seen as creating a crisis for Liberalism even before the First World War. The reforms on the other hand, including Old Age Pensions and the first unemployment and health insurance schemes, constituted precedents for welfare legislation through to the 1940s. Consult Chapter 8 on this and on the early history of the Labour Party.

Any topic on British history between 1918 and 1939 requires an informed awareness of the principal effects of the First World War on British society, including its effect on the role of women, on Ireland, on the growth of Trade Unions and of course in the deaths of one million men. The consequences of war on the economy, undermining industrial competitiveness and leading to the loss of overseas markets were even more dramatic, emphasising problems already emerging before 1914 and creating the framework for post-war unemployment problems. Note also the tenfold rise in the national debt which so appalled contemporaries that it inhibited 'extravagant' solutions to social evils.

The increased role for central government was the most important feature of the effort to win the war; many pre-war ideals had to be abandoned with traumatic effect on the Liberal Party. The war was won under a coalition government which continued its existence after the war. Their promotion of a large increase in the electorate through the 1918 Representation of the People Act changed the pattern of election politics and its main provisions deserve to be noted. The issues in and the outcome of the 1918 election are essential for understanding the political pattern during the next four years. You could then prepare a list of the dates of inter-war General Elections and know, in broad Party terms the outcome of each. (see the 'Useful Information' section later in this chapter.)

ESSENTIAL PRINCIPLES

COALITION GOVERNMENT

1918–22

"A Conservative dominated Coalition."

Assessments of political life in these years are usually related to the career of Lloyd George. Depending on the period covered by your syllabus it would be wise to have back-up material prepared on his career prior to 1918 (principally his roles as pre-war Chancellor and in the attack on the Lords, and his roles as Minister of Munitions and Prime Minister during the war). The continuation of the wartime coalition in the election of 1918 and the outcome, with Lloyd George as the Liberal head of a Conservative dominated coalition government, cut off from his radical roots, are all important. Then make a list of the issues with which Lloyd George was involved as Prime Minister from 1918:

- the Versailles Peace Settlement
- the Irish problem (continued)
- the economy
- social reform
- extravagance and corruption
- social unrest at home
- unwelcome aggressiveness abroad (the Chanak crisis)

"Lloyd George the dynamic leader."

Relate these to the growing distrust of him amongst his Conservative supporters. Detailed understanding of the 1922 Conservative rejection of Lloyd George is essential for the career of Baldwin as well as that of the Prime Minister.

You should then pause and think how you would respond to an invitation to list the positive achievements of the Coalition Government. It has not generally been given a good press. Is this just? The 'Outline Answer' to Question 1 on page 98 offers one series of approaches to the topic.

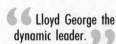

ECLIPSE OF THE LIBERAL PARTY

Explanations of this have many strands, which the 'Student's Answer' on page 101 attempts to draw together.

BEFORE 1914

"Working out the chronology of Liberal decline."

A beginning can be made before 1914, for George Dangerfield in the splendidly entitled *Strange Death of Liberal England* has argued that already by that date the end was ordained, stressing the grave problems which the party faced:

- Its free trade, *laissez-faire* economics under pressure from rising social expectations (symbolised by the rise of the Labour Party) and from the growing pressure of foreign competition on the economy.
- Labour unrest.
- The Suffragettes.
- Ireland (an especially grave problem).

The Liberals were faced with problems that were apparently insoluble without destroying the central tenets of their philosophy. It is a challenging and stimulating argument, elegantly written, but it does rest too heavily on an underestimate of the ability of the Liberals to adapt to circumstances. One has to recognise the threats to their position by 1914 without exaggerating them (the Labour Party for example was making but little progress from 1911 to 1914) and then look on to what happened to the Party during the First World War.

THE IMPACT OF WAR

Fighting a total war imposed great strains on some of the cherished beliefs of the Liberals in freedom and limited government powers and expenditure, some pacifists were driven from office or out of the party. The pressures of the war eventually forced a coalition government into existence, with Lloyd George as Prime Minister, provoking a fatal split with the last ever truly Liberal Prime Minister, Asquith. You must know enough of the detail of the events, and the subsequent bitter rivalry of the two men, to be able to offer an analysis on how significant purely personal rivalry and animosity were in destroying the Party. This will need balancing against other causes.

AFTER THE WAR

Other factors could include the failure of local Liberal associations to draw in working men, the collapse after the war of both Liberal local organisation and its presence in local government, poor finances, the loss of support to Left and Right (work out an argument on why this occurred in each direction) and so on to the disastrous effect of the British electoral system on third parties. Work out the chronology of decline against the dates of General Elections and the rise of the Labour Party. At some time in the 1920s the decline passed a critical point, perhaps in 1924 when Labour formed its first government (was the Liberal support for this a fatal mistake?) or perhaps by 1929 when Lloyd George's great effort ended with many votes but few seats. Few would feel it worthwhile to trace the decline beyond 1929.

LABOUR'S RECORD

"Labour and Liberal fortunes intertwined."

This is the other side of the coin of Liberal decline: be ready to use much of the same material in the two different contexts. The pre-1914 origins of the Labour Party and indeed the social developments of the late nineteenth century which provided their historical context are clearly important. Trade Union expansion during the war together with the rising tide of social expectations should also be noted. There was nothing inevitable in the emergence of a frankly class-based party but the working-class expectations of the last years of the nineteenth century, neglected by the Liberals, made it likely. Review the state of the Labour Party in 1918, recovering from the divisions caused by the war and producing a new constitution, based for the first time on socialist principles, and assess its likely appeal to the post-war electorate as enlarged by the 1918 Act. That is the starting point: Liberal weaknesses are the essential background, at least, to subsequent developments.

The limited nature of the achievements of the first Labour government (1924) may need explanation: the collapse of the second (1929–31), and its damaging effect on the Party through to 1939, is more important. Information on the election campaigns of 1923 and 1929, both of which brought the Labour Party to office, will round out the topic.

CONSERVATIVE DOMINATION

"Factors favouring the Conservatives."

Liberal and Labour weaknesses are part of any explanation of Conservative domination of political life. So is the political skill of the Conservative leader Stanley Baldwin, both in winning elections and calming crises, and you should have examples of his expertise available for quotation, for example:

- his handling of the General Strike
- his central part in Conservative electoral strategy in 1929
- his role in the political crisis of 1931
- his role in the 1936 abdication of Edward VIII

As the Liberals crumbled the Conservatives attracted the majority of their middle-class voters and anything, positive or negative, which helps to explain this is important (Baldwin's reassuring calm and a fear amongst middle-class voters of the red menace of socialism, often deliberately exploited by the Conservatives, come in here). Right-wing control of much of the media clearly helped, even the cinema newsreels were not totally unbiased. The desire for stability in troubled times is part of the explanation.

THE GENERAL STRIKE

"The General Strike illuminates many other issues."

This has in past papers been a popular topic but in recent years it has been offered less frequently. Your knowledge of the Labour Party's fortunes will be a starting point but necessary background includes knowledge of trade unions and labour relations, especially in coal-mining, at least from 1918. The actual events of the 1926 strike are dramatic and easily followed. Questions could be on its causes, on the objectives of the strikers, miners and others, on whether or not it should be seen as a political threat to the State, and inviting an explanation of the outcome. If you have prepared all this then be ready with some comments on the effect of the strike, and its aftermath, the Trade Disputes Act of 1927, on unions and political life over the next few years. If you decide to avoid a specific question on the Strike then remember outline knowledge of it will be valuable in illuminating various aspects of inter-war life and politics, including an assessment of the careers of Churchill and Baldwin.

FORMATION OF THE NATIONAL GOVERNMENT

“An important topic.”

The work of the second Labour government from 1929 and the international economic effects of the Wall Street Crash of that year provide the background to what has become one of the most debated political issues from these years. You need to be able to offer a brief explanation of the British financial crisis which led to the resignation of the Labour Government: in this concentrate on explaining the political tensions the crisis created within both the Labour Party and the Labour government until the situation became incapable of resolution. There will probably not be time for long accounts of all that had happened since the Wall Street Crash and much of this may well only be of marginal relevance, for in 1931 it was essentially a political crisis. The role of Ramsay MacDonald and his Chancellor Snowden were central and the effects on the Labour Party catastrophic. The election of 1931 however provided a massive vote of confidence in the newly-formed National Government. Awareness of the economic and social policies of that government, to at least 1935, could widen the range of questions available to you.

NATIONAL GOVERNMENTS

1931–1939

Study of the economic policy will involve understanding of some easily grasped technical terms such as *Gold Standard*, *Bank Rate* and *National Debt stock*. Both economic and social policies were based on financial stringency in the face of apparently imminent economic catastrophe. You need to understand why this was later criticised as quite inappropriate by followers of the economist *Keynes*. Remember that his most important work, *The General Theory of Employment, Interest and Money* was only published in 1936, some years after the emergence of the crisis. You should also note that more recently it has been argued that Keynesian solutions based on cheap money would not have solved the economic problems because these really arose from the collapse of overseas markets.

“Link 1930s politics to the economic and social background.”

These were the years of depression and unemployment which stand as major topic areas in their own right: government policy made little impact on ‘the Depression’ and it has been much criticised for its inactivity, you must judge how fairly. This area of politics is only worth preparing for examination purposes if you are also prepared to answer questions on the very varied geographic and social effects of the Depression and on the slow economic recovery of the late 1930s generally. The decade is one where political activity at home is dominated by the social and economic background. One standard question involves considering how far there were compensating features to the Depression.

FOREIGN POLICY AND DEFENCE RECORD

“Churchill's charges.”

This is a very popular topic and important aspects of it are discussed in the ‘Tutor's Answer’ to Question 3 later in this chapter. The best start is to understand Churchill's trenchant criticisms of both defence and foreign policy and then, from your reading, work out a case for:

Baldwin – largely on defence preparations, and **Chamberlain** – largely to charges against his foreign policy of appeasing the Dictators which culminated at Munich.

In what ways could they have done more and would public opinion have allowed it? Understanding of the foreign policy would be helped by study of a map of pre-1939 Europe. The bonus could be the prospect of making an alternative use of your knowledge in a European history paper: you are unlikely to have the chance to use it twice.

“A case can be made for Chamberlain.”

There was too much hindsight in Churchill's charges for them to be totally satisfactory and you are likely to do best if you work out where you wish to strike the balance of your own judgement rather than by learning lots of quotations and references to the views of distinguished historians. For revision purposes construct an opposing argument on why Churchill was not listened to by people who mattered in pre-war political life. The quality of your argument and of your supporting references, and not the terms of the verdicts themselves, will decide your mark, for in this debate there remains much room still for differences of opinion.

PROSPECTS FOR FASCISM

"A popular topic."

IN BRITAIN

This topic has a frequency in examination papers which outstrips its importance at the time. Dramatic incidents, the glamour attached to the fascist leader, Mosley, the subsequent war against Nazi Germany and the continuing use of charges of 'Fascist' against any possible political enemy on the Right, have all contributed to this state of affairs. It is an almost self-contained topic, the significant features of which are easily established. For these reasons it could be a useful extra choice as an examination topic. A check on past papers would be a sensible preliminary step. Questions come both on the appeal of fascism in the 1930s and on the reasons for its ultimate failure and are often geared to assessments of Mosley personally.

PERSONAL ASSESSMENTS

Such assessments largely involve thinking about the main episodes of inter-war history within new frameworks. Having studied the politics of these years it would be foolish not to be ready for a biographically structured question, particularly on one of the three major party leaders. A full assessment of Lloyd George, unrestricted by dates, would be vast, involving knowledge of his career both before and during the First World War (see Chapter 8 for part of this).

STANLEY BALDWIN (1867–1947)

Prime Minister 1923–1924, 1924–1929, 1935–1937
1922 Helped to bring Lloyd George down.
1923 Quixotic decision to fight election over protectionism.
1926 Had to handle the General Strike.
1931–1935 Deputy to MacDonald in the National Government.
1936 Resolved the Abdication Crisis.

LLOYD GEORGE (1863–1945)

Prime Minister 1916–1922
1916 Manoeuvred the downfall of Asquith. Gave new impetus to war effort.
1918 Coupon Election: head of Conservative dominated Coalition Government.
1919 Triumph at the Paris Peace Conference.
1921 Growing discontent amongst his Conservative supporters over setting up of Irish Free State and the sale of honours. Increasing economic problems.
1922 Conservatives withdrew from Coalition. Lloyd George resigned and never held office again.
1929 Failure of Lloyd George – inspired Liberal revival with six million votes but only 59 seats.

RAMSAY MACDONALD (1866–1937)

Prime Minister 1924, 1929–1931, (Labour), 1931–1935 (National)
1911–1914 Leader of Labour Party. Resigned 1914 because against war.
1914–1918 Pacifist: lost Commons seat 1918.
1922 Re-elected to Commons: became leader of the Labour Party.
1924 First government office was as PM and Foreign Secretary.
1931 Controversial decision to form a National Government after Labour Cabinet failed to agree measures to deal with economic crisis.

USEFUL INFORMATION

1918 Nov End of the First World War
Representation of the People Act greatly extended the electorate to all men over 21 and women over 30.
Dec **General Election** (the 'Coupon Election'): victory for the Lloyd George – Conservative Coalition.
Coalition supporters gained 526 seats (Conservative 389, Liberal 133, Labour 4). Their opponents 181 (Labour 59, Asquith Liberals 28, Sinn Fein 73, Others 21).

SWANSEA COLLEGE
LEARNING CENTRE
TYCOCH ROAD

1918–1922	**Coalition Government: Lloyd George Prime Minister**
1919	Irish Sinn Fein members set up own Parliament in Dublin.
	Peace Treaty of Versailles
1921	Post-war boom came to an end: onset of unemployment, never to fall below a million pre-1940.
1922	Conservative backbenchers voted to leave Coalition.
	Lloyd George resigned
	General Election: Conservative victory.
	Conservatives 347 seats, Labour 142, Lloyd George Liberals 57, Asquith Liberals 60
1922–1923	**Bonar Law Prime Minister** (until May 1923)
1923	**Stanley Baldwin Conservative Prime Minister,** converted to protectionism, fought general election and lost overall majority.
Dec	**General Election:** Conservative victory. Conservatives 260 seats, Labour 191, Liberals 159. Liberals did not support vote of confidence in Baldwin's government so he resigned. Labour formed a minority government.
1924 Jan	**Ramsay MacDonald Prime Minister**
	Labour minority government. Aimed at moderation and respectability. Housing Act only important legislation. MacDonald refused inquiry into failure to prosecute the communist Campbell over alleged inciting mutiny and lost vote of confidence.
Oct	**General Election:** Conservative victory with 419 seats, Labour 151, Liberals 40. Zinoviev letter kept communist threat alive.
1924–1929	**Baldwin Prime Minister**
1925	Return to Gold Standard. Samuel Commission on coal industry.
1926 May	General Strike
1927	Trade Union Act
1928	Votes given to women at 21
1929	**General Election:** Labour victory. Labour 288 seats, Conservatives 260, Liberals 59.
1929–1931	**Ramsay MacDonald Prime Minister**
	Second Labour minority Government.
1929–1931	Wall Street Crash affected world trade and led to growing unemployment.
	Foreign money started to be pulled out of London.
1931	May Committee proposed cuts in public expenditure.
	Cabinet could not agree on cuts and resigned.
	National Government formed. MacDonald Prime Minister
	General Election: National Government victory. Government won 554 seats (473 of which were Conservatives, rest National Liberals and National Labour Opposition), Labour 52, Lloyd George Liberals 4.
1932	Free Trade abandoned. (Ottawa imperial trade preference agreements).
	Oswald Mosley founded British Union of Fascists.
1934	India obtained Dominion status
1935	MacDonald resigned
1935–1937	**Baldwin Prime Minister**
1935	**General Election:** National Government victory. Some Labour recovery with 158 seats but sweeping 'National' victory overall. Government increasingly seen as a Conservative one.
1936 Jan	Death of George V
	Re-armament under way
	Jarrow hunger march
Dec	Abdication of Edward VIII. Accession of George VI (to 1952).
1937	Baldwin resigned
1937–1940	**Neville Chamberlain Prime Minister**
1938 Sept	The Munich Agreements made with Hitler
1939 Mar	Hitler invaded the rump of Czechoslovakia
1939 Sept	War declared on Germany
1940 May	Chamberlain resigned
1940–1945	**Churchill Prime Minister: Coalition Government**

EXAMINATION QUESTIONS

Q1 Why was Lloyd George's coalition government formed in 1916, continued in 1918, but broken up after only four years of peace? (London 1990)

Q2 'The divisions within the party explain its lack of success.' Discuss this view of the Labour party in and out of office between the wars. (Cambridge 1989)

Q3 Why did 'appeasement' prevail in British foreign policy in the 1930s? (Welsh 1989)

Q4 Why were the Conservatives so often in office in the inter-war years? (NEAB 1989)

Q5 Why did the Liberal Party cease to be able to form a government after the First World War? (London 1988)

Q6 Document Question 'Baldwin and Protection, 1923' (NEAB 1989)

Read the extract below and then answer the questions which follow.

The Issue of Protection: A report of Baldwin's speech at Plymouth, 25 October 1923

. . . I will pass on . . . to the main subject which I wish to discuss with you, the gravest subject in the country today, that of the unemployment of our people. (Cheers.) . . . I told you that we must consider seriously together tonight, the new facts, new since the war, an increased population in a country already industrialised to the saturation point, and secondly, we are beginning to realise now, what it was difficult to realise two years ago and what no one realised at the time of the Armistice, that it will be a long, long time before the economic reconstruction of Europe is complete. I am not going to weary you tonight with telling you what the condition of Europe means to the trade of the world and the trade of our country. you know it; but it will be years before conditions are normal, and during that time we have to find work for our people. And we have to remember this, that if, and when, such economic reconstruction is completed that Germany can pay reparations, we have to remember that whatever those reparations are, be the amount great or be it small, those reparations can only be paid by the trade balance of Germany, that is by her balance of exports.

Now, in saying this, let us not forget that Germany has lost by the Peace Treaty considerable portions of her industrial territory, which produced her raw materials, and she lost a considerable area of agricultural territory. The result is, when she begins to function economically, she will probably have to import more food and more raw materials than she did before the war, and so it follows that her exports must increase to pay for these extra imports, as well as to pay for reparations . . . The question is, where are these exports going . . .

The chief industrial country is ours, the country with most open market is ours, and we shall be shock-absorbers for the whole world . . .

Dealing with Mr Bonar Law's pledge given a year ago that there should be no fundamental change in the fiscal arrangements of the country, Mr Baldwin said:

That pledge binds me, and in this Parliament there will be no fundamental change. I take those words strictly: I am not a man to play with a pledge, but I cannot see myself that any slight extension or adaptation of principles hitherto sanctioned in the legislature are breaches of that pledge. But if at any time he was challenged, he was always willing to take a verdict. (Loud cheers.)

The unemployment problem was the crucial problem of our country. He regarded it as such. He could fight it. He was willing to fight it, but he could not fight it without weapons. He had come to the conclusion that if we went pottering along as we were we should have grave unemployment with us to the end of time, and he had come to the conclusion himself that the only way to fight the subject was by protecting the home market. (Prolonged cheers, and cries of 'Good old Baldwin'.) He is not a clever man. He knew nothing of political tactics, but he said this, that, having come to the conclusion himself, he felt the only honest and right thing as the Leader of a democratic party, was to tell them at the first opportunity he had what he thought, and submit it to their judgement. (Cheers).

They were fighting something more difficult today than Germans – namely, poverty and unemployment. To fight against unemployment was vital. By its result the country would stand or fall. There could be neither peace, nor happiness, until we had got the better of unemployment. A man without employment was a man without hope or faith. Without hope or faith a man was without love – love of men, of home, and country. Love was the only power which moved the world to betterment. (Cheers.)

a) Explain the meaning of the two phrases underlined. *(4)*

b) 'In a speech by Stanley Baldwin the presentation and tone were more important than the factual content.' Discuss this statement in the light of the extract. *(6)*

c) In the context of the debate on Protection since before the First World War, how effectively did Baldwin argue the case for Protection in this speech? *(7)*

d) How far did this speech mark a turning-point in the history of the post-War Conservative Party? *(8)*

(Total 25 marks)

OUTLINE ANSWERS

Question 1

Equal attention to each of the three parts of the question –

1916: formation because of war situation, loss of confidence in Asquith, role of Conservatives, record of Lloyd George at munitions, his energy, his ambition. A response to a national crisis or a personal coup?

1918: Lloyd George seemed indispensable to the Conservatives as the man who had won the war. His own electoral base was lost because of 'his' destruction of the Liberal Party so he had little choice. Euphoria of victory and efficacy of the 'Coupon' did the rest in the Election.

1922: the growing disillusionment and suspicion, economy, corruption, foreign adventures, especially Chanak, Ireland, all led to growing Conservative distrust of Lloyd George. Yet it needed an unlikely backbench revolt to force the climax, role of Baldwin and Beaverbrook.

Conclusion: Lloyd George, indispensable in war, had become a dangerous liability to the Conservatives in peace.

Question 2

Introduction: until 1931 there seems to be little merit in this proposition. Equally it is arguable that the Labour Party between the wars enjoyed significant success.

After 1918: there was an agreed constitution and agreed policy objectives. In 1922 MacDonald was accepted as party leader to general acclaim and this was followed remarkably quickly by the first Labour government – a success story to date. First Labour Government achieved little but this because of its minority position. No evidence divisions affected it, despite dark mutterings that it was too respectable.

"Labour not a divided party."

1926: a few favoured a pro-General Strike policy but the real split was in the wider Labour movement and not within the party. Support for the strike would have ended the chances of electoral victory and turned Labour into a party of direct action. It seems unlikely, in view of the large numbers who had voted Conservative in 1924 against precisely this threat, that this would have led to success.

1929: the reward for moderation came in the 1929 election, again a success. The limited nature of the 1929–1931 government's achievements had, until the end, nothing to do with divisions but with lack of ideas on economic policy or a parliamentary majority.

"Except in 1931."

1931: arguable that divisions became more a problem by 1931. Discuss inability of Cabinet to agree on economic measures. This was based on a real split in the party between those who placed class loyalties above what others saw as national needs. It drove the party to the brink of disaster and a decade of impotent opposition. Discuss formation of National Government, MacDonald's role to 1935 and the troubles within the tiny opposition Labour Party. Quote election figures to show Labour's plight.

1935: note the recovery of the 1935 election. This plus the revival in trade unionism are signs of future success, in practice delayed to 1945 but the seeds of 1945 were sown in the late 1930s and not just in the war.

Conclusion: To expect a lot more success than Labour enjoyed would be to ignore too many adverse factors external to the party, especially all those favouring the Conservatives. Alongside these, with the sad exception of 1931, if Labour lacked success, which can be disputed, then internal divisions did little to cause this.

Question 3

See the 'Tutor's Answer' below.

Question 4

- Anti-Conservative vote was split and neither Labour or Liberals able to get on top pre-1929 (main reason).
- Post-1931 Conservative domination sheltered under the umbrella of the National Government.
- First past the post election system exaggerated any election victory; give examples from what happened in the 1924 election.
- Conservatives seemed to the majority of people to be the best guarantors of stability in troubled times:
  - fear of Red revolution
  - social and economic crises
  - burden of debt
  - foreign uncertainties
- Key role of Baldwin as the man you can trust; illustrate this from his handling the General Strike.
- Media right-wing, ownership of newspapers but also unspoken assumptions of cinema newsreels.

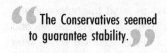

"The Conservatives seemed to guarantee stability."

Conclusion: flight of enough ex-Liberal voters to the Right and the bad luck and incapacity of Labour to grasp their best chance in 1929–31 are the key parts of the explanation.

Question 5

See the 'Student's Answer' below.

Question 6

Document Question: *Baldwin and Protection, 1923* (JMB 1989)

Tutor's comments on document question

You are again urged to attempt your own informal answers to the sub-questions before reading further. First read the document carefully.

a) Shock absorbers presumably relates to others (Germany) flooding British free trade markets with their goods in order to solve their economic problems. 'Willing to take a verdict' – read the three lines above carefully, it seems to refer to the possibility of a confidence vote in the Commons rather than a General Election verdict.

b) The document is a very personal statement playing on his own image as not a clever but surely a reliable man, a patriot, a man of honour, a man of compassion. Work on the document to see if you can see appropriate references to use in support of these points. Are there others? There doesn't seem to be much factual content on what he proposes to do – does there?

c) Protectionism had been an election loser before the war. Baldwin is trying to argue that things have changed since pre-war days: the war, the effects of the peace treaty, the unemployment problem. We live in new and very grave times. Then came the appeal to patriotism and to compassion. He seems effectively to have proposed that new times need new remedies. It cannot however be said that, in this extract, he explained clearly how protection would work. Perhaps lines 16 to 24 come nearest to giving some indications, though in a negative way.

d) This question relies heavily on own knowledge much more than the London Board document question in Chapter 5. This illustrates the important point that the approach of the examination boards to document (extract) questions is not identical.

Note: You really do need to see your own board's past papers well before the examination.

The speech leads on to the December 1923 election which Baldwin called to secure a mandate for the introduction of protectionist policies and which let in the first Labour Government. Thereafter the Conservatives avoided protectionism until the National Government took it up after 1931. It looked a major turning-point but it wasn't.

Not much of this of course can be deduced from within the given document.

A TUTOR'S ANSWER TO QUESTION 3

According to Winston Churchill's later account appeasement prevailed because of the blindness of British politicians to Hitler's real intentions and because of their timidity in not standing up to successive acts of German aggression. Personal defects loom large in this explanation for, with the benefit of hindsight, it seemed so obvious what the outcome of a craven failure to stand up to Hitler's ruthless ambitions was going to be. As the Second World War has faded into history it is possible to make out a better case for those who favoured appeasement, and notably Neville Chamberlain amongst them, than Churchill would ever have allowed.

Appeasement had so few critics and aroused no massive public hostility because as a policy it was well in tune with the public mood of the thirties. It was not just a question of a few pacifists or motions at the Oxford Union or a Fulham bye-election result, but something more widespread. The horrors of the First World War were much written about and were still a bitter personal memory for many, cinema newsreels from Spain nightly revealed the future horrors of aerial bombardment of civilian targets, for it was not just Baldwin who believed the bomber would always get through. In any case the burdens of unemployment and the enormous National Debt seemed to undermine any hope of resolute action in foreign policy. There was also a general feeling that Germany might have been harshly treated at Versailles and that on certain issues, for example the re-militarisation of the Rhineland, might have quite a good case. Without this prevailing mood the illusions of the political establishment might have been less firmly set.

“Why appeasement commanded popular support.”

Appeasement prevailed however because the political leadership of the National, really Conservative, Government and their leading advisers favoured it or indeed saw no alternative to it. The key figure was Neville Chamberlain. He fully shared the public horror at the thought of the destruction which another war would bring and of how a vigorous, and therefore expensive, defence and foreign policy would distract from pressing problems at home. He was a decent man who held a sincere belief that reasonable negotiation and goodwill could overcome the diplomatic problems of the day. In any case there was no thinkable alternative. Faced with German grievances and Hitler's ruthlessness this was probably very naive but others wanted to believe it as much as he, witness the extraordinary enthusiasm for the useless scrap of paper he brought back from Munich. He had vision and he had courage but his policy failed and he became the chief victim of the burgeoning Churchillian legend.

“It was not just Chamberlain's policy.”

If the policy had been Chamberlain's alone it would not have survived for long. It did prevail, through to at least the spring of 1939 and, for a few, into the months of the Phoney War, because it was embraced and promoted by so many figures of the political and media establishment. Only Reynolds News amongst all the national newspapers, and owned by the Scottish Co-op, spoke out against the deal struck at Munich. *The Times* under Geoffrey Dawson manipulated both news and opinion columns to pursue an appeasement policy but almost all papers maintained at best a craven policy of not rocking the appeasement boat by being nasty about Hitler. Newspaper proprietors were to the fore in creating this climate of opinion which so effectively and for so long enabled appeasement to prevail.

“A right-wing press.”

There were good reasons, and bad, why this state of affairs came about. The Press was dominated by right-wing proprietors who were deeply suspicious of the 'Red menace' from the Soviet Union and from communists at home. They saw Hitler's domestic achievements and saw him as a bulwark against communism. They were not alone. Some, like Mosley and perhaps Lloyd George, saw lessons which could be applied to English problems. Hitler flattered and deluded them and, until very late in the thirties they closed their eyes to the stories coming out of Germany about the treatment of the Jews. Strong latent anti-semitism in British society made the Jews, in any case, an unlikely rallying point for national outrage. So the unattractive features of National Socialism were glossed over and

German territorial ambitions were made to seem a reasonable response to its treatment at Versailles. The Anschluss was acceptable because the Austrians were Germans and clearly wanted it, but those same sentiments could, in September 1938, be cruelly exploited to undermine any will to help the Czechs. Not that many, if it meant war, had that will (and this despite many later convenient personal memories to the contrary).

“A case to be made for Germany.”

A Parliamentary Opposition challenging appeasement might have brought it to an end earlier but the Labour Party, natural enemies it might have been thought of fascism, did little to stiffen Chamberlain's resolution. Some members were pacifists, others had a muddled belief in collective security under the League of Nations, but had little will to provide the arms to back the League. Churchill was the voice in the wilderness and for this there were good reasons in his political record. From Tonypandy to the General Strike he had done nothing to merit any support from the Unions or the Labour Party. His extremism over granting some measure of self-rule in India and his attempt to create a 'King's party' at the time of the abdication isolated him from the mainstream of the Conservative Party. He appeared a bellicose troublemaker, the soundness of whose judgement was increasingly open to question.

“There were good reasons to ignore Churchill.”

Few men of political stature questioned the need to avoid war and for most of them a deal with Hitler was a small price to pay, especially as it would be the Czech nation and not they who would be paying. The men of power manipulated the public mood unscrupulously as the decade advanced but essentially public opinion was on the side of peace and, until his policy had evidently failed and this only as late as the spring of 1939, this meant supporting the efforts of the Prime Minister. In many ways Chamberlain was the most honourable of the appeasers, deluded but not lacking courage. His views would not have prevailed if they had not had the support of the vast majority of the politically powerful and had not caught the public mood.

A STUDENT'S ANSWER TO QUESTION 5

“Explain more fully why this was so.”

Fighting the war caused an irretrievable split in the Liberal Party so that its most dynamic leader, Lloyd George, in 1918 protected his own position as Prime Minister by remaining in a Coalition with the Conservatives. This action perpetuated the split after the war and seriously damaged the Liberals in the Elections of 1918 and 1922. By the time the cracks had been papered over the Labour Party had emerged as the more credible anti-Conservative party and all the later efforts of Lloyd George to retrieve this came to nothing.

The Liberals were divided in the the 1922 election which showed Labour moving ahead of their two wings combined in the number of seats won. In the 1923 Election, Labour won 191 seats and the Liberals, at last re-united, won 159 and here the Liberals made *a fatal mistake* when they let Labour form the Government because they were also a free trade party opposed to the protectionist Tories. This decision made the Labour party a credible alternative to the Tories and the results were seen in 1924 when ex-Liberals who were afraid of the red menace of socialism voted Conservative and many reform minded Liberals voted Labour as the anti-Conservative party most likely to win. In 1929 the Liberals made their only determined energetic attempt to win a post-war General Election, with interesting new proposals to solve the country's economic problems. They did well, gaining about 5 million votes but by now too many of the voters felt that the real struggle was between Conservatives and Labour, each of which got 8 million votes. But the Liberal votes were too thinly spread and they came second in many constituencies. They gained only 59 seats to Labour's 228 and the Conservatives' 260. They were the victims of the 'first past the post' election system and were now obviously the weakest of the three parties. They never recovered from this.

“So it perhaps deserves a longer comment.”

“Expand the reasoning here.”

The Lloyd George Asquith split was very important in 'letting Labour in' but it was not the only reason for the Liberal decline after the war. Some historians argue that their decline started before 1914 when the working class Labour Party was formed. Liberal ideas of free trade and laissez-faire were out of date. After the war they had no answers to the economic problems until too late, in 1929. The Labour Party after 1918 had a much more effective economic policy based on nationalisation. Fighting the war also upset many Liberal principles of freedom and undermined the party's philosophy.

"Good material deserving fuller treatment."

There were other Liberal mistakes. They had been very bad at bringing working class members into the Party and when the number of working class voters greatly increased in 1918 this helped Labour which had links with the Trade Unions. They were poor at maintaining their local organisations and did not pay as much attention as Labour and the Tories to fighting local government elections. Although Lloyd George made much money from the sale of honours the Liberals were always short of funds compared with the other two parties with their business and union connections.

"Some reference to why Labour rose would widen the answer."

So the Liberals largely brought about their own election downfall and for this reason ceased to be able to form a government.

EXAMINER COMMENT

This is a good answer which offers a wide range of factors directly relevant to the question. Some attempt to indicate which, in the writer's view were the more important reasons, and to suggest why, would have given an opportunity to develop parts of the answer more fully. As it is it reads a bit like a list instead of a balanced argument. One major omission lies in the absence of any reference to the strengths of the other parties and how and when this had an impact on Liberal fortunes. It is still a good answer.

USEFUL SOURCES OF INFORMATION

General reading

A Marwick, *Britain in the Century of Total War*, 1968
A J P Taylor, *English History 1914–1945*, Oxford University Press 1965
J B Watson, *Success in British History since 1914*, John Murray 1983

Further reading

P Adelman, *The Decline of the Liberal Party 1910–1931*, Longman 1982
M Beloff, *Wars and Welfare: Britain 1914–1945*, Arnold 1984
A Farmer, *Britain: Foreign and Imperial Affairs 1919–1939, Hodder & Stoughton 1992*
C L Mowat, *Britain Between the Wars, 1918–1940*, Methuen, 1946 (paperback edition 1968)
R Pearce, Britain: Domestic Policies 1918–1939, Hodder & Stoughton 1993
M Pugh, *The Making of Modern British Politics 1867–1939*, Blackwell 1982
J Stevenson, *The Pelican Social History of Britain: British Society 1914–1945*, Penguin 1984

Linked topic areas

- The effects of the First World War on Britain
- The Versailles Peace Treaty (for European examination papers)
- The British economy between the wars
- Social problems and social policy between the wars
- The depression of the 1930s
- The causes of the Second World War (see Chapter 22)

CHAPTER 10

POLITICS AND SOCIETY 1939–1951

GETTING STARTED

This topic requires an understanding of the deep scars left by memories of the miseries of unemployment in the 1930s and by the feeling that the Conservative dominated pre-war governments had blundered into a war for which the country was ill-prepared. The effects on British society of fighting a total war are of central importance with the emergence of a sense that things must be better ordered in the future. Outline knowledge is needed of pre-1914 Liberal insurance and pension provisions and of the emergence, in the inter-war years, of the Labour Party as the principal left-wing party, this following its commitment, in 1918, to a socialist reform programme. You should be aware that the role of the state in people's lives had been increasing during the earlier decades of the century, as indeed had people's expectations of the responsibilities of the state.

The military struggle from 1938 to 1945 is not included here for it is best studied in the international setting. Having an outline chronology of the main events will however be useful. This should in particular include a grasp of events in the period between the evacuation from Dunkirk in May/June 1940 and the Japanese attack on Pearl Harbor in December 1941 when Britain came so close to defeat but when it also at last committed itself to total war with long term consequences for its social and political life.

You need to look at a political map of the world in 1945 if only to realise how much of it was still shaded in the pink of the British Empire: post-war British concern to be a world power then falls more easily into place. The long term results of the war on British military power, and its destruction of the British economy, are essential for an understanding of British history after 1945. The beginnings of the Cold War and Britain's continuing commitment to the United States alliance provided the ongoing international context.

It will be important to understand how the British parliamentary and government system works, particularly in relation to electoral arrangements and to the passing of legislation. The standard vocabulary of British politics should be understood and used confidently.

ESSENTIAL PRINCIPLES

THE WAR EFFORT AT HOME

"The impact of fighting a total war."

The dramatic effects on the lives of the mass of the people of fighting a total war are important both in their own right and for an understanding of post-war society. A mass of detailed information is available to illustrate the ways and the extent to which fighting the war, first for survival and then through to victory, changed the nature of society and the lives of everyone involved. Conscription began on a small scale months before war was declared and the direction of all male and unmarried female labour was in place by 1941. Food was rationed by January 1940, furniture was strictly controlled and housebuilding came to an end, petrol was limited to essential users. Most civilians were involved in voluntary duties extra to their normal work. All production was planned and controlled to assist the war effort and a great drive made towards agricultural self-sufficiency. From May 1940 the normal patterns of party political life were suspended. A complete picture of the British nation at war requires also recognition of the hardships imposed on the people through evacuation of schoolchildren, air raids and the innumerable controls on their lives and indeed through the deaths of 250,000 people. From 1942 the arrival of growing numbers of US soldiers had its own impact on what had often been until then a relatively closed society.

Exam questions

"Two typical questions."

It is important that the readily available mass of detail is set into a series of structures or it will be difficult to use in essays and examinations. Be ready to adapt it to two different types of questions, those requiring an evaluation of the effectiveness of the effort to mobilise society and the economy for war and, more frequently, those wanting an exploration of how the wartime experience shaped post-war political life and social and economic reconstruction.

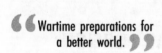

WARTIME PLANS

RECONSTRUCTION

These arose from the total commitment to the war. It became important to harness the idealism of the people to the cause of victory by holding up the prospect of a better life, worth fighting for, after the war.

The Beveridge Report

"Wartime preparations for a better world."

The most important proposals, certainly the ones which attracted the most attention at the time, were contained in the Beveridge Report (1942) proposing to fight the five giants of *Want*, *Disease*, *Ignorance*, *Squalor*, and *Idleness* by means of a comprehensive scheme of national insurance and the creation of a national health service. It was based on the assumption that governments would be active in leading the fight and in organising the nation. The Report has been described as 'providing a framework for social revolution'. The proposals and their impact deserve to be mastered in detail.

The 1944 Education Act

The other major development was the passing of the 1944 Education Act under the inspiration of R A Butler. Again the proposals, and their impact after the war, are of major significance.

The Family Allowances Act

The passing of the Family Allowances Act of 1945, occurring prior to the General Election was another sign of this wartime determination to avoid a return to the pre-war miseries endured by so many people.

Be ready to explain why these plans and legislation were developed in time of war and also how they affected post-war society.

1945 ELECTION

This took place in July, after the defeat of Germany but before the end of the war with Japan, which at the time of the election looked as though it might still last for years. The scale of the Labour victory came as a great surprise and explanations of it are a common focus for examination questions. Answering questions of this type requires knowledge of both the pre-war and wartime experiences of the nation.

“A Great Electoral Swing to the Left.”

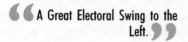

Note: A long list of factors explaining the result can, and should, be drawn up. The fact remains that the outcome was a great surprise and to many a great shock. It is only historians, blessed with hindsight, who are able to explain it away. Their explanations can become so convincing that it is a useful exercise to reflect on why anyone persisted in voting Conservative.

- Labour polled 12 million votes (47.8%) and won 393 seats.
- The Conservatives polled 10 million votes (39.8% of the votes cast) and won 213 seats.
- The Liberals polled 2.2 million votes (9%) and won 12 seats.

Exam questions

Be ready for a question asking you to explain this outcome. (One attempt is offered in the ‘Tutor’s Answer’ to Question 1 later in this chapter.)

LABOUR’S WELFARE MEASURES

The 1945 Election victory had owed much to the belief that Labour would take effective steps to ensure that the miseries of the 1930s would not return.

WELFARE PROPOSALS

Their welfare proposals, resting on the proposals in the Beveridge Report, centred on the National Insurance and the National Health Service Acts of 1946 and the National Assistance Act of 1948. You may well need to draw connections between pre-war life, wartime hardships, the Beveridge Report, the Election result and this post-war legislation. This could include an evaluation of the work of the Minister of Health *Aneurin Bevan* (remember that he was also responsible for housing). Be ready to discuss the impact made by the welfare proposals on the lives of ordinary people.

Associated legislation

There was associated legislation in other fields: the New Towns Act of 1946, the Town and Country planning Act of 1947 and the Children’s Act of 1948. It was also in these years that the 1944 Education Act came to be implemented (in 1947 for example the minimum school-leaving age rose from 14 to 15).

Social revolution

In total these measures came near to constituting a social revolution, involving a considerable extension of government activity and expenditure. They set the social agenda for at least 30 years. Have ready a brief working definition of the term *Welfare State* for example:

> ‘The central point of a welfare state is the idea of comprehensive social services and social security provision.’

The ‘Outline Answer’ to Question 3 may give you some help with this topic.

LABOUR AND THE ECONOMY

It is essential to understand the devastating impact of the war on the British economy, especially its industrial base and its transport system, and to be able to illustrate the continuing post-war austerity which resulted. Neither the Government’s economic achievements nor its failures make much sense unless set in this troubled context of:

“A grim economic outlook.”

- food and fuel shortages
- a persistent balance of trade deficit
- loans from the USA and Canada
- one of the worst winters on record in 1947

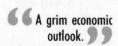

All this alongside continuing rationing, controls and conscription.

In considering the Labour Government’s economic record be able to comment on and assess the roles of three of its members: *Dalton*, *Shinwell* and *Cripps*.

Exam questions

Draw up a list of the Government’s *nationalisation legislation* and be prepared to comment on each proposal and its passage into law at paragraph length at least. (See both the 'Useful Information' and the 'Student Answer' sections of this chapter). Questions on the nationalisation programme and on the post-1945 economic difficulties appear in examination papers with equal frequency. It would be unwise to prepare for one and not the other.

POST-WAR FOREIGN AND IMPERIAL POLICY

First check that such policies figure as a significant part of past examination papers for their study will open up a vast new area of information and reading. Policy in regard to the USA and the USSR, with the developing Cold War, impinges on domestic policy with conscription, defence expenditure and the Korean War. It includes consideration of Marshall Aid, the Berlin Airlift and the formation of NATO. These matters are best studied in an international context in preparation for European and World history papers, and relevant parts of Chapters 23, 24, 26 will provide an introduction.

INDIA AND INDEPENDENCE

"Independence for India marked an imperial turning point."

In Imperial Policy the most important single event was the granting of independence to British India, marking the beginning of great changes in the size and the nature of the British Commonwealth. It should be included in any overall assessment of the achievements of these years. Happenings in Palestine and Iran provided other issues to occupy the Foreign Secretary, Ernest Bevin.

THE LABOUR GOVERNMENT

It is worthwhile, with regard to these eventful years, to master the names and the areas of responsibility of each of the leading ministers and to form an overall assessment of the capabilities and achievements of the Prime Minister, Clem Attlee, and his team. In addition to the welfare and nationalisation legislation there was:

- Trade Disputes Act, 1946
- Atomic Energy Act, 1946
- The Representation of the People Act in 1948 and a Monopolies Act, and in 1949 a Parliament Act

All were major pieces of legislation.

1950 AND 1951 ELECTIONS

"The Conservatives began to fight back."

By 1949 Conservative resistance was fiercer and its confidence rising. The international context was darkening and the internal economic problems remained largely unresolved. Austerity and controls increasingly rankled and were exploited by the Opposition and a largely right-wing press. The devaluation of the pound in 1949, arising from the failure, despite great efforts to boost exports, to bridge the adverse international trade gap, was generally represented as illustrating the economic failings of the government.

The Election Results

	Conservatives	Labour	Liberals
1950	12.5 million votes (43.5% of votes cast) 298 seats won	13.3 million votes (46.5% of votes cast) 315 seats won	2.6 million votes (9.1% of votes cast) 9 seats won
1951	13.7 million votes (48% of votes cast) 321 seats won	13.9 million votes (48.8% of votes cast) 295 seats won	0.7 million votes (2.5% of votes cast) 6 seats won

"Explaining the 1951 Election."

The swing against Labour in 1950 needs explaining. The small Commons majority which ensued placed much strain on Ministers, some of whom had been in office since 1940. Re-armament policies, a product of growing international problems, and their effects produced growing discord in the Labour ranks. The details are important for they drove Attlee, in 1951, into an unnecessary election. The small Conservative majority in the election rested heavily on the collapse of the Liberal vote which on this occasion went to the Right. Labour's support remained loyal and it obtained a record number of votes. It was nevertheless not to hold office again for thirteen years.

Revision exercise

A useful revision exercise would be to take the outline election results for 1945, 1950 and 1951 and construct an explanation of the outcome in each case. The 'Outline Answer' to Question 5 will give you a start.

USEFUL INFORMATION

1939	Sept	Britain declared war on Germany.
		Evacuation of many children from cities. Identity cards and rationing of food and clothing.
		Controls on manpower and extension of voluntary services introduced and developed over next two years.
1940	May	**Coalition Government under Winston Churchill**
	June	Dunkirk evacuation
		The 'Blitz'
1941	June	Germany attacked the USSR
	Dec	War against Japan; US at war with Germany.
1942		The Beveridge Report
1944		The (Butler) Education Act reorganised secondary schooling, provisions only operated after the war ended.
1945		Family Allowances Act
	May	War in Europe ended.
	July	General Election
1945–1951		**Attlee Prime Minister**
1945–1	Aug	War with Japan ended.
		Britain obtained loans from USA and Canada to buy food and raw materials.
1946		**Bank of England nationalised**: shareholder compensation by being given Government Stock set pattern for later nationalisaton measures.
		Trade Disputes Act repealed 1927 Act and so required union members to opt out of the political levy.
		National Insurance Act: compulsory contribution to pay for Health Service and for unemployment, sickness, maternity, retirement benefits.
		Coal Industry nationalised: little dispute over the measure, National Coal Board set up, industry faced many problems from earlier lack of investment.
		National Health Service Act: implemented the Beveridge Report, comprehensive cover, free medical provision. Bevan brought it in, after much opposition from the medical profession.
		New Towns Act: to provide for building of new towns by development corporations; Stevenage was the first.
1946–1947		Very severe winter weather paralysed transport and caused coal shortages and electricity cuts. Government blamed for poor planning. Minister of Fuel & Power, Shinwell, sacked.
1947	Nov	Budget leak led to Chancellor Dalton resigning. Stafford Cripps became Chancellor, promoted Austerity programme, longer hours of work, curbs on government spending, income tax **45p** in the pound.
		Marshal Plan brought US aid to Europe.
		British India granted independence.
		Road, Rail and Canal Transport nationalised: to be run by the British Transport Commission: lorry owners and Conservatives fiercely opposed the measure.
		Electricity Industry nationalised: placed under the British Electricity Authority with 15 regional boards; strong Conservative opposition.
		Town and Country Planning Act: local authorities had to draw up development plans.
1948		National Assistance Act: to cover cases not under the National Insurance Act; it meant the end of the Poor Law.
		Gas Industry nationalised: placed under the Gas Council with 12 Area Gas Boards.
		Berlin Airlift (July to May 1949) marked serious development of the Cold War.
		British Nationality Act: declared all Commonwealth citizens to be British subjects.

Representation of the People Act: university seats and second votes for graduates abolished.

1949 North Atlantic Treaty Organisation founded.
Pound devalued (from $4.03 to $2.80 to the £) to help exports and close the 'dollar gap' in trade figures.
Parliament Act (held up by Lords for two years): it reduced the Lords' delaying power from two years to one.
Iron and Steel Industry nationalised: to be run by the British Iron & Steel Corporation, bitterly opposed by owners and by the Conservatives. This was Labour's last nationalisation measure.

1950 **General Election**
Korean War began pushing up international commodity prices with renewed adverse effect on British balance of trade.
Bevan and Wilson resigned from government over first introduction of Health Service charges.

1951 **General Election**
Churchill became Prime Minister.

EXAMINATION QUESTIONS

Q1 How do you account for the decisive Labour victory in the 1945 General Election? (Northern Ireland 1989)

Q2 How controversial was the programme of nationalisation carried out by the Attlee governments of 1945–1951? (London 1989)

Q3 How far do you agree that, by 1951 the reforms, introduced by the Labour Governments since 1945, had done little to improve the everyday lives of the British people? (Welsh 1989)

Q4 How successful was the Labour Government, from 1945 to 1950, in dealing with foreign policy problems with which it was faced? (London 1989)

Q5 Account for the Conservative victory in the 1951 General Election. (London 1990)

OUTLINE ANSWERS

Question 1

See the 'Tutor's Answer', at the end of this section.

Question 2

See the 'Student's Answer' at the end of this section.

Question 3

Identify: the reforms to be considered.
Consider in turn the provision of: National Insurance
National Health Service
National Assistance Act
Housing

"Note the end date of the essay."

Set these in the context of previous provision and extent of problems.

Argue: effects in these areas are dramatic; illustrate this by reference to life in 1930s and to the problems left by war. Add that the terms of the 1944 Education Act were actually implemented in these years with considerable effect on the lives of secondary schoolchildren in particular.

Agree: that many other problems less affected and that Government's powers in these areas more limited and more time needed, for example, food, fuel, but also cite other problem areas of life (transport, education, lack of material possessions, drabness of life in 1940s).

Conclusion: stress that even where relevant legislation passed this alone would not solve the problem. Foundations may have been of value for future but if life so much better why did Labour lose office?

Question 4

"Many international problems."

Introduction: briefly indicate what the problems were. All the problems related to Britain's exhaustion after the war and how it was to find a role in a world dominated by the superpowers of the USA and USSR. Related to this were the specific problems like how to respond to the USSR's perceived expansionism in Europe. Other problems included: the British mandate in Palestine; disputes over oil with Iran; reacting to the communist takeover of China; the Korean War. A separate major problem arose from Britain's imperial past and related to the demands for independence in British India.

Take problems in turn and consider success, for example:

To find a new role Labour firmly attached Britain to the US alliance, this very successful in countering USSR threat, explain how: Berlin Airlift, NATO. Price to be paid was increasing loss of independent initiative.

Note: Expansion of all this to form the bulk of the essay.

Palestine: unsuccessful, Britain scrambled out of commitments beyond its resources and willpower.

Iran: apparent success for time being but no long-term protection for oil supplies.

India: from British point of view (Churchill excepted) a successful unloading of impossible commitments.

"An alliance at a price."

China and Korea: with the former, Britain took a separate line from the US but this gave no future protection to the remains of the Empire in the Far East and how to provide this was a problem never to be solved. With Korea, Britain acted as the junior partner of the US which illustrated the price to be paid in return for solving our most pressing foreign policy problems through attachment to the American alliance.

Question 5

Give the outline election results for the three main parties. Argue that they need relating to the 1950 results.

"Explaining the 1951 Election."

Explain: problems Labour grappled at home and how continuing controls gave the Opposition an opening. Also loss of momentum after vast programme of legislation. Some swing back after 1945 always likely. Be more detailed on 1951, Labour resignations, small majority, Attlee in office since 1940, tired of the fight and fought an election he could have avoided. Growing Conservative confidence.

Conclusion: analyse voting, for technical factors were important, especially the collapse of the Liberals, the reasons for them switching to the Conservatives is the key to the outcome. In main Labour voters remained loyal.

A TUTOR'S ANSWER TO QUESTION 1

Labour's victory in 1945 stunned many contemporaries. The Conservative campaign, relying heavily on Churchill's reputation as the man who had led the nation to victory had been extensively reported by a largely sympathetic Press and had taken on the apparent momentum of a victory parade. The first ever Gallup Poll had predicted a Labour win but this had been almost totally ignored in the excitement of the campaign.

Since 1945 historians have sought to explain what happened in what is now seen as the biggest lurch to the political left ever undertaken by British voters. These explanations have had to come to terms not only with the fact of a Labour victory but also with its decisive nature. Labour, with almost 48 per cent of the votes cast had taken 393 of the 640 seats in the Commons, 180 more than had the Conservatives with the Liberals reduced to a rump of 12.

"1945 a rejection of the 1930s?"

The scale of the victory can be seen as a rejection of the social and economic miseries of the 1930s which, along with an inept foreign policy in that decade, had been largely blamed on the Conservative dominated governments of the pre-war period. It can also be seen as a consequence of the changes forced on British society through the efforts needed to see a total war through to total victory. A number of 'technical', personal and even accidental matters which occurred during the election campaign may also have contributed to the outcome.

The social ills brought on by the economic depression of the early 1930s had had an uneven impact, socially and geographically, but the most dramatic effects of long-term mass unemployment in the old staple industries coupled with the apparent inability or unwillingness of the government to counteract it had sharpened class attitudes in politics. The common hardships to be endured in war made a return to these miseries and this indifference intolerable to more than just those who had suffered most. The Hunger Marches had become a potent symbol of the need for change.

Labour was the chief beneficiary of these memories and, as Trade Union strength revived even before the war, so did the electoral prospects of the Labour Party. The crushing defeats of 1931 and even 1935 had been exaggerated by internal division and external economic crisis and, but for the outbreak of war, there had been every prospect of significant Labour gains in an election which should have been held by 1940 at the latest. The 'normal' swings of party electoral fortune would have helped Labour as would the spectre of fascism at home and abroad. One element in the surprising decisiveness of the 1945 results arises from a failure to recognise these pre-war tendencies and to remember that ten years had elapsed since the last General Election.

"And a product of the war effort."

The lives of everyone in the country were affected by the war, through conscription, the direction of even female labour, rationing and material shortages and indeed through exposure to the considerable hazards of German bombing. From a range of sacrifices shared by military and civilians there emerged a common sense of purpose, directed first to the notion of victory over what were increasingly seen as the forces of evil and then to the view that these sacrifices must lead to a better world. At this point the memories of the thirties were again important. The memories of government inactivity at that time were in marked contrast to the energy now directed by the State to the cause of victory in war. A State which could organise on this scale for war could be expected to do the same to provide a better peace. This was the growing mood as the war entered its last phase.

It was the Labour Party which managed in 1945 to benefit from these hopes and fears and turn them into electoral victory but precisely why this proved to be the case is less easily explained. Here personality, chance and accident all perhaps played their part.

"Why did Labour benefit from the mood of the time?"

Conservatives later argued that Labour benefited greatly from keeping its party organisation operational during the war and that this was in turn enhanced by the inevitably increased role in war of the Trade Unions. The Conservatives it is clear, in this explanation at least, got on with the patriotic job of winning the war. Similar lines of explanation include reference to the left-wing views to which soldiers were exposed through the activities of young left-wing education officers and through the leftish ideas expounded in film and on the wireless by young intellectuals of the Central Office of Information. The significance of J B Priestley usually looms large in such analysis.

"Conservative reliance on Churchill."

The Conservative election campaign relied heavily on Churchill's personality and reputation with many candidates centring their own campaigns on precisely this point with slogans that 'A vote for X is a vote for Churchill'. Too many voters however remembered Churchill's controversial reactionary reputation in many fields, and perhaps also recalled the use of slogans and a personality cult by Lloyd George at the end of the First World War, for this campaign strategy to be at all effective. The Conservatives gave the impression of being lukewarm on the Beveridge welfare proposals, strong on foreign affairs, imperial resonsibilities and balancing budgets, and none of these struck a clear chord with the voters. There were also silly mistakes in the Conservative campaign. In particular the attempt to label Labour as likely to employ a 'Gestapo' to implement policy was counter-productive. Attlee and his colleagues, who had played such an important part in winning the war, simply didn't fit the alleged role.

"Labour's social programme the more convincing."

Labour, on the other hand, with its campaign manifesto 'Let Us Face The Future' with its emphasis on housing, employment and social security seemed to promise active and caring government which could so easily be contrasted to the previous record of the Conservatives. Labour had played a full part in wartime government so there seemed every reason to believe that they could deliver their promises. It was not a programme totally different from that of the Tories but in the context of the time the commitment seemed so much more convincing.

"The Liberal collapse."

The continuing slump in Liberal fortunes this time helped Labour for with Russia as a still valued wartime ally the 'Red menace' seemed a less relevant threat to stability than it had in pre-war elections. It seems that disillusioned Liberals, or enough of them to matter, were for this reason prepared to move to the left. Then other technical factors emphasised the extent of the Labour victory, most notoriously the first past the post electoral system which transformed 48 per cent of the votes in to 60 plus per cent of seats in the Commons. It has also been claimed that Labour held an undue proportion of small decaying city centre seats and that, in this way the electoral system discriminated against the Tories.

It seems likely that the Election hinged on Labour capturing the wartime desire for a better future and giving the impression that it was more likely to deliver this than were the Conservatives. Their team and their programme seemed more in tune with the times. The extent of the swing to Labour must be kept in perspective for not everyone saw their case as overwhelming and ten million voters still preferred to vote Conservative.

A STUDENT'S ANSWER TO QUESTION 2

"A very indirect introduction."

The Attlee government of 1945, elected after the Second World War had many measures to its credit including the nationalisation of many industries and the creation of the National Health Service and a system of national insurance. The victory of 1945 had owed much to the mood in the country in the last years of the war and on the back of the 1945 mandate the Labour Party carried out a great series of reforms. The main measures of nationalisation included the Bank of England, electricity and gas, transport, coal and iron and steel. These can be considered in turn.

"Why not start here?"

The Bank of England was nationalised in 1946 and this caused little controversy, the central banks of most other countries were already in public control and this measure did not affect the rest of the banking system. Churchill said he would not oppose it and there was little debate in Parliament. Labour supporters were delighted for they felt that the Bank had betrayed their party in 1931. Electricity too was uncontroversial because there had already been some control since before the war and because the owners were generously compensated they did not lead a campaign of protest. Gas led to a much greater row and passed only after heated debates. In transport the nationalisation of the airlines went through easily as plans already existed for further amalgamation of small companies. Exactly the same was true of the railways where the idea of removing wasteful competition commanded wide support and the Trade Unions were very much in favour. Road transport was however fiercely argued over with the Conservatives defending the interests of the small lorry operators so that the government gave in and allowed these to continue. The industry Labour most wanted to nationalise was coal where industrial relations had always been very bitter. The Conservatives offered very little resistance and the Liberals supported the measure. Once more the owners were generously compensated.

"An overlong paragraph?"

Iron and steel produced much more controversy. They had never been high amongst Labour's priorities and were, unlike earlier industries which had been nationalised, manufacturing industries. Steel was profitable and the steel unions were not enthusiastic to have the industry nationalised. Within the Cabinet Morrison opposed steel nationalisation. The Bill to nationalise steel was rejected by the Lords and had to be re-introduced despite the continuing opposition of a few ministers and backbenchers.

"Stress the chronology more."

It was the early nationalisation Bills which went through Parliament most easily. This was because the Conservatives saw that the voters had been in favour of such measures and decided not to

> resist Labour's introduction of them. Later the Conservatives began to re-gain their confidence and started to resist nationalisation more fiercely as the Government's other problems increased. At the same time the momentum for reform slowed down and even the Labour Party became disheartened by the problems it faced. For these reasons nationalisation became more controversial as time went on.

EXAMINER COMMENT

This is a closely packed essay with solidly relevant knowledge. It suggests a student well-prepared for this topic. It avoids just describing what happened because it contains a great number of brief relevant comments.

The analysis, however, needs expanding and the controversies need setting in a wider context. The essay eventually argues that controversy grew as time progressed. This was certainly the case but the argument would have seemed more convincing if some dates had been introduced and commented on, for example:

> 'The nationalisation legislation of 1946 and 1947 went through Parliament with relatively little controversy but the sharper disputes over road haulage in 1947 and gas in 1948 marked a change in mood which led on to the acrimonious debates over steel in 1949.'

There are some sensible direct points made, 'Iron and Steel produced much more controversy' which highlights a key turning point in the discussion. But then comes what is arguably the weakest part of the answer and this on what is in fact the central controversy of the period. The extent and sharpness of the divisions within Labour need to be established more clearly (this was in some ways the most interesting of the controversies) and the argument over the extent and structure of the nationalised steel industry, even amongst supporters of nationalisation, would have been a welcome addition. Above all though the essay needs at this point to elaborate how these divisions encouraged Conservative and other opponents and the key role of the House of Lords in all this. The links between this controversy and that over the powers of the Lords and indeed, the shadow of a forthcoming election would have provided the wider context of the answer.

The last paragraph could have developed the reference to the extent of the Labour victory in 1945, making the point that the electorate had been fully aware of Labour's proposals and that this perhaps limited the Opposition's ability to resist to the last ditch, even if that ditch were in the Lords. The economic background is not picked up. At the end of the war the coal industry and the railways in particular were in such a lamentable state that there appeared to be strong reasons for re-organisation and capital investment programmes under state control which pressed into silence many of those who, on ideological grounds, were most opposed to nationalisation.

In summary it is an informed, directly relevant, essay with a sensible structure. These qualities would ensure it a pass mark but a little development of the commentary at some key points could raise that mark significantly without requiring much more depth or range of knowledge to be available.

USEFUL SOURCES OF INFORMATION

General reading

C J Bartlett, *A History of Post-War Britain, 1945–1974*, Longman 1977
D Childs, *Britain since 1945, A Political History*, Methuen (2nd edition) 1986
L C B Seaman, *Post-Victorian Britain, 1902–1951*, Methuen 1966
A J P Taylor, *English History 1914–1945*, Oxford University Press 1965: a classic piece of historical writing, use the contents pages to help you dip into it. In most libraries.
J B Watson, *Success in British History since 1914*, John Murray 1983

Further reading

P Addison, *The Road to 1945: British Politics and the Second World War,* Quartet 1977
P Addison, *Now the War is over: a social history of Britain 1945–1951*, BBC/Cape 1985
P Hennessy, *Never Again: Britain 1945 –1951,* Cape 1992
A Marwick, *Britain in the Century of Total War,* Penguin 1970: develops his vigorously argued thesis of war as the engine of social and economic change.
K O Morgan, *The People's Peace: British History 1945 –1989,* Oxford University Press 1990
K O Morgan, *Labour in Power 1945–1951*, Oxford University Press 1984: a major work, useful for reference on important topics.
M Sissons & P French, *Age of Austerity 1945–1951*, Penguin 1963: a fascinating series of essays on everyday post-war life.

Linked topic areas

- Life in Britain in the 1930s
- The causes of the Second World War
- The course and outcome of the Second World War
- British Imperial history after 1945
- The Cold War (see Chapters 23 and 24)
- British society and politics after 1951 (see Chapter 11)

CHAPTER 11

BRITISH HISTORY 1950 – 1993

GETTING STARTED

A sensible starting point would be to look through Chapter 10 on the Second World War and the period of Labour government from 1945 to 1951, as the agenda for much of British political, social and economic history until 1979, at least, was set during the 1940s. The creation of the Welfare State and the programme of nationalisation were central to this. The economic difficulties which have plagued Britain since the end of the Second World War have been of such recurring importance in political life that even non-economists will find it necessary to understand the outline vocabulary employed in their analysis. Textbooks try to be user friendly in these matters but an intelligent interest in newspaper coverage of present day economic affairs could greatly ease your understanding of the historical background, even if only by making the vocabulary employed a little more familiar. There is no need to assume that the study of economics at A-level is at all necessary, though the study of recent British history may well be helpful to economists.

Alongside an understanding of the major economic issues you should acquire familiarity with the normal vocabulary of political life based on an understanding of British political processes. There seems little point in studying this very recent period of history unless you are interested in current events in the broadest sense. Given that interest it is a very rewarding period to study, not least for the vast range of evidence available to the historian. It was in the middle years of the century that the range of visual evidence available was greatly increased and you should try in your studies to make full use of newsreel and film coverage. Make a virtue out of discussing past events and experiences with those who lived through them; not to take what you are told at face value but to set against the textbook generalisations and to bring them to life. No earlier period of study will offer you the same opportunities to research your own history.

Finally it would be sensible to spend a little time looking at an atlas of the modern world and to keep one available during the course of your studies. Examination howlers which have the Suez Canal running into the Persian Gulf may cheer up the examiner but are unlikely to create a feeling of confidence in your more specifically historical judgements.

ESSENTIAL PRINCIPLES

THIRTEEN CONSERVATIVE YEARS

1951–1964

This topic opens with the recovery of Conservative fortunes in the 1950 and 1951 Elections. They increased their number of MPs in 1955 and again in 1959. By 1964 Labour's election charge was that these had been 'thirteen wasted years' and this could provide a peg on which to hang your assessment of the Conservative achievement.

THE PRIME MINISTERS

A substantial start could be made by summarising the careers in this period of the four Conservative Prime Ministers, though *Macmillan* (1957–1963) is the one most likely to figure as the subject of a biographical question. *Churchill* (1951–1955) was a shadowy figure at this stage of his long career and *Eden* (1955–1957) seems forever destined to be judged by his actions over Suez; whilst *Douglas-Home* (1963–1964) left no permanent mark and is less important than the 'Prime Minister who never was', namely *R A Butler*.

1955 ELECTION

In the election of 1955 the Conservatives gained 344 seats (23 more than in 1951) with 49.7 per cent of the vote and Labour 277 (1951–295) and 46.4 per cent. By 1959, despite the Suez affair and leadership problems, the Conservatives held 365 seats (49.4 per cent of the vote) and Labour 258 (44.1 per cent). These were dire days for the Liberals who won 6 seats on each occasion though their percentage of the vote rose from 2.1 per cent in 1955 to 4.6 per cent in 1959. It would be useful to construct an explanation of this record of Conservative success as this would involve the travails in these years of their Labour opponents and also the general experience of growing prosperity after the austerity of the immediate post-war years. The establishment of commercial television is perhaps the best symbol of the fifties.

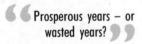

"Prosperous years – or wasted years?"

LABOUR 1964–1970

"Labour divisions in the 1950s."

In any judgement of the record of the Labour governments after 1964 remember the legacy of the great ministry of 1945–1951. The memory of their achievements then, often seemed to dictate both policy and tactics. The 1950s had been a disastrous decade for the party with long-running splits caused by differences over foreign policy, re-armament, nuclear weapons and what constituted a truly socialist domestic policy. The roles of *Aneurin Bevan* and *Hugh Gaitskell* are the clearest route to an understanding of the issues at stake and the debilitating effect the quarrels had on the party's electoral fortunes. Labour looked a one class party, refusing to abandon its nationalisation ideals and temporarily committed to unilateral nuclear disarmament. From 1960 they were also confronted by a revival in Liberal fortunes and seemed to face a grim future.

HAROLD WILSON

Harold Wilson's contribution to the party must be set in this context. As Prime Minister from 1964 to 1970, unlike Attlee, he adopted a very high profile amongst his colleagues and in public. He deserves much credit both for the successes and the failures of these years.

A major triumph was the result of the 1966 Election increasing the Labour majority over the Conservatives from 13 to 111 seats, which represented a great tactical victory over the new Conservative leader Edward Heath and squeezed back the Liberal revival of the early 1960s. There followed a period of growing economic difficulties which led in 1967 to a damaging devaluation of the pound and, as economic difficulties grew worse, problems arose in Rhodesia, with the Trade Unions and, in 1969, in Northern Ireland. From the high hopes and the rhetoric of 1964–1966 the scene darkened with remarkable suddenness. Wilson was the major political figure of the period. Be ready to judge both his personal achievement in politics and the record of his governments both at this point and from 1974 to 1976.

"Wilson a major political figure."

Few pollsters predicted the Conservative win in the 1970 election for, under Wilson, Labour seemed to have emerged as the natural party of government, the role that had belonged to the Conservatives in the 1950s.

THE HEATH GOVERNMENT

1970–1974

In 1970 the Conservatives came to power committed to a programme of radical political and economic change. The achievements were, with the notable exception of *entry to the European Community* few.

"Britain entered the European Community."

Heath made his own difficulties with the Trade Unions over wage restraint and through support for uncompetitive firms. There was no effective administrative reform and the promised de-nationalisation measures proved laughably minor. The troubles in Northern Ireland continued and the oil crisis of 1973 heralded in a series of economic difficulties. Then came the miners' strike and Heath's unnecessary calling of an election which, in February 1974, he lost. The Labour Party had only four more seats than the Conservatives and Heath tried vainly to do a deal with the Liberals which would have left him in office.

"Thatcher elected Conservative leader."

The loss of the election was quite quickly to lead to Heath's replacement, in the first ever election for a Conservative Party leader, by the comparatively unknown outsider, Margaret Thatcher. It is difficult to see his government's failure to live up to the promises of a new direction in political life as anything more than a stage on the way to post-1979 Thatcherism.

Exam questions

The most probable examination questions on Heath will rest on an invitation to consider his own responsibility for the fate of his government as opposed to that of the admittedly difficult circumstances with which he was faced.

LABOUR 1974–1979

Wilson was Prime Minister until his resignation in 1976. After the February 1974 election he called a second election in October and gained a 42-seat majority over the Conservatives, but strong minor party support (39 seats) and then bye-election defeats denied Labour an overall majority.

EC REFERENDUM

In 1975 a referendum was held on continued membership of the European Community which was supported by a two-to-one majority. This is the point at which to prepare an overall assessment of Harold Wilson's political career and achievements. The length of his periods in office, if nothing else, suggests that he will become a favoured target in examination questions.

CALLAGHAN GOVERNMENT

Callaghan's government (1976–1979) faced many problems with sharp inflation and numerous industrial disputes. In 1976 it had to turn to the International Monetary Fund for economic support. The terms were tough and created strains within the government and the party. A pact with the Liberals helped in Parliament though the potential benefits to the Liberals proved illusory. The government made proposals for devolution of government in both Scotland and Wales but in neither case did the stipulated 40 per cent of the total electorate vote in favour of them. The fragile Parliamentary majority led to the loss of a vote of confidence. This against a background of growing industrial unrest, the much noted *'winter of discontent'*.

"The 'winter of discontent'."

1979 is another sensible point at which to carry out an overall survey of the political scene. James Callaghan seems likely to be less popular with examiners than Wilson, and his problems to loom larger than his achievements, but nevertheless be ready to comment on the Labour record from 1964 through to 1979.

CONSERVATIVES 1974–1979

"Mixed Conservative fortunes from 1964 to 1979."

The same period had been almost as unhappy for the Conservatives as the preceding thirteen years had been for Labour but in 1979 the latter paid dearly for a sense of disintegration detected by numbers of voters. In the 1979 election the total Conservative vote (10.5 million in 1974) was 13.7 million and they won 339 seats (1974 – 277). Labour's vote was almost identical in both elections (11.5 million) but their seats fell from 319 to 269. Liberal votes fell by a million (5.3 to 4.3) and the number of their MPs from 13 to 11 but the Nationalists lost 10 of their 14 seats of 1974.

1979 – A POLITICAL TURNING POINT?

"The end of the post-war consensus?"

Margaret Thatcher had promised a new sense of political direction and the length of her stay in office may well ensure that that is how it is seen by future historians. Whether all who voted for the Conservatives in 1979 realised how radical their policies were to become is not certain but, with the benefit of hindsight, which is always a dangerous commodity, it seems valid to see the 1979 election as marking the end of a post-war political consensus between the major parties as to the purposes and the legitimate interests of government.

IMPERIAL AND FOREIGN AFFAIRS

"Britain's international position under threat."

1950–1980

Here too the context had been established by Britain's role and experiences in the Second World War. For almost any question on Britain in the international setting during the second half of the twentieth century it will be useful to be able to illustrate and to discuss how the impact of war cruelly exposed its inability to maintain the worldwide role inherited from an earlier imperial age. By 1945 Britain's military potential was dwarfed by that of the new superpowers, its economy was shattered and its foreign debt enormous. In 1947, partly in recognition of these realities, Attlee's Labour government had hastened the granting of independence to British India. Questions on the dismantling of the Empire are likely to take 1945 as their starting point so make it yours, taking in also the complications involved in bringing to an end in 1948 the old British League of Nations mandate in Palestine. After the war it became normal to talk about the British Commonwealth rather than the British Empire: in the 1950s the 'British' was quietly dropped.

THE ENDING OF EMPIRE

Britain lacked the resources either to hold or to develop the colonies. Attempts at federations in Africa and the West Indies were unsuccessful and the Suez crisis of 1956 (see the 'Document Question' later in this chapter) undermined even Conservative desires to retain a colonial empire. A full survey of the end of the British Empire should take in events in Malaya and Cyprus, but, in the 1960s, the focus was increasingly on the affairs of the colonies in Africa. These in turn came to centre on what became known as the 'Rhodesian problem', which, for those studying the end of the Empire in Africa, is the most important single topic. In 1961 the newly created Republic of South Africa withdrew from the Commonwealth and this opened up a new series of relationships with Britain and the rest of the Commonwealth which centred on what was to be done about the new republic's apartheid policies.

Exam questions

"Use the crises to show the problems."

Foreign affairs were conducted under the shadow of the Cold War and the reality that Britain could no longer claim to be in the first rank of the world powers. The two most important British foreign policy themes are the much cherished 'special relationship' with the USA and the long flirtation with the European Community. These, together with the story of the end of the Imperial dream, will provide the basis for most questions on Britain's declining international role. At any one time be ready to offer some comment on the foreign/imperial policy of particular ministries, Conservative and Labour, in case these are needed to answer general questions evaluating their achievement. Eden and Suez, Wilson and Rhodesia, Macmillan and the Common Market, Thatcher and the Falklands are possible examples.

THE ECONOMY

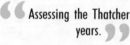

“Economic policy has moved to the heart of government.”

Far more important than foreign affairs in assessing the work of ministries is their success, or more usually their failure, to resolve the economic problems besetting the country at the time. The success or failure of economic policies has become the touchstone by which, first the electorate and then the historians, judge political achievement. You will need to be able, even in non-economic essays, to offer a verdict on the economic record of successive ministries. It cannot be avoided for it also regularly impinges on the successful resolution of most social problems.

Any analysis of economic issues needs to include an informed understanding of issues such as:

- trade deficits
- visible and invisible trade
- economic growth rates
- inflation

You do not need to be an economist but you do have to be prepared to take an intelligent interest in economic affairs.

SOCIAL TRENDS

Exam questions

Inevitably social history examination questions can be so diverse as to defy prediction but two themes may prove particularly popular viz:

- The emergence of a youth culture from the 1950s.
- The emergence of a multicultural society in Britain, the reasons for this, the problems and promises of a multicultural society, race relations, immigration issues, together with all the accompanying legislation.

“For examination purposes take a long view on social matters.”

The provision of education, and of welfare and health, continue to lead the political agenda and so seem likely to be prominent in future history examination papers. Remember to check from past papers that social issues do appear and note that such questions frequently cover a much wider period of time than do more specifically political questions.

NORTHERN IRELAND

Exam questions

The disturbed history of the Province since the late 1960s is still difficult to view with historical objectivity. Establish first that the syllabus of your paper and the offerings in past examinations make it a reasonable prospect for study and revision purposes. It could offer a self-contained topic but it will require a look back in Irish history to at least the 1912–1921 period to understand the full implications. You will need to understand the history of what is now the Republic of Ireland across the same period. It will be worth preparing for by those with an interest in the topic but they will need to be able to separate historical analysis from current political speculation and commentary.

THE THATCHER YEARS

1979–1990

Few, in 1979, would have seen the Conservative election victory as a key turning point in British political life since 1945. It has been the radical policies pursued by the governments led by Margaret Thatcher and their subsequent election victories in 1983 and 1987 that have made it so.

Exam questions

“Assessing the Thatcher years.”

As history examiners bring their syllabuses closer to the present it is already clear that assessments of the purposes and the achievements of the Thatcher years will provide topics of major importance in examination papers. The record is sufficiently controversial that it will be necessary, for some years yet, to keep a cool head when the verdict is being delivered. A start to many questions could be made by understanding how Margaret Thatcher took the Conservative leadership from Edward Heath and then, by looking at the political record since 1979, preparing a very brief case arguing that 1979 marked the first new political starting point since 1945. If you then reflect on how truly this can be claimed in relation to the economy, social policy, international affairs you will have gone a long way to prepare yourself for the sort of questions historians will soon be asking about the period.

How would you respond, within the format of a history essay, to a question inviting you to assess how successfully the Thatcher governments promoted the country's real (economic, social or international) interests and what evidence you would use to support your point of view? Then honestly seek out the strongest piece of contrary evidence and take account of it within your case. Another range of questions is likely to involve personal assessments of Mrs Thatcher's political style and achievement and these too will require a measured historical response.

USEFUL INFORMATION

1951	**General Election** (see Chapter 10)
1951–1955	**Churchill Prime Minister**
1953	Iron and Steel Act started the process of denationalising the industry.
	Transport Act denationalised road transport.
	Other nationalised industries remained in state control.
1952	Death of George VI. Accession of Elizabeth II.
1954	End of food rationing
	Television Act set up ITV
1955	**General Election**: Conservative majority increased.
1955–1957	**Eden Prime Minister**
1956	The Suez Crisis (see 'Document Question').
	Death penalty limited to specific types of murder.
1957	Resignation of Eden
1957–1963	**Macmillan Prime Minister**
1958	First serious racial clashes in Notting Hill and Nottingham.
1959	**General Election**: further increase in Conservative majority.
1960	End of conscription.
	Betting shops and casinos made legal for the first time.
1962	Orpington bye-election marked the 1960s high point of the Liberal revival.
	Commonwealth Immigrants Act restricted immigration.
1963	Beeching Report started process of closing 5000 miles of unprofitable rail track.
	De Gaulle vetoed Britain's application to join the EEC.
1963	The Profumo affair
	Retirement of Macmillan
1963–1964	**Douglas-Home Prime Minister**
1964	Opening of the Rhodesian independence issue with election of Ian Smith as Prime Minister of that British colony.
1964	**General Election**: narrow overall Labour majority with 317 seats and 12.2 million votes, Conservatives 304 with 12.0 million, Liberals 9 with 3.2 million.
1964–1970	**Wilson Prime Minister**
1965	End of death penalty
1966	**General Election:** Labour majority of more than 100 over Conservatives. Labour 364 seats with 13.1 million votes, Conservatives 253 with 11.4 million, Liberals 12 with 2.3 million.
	First Race Relations Act set up the Race Relations Board.
1967	Steel industry renationalised (British Steel Corporation set up).
1968	Commonwealth Immigration Act restricted the right of entry of British passport holders without substantial connection with the country. This was a response to the prospect of large-scale Asian immigration from Kenya and Uganda.
	Second Race Relations Act.
	Enoch Powell's speech on immigration dramatised the issue.
1970	**General Election**: generally unexpected Conservative victory. Conservatives 330 seats with 13.1 million votes, Labour 287 with 12.2 million, Liberals 6 with 2.1 million.
1970–1974	**Heath Prime Minister**
1971	Immigration Act provided a control system for all immigrants
1974 Feb	**General Election**: Conservatives 297 seats with 11.9 million votes, Labour 301 with 11.6, Liberals 14 with 6.1 million, Nationalists 9 with 0.8 million.
1974–1976	**Wilson Prime Minister**
1974 Oct	**General Election**: Labour 319 seats with 11.5 million votes, Conservatives 277 with 10.5 million, Liberals 13 with 5.3 million, Nationalists 14 with 1.0 million.

1976–1979 Callaghan Prime Minister
1976 Third Race Relations Act
1979 **General Election**: Conservatives 339 seats with 13.7 million votes, Labour 269 with 11.5 million, Liberals 11 with 4.3 million, Nationalists 4 with 0.6 million.

1979–1990 Thatcher Prime Minister
Radical economic policies, monetarism, privatisation, three million unemployed, income tax reductions, VAT increased.
1981 SDP formed by dissident Labour MPs
1982 Falklands War
1983 **General Election**: increased Conservative majority, Conservatives 397 seats with 13 million votes, Labour 209 with 8.45 million, Liberals and SDP 23 with 7.8 million. Note how Liberal/SDP vote increase has hit the Labour vote but has led, on a reduced vote, to the election of more Conservative MPs.
Further privatisation proposals followed the election.
1987 **General Election:** Conservatives retained most of their gains. Conservatives 374 seats with 13.7 million votes, Labour 227 with 10 million. Alliance (Liberals 17, SDP 6) 23 with 7.3 million. Centre party advance blocked by Labour recovery.
1989 Signs of a recovery in Labour's fortunes raised the prospect that the Conservative's long tenure of power might be under threat at the next General Election.
1990 SDP disbanded.
Mrs Thatcher resigned after failure to win necessary majority in Party leadership election provoked by Michael Heseltine. John Major subsequently elected Party leader and became Prime Minister.

1990 – Major Prime Minister
1992 Unexpected Conservative General Election victory despite economic recession.
1993 Recession persisted; worst economic situation since 1930s. Deep divisions in Conservative Party over attitudes to Europe and Maastricht Treaty.

EXAMINATION QUESTIONS

Q1 What principles motivated Conservative governments in the period 1951–64? (Welsh 1989)

Q2 Assess the evidence for the claim that 'by the early 1960s Britain was becoming more 'European' and less 'imperial''? (Northern Ireland 1988)

Q3 What factors appeared by 1974 to be causing increasing disillusionment with traditional two-party politics in Britain? (London 1990)

Q4 On what grounds might a historian regard the 1960s and the 1970s as years of 'wasted opportunity' for Britain? (Oxford 1989)

Q5 Document question: 'The Suez Crisis 1956' (London 1990)

Study Documents 1, 2 and 3 below and then answer questions (a) to (f) which follow:

Document 1

The uproar which we anticipated has been taking place in London and Paris. This tremendous uproar is not supported by reason or logic. It is backed only by imperialist methods, by the habits of blood-sucking and of usurping rights, and by interference in the affairs of other countries. An unjustified uproar arose in London, and yesterday Britain submitted a protest to Egypt. I wonder what was the basis of this protest by Britain to Egypt? The Suez Canal Company is an Egyptian company, subject to Egyptian sovereignty. When we nationalised the Suez Canal Company, we only nationalised an Egyptian limited company, and by doing so we exercised a right which stems from the very core of Egyptian sovereignty . . . The Suez Canal Company is a limited company, awarded a concession by the Egyptian Government in 1865 to carry out its tasks. Today we withdraw the concession in order to do the job ourselves . . .

Compatriots, we shall maintain our independence and sovereignty. The Suez Canal Company has become our property, and the Egyptian flag flies over it. We shall hold it with our blood and strength, and we shall meet aggression with aggression and evil with evil.

(President Nasser, speaking 28 July 1956)

Document 2

British public opinion should be united behind us in treating what has happened as unacceptable . . . We cannot have this Canal under the control of this dictator, subject to his whims. He showed his irresponsibility by announcing his decision as a method of retaliation to something that happened affecting the internal economy of Egypt. His threat to imprison the employees, his utter disregard for the finances of the Canal show that he cannot be trusted to manage it. He seems totally unable to realise that the Canal will need capital in the coming years, rather than be able to produce it for other projects.

If we lie down under this behaviour, he will have our oil supplies in his grasp. He will have the capacity to interfere at will with seaborne movements, troops, supplies and trade. What he has done will be an example to other countries.

(Selwyn Lloyd, British Foreign Secretary, speaking to the Conservative Foreign Affairs Committee, 31 July 1956)

Document 3

The Governments of the United Kingdom and France have taken note of the outbreak of hostilities between Israel and Egypt. This event threatens to disrupt the freedom of navigation through the Suez Canal . . . They accordingly request the Government of Egypt:

a) to stop all warlike action on land, sea and air forthwith;
b) to withdraw all Egyptian military forces to a distance of ten miles from the Canal; and
c) . . . to accept the temporary occupation by Anglo-French forces of key positions at Port Said, Ismailia and Suez.

(Anglo-French ultimatum to Egypt, 30 October 1956)

a) What was meant in these documents by *each* of the following:
   i) 'sovereignty' (lines 7/9/13)
   ii) 'nationalised' (lines 7 and 8)
   iii) 'capital' (line 23) (*3*)

b) i) From your own knowledge, explain Selwyn Lloyd's point in Document 2 about Nasser acting in 'retaliation' (line 20).
   ii) What did Selwyn Lloyd mean when he said, 'he will have our oil supplies in his grasp' (line 25)? (*3*)

c) In what way does Document 1 (lines 1–15) provide evidence to support the view that Nasser was (i) a nationalist, and (ii) a demagogue? (*5*)

d) What evidence in Documents 2 and 3 (lines 17–34) might support Nasser's charge that 'London and Paris' were using 'imperialist methods' (lines 1 and 3)? (*5*)

e) Why should Selwyn Lloyd and others at this time have been concerned about 'an example to other countries? (line 27) (*3*)

f) Making use of these documents and of your own knowledge, discuss the allegation that Britain, France and Israel in 1956 jointly conspired to bring about the downfall of President Nasser of Egypt. (*6*)

OUTLINE ANSWERS

Question 1

"Conservative principles."

Introduction: this cannot be a block answer for some principles were more important to some Conservatives than to others. Equally the motivating power of some principles changed over the 13-year period. Certain generally accepted principles can however be noted.

1 An emphasis on: Conservative freedom at home; end of rationing; conscription; rent controls.
2 A linked desire to roll back the state though in fact this had limited results, for example: breaking the BBC's monopoly; the limited measures of denationalisation.
3 But post-war Conservatives accepted a positive role in managing the economy and in providing for the welfare of the people, for example the extended house-building programme; the attempt to control inflation by taxation and interest rate policies.
4 The Conservatives were pledged to the American alliance and to preserving the Empire. The former survived the Suez campaign of 1956 but the latter was much weakened by that experience. The 'European principle' was only embraced towards the end of the period. They were, however, totally committed to the independent nuclear deterrent.

Question 2

Consider: evidence for *'less imperial'* first: there remained a great nostalgia for empire, especially on the political right but Churchill, the romantic imperialist, was out of power. Suez had marked a turning point so far as practical politics were concerned, examine its effects on even Conservative opinion.

After 1956: move to end the colonial inheritance got under way, for example: 1957 Ghana and Malaya; 1960 Nigeria, Sierra Leone and Tanganyika. This was the beginning of the 1960s flood of grants of independence including Caribbean islands. Some attempts to hold on in Kenya, and more seriously for strategic reasons, in Cyprus but in the main first part of proposition is valid.

"Commonwealth or Common Market?"

Assess: whether *'more European'*: Macmillan first Prime Minister to look for a European future for Britain but many Britons were lukewarm. De Gaulle's assessment that Britain not ready to join the EEC was probably just. Not wanting to sacrifice political independence Britain had helped set up EFTA as late as 1959 rather than join the EEC. Only the tiny Liberal Party had been pro-EEC prior to Macmillan's 1961 attempt which smacked of political expediency in a world of superpowers rather than a genuine European commitment.

Conclusion: Britain, no longer a great power, had little choice but to be less imperial eventually but, in the early 1960s, it was not really committed to turning to Europe. In 1975 in a referendum Britons voted two to one to stay in the European Community, it seems unlikely that Macmillan would have dared to risk a referendum 14 years earlier.

Question 3

Introduction: give voting figures and seats of Liberals and Nationalists in the two elections of 1974. There had been a shift since 1970, quote figures to illustrate but it needs to be kept in proportion for 1979 saw some reversal.

Factors: largely relate to perceived weaknesses in the major parties; for example Labour seen as a class-based backward-looking party; Heath's Conservative record since 1970 was not impressive. Neither major party had solved the many economic problems.

"Third Party politics."

Wales and Scotland: this discontent led to a general surge in third party support. Circumstances in Wales and even more in Scotland encouraged a nationalist upsurge, London had neglected their interests and the demand grew to run their own affairs. Northern Ireland was a special case based on the Province's deep political divisions.

England: the Liberals were the beneficiaries but could only really harness the discontent in a few constituencies, many remained loyal to the major parties and the voting system worked against the Liberals.

Conclusion: arguably the disillusionment was a minority affair, more apparent than real, a protest vote which did nothing to prevent Labour providing effective government from 1974 to 1979 or the Conservatives after 1979.

Question 4

"Assessing the 1960s and 1970s record."

Grounds could be economic or social. The idea of *'wasted opportunity'* implies that there were permanent solutions to Britain's problems which were missed. This is probably not true.

Economic: take the economic problems which survived the decades, for example: entry to the EC did not cure economic ills; industrial inefficiency; lack of economic growth compared with West Germany; trade deficits; currency weaknesses all persisted. Develop and illustrate this theme.

Social: social opportunities missed were most notably the opportunity to develop a full multi-cultural society on a harmonious basis: explore this. Other social opportunities were perhaps more pipe dreams, the stuff of political rhetoric rather than practical possibilities, for example: the conquest of poverty.

International: internationally there were few real opportunities missed for most had already been closed down before 1960 and the dual compromise of a Commonwealth and lukewarm entry to the EC was probably the best Britain could hope for.

Public opinion: individuals and pressure groups could see all sorts of missed opportunities but for nations the practical prospects are usually more narrowly confined.

A TUTOR'S ANSWER TO QUESTION 5

a) i) A country with total governing power over its own affairs.
ii) Taken into state control.
iii) Money for investment.

b) i) Selwyn Lloyd was suggesting that Nasser's seizure of the Canal was in retaliation for the earlier British decision to withdraw from its commitments to help finance the Egyptian building of the Aswan High Dam.
ii) Much of British oil came from the Middle East through the Suez Canal which Nasser had nationalised; hence the reference.

c) i) Nasser probably was a genuine nationalist and it was certainly a good moment to arouse Egyptian national feelings. His references to the imperialist methods, his repetition of 'Egyptian' and his emphasis on the legal, moral and contractual basis of Egypt's claims on the canal are all nationalist in inspiration. His insistence on the sovereignty and independence of his country and his reference to its flag flying over the canal reinforce the appeal to the national feeling of his people.
ii) Nasser was speaking at a moment of national crisis and is using all his power as an orator to rally support for his perhaps risky nationalisation of the Canal. The blood-sucking habits of his country's enemies raises the emotional temperature at the start, their arguments are 'uproar' and 'interference'. The repetition of 'Egyptian' underlines his message and his dramatic 'Today we withdraw the concession . . .' rounds it off but the real flourish of rhetoric is reached with 'We shall hold it with our blood . . .' meeting 'aggression with aggression and evil with evil'. It was a public rallying cry for national resistance to the foreigner in which reason played little part but where the language and the emphasis were both intended to stir up his audience's emotions.

d) Selwyn Lloyd's tone in Document 2 is unpleasantly patronising, as though when speaking about both Egypt and its leader he is concerned with some lesser breed – 'irresponsible', 'untrustworthy', 'unable to grasp simple economic truths'. The second paragraph is concerned solely with British interests and it is clear that the speaker considers these paramount even when running through the heart of a foreign independent country. The ultimatum, Document 3, assumes the right to order and instruct the Egyptian government and its troops on what they are to do within their own territory at the moment when it has been invaded by Israel. All is justified in the name of free navigation of the Canal. British troops had only withdrawn from the Canal Zone two years earlier and Britain had, prior to that, long exercised control of Egypt. In these circumstances Nasser was likely to be over-sensitive to the notion of imperial pressure. There is however enough evidence in the two documents, with their underlying assumption that Britain can act as it thinks fit on Egyptian soil in order to protect British interests, to substantiate Nasser's charge.

e) If Nasser got away with his resistance to European interests then it could arouse nationalist feelings elsewhere which would be inconvenient, at least, to the two old colonial powers, Britain and France. Britain had already had serious problems maintaining its pre-eminent position in the valuable Iranian oilfields and there were the first murmurings of nationalism in Cyprus and with the Mau Mau in Kenya. France had just lost its Indochina possessions and was becoming entangled, close to Egypt, with the forces of Algerian nationalism. Neither country had the resources to view calmly the prospect of escalating nationalist demands.

f) The evidence in the documents does not establish the charge; it is hardly likely to, for at the time all three countries named as conspirators spiritedly denied collusion and it was only long after the event that evidence emerged which for all reasonable purposes suggested that the charge is indeed valid. Document 1 is clearly a partisan statement on behalf of Egypt and, however colourful its charges and its language cannot be taken as in any way conclusive. In fact in this extract from the speech Nasser does not take up the charge, which he certainly believed, that his country was the victim of a conspiracy involving Israel as well. He certainly believed that his country's sovereignty, and thus inevitably his own position, was threatened by the joint action of France and Britain but, when he is speaking, the invasion which climaxed any proposed conspiracy was still weeks away.

The British Foreign Secretary is, in Document 2, far too clever to provide evidence of any planned conspiracy; his is a moral tale. The unwitting evidence of Document 3 certainly suggests a well thought out Anglo-French response to the situation caused by the 'unexpected' Israeli attack. On its own it is suggestive rather than conclusive. The second clause on withdrawals from the canal area only becomes really significant when it is known that at the time in question the Egyptian forces were still across on the Israeli side of the canal and were being required to withdraw to allow the Israeli troops to move forward. If the third clause had been enforced it is difficult to see how the Egyptians could ever have removed the foreign troops or how Nasser could have survived the humiliation of defeat.

Many years after these events first French and more reluctantly British sources have revealed prior talks with the Israelis about contingencies. Even thirty plus years after the affair many relevant British records are unavailable to historians so that we cannot be sure who precisely knew what and how long before the event. On balance of probabilities it seems very likely, certainly not from these documents but from the other, later, evidence that there was a conspiracy at some level.

USEFUL SOURCES OF INFORMATION

General reading

D Childs, *Britain since 1945: a political history*, Routledge 1993

P J Madgwick, D Steeds & L J Williams, *Britain since 1945*, Hutchinson 1982

J B Watson, *Success in British History since 1914*, John Murray 1983

Further reading

M E Chamberlain, *Decolonization: The Fall of the European Empires*, Blackwell for the Historical Association 1985

A Marwick, *British Society since 1945*, Penguin 1982

B Pimlott, *Harold Wilson*, Harper Collins 1992 : this is placed here as one example of a large number of political biographies and autobiographies which range across the period. Dipping into some of them can be very interesting but do not get carried away, for the opportunity to use them directly in examination and essay work may be quite limited.

A Sampson, *The Changing Anatomy of Britain*, Hodder & Stoughton 1982

Linked topic areas

- British society and politics 1945–1951 (see Chapter 10)
- Western Europe since 1945 (see Chapter 26)
- The Cold War (see Chapter 23 on the USSR)
- Anglo-American relations (see Chapter 24 on the USA)
- The end of European imperialism

CHAPTER 12

EUROPE: THE 1815 SETTLEMENT

GETTING STARTED

The political arrangement of Europe following the defeat of Napoleon provides the setting for the study of European political history until well into the second half of the nineteenth century. For this reason alone it is worth understanding the more important provisions. The Settlement is also a topic much favoured by examiners. With a syllabus which starts before 1815 many questions are set which require a look back into the late eighteenth century to assess how far the statesmen were motivated by a desire for restoration of that older Europe. A syllabus opening in 1815 limits the examiners in this respect so adapt your revision pattern to the syllabus. Unless you are studying pre-1815 Europe as an examination topic you will have to take care that you do not spend too long on introductory material.

The French Revolution is held to have released new political forces, notably *liberalism*, which was important in the nineteenth century: establish a working definition of 'liberalism' – constitutional government, the rule of law, civic rights and on to economic ideas like freedom of trade – look it up in a good dictionary and in a textbook index. The turmoil of the Napoleonic wars is held to have encouraged the growth of *nationalism* – the desire for people of the same national identity to be able to form a nation state – again, by the same means, be able to use this term confidently.

As immediate background to the Peace Settlement you should be aware that Napoleon's military adventures had put Europe in turmoil for over a decade, destroying old empires and creating new states and leaving a huge agenda of problems to be sorted out. The manner of his defeat, from 1812, is important for an understanding of the peace terms, particularly those affecting France.

Start by looking at a political sketch map of the state boundaries of Europe after the statesmen of Europe had done their work. It will make commentaries on this work much easier to understand.

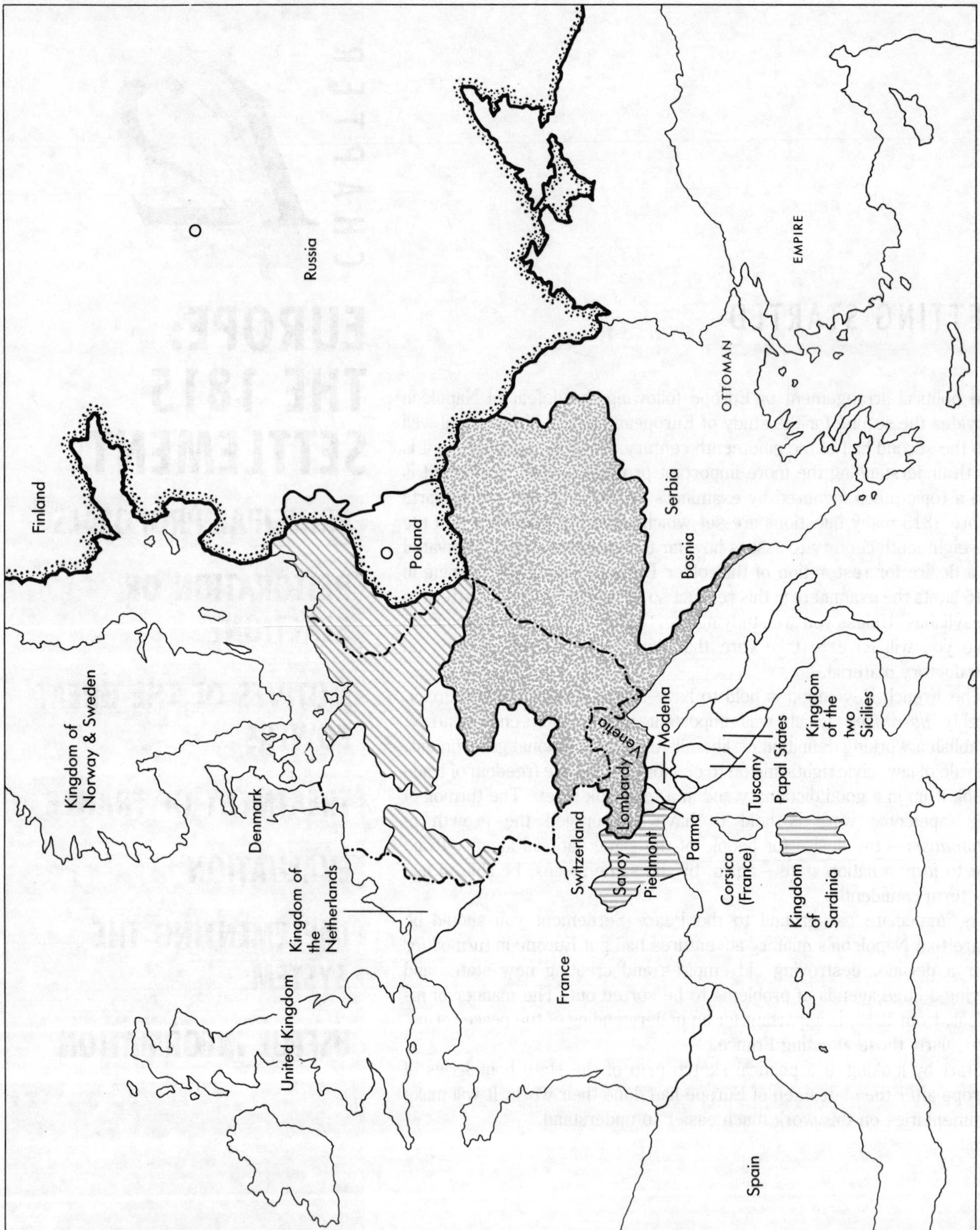

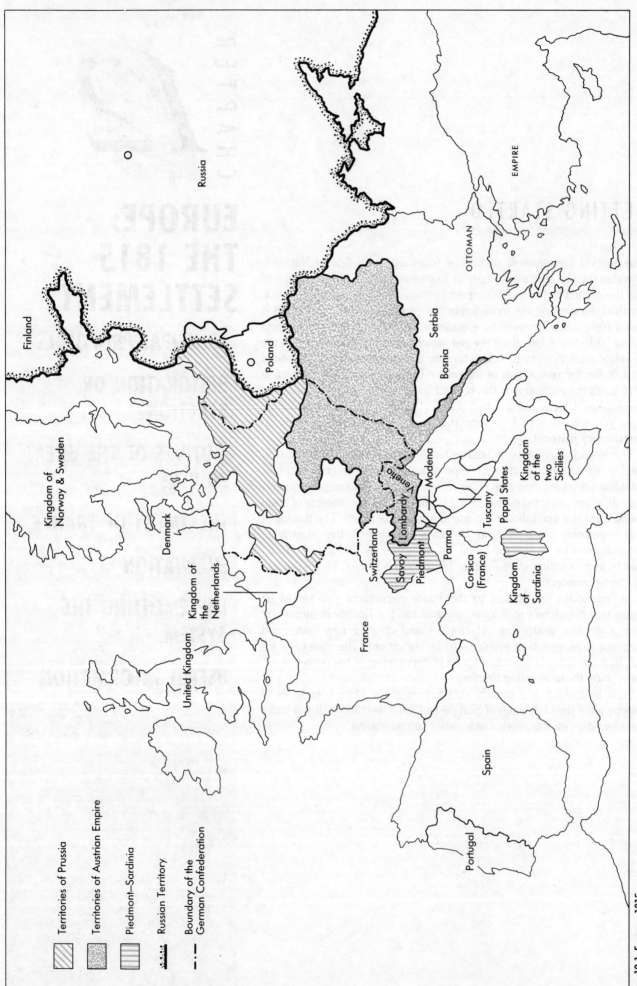

Fig. 12.1 Europe: 1815

ESSENTIAL PRINCIPLES

PRINCIPAL PROPOSALS

The major terms are indicated in the 'Useful Information' section at the end of this chapter and you will find that most textbooks also contain clear summaries of the territorial arrangements. They will make much more sense when related to a post-Settlement map of Europe and grouped into categories, for example:

- Arrangements to guard against future French aggression.
- Rewards to the Allies.
- The restoration of legitimate rulers.

"Knowing the terms is not enough."

Too many candidates can recite the terms but are less able to offer ideas and comments on them; this is of very limited value. The terms were much argued over, they reflected conflicting claims and the comparative strengths of the protagonists. You must be able to offer comments on their significance, for example:

- Prussia's territorial gains made it by far the largest and strongest state in north Germany; all its new lands were German.
- Austrian gains were more scattered and in the main non-German. This was to prove of crucial importance for the unification of Germany fifty years later.

A great European occasion

During the Settlement, a glittering social occasion lasting for months, Napoleon's return to France and his last adventure which ended at Waterloo, and the more successful intrigues of the French representative, Talleyrand, in Vienna, greatly affected the outcome of the Settlement. It was also a great European political occasion, packed with personalities and intrigue, and not a game of chess conducted on rational principles: your comments will have greater impact if you bear this in mind.

TWO ALLIANCES

As well as the territorial arrangements and those for the governing of states, it is important to be able to consider the origins, purpose and defects of the two alliance 'systems' which were set up at Vienna:

- The Holy Alliance: set up by Tsar Alexander I.
- The Quadruple Alliance.

RESTORATION OR REACTION?

"This is a common question."

A restoration of the old order? A reactionary settlement? This question is less likely to arise if the syllabus starts in 1815. In learning the principal terms of the Settlement one valuable exercise is to put them in categories of those which support this claim and those which, in your view either contradict it or suggest that other influences were also important. It is unlikely that any one simple theory or proposition will explain all the complexities of such an occasion so be prepared to indicate ways in which the explanation proposed above needs strengthening.

RESTORATION

The maintenance of French territorial integrity and the restoration of its Bourbon rulers, also the restoration of traditional rulers in Italy, seem to support the idea that essentially the arrangements were backward looking, so does the way the national aspirations of the Belgians and the Poles were ignored. The further enlargement of the great eighteenth century states, Russia, Prussia, the Austrian Empire, suggests the same. The manner in which the settlement was conducted, dominated by secret deals amongst a handful of great statesmen is certainly reminiscent of eighteenth century diplomacy.

REACTION

The suggestion that it was a reactionary settlement is clearly not entirely wrong but is this the total explanation, the only motive? Go through the terms again with this question in mind.

"Were Liberalism and Nationalism ignored?"

The accusation which arises from this is that the Settlement, in pursuing its reactionary aims ignored the aspirations of Liberalism and Nationalism but it would be wise not to over-emphasise the strength, in 1815, of these later powerful political emotions.

MOTIVES OF THE GREAT POWERS

"Be able to comment on the national ambitions."

Questions in this category are sometimes worded in terms of the statesmen of Europe so you should know the names, at least of the representatives of the major powers (see 'Useful Information' at the end of this chapter). You need in practice to be able to comment on each one in their roles as spokesmen for the interests of their states. Because so many of the arrangements were first negotiated through separate deals it is essential that the national aspirations or ambitions of the Great Powers and the role of their key spokesmen are understood. The material will not be entirely new: it is a case of re-ordering yet again under new headings – this time under the ambitions of each of the powers; do not forget that for Britain in particular some important issues were non-European.

A BALANCE OF POWER?

"Another common question."

A popular question is to propose that what the statesmen sought was a balance of power in Europe and then to invite discussion of this. The most effective response is probably to argue that, collectively, they were not prepared to see any one nation become overpowerful, but that in practice this usually meant in any one region rather than in Europe overall (Prussia in Germany or Russia in eastern Europe generally are good examples). The arrangements in regard to France and its neighbouring territories may well have been based on an exaggerated estimate of France's ability once more to disrupt the peace of Europe and so can arguably be seen as part of a plan to establish a balance of power.

"Peace and stability major aims."

You could also argue that, unsurprisingly after a generation of turmoil threatening their own status, they were anxious to establish political stability between nations and that peace was inevitably part of this. A balance of power was only one part of this wider aim with buffer states to keep France in check, or the restoration of ancient Habsburg dynasties to keep Italy stable, as equally important aspects.

TREATMENT OF FRANCE

"A starting point for later French history."

This was lenient, more so before Napoleon's Waterloo campaign than after. The reasons why this was so need to be understood but thereafter this material is most valuable to students who also wish to prepare for the regular questions which appear on French history after 1815. If you decide to do this it would be the most effective use of your time to take the topic on to 1848 at least. The 1815 arrangement for France then becomes merely a starting point for a further series of topics (see also Chapter 13).

EVALUATION

ASSESSING ITS EFFECTIVENESS

The work of the statesmen at Vienna is sometimes, but quite artificially, compared to that of their successors at Versailles in 1919. This can be to their advantage but it would be more valuable to work over the notes taken from your reading on the Settlement (with the map!) and consider how satisfactory, or at least how long-lived each of the arrangements were. Your views could then usefully be considered alongside those in the next section on implementing the settlement.

"Vienna the basis for many other examination topics."

All this of course involves a series of excursions into nineteenth century history but, equally, this could have a double value in opening up a further range of examination topics. In broad terms such a survey will indicate that many of the arrangements, notably in eastern Europe, Germany and Italy, survived into the second half of the century and that in that period there were, with the possible exception of the Crimea, no major European wars. The suppression of nationalist and liberal aspirations was the price to be paid for this, but that would not in any case have displeased the statesmen at Vienna.

CHANGES

Pre-1850

There were changes in the arrangements before 1850, Greece, Belgium and the Spanish colonies being the important examples and the crushing of uprisings in Naples, Piedmont and Spain in 1821–1823 and the failure of the Polish revolt of 1830 the best examples of the status quo being preserved. The workings of the Quadruple Alliance, through the Congress System, and the work of Metternich to bolster up the Vienna arrangements are referred to in the next section of these notes.

Post-1850

"The end of the Vienna arrangements."

After 1850 the Vienna system was increasingly dented with the Crimean War, dividing Russia from the Austrian Empire, acting as a more important catalyst of change than had the 1848 Revolutions (another topic in their own right), leading on, by 1871, to the unification of both Italy and Germany, quite contrary to the spirit of 1815. The great military victories of Prussia over the Austrian Empire (1866) and France (1870) mark a new starting point in European international arrangements and the end of Vienna. You need only the bare outline of these great events to apply them to a critique of the achievement of the statesmen at Vienna. The terms of the assessment can be your own but you must be able to buttress it with informed comments and illustration. It may well be an ideal topic for collective revision by a group of students.

IMPLEMENTING THE SYSTEM

THE CONGRESS SYSTEM

1815–1822

This was used by the continental powers to put down uprisings that might destroy the peace of Europe which in practice came to mean all uprisings. By 1821 Britain was separating itself from these polices, even before Castlereagh was replaced by Canning as Foreign Secretary. Until 1822 the Congresses had considerable success in maintaining the Vienna arrangements. The workings, the achievements and the eventual break-up of the System is a common examination topic which can also appear in British history papers as a substantial part of a question on the foreign policies of Castlereagh (to 1822) and Canning (from 1822 to 1827). It is therefore worth pointing out that, in terms of putting British interests first, the two have more in common than might appear.

"Useful background for British foreign policy."

THE GREEK REVOLT

Be ready to explain why the Greeks were able to obtain their independence: this involves both their own efforts and the actions of Britain, France and Russia. The topic is considered at greater length in Chapter 15. Be ready to explain why the issue divided the Congress powers and was largely responsible for ending their meetings. This needs linking to Britain's earlier dissatisfaction with the actions of the other powers.

THE WORK OF METTERNICH

Note: Any full assessment of this must include his work at the Vienna Settlement and as the leading figure in the Congresses.

"The most important European statesman."

Within the Austrian Empire: he was, until 1848, the key figure in maintaining the *status quo*, supporting conservative forces, blocking nationalist aspirations, maintaining the repressive bureaucracy and the absolutist political system. It can be seen as a largely negative role, protecting the ramshackle Empire from the nationalist and liberal forces which, once unleashed, would surely engulf it.

Within the German Confederation: which he had from the first sought to keep weak. The last thing he wished was for it to become an instrument for nationalist dreams and he used the conservative State authorities to ensure this. The Carlsbad Decrees of 1819 and the suppression from 1830 of the Young Germany movement are the best illustrations of the repressive policies he promoted. The key to policy was that any growth of nationalism, in the Confederation or in the Austrian Empire itself, would surely act to the detriment of the latter, consisting as it did of so many nationalities.

In Italy: Metternich performed precisely the same role, crushing the Carbonari in 1821 and repressing the Young Italy movement after 1830. Thanks largely to Metternich nationalist aspirations had made little real progress in either Germany or Italy by 1848.

In Eastern Europe: Metternich had the invaluable presence of the Russian Tsars as allies in his repressive policies, they let him down only in relation to the Greek Revolt.

REVOLTS IN 1830

Questions here usually take the form of questions on either the Belgians securing their independence or the Poles failing to do so. In both cases the actions and policies of the neighbouring Great Powers were crucial.

Revision exercise

A useful form of revision would be to rehearse the reasons, internal and external, why the Belgians succeeded and the Poles failed. For the events in France in 1830 see Chapter 13.

REVOLUTIONARY UPHEAVALS 1848–1849

It was the number of outbreaks which made 1848 so remarkable. There was no co-ordination but they were a common, often a copied, reaction to the years of repression.

In France: they led to the Second Republic (see Chapter 13).

In Italy and Germany: they came to nought but form an essential field of study if you intend to offer examination questions on the later unification of these countries.

Events in 1848

"1848: events in Austria decisive."

In terms of 1848 for its own sake it is worth making a list of the revolutions, noting the outcome in each case and then be ready to argue a general case why overall they produced so few results of permanent significance. The best overview for this exercise is probably Vienna: work out how, from the low point of the overthrow of Metternich, the Austrian Imperial authorities re-built their position throughout their lands and went on to re-assert their pre-eminence in Germany and Italy. By the end of 1849, outside France, little had changed. Could this be claimed to be a measure of the greatness of Metternich's achievement across the previous decades?

USEFUL INFORMATION

1814		Napoleon abdicated. Sent to Elba.
		Bourbon monarchy restored in France.
		First Treaty of Paris. France returned to 1792 frontiers.
1815		The Congress of Vienna
		Return of Napoleon to battle of Waterloo.
	June	Treaty of Vienna: harder terms imposed on France.
	Sept	**Holy Alliance** drawn up at instigation of the Tsar Alexander I: a brotherhood of monarchs based on Christian principles. Britain avoided joining.
	Nov	**Quadruple Alliance** of Austria, Great Britain, Prussia and Russia for defence against future French aggression and to meet periodically to discuss problems.

Leading delegates at Vienna:

Austria	Metternich
France	Talleyrand
Great Britain	Castlereagh
Prussia	Hardenberg
Russia	Tsar Alexander I

The main terms of the Treaty of Vienna

1 Preventing future French aggression by placing stronger states on its borders
- Austrian Netherlands merged with Holland
- Prussia gained Rhineland states
- Piedmont obtained Savoy and Genoa
- Creating the German Confederation of 39 states from the previous 300

2 Rewarding the Allies who had fought Napoleon
- Austria obtained Venetia and Lombardy
- Prussia obtained two-fifths of Saxony, Swedish Pomerania and other North German lands
- Russia gained control over Finland and Poland
- Britain obtained European islands: Heligoland, Ionian Islands, Malta; West Indian islands: St. Lucia, Tobago (from France), Trinidad (from Spain); Cape of Good Hope, Ceylon and Guyana (South America), from the Dutch; Indian Ocean islands of Mauritius and the Seychelles from France

3 Restoration of legitimate rulers
- Bourbon kings restored in Naples
- Habsburg rulers restored in Tuscany and Modena
- Papal States re-established

4 Further clauses
- Norway transferred from Denmark to Sweden
- International declaration against the slave trade

(*Note:* Several of the clauses under 2 and 3 above also served to meet the fear of future French aggression referred to in 1. Think which terms you may wish to use to illustrate this. The restoration of the Bourbon monarchy in France was certainly intended by the Allies to promote the same end, see Chapter 13).

1818	Congress of Aix-La-Chapelle: army of occupation withdrawn from France. France joined Quintuple Alliance.
1820	Congress of Troppau and . . .
1821	Congress of Laibach: alarmed by revolts in Italian states, Spain and Portugal, Russia, Prussia and Austria pledged to act together against revolts which threatened European peace. England disagreed; this first split in post-war unity of Allies. Beginning of Greek revolt against the Turks
1822	Congress of Verona: called because of troubles in Greece and Spain. Canning had replaced Castlereagh and denounced the interference of the continental powers. End for practical purposes of the Congress system.
1823	The Monroe Doctrine protected the ex-Spanish colonies against European re-occupation.
1827	Treaty of London between Britain, France and Russia secured Greek independence.
1830	Revolts in Paris overthrew the restored Bourbons Belgians gained independence from the Dutch Polish revolt against Russian rule failed Unrest in German Confederation and in Italy repressed
1848	Year of Revolutions in Europe but, with the exception of France, the old order was successfully restored.
1854–1856	Crimean War
1859–1861	Italian Unification (basis laid in these years)
1866	Prussian defeat of Austria
1870	Prussian defeat of France
1871	Establishment of the German Empire

EXAMINATION QUESTIONS

Q1 'Great-power politics rather than principles dominated the Vienna Settlement of 1815.' Discuss. (Oxford 1989)

Q2 Why, and with what success, did the Vienna Settlement lead to the suppression of nationalism in Europe between 1815 and 1830? (Cambridge 1989)

Q3 'Conservative but not reactionary.' How well does the peace settlement of 1814–1815 deserve this description? (Welsh 1989)

Q4 To what extent, and with what success, did the framers of the Treaty of Vienna, 1815, seek to restore the political balance existing in the late eighteenth century? (London 1990)

Q5 'The peace settlement of 1814–15 was shaped by the statesmen's anxieties about the European balance of power.' What do you understand by this statement, and with what evidence can you illustrate it? (London 1989)

Q6 'A happy union of principle and expediency.' Discuss this assessment of the Vienna Settlement. (Oxford 1986)

OUTLINE ANSWERS

Question 1

See the 'Tutor's Answer' below.

Question 2

- Argue that at Vienna nationalism was suppressed because to make concessions to it would have undermined the position of the Great Powers whose interests were dominant in the Settlement.
- Give a range of examples of how this was done (in Italy, Germany, Netherlands, Poland, Finland) and how it was Great Power interests which were the key in each case.

"Nationalist feeling in 1815 not all that potent?"

- Point out that nationalism not all that strong at the time – quote German and Italian examples.
- Success to 1830: very successful in some instances; Italian states 1821, Spain 1823, German Confederation and the Carlsbad Decrees. Largely due to the work of Metternich.
- Failures were Spanish colonies and Greece: both in a sense special cases (explain why).
- In 1830 Belgians seemed to point up a new nationalist dawn but Poles indicated power of the Great States to delay this was still far from exhausted.

Question 3

Note: Definition of terms is all-important.

Conservative: desiring to preserve the existing state of affairs.

Reactionary: desiring to revert to an earlier state of affairs, to reverse current tendencies.

- Difficult to apply fine distinctions after all the changes of the French Revolutionary and Napoleonic years.

"A reactionary settlement . . ."

- Reaction: there are elements of reaction in the Settlement in the efforts (give examples) to restore European States to their legitimate rulers and also in the aim of replacing the control of power in Europe to the traditional Great Powers (again give examples). Settlement certainly made no concessions to new forces of liberalism and nationalism. Secret diplomacy and separate deals amongst the leading 'Powers' also a return to the traditional diplomatic methods of the eighteenth century.

". . . or merely a conservative one?"

- Conservation: but Settlement was also conservative in the sense of keeping the peace which had at last been established and many of the terms can be seen fairly in this light (give examples) rather than as reaction for its own sake. Perhaps also conservative in the sense of keeping a 'balance of power' in Europe to avoid further turmoil.

Conclusion: arguably both conservative and reactionary, and difficult to separate the two because the main point is that the Settlement was dominated by the old 'Powers' of the eighteenth century who placed their interests at the top of the agenda.

Question 4

"This question is often asked."

Introduction: Identify the late eighteenth century political balance; briefly expand by reference to the four great continental powers after 1763 and before 1789. Balance in eastern Europe and in Central Europe, France checked in the west by English antagonism.

Extent of restoration: quite considerable:

- Prussia gains, for example: Saxony to redress Russian territorial move west.
- Stand of Russia and Austria in Balkans by preserving Ottoman position.
- Stress west European balance by buffer states around France.
- Political balance within nations by returning and bolstering traditional rulers, in Italy for instance.
- Main change in Germanic Confederation; did not affect European balance but yet brought stability to central Europe.

Success: quite considerable; internally until 1848 revolutions, quote work of Metternich, in great power balance until decades after Crimean War with unification of Italy and Germany and 1866 and 1870 wars (explain significance of).

Question 5

See the 'Student's Answer' below.

Question 6

"A question of motives – principles or expedients."

- Agree both principle and expediency present.
- Discuss and illustrate operation of principles:
  - promoting balance of power
  - restoring the eighteenth century international arrangements
  - securing stability and peace in Europe.
- Mention anti-slave trade arrangments.
- Expedients; conveniently ignoring the, admittedly muted, demands of liberalism and nationalism, sometimes to achieve principles above.
- Rewarding the victors, give examples.
- Offer restoration of Bourbons to France as largely expediency with wishes of people ignored, and yet this too supported principles above.
- Was it happy? For national aspirations no, give most striking examples of troubles through to 1848.
- It did bring, however, a long period without major wars through achieving a political balance which lasted for at least half a century. A happier Europe than in the years of revolutionary and Napoleonic turmoil.

Note: The 'Tutor's Answer' that follows deals with a similar question.

A TUTOR'S ANSWER TO QUESTION 1

It is hardly surprising that the Settlement was dominated by the Great Powers for it was they who, at great cost, had defeated Napoleon and only they who had the strength to bring the turmoil that he had created to an end. So the most delicate negotiations and the key decisions took place, outside the formal sessions of the Conference, between the statesmen representing the victorious powers, Austria, Britain, Prussia and Russia. The scheming of Talleyrand won France a place in the inner discussions but the representatives of the lesser nations were kept away from the decision-making to amuse themselves at Vienna's countless glittering social occasions. The Settlement is often studied through a survey of Great Power representatives, motives, tactics and rewards. At the end of this essay it will be argued that this situation does not necessarily mean that principles had no part to play in shaping the settlement of Europe. A lot may depend on how one defines a principle.

The territorial arrangements arrived at offer a clear indication of the significant part played by Great Power politics. The Tsar Alexander pursued the traditional Russian policy of expansion westwards in order to provide deeper defences for the heart of his kingdom, securing both Finland and Poland for his pains. Hardenberg of Prussia had great ambitions to obtain all of Saxony, if only to compensate for Russia's lurch to the west. Prussian claims provoked the most serious crisis of the Settlement and, by allowing Talleyrand to play on Austrian fears of Prussian expansion, one which enabled France to join the war's victors at the settlement table. Prussia had to compromise but only after compensation had been gained at the expense of Sweden and several small German states. Austrian gains in Italy, Lombardy and Venetia, intended to compensate for giving up the troubled Netherlands, smack of the same large power aggrandisement.

"The Great Powers wanted to be compensated."

What the Great Powers wanted in the way of territory they appeared to get unless they ran up against the counter interests of one of their peers and compromise and compensation were, after a generation of war, inevitable. British territorial gains though outside Europe, in Ceylon and South Africa principally, have a similar ring of ensuring the reward of the powers for their efforts.

Outside the immediate territorial gains of the Great Powers there is more room for debate on what constituted the dominating themes of the Settlement. The aggregation of hundreds of small German states into the 39 of the Germanic Confederation was arguably a commendable attempt to provide political stability in Central Europe. More cynically it was convenient for the Great Powers of Prussia and Austria because it left the region open to either of them to dominate in the future without provoking an immediate crisis between them as the Saxon issue had done.

"They also wanted a stable Europe."

Contrasting arguments can also be developed in regard to the arrangements for Italy, where it has been suggested above that Austrian territorial gains were a sop to its great power ambitions. They could however be defended as providing both political stability and defence against future French attacks for the region. The restoration of Habsburg and Bourbon rulers to the lesser Italian states could be seen in the same light.

Play has been made of the notion, for it is scarcely a principle, that one intention of the Allies was to create a buffer-zone around France in order to prevent aggression by it in future. Certainly one of the aims of the Powers at Vienna, and this could well be seen as a principle, was to restore stability and peace to Europe. The 'buffer states', the combined Netherlands, Austrian Italy, the Prussian Rhineland were a part of this strategy which can be seen as a matter of principle but which was also in the interests of the European Powers.

Similar arguments can be made relevant to other arrangements arrived at during the Settlement. The Quadruple Alliance was self-consciously a great power arrangement whereby *they* would meet to settle future disputes at an early stage, no doubt largely to maintain a *status quo* that was very much in their own interest. And yet the idea of Great Powers meeting to avert conflict has a principled, modern ring to it. The same could be said for the Tsar's Holy Alliance, only the principles were more vague and the self-interest more difficult to conceal. Britain's refusal to join was certainly more a matter of convenience than of principle. Though some may have liked to have claimed the contrary.

"The Alliance systems – self-interest and principle at work?"

In all this it is difficult to argue that the Balance of Power in Europe was ever raised as a matter of principle or ever systematically pursued. No-one wanted overpowerful neighbours but this was self-interest; not principle.

The best example of principles not being totally forgotten rests upon Britain's persistent campaign to have the slave-trade declared illegal by the participants at the Settlement. That, and the later efforts at naval enforcement, are the other side of the coin to Britain's substantial colonial gains.

In 1815 the great political ideas, or principles, for the future were those born in the previous revolutions and wars – that is liberalism and nationalism. At Vienna these were conveniently forgotten, ignored or suppressed. The suggestion that suppression was cynically and deliberately carried out on a large scale by the statesmen of the Great Powers gives to these new political forces an identity and a strength which in 1815 they did not possess. The statesmen, with Metternich of Austria pre-eminent amongst them, it can be argued, sought the restoration of older principles through the restoration of legitimate rulers to their possession and to protection of the interests of their subjects.

Inevitably then, the Great Powers dominated the Settlement and used it to reward themselves for their efforts against Napoleon. This does not mean that their settlement was unprincipled, in the sense of being totally cynical, or that it was without any basis in principle even if that was only the search for stability, by the attempted restoration of the political arrangements which had characterised the eighteenth century.

A STUDENT'S ANSWER TO QUESTION 5

"A good attempt at a definition."

A balance of power between countries occurs when no one power is able to do what it wants because no other power, alone or in alliance with other countries, is able to resist its demands. In Europe from 1805 to 1812 this balance had broken down and the French under Napoleon were so strong that it was impossible for the other countries, Britain, Austria, Prussia and Russia to stand up to its military might. This went on until 1812 when the disastrous attack on Moscow destroyed French military supremacy. After the defeat of Napoleon the victorious Allies were determined that this upsetting of the balance, and so the peace, of Europe must not happen again. They were mainly concerned that it would be the French who would destroy the balance and this feeling was strengthened by Napoleon's 100 Days Campaign. It now looked as though the French could not be trusted. It is also true that the statesmen of the different Allies did not totally trust each other and so, in the Settlement they were anxious to make sure that no one country among the Allies would gain too much and so become too powerful. Certainly none of the countries wanted a balance of power which threatened them.

"The statesmen were fearful of France."

To prevent France from becoming a threat the Allies planted buffer states around its borders, Belgium was joined to Holland, Venice and Lombardy were given to Austria, Prussia got lands near the Rhine and all the German states were joined into the German Confederation with only 39 members instead of 300. An occupying army was put into France and the country was required to pay money to the Allies to compensate for all their losses. In the end this was all lifted and the army was withdrawn. The restoring of the Bourbon monarchy to France was another way in which it was hoped that the French would forget Napoleon and settle down peacefully. The old rulers were also restored in Italy in order to bring stability back to that area.

"They also quarrelled over Central Europe."

Between the Allies there were also suspicions about the balance of power. The chief problem was the ambition of Russia which had done so much to defeat the French and which had by far the largest army of the Allies. She got Poland which brought her well into Central Europe and which alarmed Austria and Prussia. The Prussians were strengthened by being given a lot of Saxony in the north of Germany, this compensated her for losing Polish lands to Russia. It worried the Austrians who now feared Prussia becoming too powerful in Germany and the Austrians worked to protect the other German states from Prussian takeover.

Britain was less worried about events on the continent but looked for rewards, for all her fighting against Napoleon, outside Europe. With the World's largest navy to defend her she did not have to worry as much as the other powers about a balance of power for protection.

"The territorial changes which show this need to be indicated."

"The essay lacks substance."

So it is true that the countries of Europe wanted to restore a balance of power. Of course they all wanted the balance to be tilted in their favour. It was the Russians who came nearest to this with their gains in Eastern Europe. The Prussians did quite well but the Austrians held them in check for the moment. After being defeated France had to accept what was imposed on her.

Examiner comments

It is brief but effective. The balance of power is well defined and this lifts the rest of the essay. Few candidates would see the need for an early definition and be able to give it so directly. The essay is immediately marked out as likely to be above average. The big disappointment is that, although the statesmen are directly referred to in the question, none of them is mentioned. An informed candidate would have commented on the statesmen and what each sought (i.e. their 'anxieties') in the settlement. In fact they may well not have been anxious about the balance of power but other matters: this possibility is ignored and the question is unchallenged.

The illustrations of the proposition in the question would have been much sharper if they had been related to the individual statesmen but they are sensible and relevant enough to show that the candidate is quite informed about the terms and the purpose of the Settlement. The answer is quite brief, it needs more detail to illustrate how the balance was struck but it is direct from the start. Probably a C grade answer?

USEFUL SOURCES OF INFORMATION

General reading

A Ramm, *Europe in the Nineteenth Century 1789–1905*, Longman 1984

J B Watson, *Success in European History 1815–1941*, John Murray 1981

A Wood, *Europe 1815–1960*, Longman 1984

Further reading

J Lowe, *The Concert of Europe: International Relations 1814–70*, Hodder & Stoughton 1990

L C B Seaman, *From Vienna to Versailles*, Methuen 1972

D Thomson, *Europe since Napoleon*, Penguin 1977

Linked topic areas

- The defeat of Napoleon
- British foreign policy under Castlereagh, Canning and Palmerston
- The Congress System
- Greek independence and the beginnings of the Eastern Question (see Chapter 15)
- France 1815–1848 (see Chapter 13)
- The 1848 Revolutions

CHAPTER 13

FRENCH HISTORY 1815–1870

- RESTORATION OF THE BOURBONS
- CHARLES X
- LOUIS PHILIPPE
- THE 1848 REVOLUTION
- THE SECOND REPUBLIC 1848–1852
- NAPOLEON III
- KEY TURNING POINT
- GENERAL THEMES
- USEFUL INFORMATION

GETTING STARTED

Any study of French history in the nineteenth century needs to take account of the political and social consequences of the French Revolution and of the Napoleonic period which followed. The events from 1789 to 1815 left a permanent mark on French life. In assessing the political fortunes of individuals and regimes, as well as in accounting for the course of events, you must be able to set your comments in the framework of the experiences and memories of the revolutionary years.

The Revolution benefited many in its redistribution of land and its destruction of social privilege. It created a Left in French politics, from the professions and the artisans in the towns which was to remain deeply suspicious of any sign of reaction and was itself committed to promoting political freedom and advancing democratic politics. Those who thought in this way were to remain profoundly distrustful of both monarchs and of those who tried to set up right-wing governments in the Napoleonic tradition.

Reaction to the Revolution produced a desire for stability which was to prove an important political ingredient whenever the revolutionary tradition appeared to threaten the country's social and economic security. Sometimes it led to a resurgence of monarchical support, at other times the heirs of Napoleon benefited. Memories of the glory and the ultimate tragedy of the Napoleonic period were a crosscurrent in these manoeuvres of the political Right, sometimes frightening and sometimes exciting Frenchmen into quite different views of political adventurers in the Napoleonic tradition.

It was a society marked by deep political divisions, arising from the historical traditions of those epic years, and it would need considerable skill, great strength and determination and a slice of luck to rule it effectively in critical times. Read enough about the Revolution and about Napoleon to fit your views about them into your analysis of later episodes when this appears relevant, as it frequently will.

ESSENTIAL PRINCIPLES

RESTORATION OF THE BOURBONS

"An important examination topic."

This important examination topic is the subject of the 'Tutor's Answer' at the end of this chapter.

It is essential to be able to explain the key role of the Allies who had defeated Napoleon in bringing about the restoration of the Bourbon Monarchy. Their motives in this formed part of their approach to the re-settlement of Europe generally (see Chapter 12). Understand the changes in the treatment of France brought about by Napoleon's escape from Elba and the turmoil caused by the Hundred Days Campaign.

REIGN OF LOUIS XVIII

"The general situation in Europe was the key."

The restored Louis XVIII had to be acceptable to the politically important classes in France, a tiny minority of the total population but one which had often benefited from the political changes of the previous decades. To this end he was prepared to accept the terms of the Charter (see 'Useful Information' later in this chapter) drawn up by leading Napoleonic figures and his own advisers as the basis of constitutional rule.

Exam questions

Be aware of the main terms of the Charter so that you are able to comment on the extent to which Louis and then Charles X observed it as the basis for their regimes. You then need to be able to offer an assessment of how effectively Louis XVIII ruled France which comes down to his success in re-establishing the position of the Bourbons who had owed their return to the throne entirely to the action of France's recently implacable enemies. Examination candidates are frequently asked to compare and contrast Louis XVIII with Charles X in these matters. You need enough knowledge of both reigns to give substance to your ideas. Weaker answers in this area are often marked by lack of knowledge.

CHARLES X

AND THE BOURBON MONARCHY

"Set the reaction against the revolutionary tradition."

You should also be ready to explain how Charles's own weakness in 1830 contributed to the end of the restored Bourbon monarchy. Be ready to do more than list Charles's mistakes; set them in the context of the political life of post-Revolutionary France. Show how, by antagonising the classes who had benefited from the changes after 1789, Charles lost the support of the very groups for whom Louis XVIII had committed himself to the Charter as the basis for the Bourbon Restoration.

Revision exercise

The 'Tutor's Answer' on page 144 is again relevant here. In revision prepare a list of Charles's mistakes which were based on a wish to return to the ways of the Ancien Regime of the eighteenth century and symbolically included the traditional religious Coronation and restoring the old authority of the Catholic Church. Compensating the emigré nobles for lost lands and interfering with interest rates antagonised the middle class on whom the restored Bourbons had to rely. When opposition grew his policies became more overtly reactionary with Prince Polignac's actions and the Ordinances of St Cloud of 1830 both providing the basis of a useful commentary.

LOUIS PHILIPPE

ASSESSING HIS REIGN

You need to be able to explain what happened in 1830 and why. This involves why Charles X's regime came to an end. The workers in Paris wanted a republic to be established but the bourgeoisie remembered the extremism of the First Republic in the 1790s and wanted a guarantee of stability and respect for property. Their manipulation brought Louis Philippe, Duke of Orleans to the throne and he was astute enough to make concessions to republican traditions to win the consent of the Paris workers, being sworn in as 'King of the French by the grace of God and the will of the people' and accepting the Tricolour.

Exam questions

"Orleanist weaknesses."

Most examination questions on the period 1830 to 1848 relate to the weaknesses of the Orleans monarchy, as it is usually termed, in both domestic and foreign policy, leading on in turn to why it came to an end in 1848. As with Charles X some candidates assume that a list of mistakes or weaknesses is an explanation of why there was a successful revolution in 1848. Rather than make too many notes on Louis Philippe's achievements and failures a better focus could well be to prepare, in note form, an explanation of events in France in 1848. This needs to take account of the important economic and social changes that were taking place during his reign which did much to ensure that the events of 1848 had more radical consequences than the muddled compromise of 1830. Be ready to draw attention to the growing industrialisation, the emerging urban proletariat, and the spread of the socialist ideas of Louis Blanc.

THE 1848 REVOLUTION

CAUSES AND CONSEQUENCES

"Important mid-century economic and social changes."

Place any explanation of what happened in France in 1848 in the context of the revolutionary tradition in France, looking back to the first French Revolution. Then bring in the profound economic changes which were taking place in the middle years of the century and also the consequent social problems to which there was so little response from Louis Philippe's governments. The failures of the July Monarchy can then fit into this context. Do not give the impression that all of Louis Philippe's mistakes were of equal importance in bringing about the Revolution. Economic problems at home, and the *laissez-faire* social policies of the government which largely ignored the need for social reforms, were much more important than the celebrated claim that France was bored with Louis Philippe's foreign policy, in bringing him down.

Exam questions

Any question on this topic will almost certainly require you to assess the relative importance of the causes of the Revolution. You should not just offer a list of causes but also be able to suggest an order of significance. Be ready with a plan of how you would approach such a question but do not prepare an answer to a specific question in advance for then some twist in the wording of the question may disconcert you. It is the general approach which you need to be prepared for and the 'Outline Answers' to Questions 2 and 3 will give you a start.

THE SECOND REPUBLIC 1848–1852

"The beginnings of socialism."

The 1848 Revolution and the Second Republic which emerged from it were both the work of the Parisians. There was an outburst of socialist fervour which led to the setting up of National Workshops which soon became nothing more than expensive relief agencies. These and the savage crushing of a working-class revolt by the army under General Cavaignac with the tacit support of the bourgeoisie are important episodes to use in explaining why the Republic was so short lived.

LOUIS NAPOLEON

"Louis Napoleon proved a skilful politician."

The other ingredient in its downfall which needs evaluation was the surprising achievement of the unlikely Louis Napoleon, nephew of the Emperor, in skilfully exploiting an image of the Napoleonic legend as peaceful and caring, to win the election for the Presidency of the Republic. From this base he played the populist card as the protector of the people's political rights in the face of republican efforts to reduce the franchise. This enabled him, in 1851 to extend his period as President. Skilful propaganda promoting social reforms and exploiting the unpopularity of the Assembly politicians paved the way to his announcement of the formation of the Second Empire soon to be approved in a plebiscite by 8 million votes to a quarter of a million. The new Emperor Napoleon III had out-manoeuvred those republican politicans who had thought to manipulate him to their own ends. Both the circumstances of the time, including an improving economy, and the skill and tactics of Louis Napoleon must be given due weight in the explanation of the Republic's downfall. Again any explanation should be set in the contradictory desires for liberty and stability released in the events of the 1789-1815 period. See also the 'Student's Answer' to Question 4.

NAPOLEON III

"An authoritarian regime . . ."

DOMESTIC POLICY

The Second Empire of Napoleon III (third because in Napoleonic genealogy the first Emperor's only son, who had died in 1832, was counted as Napoleon II) had no legal basis and, in its first years, owed all to the personal rule of the Emperor. It was a totally authoritarian state with a powerless and subservient parliament and strict censorship of the press. Those who wanted stability nevertheless gave it tacit support. Few gave it their active loyalty and in particular the great towns remained hostile. In the 1857 elections to the Assembly however the opponents of the regime did very badly. In the 1850s the Empire seemed to be working effectively, albeit on the basis of the Emperor's personal power. You need to be able to analyse why at that time Napoleon seemed secure.

THE LIBERAL EMPIRE

"... which became more liberal."

From 1860 Napoleon sought to make his Empire more liberal and to give his power a constitutional basis. In 1859 political exiles were allowed to return home, censorship of the press was relaxed, and in 1860 the Senate and the Assembly were given greater freedom of debate. Further relaxation followed in 1867 with his ministers required to answer questions in the Assembly. The more far-reaching reforms of 1869 seemed to give power to the Assembly and to place Napoleon above politics. The chances of the reforms creating a durable parliamentary monarchy in France remained untested for the Empire was swept away in 1870 by defeat in war. If you are asked to evaluate the regime's achievements within France it is worth remembering that in a plebiscite early in 1870 the French people overwhelmingly accepted the new 'Liberal Empire'.

FOREIGN POLICY

With no legitimate basis for his regime and burdened by the legend of Napoleonic glory the foreign policy of the Third Empire grew increasingly active, not to say reckless (see the 'Useful Information' at the end of this chapter). Napoleon's personal responsibility in this cannot be evaded. His message until 1852 had been that the Imperial tradition was a peaceful one. After 1852 he did little to make that reality. The Crimean War, or its outcome, presented in France as a great victory for French arms, was popular and probably helped the Imperial fortunes in the 1857 parliamentary elections. Thereafter little went right.

Failures

"Too many foreign adventures . . ."

You need to be able to explain how the Italian policy (Chapter 16 will give you the background) lost Napoleon Catholic support in France and yet still failed to gain him liberal support there. The Free Trade arrangements of 1860 with England, for which the Emperor was personally responsible, lost him the support of the manufacturers. The shabby and humiliating outcome of the Mexican adventure was a damaging blow to Napoleon's prestige. Most serious however was the inactivity, until too late, in the face of growing Prussian power. The balance of power in Europe was tilting irretrievably against France and the Emperor and his advisers failed to realise this. This was to be the most serious failure in foreign policy.

"... and a fatal miscalculation."

Revision exercise

You should be ready to analyse and judge the regime's foreign policy and be able to discuss how far the introduction of the 'Liberal Empire' was a bid to compensate, in terms of support for the regime, for the growing list of foreign policy failures.

KEY TURNING POINT

"1870: a decisive shift in the European balance of power."

THE DISASTER OF 1870–1871

This was a much larger issue than just the defeat, surrender and abdication of Napoleon III. It marked the crucial turning point in international relations from 1815 to 1914 and is, of course a key episode in the unification of Germany, from which standpoint it is usually offered in examination questions (see Chapter 17). The defeat was so total that it marked the abrupt end of the Empire. In French history therefore the war and its outcome are usually studied in the context of the Paris Commune and the establishment of the Third Republic, to both of which it gave rise (see Chapter 18). Napoleon III simply vanished from the scene and the French had to make a new start.

GENERAL THEMES

1815–1870

Exam questions

These will constitute only a minority of questions on French history in the period despite the fact that the examination boards are regularly urged to set questions in increasing numbers on philosophical, cultural and scientific subjects. Few candidates attempt them for the hit or miss factor of their turning up is more than a little disconcerting. They are often the home of those desperate to find a final question!

Possible themes

French history across the nineteenth century does however open up a number of general themes, both within a purely French and within a general European context. These include:

- Economic change and growth; industry and railways.
- The development of socialism as a political force. In the French context this could link to the growth of Trade Unions and Syndicalism under the Third Republic through to 1914.
- The role of the Catholic Church and anti-clerical trends in society.
- Cultural questions: the obvious one in France being related to the visual arts and particularly the Impressionist movement.

"You need to have a real interest in 'cultural' topics to do them well."

To study any of these topics you need to take a view right across the period from 1815 to 1914 and, usually in an international context. With a real interest in any of these fields you may well do brilliantly; providing that a question appears on the right topic! It is not worth just working up material for such a question on the chance of this happening. A more effective examination tactic is to stick to mainstream political, social and economic questions, always using the pattern of past papers as your guide.

USEFUL INFORMATION

1814 Allies restored the Bourbon monarchy to France.
Louis XVIII agreed to rule by the terms of **the Charter** in order to secure support in France for his return.

The Charter

Terms included:
- Freedom from arbitrary arrest.
- Fair trials.
- Equality before the law.
- Religious toleration.
- Security of property (including all bought since 1789).
- Royal ministers to be answerable to an Assembly.
- High property qualificiation for voting for the Assembly (estimated that only 1 in 300 could vote).

1815 Napoleon's Hundred Days to the battle of Waterloo
Louis XVIII returned again to Paris

1815–1824 Reign of Louis XVIII

1815 Election to the Assembly, under the very narrow property based franchise of the Charter, produced an Ultra (right-wing) majority.
Right wing purge of opponents (The White Terror). Louis managed to check the excesses.

1816–1820 Under more moderate governments constitutional rule appeared to be working more effectively. Leading minister **Decazes**.

1820	Murder of Louis' nephew the Duc de Berri forced the king to appoint a more right-wing government under Richelieu.
1820–1824	Revival of Ultra power in last years of Louis XVIII's reign.
1824–1830	**Reign of Charles X**
1824	Charles X's traditional religious coronation
	Pursuit of reactionary religious and land policies by Chief Minister **Villèle**.
1828	Charles appointed more moderate **Martignac** as Chief Minister
1829	Charles reversed policy again and appointed arch-reactionary **Prince Polignac** to be his Chief Minister.
1830	Assembly dismissed, after elections Charles suspended constitution.
	Reactionary Ordinances of St Cloud issued.
	Rising of Paris working classes. Flight of Charles.
	Bourgeois leaders installed Louis Philippe as King of the French so preventing setting up of a republic.
1830–1848	**Reign of Louis Philippe** (the Orleans Monarchy)
1832	Bourbon rebellion in La Vendée easily put down.
1834	Republican risings in Lyons and Paris fiercely put down and repressive policies applied.
1836 & 1840	Attempts by **Louis Napoleon** to overturn constitution easily dealt with.
1840s	With developing industrialisation there was a growth in socialist ideas. (1839 **Louis Blanc** wrote L'Organisation du Travail.)
1840s	Foreign policy of Louis Philippe increasingly unpopular.
1846	Harvest failed
1847	Collapse of the Paris Stock Exchange following a period of growing financial corruption and speculation.
	Beginning of middle-class Reform Banquets
1848	Banning of a Reform Banquet provoked street rioting and led to Louis Philippe's abdication.
1848–1852	**The Second Republic**
	Louis Napoleon elected President for four years: Louis Napoleon, 5.5 million votes; General Cavaignac, 1.5 million; Ledru-Rollin (a radical), 370,000; Lamartine, hero of 1848, 17,000.
1851	Coup: new Constitution extended Presidential term to ten years: approved by 7,439,000 to 640,000 in a plebiscite.
1852	Plebiscite approved transformation of the Republic into the Second Empire by 7,824,000 votes to 640,000.
1852–1870	**The Second Empire** (Napoleon III)
1854–1856	Crimean War seen in France as a great victory.
1857	Elections suggested Napoleon's rule was popular.
1858	Plombières pact with Cavour
1859	Peace of Villafranca
	From this point Napoleon's Italian policy caused increasing dissension amongst both Catholics and Liberals in France.
	Amnesty for political exiles.
1860	Free Trade treaty with Britain unpopular with manufacturers.
	First liberalisation of the Constitution introduced.
1861–1867	Mexican adventure discredited the Napoleonic legend of winning glory for France in the international arena.
1869–1870	New Liberal Empire with wide powers to the elected Assembly.
1870	Plebiscite on new liberal reforms approved them by 7,358,000 to 1,571,000 but with the great towns voting against.
	France declared war on Prussia
	Capture of Napoleon at Sedan
	Proclamation of the Third Republic

EXAMINATION QUESTIONS

Q1 Why was the Bourbon monarchy successfully restored in France in 1815? Explain how the basis of this success was destroyed by 1830. (London 1989)

Q2 Why did it prove so difficult to achieve long-lasting political stability in France between 1815 and 1852? (Northern Ireland 1988)

Q3 'It was not what he did but all that he failed to do that brought about his fall.' Discuss this verdict on Louis Philippe. (London 1990)

Q4 Why were the hopes of revolutionaries in France in 1848 not fulfilled and why was Napoleon III able to establish an autocratic regime by 1852? (Cambridge 1989)

Q5 Why was the Second French Empire a more enduring regime than the Second Republic? (Welsh 1989)

Q6 By what means, and how effectively, did Napoleon III maintain and strengthen his power in France in the years 1852–1870? (London 1989)

OUTLINE ANSWERS

Question 1

See the 'Tutor's Answer' on page 144.

Question 2

Stability: difficult to achieve because the events of the French Revolution and the Napoleonic periods had divided the French nation into supporters of deeply divided political traditions. If one side seemed to be asserting itself this usually produced a reaction.

"Charles X and the revolutionary tradition."

Theme of essay: to illustrate and comment on this, concentrating on why Charles X was replaced because he was an extreme Royalist who would not accommodate the Revolutionary legacy and opposite example of how the extremism of the Republicans drove conservative Frenchmen into the arms of Napoleon III.

The other source of instability arose from the development of industry and the emergence of an urban proletariat as a revolutionary force for instability in the 1840s, especially in 1848 – explain this.

Question 3

Introduction: agree that there is much truth in the proposition if one sees Louis Philippe as entirely responsible for the end of the July Monarchy.

Foreign policy: he had an active foreign policy which was unpopular. Indicate why his policy re Belgium, Mehemet Ali and subservience to Britain were so unpopular. However this did not lose him the throne.

Repression of potential opposition: give examples; censorship, banning of Reform Banquet; this last provided the spark which led to the end of his monarchy but no more than that.

"The causes of Louis Philippe's fall."

Failures: the problems he failed to address were those that proved fatal, for example

- He never put himself at the head of a royalist party (comment on his uninspiring personality and the contempt for him).
- He failed to make enough political concessions to the middle classes to win even their tolerance of his regime.
- He failed to offer any social reforms in time of economic change and emergence of socialism.
- He failed in the end even to fight to retain control.

"Not just his fault – review the general situation."

Conclusion: question implies it was all his fault, one way or the other, and this not true. France deeply divided politically, Orleans monarchy always a lukewarm compromise, (illustrate this by reference to opposing groups), meant there would be few to help if things went wrong. Bad harvests and economic recession of late 1840s were what went wrong and were scarcely his fault.

Question 4

See the 'Student's Answer' on page 146.

Question 5

Introduction: Thrust of answer seems to be on Second Empire but reference to Second Republic requires some explanation of why it was so short-lived (a condensed version of the ideas offered by the student answer to Question 4 below provides all the argument needed for this part of Question 5).

"Why the Second Empire survived."

Argument: then why was the Second Empire more enduring. Argue that it *survived* for so long because it gave the French stability and an illusion of international glory (Crimean War) and so was very popular. Even when glory faded and opposition grew for an autocratic regime Empire proved very responsive to the people's wishes – liberal reforms of 1860 and 1869. *Enduring* because it remained popular, quote 1869 plebiscite to illustrate this.

Conclusion: it can be argued that Napoleon blinded the French to reality to achieve this popularity but at least he linked his regime with the wishes for stability and national pride of the mass of the ordinary citizens in a way which the Second Republic totally failed to do. That is why his regime proved more enduring.

Question 6

Means: explain the means first – be careful not to go on too long.

- The 1852 constitution which he brought in gave him unlimited power (explain terms) and the basis for first years.
- Most interesting constitutional attempts were in fact not to strengthen but perhaps an effort to lengthen his power. Explain:
  - the liberalisation of 1859–60
  - the liberal Empire of 1869–70.
- Economic and social reforming policies (give examples) also aimed to bring popular support.
- Sought to bolster his position at home by his foreign policy particularly in the Crimean War, Italy and Mexico.

How effectively: take each of the above in turn and comment.

- All constitutional changes approved by huge plebiscite majorities (give some details) so appear to have been effective right to the end.
- What his powers would have become under 1869–70 arrangements we will never know, presumably less but, he no doubt intended, more secure.
- Economic and social reforms meant that he avoided an 1848 type uprising though 1860 Free Trade agreement with Britain lost him middle-class support to a dangerous extent.
- Foreign policy:
  - Crimean War helped his support in 1857 election to Assembly
  - Italian policy annoyed Catholics without pleasing Liberals (explain how)
  - Mexican adventure led to disastrous loss of prestige
  - Empire collapsed because of his failure to perceive and to deal effectively with the rise of Prussia – in this respect not at all effective.

A TUTOR'S ANSWER TO QUESTION 1

The first prerequisite for the restoration of the Bourbon monarchy was the total defeat of Napoleon by the Allies and their subsequent willingness to see the traditional rulers of France replace the warring Emperor. The success of the restoration then depended on the actions of Louis XVIII in the years immediately after his accession to the throne, through to 1820 approximately. The basis of this success was being undermined before Louis' death in 1824 but the central focus of the second half of this question must be on the short reign of his successor Charles X and especially on the years 1829 to 1830.

"The Allies put Louis XVIII there."

Louis XVIII was put on the throne of France because, after a period of turmoil and war which had had its roots in French instability and then in French aggression and which had lasted for twenty-five years, it seemed to those Powers who had eventually and at great cost triumphed over France, that the cause of future European peace and stability would be best served by restoring France's Bourbon monarchy. This was in turn part of a wider desire amongst some of the Allies to see a general restoration of the stable European order of pre-Revolutionary Europe. Napoleon's last adventure from Elba to Waterloo strengthened this resolve for stability and, fortunately for Louis, this was still seen as best served by a Bourbon restoration. The terms now were much more onerous and the imposition of an army of occupation until a war indemnity was paid made this a sharp reality. It made acceptance of the restoration by the French nation more problematic. The survival of the restored regime would depend on how successful it was in learning to live with and to obtain at least the toleration of the new forces in French life which had been unleashed by the Revolutionary and Napoleonic experiences.

Louis had, in 1814, agreed to rule by the terms of the Charter drawn up by his representatives and those of the Napoleonic establishment. Its liberal appearance was helpful if at times misleading but religious and personal freedom and equality before the law, freedom of opinion and security of property from confiscation were all reassuring to those who had benefited from the last 25 years of change. The parliament that was set up had little freedom of action and was elected on a very narrow franchise based on property qualifications. The Charter however ensured the acquiescence of the middle ranks of French society who had a great wish for stability but much to lose in any full scale reaction to restore the Ancien Regime.

Louis was also assisted by the exhaustion and the apathy brought on by the appalling cost, in lives and taxes, of Napoleon's adventures. This gave him time to establish his regime. His mistakes were trivial, flags and the like, but his dangers great. The Assembly elected in 1815 was dominated by the Ultras who now organised the 'White Terror' of revenge against known supporters of previous regimes. At this point Louis could well, with Ultra support, have carried out a coup to restore the power and trappings of the Ancien Regime. To his great credit he turned his back on this temptation and, by supporting the moderate ministry of Decazes from 1816 to 1820, probably played the key role in the successful restoration of the Bourbons as a regime which was acceptable to enough Frenchmen to ensure its survival. He was assisted by good harvests and general economic recovery but his own good sense in limiting, so far as he was able, the excesses of the privileged survivors of pre-revolutionary France, has been given less than just recognition in the restoration of the Bourbon regime.

“But he deserves much credit for securing the regime.”

The assassination of Louis' nephew the Duc de Berri marked a turning point, for from 1820 Louis, older and a sick man, proved unable to resist reactionary pressure. By the time of his death in 1824 the regime had a less liberal appearance and the way was already marked for the full royalist reaction which Charles X intended to mount.

“A clear start to part 2 of the essay.”

The end of the Bourbons may simply be explained in the suggestion that, in his eagerness to restore the full glory of the Ancien Regime, Charles X forgot the Revolution and failed to realise that it had created strong feelings in France that would resist any apparent attempt to restore the past. Charles' early policies were foolish and provocative: the coronation in the ancient religious form, the dramatic increase in the powers of the Catholic Church, the generous compensation for the returning nobility who had lost their lands, all aroused the suspicions of the urban middle class who were further outraged by reductions in the interest paid on their government investments. In all this Charles had dangerously narrowed the basis of his support but had not yet endangered his throne. Indeed all might have been well, with the appointment in 1828 of the moderate Martignac as Chief Minister, for sensible moderation might still have kept him the support of the middle classes.

In 1829 however Charles turned his back on any attempt to hold the loyalty of the new France when he appointed the arch-symbol of the old reactionary regime, Prince Polignac as his Chief Minister, a man who sought his policies in the realms of religious mysticism. Much of the blame for what followed must rest with Charles for, when even the narrowly based Assembly called for Polignac to be dismissed Charles dissolved the Assembly. The elections which followed provided an even more recalcitrant Assembly with more opposition members and so Charles suspended the constitution and, in the Ordinances of St Cloud created a new one under which less than one in a thousand of the population would have the vote. The basis of his support in France, as demonstrated by this episode, could scarcely have been narrower. With moderate policies all those who had a vested interest in stability, notably the middle classes and perhaps the peasants, would have continued to tolerate the Bourbon regime. It is difficult to avoid the conclusion that Charles X had, perversely and blindly, thrown all this away. Unlike his brother he had not been prepared to compromise with the new forces in post-Revolutionary France.

“Charles X's share of the responsibility.”

"But more to it than just this."

This is not however the total explanation of the downfall of the regime in 1830. It was not those who had once had some share in political life under Louis XVIII, and who now saw Charles snatching this and perhaps other liberties away, who now drove the last Bourbon from the throne of France. This role fell to the working classes of Paris, made desperate by worsening economic times. In the last fifteen years Paris had grown enormously through immigration from the countryside, thousands could find no work and faced starvation. They raised the barricades in the streets and shouted for revolution and, in three days they had won.

"A regime without supporters."

Neither the army nor Charles himself had any stomach for a fight and soon lost control of the capital to the mob. It might be argued that Charles lost his throne because he failed to ensure the loyalty and availability of his army before he embarked on a deliberately provocative series of policies. With equal validity it could be argued that the Regime's failure to ease the economic plight of those outside the political system, and especially the Parisian working class amongst them, did more to bring about his downfall than any of his reactionary political proposals. What the latter did ensure was that none would be found to take up the regime's cause when the moment of crisis came. Charles' personal failure to offer resistance to the tide of events simply ensured the Bourbon regime ended swiftly and with the minimum of bloodshed.

A STUDENT'S ANSWER TO QUESTION 4

There were in 1848 two broad types of revolutionary in France. The middle-class intellectuals who despised Louis Philippe and who wanted to see the monarchy replaced by a Republic with a much wider franchise than under Louis Philippe. This would give political power to the middle-class and continue to provide political stability and safeguard property. The other sort of revolutionary were members of the Paris working-class and were followers of the socialist leader Louis Blanc. They wanted a much more far-reaching revolution with votes for all men and they also wanted a social and an economic revolution which would give them work and a living wage rather than the heavy unemployment of the last few years. All that they shared with the middle-class revolutionaries was that they did not want a monarchy any longer.

"Identifies the revolutionaries."

The division between these two groups, which became more and more bitter, is the main reason why neither got what it wanted and why Napoleon had the chance to become Emperor. At first the more extreme revolutionaries got their way, the mob forced through the idea of universal suffrage to choose a new parliament. Their leader Louis Blanc was unpopular with the middle class but he was so popular with the Paris working-class that they had to accept him as a member of the government, where he forced through the idea of National Workshops providing work for the people of Paris, these soon turned into a very expensive form of poor relief. In the elections the moderates did very well and used their success to remove Louis Blanc from the government. This led to civil war in Paris as the socialists fought to restore the ideas of Louis Blanc.

"This is developing a coherent argument."

The revolt was put down with great bloodshed by General Cavaignac, whom the government had given absolute power to destroy this threat to political stability and the safety of property. The people's fears made them want security and this encouraged them to vote for Napoleon as President. The fatal mistake of the republicans had been to make a constitution where the President of the Republic was voted for by the people. This gave Napoleon his chance.

He was the heir to the Napoleonic legend at a time when France remembered the glories of the great Napoleon but had forgotten all the miseries he had brought upon the country. He offered the French glory after the weak policies of Louis Philippe and he also offered the frightened middle class the chance of a secure stable government which would protect them from socialists and Paris mobs. He gained five and a half million votes against Cavaignac's one and a half million with the radicals nowhere. He was able to win like this because the socialists and the Paris mob had frightened the respectable classes. It was not just the middle-class who voted for Napoleon but also the respectable workers outside Paris and the peasants. He put forward the idea that the Napoleonic tradition had been one of caring for the people and that he would introduce the social reforms that were so badly overdue since Louis Philippe's time. Only the extremists in Paris wanted a socialist paradise and their violence frightened the rest of France into voting for Napoleon in order to ensure stability.

"Louis Napoleon's skilful exploitation of the Republic's weaknesses."

It is now easy to see how Napoleon went on to establish his own personal power and the Empire. He used his own popularity and the divisions amongst his enemies to advance his own power. He was a patriot but also very ambitious for himself. He had been elected President for four years and the Constitution would not allow him to be re-elected. When he tried to change this the Assembly did not support him with the two-thirds majority needed so he dissolved the Assembly and appealed, in a referendum, to the people to support the extension of his powers for ten years. He again relied on his own popularity and on his uncle's legend and he was not disappointed. Seven and a half million people voted for him in the referendum and 640,000 voted 'No'.

Napoleon III had out-manoeuvred the republican Assembly for as well as being in office for ten years the referendum also confirmed an increase in his own powers and the establishment of a Senate to balance the Assembly. This Senate was from the start controlled by Napoleon and in less than a year it suggested that he be made Emperor. Another referendum was held and the proposal was supported by almost eight million votes to a quarter of a million.

"A good essay."

To sum up it can be said that the divided republicans and especially the extremism of some of the Parisians gave Napoleon his chance to become President. They also gave him the means, by having the president elected by all men, to use his family's legend to win. He then adapted the election idea into the form of the two plebiscites to gain autocratic power, again using the desire of most French people for stability and also promising the prospect of a little Napoleonic glory as well.

Examiner comments

A very pleasing essay packed with ideas and comments! It deserves a good mark. In the first part, on the republican disappointment, the work of Lamartine and the dashing of his hopes deserves some comment as he was the leading moderate republican (who got only 17,000 votes in the Presidential election!). A comment on why the monarchists never got in Napoleon's way, (after all they could have offered stability against extremists as well as he did) would have been valuable even if it was limited to saying that they were no obstacle because they were split between the supporters of the Bourbon Comte de Chambord and a number of relatives of Louis Philippe. With no reference at all to them it looks as though they have been forgotten. It remains a minor blemish on a good essay.

USEFUL SOURCES OF INFORMATION

General reading

A Ramm, *Europe in the Nineteenth Century*, Longman 1984
J B Watson, *Success in European History 1815–1941*, John Murray 1981
A Wood, *Europe 1815–1960*, Longman 1984

Further reading

A Cobban, *A History of Modern France; Volume 2 1799–1945*, Penguin 1961
J A S Grenville, *Europe Reshaped, 1848–1878*, Fontana 1976
K Randell, *France: Monarchy, Republic and Empire 1814–1870*, Arnold 1986

Linked topic areas

- The defeat of Napoleon I
- The Vienna Peace Settlement (Chapter 12)
- Belgian independence 1830
- Mehemet Ali and the Eastern Question (Chapter 15)
- The 1848 Revolutions across Europe
- The Crimean War
- Italian unification (Chapter 16)
- The rise of Prussia to 1870 (Chapter 17)
- The beginnings of socialism in Europe

CHAPTER

14

RUSSIAN HISTORY 1815–1914

GETTING STARTED

Look at a globe, look at a map of Russia, note its size and the main geographic features. They are relevant to many explanations of events and developments in Russian history but they are rarely referred to by examination candidates or when mentioned they produce more than their fair share of factual errors. The Caspian Sea fleet, assuming that it existed, would with difficulty have sailed to challenge the Japanese in 1904! Know enough about Russian society and the economy in the nineteenth century to make use of it in answering political questions, especially on the effects of the emancipation of the serfs and on the growth of opposition to Tsarist rule.

The first Russian census was taken in 1897; it was subject to many errors and perhaps in some instances double counting but it recorded 125 million inhabitants drawn from over 100 national groups with 55 million Russians, 22 million Ukrainians, 8 million Poles and 5 million Jews. Westwood (see 'Useful Sources of Information' at the end of chapter) estimates that it had grown from 86 millions in 1870 when 11 per cent lived in towns, a proportion that grew to 15 per cent by 1897. At the end of the century Russia was still overwhelmingly an agrarian society based on peasant production on holdings which, from generation to generation, became more sub-divided; thanks to climatic disasters and rising population, the prospect of famine was never far away. Heavy industry, especially steel production, did expand from the mid-nineteenth century but it was by west European standards primitive in the extreme, a labour-intensive industry with appalling working conditions. The social structure was by west European standards remarkably rigid. The Tsar and the nobility owned vast estates and kept themselves separate from the small middle-class. The peasants ceased to be serfs in 1861 but they remained poverty stricken and trapped on the land; by the 1897 census it was estimated that only one in five of the population could read and this in a land with quite a developed system of higher education and high cultural traditions in music and literature.

Finally you need to note the central role played in the Tsarist state by the Orthodox Church. It almost invariably acted as a brake on any form of social or political progress, both in its role as a major owner of land and through its influence at the Court.

ESSENTIAL PRINCIPLES

RUSSIAN AUTOCRACY

ALEXANDER I

The burning of Moscow in 1812 to thwart Napoleon opened a new phase of Russian history. It produced an outburst of national feeling which at times Tsar Alexander I seemed prepared to accommodate with a series of liberal constitutional reforms. Alexander personally led the Russian army to liberate Europe and made a very favourable impression in Paris and in Britain; the lenient treatment of the defeated France owed much to him. He had a reputation as an enlightened thinker but the reforms he introduced amounted to minor tinkering, except perhaps in Poland whose separate status he protected and where he established relatively liberal constitutional arrangements, with a parliament which he intended to be a model for one in Russia itself. He was half-hearted in all this, seeing the parliaments merely as discussion bodies. Russia was to be, throughout the century, a despotic state.

"Alexander I – potentially a liberal?"

The other side of his character was marked by deep piety and this led him to the foundation of the Holy Alliance and from 1820 to a decidedly more reactionary stance at home, restricting the universities and freedom of speech. He has been described as brilliant and unstable. He promised much but neither socially or constitutionally achieved anything.

"But ended as a reactionary."

NICHOLAS I

Nicholas I's accession to the throne was marked by the Decembrist revolt which encouraged him to embark on a long reign of repression of any signs of dissent against the powers and position of the Tsar and the Orthodox Church. Amongst the small educated class however the first signs of socialist ideas were established in his reign and in *Michael Herzen* the first of a long line of revolutionary opponents of the regime appeared. Some opponents of the Tsar looked to west European liberalism for inspiration, others looked to older Russian traditions. Under Nicholas's repression none made much progress but neither did the Russian state. The defeat in the Crimean War revealed how backward and inefficient Russia had remained during a half century of dramatic changes in the rest of Europe.

"Nicholas I – repression and stagnation."

Exam questions

To answer questions on Russian political history in the period to 1855 it is essential to have enough general information and ideas on Russian society to interpret, and indeed to supplement, the rather slim and essentially negative achievements of the two Tsars. Examination answers on this period of Russian history tend to be marked by superficiality and, perhaps for this reason, it is much less popular with either examiners or candidates than the later period.

"Too many candidates lack knowledge of Russian history topics."

ALEXANDER II

REFORMS 1855–1881

Inefficiency in the Crimean War and the consequent defeat revealed the weakness of Russia which the repression of Nicholas I had hidden. Alexander II had to obtain peace and to rebuild the Russian forces. His reforming period is spread over the next ten years, after which he reverted to repressive policies on the same lines as his father. The reforms were, however, important and deserve serious assessment (see the 'Useful Information' section and the 'Tutor's Answer' at the end of this chapter).

REACTION

The Poles rebelled in 1863 and this provided the excuse for repression which was in full swing within a year or so. The national aspirations of non-Russians became a particular target for oppression. After an assassination attempt on him in 1866 Alexander's grip on potential dissidents tightened, press censorship became more restrictive and juries were discarded in political trials. The regime was however inefficient and opposition survived and grew, notably the *Narodniks* from whom the later Social Revolutionaries developed

"Alexander II reverts to reaction."

and anarchist groups like the *Nihilists*. Liberalism as a source of opposition had limited influence, a reflection of the weakness of the Russian middle-class. In 1881 the assassins were at last successful. By that date Alexander II's reputation as a reformer, 'the Liberator', was somewhat tarnished by his later repressive policies.

Exam questions

"A very common examination topic."

This is the most popular examination topic in nineteenth century Russian history. The previous reigns could well be studied simply as background to Alexander II. Certainly you need a brief summary of Russian backwardness, social and economic, but also, after learning what Alexander II did you need to be able to set his work in that context and to offer a judgement of what he had achieved and what remained to be done.

ALEXANDER III

REACTION 1881–1894

It is very unlikely that you will face a question on Alexander III alone but the continuation and indeed increased rigour of repression did set the scene for the more important reign of Nicholas II. Alexander III's chief service to Russia was in 1892 to appoint *Witte* as Finance Minister and he, in the next reign, did much to strengthen the economy. Alexander rejected all suggestions for political reform and the reign contained no worthwhile social reform. Repression was its keynote and it is worth noting that the first Marxist group appeared in Russia at this time.

NICHOLAS II

1894–1914

Nicholas was committed to his father's policies of repressive preservation of the autocracy. The early years of the reign saw the development of a number of opposition groups who played significant parts in later events, note in particular:

"Opposition groups emerge."

- The Socialist Revolutionaries who became the SR Party in 1907.
- The western democratic style Cadets.
- The Marxist Social Democrats.

Lenin's early political career developed in this period and in 1900 he left Russia to continue the struggle from abroad. In 1903 came the momentous Social Democrat meeting at which Lenin's *Bolsheviks* divided from the *Mensheviks*. Anyone with a serious intention of writing about later revolutionary activity through to 1917 should at this stage come to an understanding of the status of each of these opposition groups.

THE REVOLUTION OF 1905

"Another common examination topic."

The other major political topic of these years concerns the Revolution of 1905, arising from appalling social and economic conditions, political repression and reaction to defeat in the war against Japan. You need to have a full understanding of what occurred in that year. The events and the outcome provide vivid historical narrative but you must be ready to analyse the causes and comment on the significance of the rather limited constitutional changes (the Duma) to which it gave rise. Above all be ready to discuss why it appears to mark a decisive stage in the final fate of Tsardom.

Exam questions

Questions sometimes refer to the events of 1905 as a watershed; too many candidates fail to identify the meaning of this term, so it might be worth some reflection now. In this context 'the slope down which the waters flowed to the revolutions of 1917' might be the most useful loose definition. Having read up the events of 1905 and taken your study of Russia through to 1917 come back to the earlier year and reflect on the period in these terms. How do you, in an examination, wish to relate the two revolutions? This would at least discourage you from merely describing what happened in 1905!

THE OCTOBER MANIFESTO

The disorders of the summer of 1905 were so great that the Tsar issued the October Manifesto setting up a national Duma on a liberal basis with a wide franchise and extensive powers in approving laws and safeguarding the rule of law. This was based on the advice from Witte who became Chief Minister: it succeeded in dividing the Tsar's opponents and the Cadet Party was prepared to work within the new Constitution. The workers' Soviets, set up in the cities, and the peasant uprisings could now be crushed by the armed forces which on this occasion had remained overwhelmingly loyal. Lenin and the other SD leaders arrived too late to influence events but the potential of the workers' Soviets was noted by him.

THE STATE DUMAS

The most straightforward way to study political life from 1905 to 1914 as the First Duma was followed by the Second, Third and Fourth (see the 'Useful Information' section at the end of the chapter) is by drawing up a commentary on Nicholas's actions as he struggled to preserve the royal autocracy intact. Include:

"1914 – a good vantage point from which to review the state of Russia."

- The dismissal of Witte.
- Be ready to comment on the work of the only other notable minister, *Stolypin*, with his policies of political repression and economic, especially agricultural, reform.
- Assess how secure and how effective the Tsar and his system of government were on the eve of war.
- Evaluate if it was just the strain of the war that destroyed the autocracy which was gradually evolving a working relationship with the Fourth Duma or if the masses were already so alienated that the war merely accelerated events.

Note: There is, of course, no certain answer to such questions but having some ideas of your own concerning them could sharpen up your essays immeasurably. Part of your calculation needs to include some ideas on the power of the different groups opposing the Tsar.

THE ECONOMY

Exam questions

Examination candidates are often asked to discuss the proposal that the reign of Nicholas II was marked by significant economic growth. There is more to this than just the policies of Witte and Stolypin, though this is frequently all that candidates offer. Questions on the economic policies of the two ministers are also quite common and the same revision material can help open up both types of question, though there is then the danger that the question actually set is not focused upon sufficiently directly. It is not difficult to collect some useful examples of the state of the Russian economy at this time for most historians are interested in how it performed during the war and what part economic collapse played in bringing about the end of Tsardom. The 'Useful Information' section below contains some economic data. The economic reforms of Witte and Stolypin should of course be studied in the context of their overall achievements.

RUSSIA AND THE FIRST WORLD WAR

"Link this topic to the causes of the First World War."

Russian foreign policy under Nicholas II is best studied as an extension of the nineteenth century Eastern Question and as one of the threads leading to the First World War. Chapters 15 and 19 will both be helpful in providing these contexts. It is important to understand Russia's ambitions and fears in the Balkans, which made relations with Austria-Hungary subject to so many crises, and the more cordial relations established, first with France and then with Britain, which in turn loosened the ties to Germany and so set the scene for Russia's part in the First World War.

This is not quite the full story and you will need to be aware of Russian expansion into the Far East which had culminated in the Russo-Japanese War, the outcome of which had sharpened Russia's interest in eastern Europe. The events of the war are usually studied in relation to the two revolutions of 1917 and are referred to in Chapter 20.

USEFUL INFORMATION

1801–1825	**Reign of Tsar Alexander I**
1812	Napoleon occupied Moscow and the burning of the city.
1814–1815	Alexander's leading role at the Peace Settlement: he founded the Holy Alliance.

1815	Alexander became king of Poland; benevolent and progressive rule.
1825	**The Decembrist Conspiracy** put down by Nicholas I.
1825–1855	**Reign of Tsar Nicholas I**
	Centralisation of the administration (Personal Chancellory of the Tsar) with a powerful police force (the Third Section), peasant education restrictions, purges of intellectuals and Universities, strict censorship.
1830	**Polish Revolution** suppressed.
1842	Following hundreds of peasant uprisings some limited reforms of noble rights over serfs and more land for royal serfs. Serfdom however remained intact.
1848	European revolutions did not affect Russia despite the development of some intellectual opposition to the repression Russian troops used to crush revolution in Hungary.
	Repression in Russia intensified after 1848.
1853	Russia invaded Turkish provinces of Moldavia and Wallachia.
1854–1856	**The Crimean War.** Incompetence of Russian Generals and poor military organisation. Over 250,000 Russians died. Loss of the Sebastopol naval base
1855–1881	**Reign of Tsar Alexander II**
1856	**Treaty of Paris** ended the war. Allies evacuated the Crimea. Black Sea declared neutral. Outcome a great humiliation for Russia and revealed how backward it was in relation to west European states. This re-inforced by the numerous peasant rebellions and the low level of agricultural output, small and inefficient industries, and lack of a commercial middle-class. Russia the only European country where serfdom remained; economic progress seemed to depend on its abolition.
1857–1858	Reforms of Alexander: Tsar founded a Russian Railway Company and a State Bank.
1861	**Emancipation of the Serfs**. They gained personal freedom and allotments of land to be paid for over 49 years. – REDEMPTION PAYMENTS
1863	**Polish Revolution** (suppressed in 1864). Poland fully integrated into Russia.
	From this point Alexander reverted to repression of critics and dissident groups.
1864	Zemstva established as a system of local government.
	Judicial system reformed
1870	Towns given self-government under councils elected by the wealthy.
1874	Army reforms introduced
1875–1878	**Crisis in Eastern Europe** (see Chapter 15)
	Emergence and growth of secret and violent political societies
1881	Alexander II assassinated.
1881–1894	**Reign of Tsar Alexander III**
	Repression continued
1894–1917	**Reign of Tsar Nicholas II**
1898	Social Democratic Party formed following Marxist ideas. Radical wing led by Lenin.
1901	Social Revolutionary Party formed
1903	Social Democratic Party split into Bolsheviks and Mensheviks.
1904	Union of Liberation, inspired by western liberalism, in 1905 they formed the Cadet Party.
1904–1905	**Russo-Japanese War**
1905 Jan	**'Bloody Sunday'** massacre of workers outside the Winter Palace led to mass strikes in Moscow and St Petersburg, peasant uprisings and mutiny on the battleship Potemkin.
Sept	Renewed with printers and railway workers.
Oct	Led to a general strike. First ever workers' Soviet set up in St Petersburg.
	Nicholas issued the October Manifesto setting up a national Duma based on a wide franchise and with wide powers.
	Witte became Chief Minister.
Dec	Workers in St Petersburg Soviet arrested
1906 Jan	Repression began
May	Witte dismissed. Fundamental Laws issued defining extensive powers

retained by the Tsar over the government, the armed forces and right to issue laws by decree if Duma not sitting.

Duma met for first time

July — Duma dismissed when it passed a vote of no confidence in the Tsar's ministers.

Stolypin became Chief Minister: introduced agrarian reform.

1907 — Second Duma sat for three months. The elections had been supervised by the government; open opposition to the Tsar led to its dismissal.

1907–1912 — Third Duma elected on a much narrower franchise; had a conservative majority and passed some modest social and administrative reforms.

1912 — Elections for the Fourth Duma

ECONOMIC INFORMATION FOR NICHOLAS II'S REIGN

Population

- 1897 (census) 125 million – by 1914 at least 155 million
- St Petersburg in 1897 – 1,250,000 inhabitants – by 1914 nearly 2,250,000 (Moscow from 1 million to 1¾ million)

Industry

A protective tariff was introduced in 1891 and behind it industrial output doubled by 1900 and continued to grow more slowly after 1900.

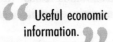

"Useful economic information."

- Railway development in the 1890s proved a stimulus to the coal and the iron industries.
- 16 million tons of coal was mined in 1900 (1890 6 million) and 35 million in 1913.
- Production of pig iron rose from 3 million tons in 1900 to over 4 million tons in 1913.
- Most industry was around the great cities of European Russia.
- Oil production, in which Russia led the World in 1900, remained static in the same period.
- Gross output totals lingered far behind that of countries like Britain and the USA.
- There were 30,000 kilometres of rail track in 1890 and 75,000 prior to the outbreak of war.

Agriculture

- Progress in agriculture was disappointing both in terms of reorganisation and output despite Stolypin's reforms.
- Grain production inevitably fluctuated with changes in weather patterns.
- Distribution was hampered by the limited transport system.
- There was a record harvest in 1913, with the growth of larger farms and some co-operative production.
- The great need was to push the surplus rural population into urban industry but the policies of neither Witte nor Stolypin, though they caused much rural unrest, had much success in this.
- The 1913 harvest, like so much in Russia on the eve of war remains an enigma, either a sign of new stability and progress or a mere flash in the pan depending on how one views events from 1914 to 1917.

EXAMINATION QUESTIONS

Q1 Why did Tsarist Russia escape unscathed from the revolutions of 1848? (Welsh 1989)

Q2 'The Great Disappointment.' Is this view of the emancipation of the serfs in nineteenth-century Russia justified? (Oxford 1986)

Q3 How effectively did the reforms of Alexander II solve the internal problems of Russia? (London 1989)

Q4 'Repression and reaction were the particular marks of the rule of the last Tsar, Nicholas II.' Discuss the validity of this verdict on his reign to 1914. (London 1990)

Q5 How extensive and how effective in promoting change was the opposition to the Tsarist system in Russia from c.1881 to 1914? (AEB 1989)

OUTLINE ANSWERS

Question 1

Introduction: explain the chief features of the 1848 Revolutions elsewhere, they were nationalist and liberal, largely middle-class led with the backing in some cases of the emerging urban working-class.

Reasons: did not occur in Russia because

- There was a very small middle-class and very little urban development, illustrate this.
- It was a social structure based on noble privilege and a downtrodden peasantry.
- The uprisings which happened regularly in Russia were local violent protests against famine or land and labour issues.
- In this social structure there was no potentially revolutionary class to be inspired by what was happening elsewhere.
- The size of the country and the poor communications further prevented the spread of politically subversive ideas.
- The regime of Nicholas I was effective in repressing dissidents and keeping control, this was the work of the Third Section, for example:
  - the non-Russian nationalities were a particular target
  - the Poles had been crushed in 1830
  - the Finns had been given enough concessions to encourage them to accept the Tsar
  - the vast Russian Army was available to prevent any rising anywhere.

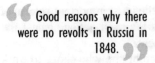

"Good reasons why there were no revolts in Russia in 1848."

Question 2

The gist of the answer is contained within the 'Tutor's Answer' to a similar question on page 156. It was a disappointment to the serfs, to those who dreamed of a modernised Russian economy and society and, because internal unrest continued, to Alexander II. Do not get swept away by the quotation: Is there nothing good to be said about the reform?

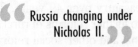

"See the 'Tutor's Answer' for relevant commentary."

Question 3

See the 'Tutor's Answer' on page 156.

Question 4

Introduction: Nicholas II was in favour of preserving the Tsarist state intact as he had inherited it, he was prepared to repress any attempt to undermine the autocracy.

In personal terms: the statement has great validity, even greater if the record of his Tsarina and her adviser Rasputin is taken into account. Nicholas never realised how much he lost with the greatest act of repression in his reign, the massacre outside the Winter Palace in 1905, briefly indicate to illustrate the theme and go on to indicate also the repression of the workers' Soviets and the crushing of rural uprisings.

Full story: argue that this is not the full story of the reign, there were signs of change and development:

- the Dumas, even if only a reluctant experiment by the Tsar
- the Third and Fourth Dumas had some achievements to their credit
- the economic progress under Witte and Stolypin also needs to be acknowledged

"Russia changing under Nicholas II."

Conclusion: by 1914 Russian society and the economy had changed markedly despite the Tsar. This change might have continued without a revolutionary outcome but for the war. Whether Nicholas II would personally have adapted to real political change remains more doubtful.

Question 5

Consider: how extensive.

List: the groups:

“Opposition to the Tsar.”

- *Narodniks* of pre-1881 becoming the Social Revolutionaries largely as a Utopian party of the peasant interests and joining with Bakunin's anarchists and Nihilists.
- *Marxists* under Plekanhov becoming the Social Democrats and splitting into Bolsheviks and Mensheviks.
- *Liberals* in the Zemstva.
- *Cadets* and the conservative *Octobrists* in the State Dumas after 1905, the latter arguably ceasing to be opponents of Tsardom but content to work for change within the Tsarist system.

Discuss: how extensive these groups were, taking view that splits and divisions weakened them and that often parties were very small and subject to effective Tsarist repression. Use Lenin having to go into exile as an example.

Argue that opposition was much widened by the events of 'Bloody Sunday' 1905, with Soviets and peasant uprisings against the system.

It was this wider opposition of the masses which produced the most important reform of the period with the introduction of the State Duma. Nicholas II's swift action against the First and Second Dumas showed the limits of that achievement.

After that however it was only those groups, Cadets and Octobrists, who chose to work within the Third and Fourth Dumas who had any reforming influence with some factory and insurance legislation but achieving nothing in the way of political reform.

“Many opponents wanted to destroy rather than reform the system.”

Conclusion: the reforming achievement of those who opposed the Tsars was very limited, partly because they were so divided amongst themselves but also because only the Cadets and the Octobrists saw themselves as committed to reform. The other parties were of a revolutionary nature, committed to replacing rather than reforming Tsardom.

A TUTOR'S ANSWER TO QUESTION 3

“Lessons from the Crimean War.”

The defeat in the Crimean War, coming right at the beginning of Alexander II's reign, brought the internal problems of Russia into sharp focus. The defeat was blamed on military and administrative incompetence but also on the backward state of the Russian economy and Russian society. Other European states were, to varying degrees, going through a period of vast economic and social development. Russia under the repressive despotism of Nicholas I had changed little and the outcome in the Crimea revealed that it could no longer be regarded as a major power. Bringing this state of affairs to an end would require an overhaul of the armed forces, the administration and, above all, the economy. The economic problems related to the primitive agricultural system characterised by low yields and an absence of innovation and by Russia's failure, by western standards, to develop modern heavy industries.

The internal problems were vast, encompassing the military, the administration and the economy. It is therefore suprising that there seemed, in 1855, to be general agreement on the fundamental reform that was required if all was to be put right. Alexander II, not a reformer by conviction, had come to the conclusion that it was the institution of peasant serfdom which prevented changes in agriculture and frustrated the labour mobility which could lead to industrial growth. A growing number of landowners also saw the advantages of a free labour market and the constant peasant uprisings and rural violence underlined the message.

“The most radical step.”

Alexander II's greatest reform was the 1861 Edict of Emancipation which set free about 40 million serfs who received a portion of the landlords' estates in a move financed by the government but based on loans to be repaid by the new peasantry over 49 years. This totally changed the social structure of the country and led on to further reforms of rural and municipal local government which in turn promoted educational and other social reforms. There was also a reorganisation of the army and a relaxation of censorship laws and a restructuring of the judicial system. Emancipation of the serfs is generally seen as the cornerstone of much of the rest of Alexander's reforming programme which, in any case, only occupied the first ten years of his reign, after which he reverted to an instinctive conservatism.

"Reform a disappointment."

If serfdom is looked at from a peasant viewpoint then Alexander's reform did little to resolve their problems, which were ones of survival. Domestic serfs received no land and were as dependent on the nobility for a living as ever. The landed serfs received less land on emancipation than they had been in possession of before; this was especially so in the fertile southern grain areas and often elsewhere they received land of a poorer quality than that retained by the nobles. They found themselves saddled with high redemption payments and, with the land organised by the *mir*, or village community, were often prevented from leaving because of their unpaid debt. With an increasing population and continued sub-division of land holdings, the peasant's lot was for many years no better than before emancipation and rural disturbances continued even into the next century. The peasants, who had over the centuries come to see the land as theirs and who now had to pay the government for it, felt cheated.

"Agricultural change slow to come."

The end of serfdom did not lead to any dramatic transformation of Russian agriculture. The free land was supervised by the mir and village custom ensured that innovation was slow to occur. The land remained organised on a strip system, often with periodic redistribution of holdings, and was left fallow for one year in three. There was no great increase in output and no growth of a prosperous peasantry on west European models. The obstacles put in the way of peasant mobility by the mir meant that there was little increase in labour mobility and, although industry continued to develop, there is no evidence that emancipation proved a great stimulus to economic development.

"A new adminstrative structure now needed."

Emancipation of the serfs removed much of the power structure of rural Russia and in 1864 led to the creation of district and provincial zemstva to provide a system of local government through elected councils. They were not democratic bodies, and the Tsar's police remained responsible for law and order, but they did useful work, not least in trebling the number of elementary schools from the 8000 at the beginning of Alexander's reign. The zemstva and the municipal councils or Dumas, started in 1870, also contributed to the provision of hospitals, prisons, poor relief and sanitation. If Russian society was to break free from the feudal power of the nobility and to establish a modern administrative framework then the zemstva provided the first step on the way.

The reform of the legal code introduced jury trials, less severe punishments and less bribery of judges. It made the law less corrupt but it did little to protect the individual from the arbitrary powers of the state. The Tsars had in any case never seen this as a problem which required attention.

The military were quite a different matter and in the aftermath of the Crimean defeat the war minister *Milyutin* carried out extensive reorganisation of the General Staff, of officer training and recruiting and, most importantly, applied the principle of conscription to all classes of society. The army remained a major cost on the state, it was far too large and exerted too much influence over policy. Despite the work of Milyutin, Russia's defences continued to rely on numbers rather than military efficiency and its defeats at the hands of the Japanese in 1904–1905 were as humiliating as those half a century earlier.

"The paradox of reform from above."

"Autocracy before modernisation."

Russia in 1855 was so backward that change could not come quickly. Its economic problems in particular had no immediate remedy. Alexander's reforms laid the basis for a transformation of society but only the basis and the provision of an efficient local administration to tackle social problems would take decades of development. Economic innovation in a backward peasant agriculture would inevitably make slow progress. Above all none of the Tsar's reforms did anything to reduce his own autocratic power or the vast influence of the reactionary Orthodox Church. Problems therefore had still to be tackled from the top because no independent reforming initiatives could be tolerated. Once Alexander II lost the will to reform then the problems were allowed to stagnate again, a process only too easily continued under his successors. The great reforms of the 1860s were never built upon because the Tsars were more anxious to retain autocracy than they were to modernise Russia whose central problems remained largely unresolved through to the days of Witte and Stolypin and beyond.

USEFUL SOURCES OF INFORMATION

General reading

A Ramm, *Europe in the Nineteenth Century 1789–1905*, Longman 1984

J B Watson, *Success in European History 1815–1941*, John Murray 1981

A Wood, *Europe 1815–1960*, Longman (Second Edition) 1984

Further reading

J N Westwood, *Endurance and Endeavour: Russian History 1812–1986*, Oxford University Press (Third Edition) 1987: a very useful, and very entertainingly written national history, an obvious book to move on to from the general European textbooks.

Linked topic areas

- The Eastern Question (see Chapter 15)
- The causes of the First World War (see Chapter 19)
- The Revolutions of 1917 (see Chapter 20)
- Soviet history 1917–1941 (see Chapter 20)

CHAPTER

15

THE EASTERN QUESTION

GREEK INDEPENDENCE

MEHEMET ALI

THE CRIMEAN WAR

CRISIS OF 1875–1878

THE OTTOMAN EMPIRE

USEFUL INFORMATION

GETTING STARTED

The Eastern Question was to create tension amongst the Powers of Europe throughout the nineteenth century. Its origins lay in the weakness of the Ottoman Empire which, in 1815, still ruled over much of the Balkans. By 1913 those European possessions had shrunk to a tiny rump. This process of decline was punctuated by a series of international crises which were usually linked to Russian ambitions in the area; these in turn aroused the suspicions not only of the Austrian Empire, whose territories bordered the Balkans to the north, but also of both Britain and France. The advice to start your study by looking at a relevant historical map has been only too frequently offered in previous chapters but with the Eastern Question a historical atlas will be an essential companion if much of the political game is to make any sense.

There was a long history of antagonism between the Orthodox Christian Russians and the Moslem Turks and since the early eighteenth century the Tsars had had territorial ambitions around the Black Sea. Many of the Ottoman Empire's subjects in the Balkans were themselves Orthodox Christians and many, also like the Russians, Slav by race. The Ottoman Empire had been at its height in the sixteenth and seventeenth centuries and by 1815 was less and less capable of providing its Balkan provinces with effective government or defending them against ambitious neighbours. The Ottoman record of brutal oppression of their Christian subjects provided a series of easily available reasons for outside intervention and concern. Before 1815 only the Serbs in the north of the Balkans had in practice broken from Turkish rule and in 1830 they obtained virtual independence with their security guaranteed by Russia.

Austrian concern was twofold: it did not want to see an expansion of Russian influence to the south nor did it wish the nationalist ambitions of the Turkish Sultan's subjects to inflame those of the diverse nationalities within its own empire. When later in the century Austria drew closer to the newly united Germany then it too would be drawn into arrangements to defend its ally's interests in the Balkans. The origins of the 1914 war were there a century before its outbreak when the Serbs had established an independent Slav nation on Austria's southern frontier.

The reason for British and French interest in the Eastern Question is not as immediately obvious but it rested more on a fear of Russian ambitions towards the eastern Mediterranean than on any affection for the Ottoman Empire. In Britain there was a deep and not always rational suspicion of Russian despotism and of the Russian threat towards the Middle East but especially of a possible Russian thrust through Afghanistan and on to British India.

ESSENTIAL PRINCIPLES

GREEK INDEPENDENCE

"An issue for the great powers."

There was Greek unrest against Turkish rule before 1815 and open rebellion in 1821. In Britain there was much sympathy for the Greeks which made it impossible merely to support the Turks in order to block any advance of Russian influence. Russia, the first to stamp on rebels elsewhere in Europe, had both political and religious reasons for meddling.

You need to read an account of the events of the 1820s, including especially the role of the ruler of Egypt, *Mehemet Ali*, on the Turkish side. Increasing Russian support for the Greeks forced the British Foreign Secretary, *Canning*, to act. Unable simply to support the Turks he chose to work with the Russians to end the conflict and to establish a truly independent Greece, as free from Russian influence as from Turkish rule. French interests in this were identical with those of Britain and the two powers worked together to bring about Greek independence. The destruction of Mehemet Ali's fleet by the British navy left the Sultan with few cards to play.

The Greeks got their independence through their own efforts and the willingness of Britain, France and Russia to find a solution agreeable to all of them and one which they enforced against the Turks.

Exam questions

If you are asked to explain why the Greeks were able to obtain their independence, a popular question, remember to include references to Turkish weaknesses and to the strength of Greek feeling, the savagely effective guerrilla war and their control of the sea. Too many students analyse the issue as entirely one amongst the 'Great Powers'. Without the Greeks themselves it would never have become an issue for the Powers. The rebellion produced interesting international cross-currents (see the 'Outline Answer' to Question 1).

This topic can also form an important part of questions on the work of the Great Powers in upholding, or in this case failing to uphold, the integrity of European states after the 1815 Vienna Settlement (see Chapter 12). It also features in British history papers in questions on Canning's foreign policy.

MEHEMET ALI

For his help to the Sultan against the Greeks, Mehemet Ali was given the island of Crete but in 1833 he decided also to seize Syria. Subsequent events are mainly of interest because of the reactions of the major powers (see the 'Outline Answer' to Question 2).

Russian support

"1834: an unwelcome Russian advance."

The Russians supported the Turks and in return, at the *Treaty of Unkiar Skelessi* in 1834, the Sultan agreed to close the Dardanelles Strait to foreign war vessels at the request of the Russian government.

1841 STRAITS CONVENTION

British policy thereafter worked to get the treaty revised and, when in 1839 the Turks were again attacked by Mehemet Ali, Palmerston, the British Foreign Secretary, made sure that Britain was involved in backing them up. The Russians were prepared to be conciliatory and the outcome was the 1841 Straits Convention which established that whilst the Ottoman Empire was at peace the Straits would be closed to all foreign warships.

"Thwarted in 1841."

The Russian advantage had been cancelled. An interesting complication had been provided by French backing for Mehemet Ali and a consequent crisis in relations with Britain. France, with Russia and Britain on this occasion taking a common line, had in the end to agree to the 1841 arrangements which included limiting their ally Mehemet Ali to his Egyptian possessions. The episode is complicated. Unless you remember the traditional interests of the Great Powers in the fate of the Ottoman Empire it will appear incomprehensible.

THE CRIMEAN WAR

This arose from the Eastern Question but it had wider consequences, for Austrian neutrality and diplomatic moves against Russia lost her the latter's support against the rising tide of national feeling in Europe. This support had helped preserve the Austrian Empire in the revolutions of 1848 and its withdrawal after the Crimean War opened new prospects for Italian and German nationalism to move against the interests of the multi-national Austrian Empire. The Vienna Settlement of 1815 was now open to major revision.

CAUSES

The causes of the initial conflict between Russia and the Ottoman Empire, involving repression in the Turkish provinces of Moldavia and Wallachia and Russian pretensions to safeguard the Holy Places in Palestine, should be set in the background of long-standing antagonism between the two countries. The reasons for British and French involvement also need to be set in context if they are to make much sense. Their response rested on the traditional suspicion of Russian intentions against the eastern Mediterranean. The diplomatic moves to support the Turks, leading to the sending of a military expedition with the unlikely task of capturing the Russian naval base of Sebastopol, and the events of the subsequent military campaign, feature regularly in questions on British history and it is worth checking past papers for this. The additional reasons for French involvement are an important strand in the foreign policy of the Emperor Napoleon III (see Chapter 13). The outcome of the war had important internal consequences for Russia and was a direct stimulus for the reforms of Alexander II (see Chapter 14). It did nothing to bring nearer a solution to the Eastern Question (see the 'Outline Answer' to Question 3).

"... but did nothing to solve the Eastern Question."

Exam questions

The Crimean War appears to have been an insignificant episode in European history but it is a topic of limited scope, easily revised in outline. If questions on it have appeared on past papers then consider revising it in either a European or British context.

CRISIS OF 1875–1878

CAUSES

"A common examination topic."

The causes of this important crisis arose from the decline of the Ottoman Empire and from traditional Russian ambitions, both of which have been already noted and which are likely to be brought into any answer on the events of these years. A new element in the situation arose from the unification of Germany in 1871. The German Empire, with Bismarck as Chancellor, was to play an important role in resolving matters on this occasion but remember that German involvement widened the potential scope of any future crisis. In 1914 it was to turn a Balkan crisis into a European war. Look at the section of Chapter 17 on Bismarck's foreign policy, read a textbook narrative of what happened from 1875 to 1878, and then analyse the part played by each of the major powers.

Sultan's misrule

"British policy under Disraeli."

The continuing misrule of the Sultan and his local representatives caused rebellions amongst the Christian subjects, first in Bosnia and Herzegovina and then in Bulgaria. Savage repression resulted but when the European Powers showed concern the Sultan, Abdul Hamid, offered constitutional reforms at a conference in Constantinople set up by the British. The aim of the British Government under Disraeli was the traditional one of bolstering the Turks in order to block the advance of Russian influence. Disraeli knew that he was unlikely to prevent foreign intervention against the Ottoman Empire unless the Sultan carried out reforms. The Sultan's promises seemed to meet the case for the moment but, once the conference had ended, these were withdrawn and the lot of the Balkan Christians was as desperate as ever it had been.

RUSSIAN ATTACK

In 1877 the Russians attacked the Ottoman Empire and after some difficulties imposed peace terms on them (*Treaty of San Stefano*) which almost pushed the Turks out of Europe and which set up a large independent state of Bulgaria which stretched from the Black Sea to the Aegean. In Britain it was assumed that this would give Russia itself easy access to the Mediterranean and war fever gripped the country. Britain seemed to be rushing towards war with Russia.

MOVES TO PEACE

"Bismarck – the key to peace."

It was Austrian anxiety to avoid a Balkan war and Bismarck's wish to maintain peace throughout Europe which led to the *Congress of Berlin*, aimed at a peaceful solution of a crisis in which Britain and Russia now seemed to be the main protagonists. The Congress led to the *Treaty of Berlin* which reduced Bulgaria to a third of the size envisaged at San Stefano. This was intended as a rebuff to Russian influence in the region and when the new Bulgaria proved resistant to Russian influence the Powers consequently raised no protest when, in 1885, it annexed neighbouring Eastern Roumelia. Certainly the Berlin arrangements did nothing to solve the problems of the region. They merely ended the crisis which had developed between Britain and Russia. The 'Tutor's Answer' to Question 4 develops some of these issues at greater length.

THE OTTOMAN EMPIRE

ITS DECLINE 1878–1913

Ottoman rule remained as savage as ever and the unrest amongst the subject Christian population continued to provoke concern and the threat of intervention from the European Powers. In the 1890s there were widespread massacres of the Armenians, south-east of the Black Sea, and also on the island of Crete. Both illustrate how far the problems associated with the decline of the Ottoman Empire were from solution.

THE BALKANS

“Good examination strategy to link the Eastern Question to the First World War.”

In 1908, in a major rebuff for Russia in its role as a guardian of Slav interests in the Balkans, Austria incorporated the two autonomous Turkish provinces of Bosnia and Herzegovina into the Habsburg Empire. This and other aspects of the Eastern Question after 1878 become a part of the answer to questions on the origins of the First World War. The continuing rivalry amongst the small Balkan nations erupted into wars against the Turks in 1912 and amongst themselves for the spoils in 1913. It was deep rivalry between Austria and Serbia that provided the spark for the First World War. It is almost certainly good examination strategy to be prepared to discuss the importance of the Eastern Question in bringing about war in 1914 and it is considered in that context in Chapter 19. Otherwise it might be better to be fully prepared for questions on the 1875 to 1878 crisis than to spend long mastering the complexities of Balkan politics after that date.

USEFUL INFORMATION

1821	Greek Independence: start of the Greek revolt against Turkish rule.
1825	Egyptian forces under Ibrahim, son of Mehemet Ali, crushed revolt.
1826	Russia and Britain agreed to work together for Greek self-government.
1827	**Treaty of London**: Britain, France and Russia agreed to threaten joint action against the Turks in Greece.
	Battle of Navarino: destruction of Egyptian fleet by British, French and Russian ships under Codrington.
1830	Powers guaranteed Greek independence
1831	**Mehemet Ali** attacked the Turks, claiming Syria as a reward for Egyptian help.
1832	Otto of Bavaria appointed King of Greece and the Turks accepted Greek independence.
1833	Sultan obtained Russian help against Egypt and latter made peace.
	Treaty of Unkiar Skelessi: defensive treaty to last 8 years between Russia and the Turks. Secret clause committed Turks to closing Dardanelles Strait to foreign warships if Russians requested. When clause leaked, Britain and France saw it as total protection for Russian Black Sea navy which could then come into the Mediterranean.
1839	Turks attacked Mehemet Ali
1840	Austria, Britain, Prussia, Russia agreed to act against him, if necessary to bring peace to the area. He made peace after the French failed to support him despite their growing interest in Egypt and their earlier encouragement of him.
1841	**The Straits Convention** was agreed by all the European Powers, it closed the Dardanelles to all foreign warships in time of peace and so checked Russian influence over the Turks.
1850	**Origins of the Crimean War**: start of the quarrel between France and Russia as Napoleon III supported French Catholic rights to look after the Christian Holy Places in Palestine and the Tsar Nicholas I asserted the right

	of the Orthodox Church to do so. This dispute escalated over the next three years causing great tension between the two countries.
1853	Failure of Russian attempts to reach agreement with Britain over both the religious dispute and the distribution of lands when the Ottoman Empire should collapse.
	Stratford de Redcliffe, British Ambassador in Constantinople, urged Turks to resist Russian pressure.
	Russian troops entered Moldavia and Wallachia to put pressure on the Sultan to uphold the ancient treaty rights of the Russians to protect the Christian subjects of the Ottoman Empire.
	Turks declared war on Russia. Turkish fleet sunk at battle of Sinope and this aroused anti-Russian sentiment in Britain.
1854–1856	**The Crimean War**: Franco-British expedition to capture the Russian naval base at Sebastopol.
1855	Alexander II became Tsar and Russians evacuated Sebastopol
	Austrian mobilisation and ultimatum to Russia
1856	**Peace of Paris**: ended the Crimean War
	■ Black Sea to be neutral with no warships or naval bases.
	■ Strait Convention on Dardanelles renewed.
	■ Turks introduced civil rights reforms for their Christian subjects. The reforms were never really operated.
	■ Moldavia and Wallachia were made virtually independent provinces of the Ottoman Empire. Russians gave up any claims there.
1862	Moldavia and Wallachia combined to become independent Rumania.
1870	Tsar Alexander II took advantage of the Franco-Prussian War to repudiate the Black Sea neutrality clause. Under Alexander II the Russians developed Panslavist policies, setting themselves up as protectors of the Slav people of the Balkans.
1875–1878	**Critical stage of the Eastern Question**
1875	Rebellions amongst the Balkan Christians especially in Bosnia and Herzegovina.
1876	Bulgarians rebelled. Ruthless Turkish repression.
1877	Russians declared war on the Turks, fought way towards Constantinople.
1878 March	**Treaty of San Stefano** imposed on the Turks.
	■ Set up a 'Big Bulgaria' stretching from the Black Sea to the Aegean Sea.
	■ Reduced Turkish lands in Europe to a fragment.
	British started naval and troop movements to counter Russian expansionism. Jingoism in Britain.
June	Bismarck called the Congress of Berlin
July	**Treaty of Berlin**
	■ 'Big Bulgaria' dismantled with the south restored to the Turks, and Eastern Roumelia a self-governing province under the Turks.
	■ Bulgaria cut back to one third its San Stefano size.
	■ Britain obtained Cyprus as a counterweight to Russian advances.
	■ Bosnia and Herzegovina were to remain in the Ottoman Empire but were to be administered by Austria.
	■ More reform promises by the Sultan, but few materialised.
1894	Turkish massacres of Armenian Christians
1897	Powers made Sultan place Crete under Greek rule (1913 united to Greece).
1908	Young Turks' revolt against Sultan soon moved from apparent liberalism to military repression.
1912	**First Balkan War**: Balkan states combined to seize almost all Turkish lands on European side of the Dardanelles.
1913	**Second Balkan War**: Balkan states quarrel amongst themselves over the territorial arrangements of 1912.
1914	Balkan nations divided in First World War: Bulgaria and Turks on German side because of enmity with Russia and Serbia. Serbia, Rumania and Greece on Russian side because of anti-Austrian feeling.

EXAMINATION QUESTIONS

Q1 Why was the Greek War of Independence regarded as a matter of grave concern by the Great Powers of Europe? (Welsh 1989)

Q2 Discuss the role of Mehemet Ali in international relations between 1825 and 1841. (Oxford 1989)

Q3 Did the Crimean War mark any significant progress in the solution of the Eastern Question? (London 1990)

Q4 Why was it possible in 1878 to settle the affairs of the Balkans without recourse to a major European war? (London 1990)

OUTLINE ANSWERS

Question 1

Introduction: answer directly that it was because it threatened to destroy the arrangements that they had made, after a generation of war, to preserve the peace of Europe and their own positions in the European Balance of Power. Different views on the issue seemed likely to destroy the Congress System.

Explain: the outline events, in one paragraph, of the Greek struggle and go on, quickly, to analyse the danger from the position of the different Powers.

Analysis: Russia, arch opponent of nationalism as a source of revolution, and yet could not stand by and see fellow Orthodox Christians persecuted by the Egyptians.

" A British history topic as well. "

- Austria (Metternich) also against nationalism and seeing Greek example as dangerous for its own subject nationalities and rest of Balkans.
- Britain and France concerned about what Russians might do which would increase the prospect of their presence in the eastern Mediterranean but facing public opinion, Britain especially, that the Greeks had to be helped. Traditional policy of being on Turkish side to thwart Russia was impossible to maintain.

Question 2

Introduction: explain Mehemet Ali's position in Egypt and in relation to the Ottoman Empire. His significance arose because the Sultan's power had so declined that he was unable to prevent attempts to dismantle the Empire.

Defence: his first role was as a defender, at a price, of the Empire against Greek nationalists. Egyptian intervention (describe) was so successful it brought the Great Powers into the issue of Greek Independence. Then Mehemet Ali's significance was limited by the destruction of his fleet and the Powers could ignore him in their arrangements for Greece.

Attack: his second role from 1833 was in his attack on the Ottoman Empire's province of Syria.

" Assessing Mehemet Ali's significance. "

Consequences: *Phase 1* – again important because it gave Russia the opportunity to establish influence at Constantinople to the consternation of Britain (explain issues and also terms of Unkiar Skelessi treaty and its effect). This phase continued from 1839 when he defeated the Turks as part of his bid for total Egyptian independence. This brought in the Great Powers again. *Phase 2* – Mehemet Ali was also important because links had been forged between Egypt and France. His adventures therefore provoked a rift between Britain and France. The final failure of France to back him was one aspect of Louis Philippe's weak foreign policy.

Outcome: In the end he did not have the military force to be a major power in the region on his own and his forces were driven from Syria. He was strong enough though to have to be bought off by the Sultan giving him hereditary rule over Egypt. His last adventure enabled Britain, in helping the Sultan against him, to get the terms of Unkiar Skelessi replaced at the 1841 Straits Convention.

Conclusion: Mehemet Ali was an important player in the decline of the Ottoman Empire but once his actions had brought in the major European Powers he was left with little opportunity to influence the outcome of their arrangements for his region.

Question 3

"The effect of the Crimean War on the Eastern Question."

Introduction: neither the war nor its outcome did anything directly to deal with the central issues embraced by the Eastern Question.

Central issues:

- The decline of the Ottoman Empire, as weak after 1856 as earlier – illustrate why this was so.
- The ambitions of Russia which were apparently only temporarily thwarted. 1870 defied neutrality of the Black Sea, embarked on reforms to strengthen the state.
- The distrust of the western powers about Russia's intentions which remained as strong as ever – give 1878 British jingoism as an illustration of this.
- The crisis of 1878 supports this view that the earlier war had done little to ease the problem – indicate its gravity briefly.

Indirect effects: the Crimean War did make some impact on the Eastern Question.

- In isolating Russia from Austria it opened up the way for a new balance of power in Europe with the unification of Germany which through to 1914 was to be a new element of major importance in the affairs of Eastern Europe.
- In 1878 this new element worked to prevent a major war over the Eastern Question but in 1914 it worked in the opposite way.

Conclusion: So it is difficult to argue that the Crimean War helped to solve the Eastern Question but it did help to transform its nature and widen its potential impact.

A TUTOR'S ANSWER TO QUESTION 4

The rivalry amongst the European Powers over the Balkans had a long history: it had provoked a war from 1854 to 1856 and was to do so again, with more devastating effect, in 1914. The most serious Balkan crisis between those dates, which had started with rebellions amongst the Sultan's Christian subjects in 1875 and which culminated in the Treaty of Berlin in 1878, was settled without an armed conflict between the Powers. It did however involve mass repression of the Christian rebels on the one hand and a war between Russia and the Ottoman Empire on the other.

"The essentials of the Eastern Question."

The issues at the heart of the crisis were long-standing and of major significance to the European Powers. They were capable of no easy solution. They arose from the declining ability of the Ottoman Empire to keep control of its Balkan possessions and to the decline of law and order within its borders. The largely Christian indigenous population found themselves subject to increasingly arbitrary and brutal government from both local and central officials. They were in any case increasingly restive under Turkish rule and the first stirrings of Balkan nationalism went back over fifty years since the Greeks and the Serbs broke free. It was always likely, as had happened in the case of the Greeks, that the Christian powers of Europe would not feel able to stand by if a crisis arose between the Moslem Sultan and his Christian subjects. The Russians had long claimed protective rights over the interests of the Orthodox Church and its members in the Ottoman Empire and, since the Crimean War, had begun to develop a new interest in the concept of Panslavism, seeing itself now as the protector of the Slav people of the Balkans.

"Russian pretensions in the Balkans."

These Russian interests in the region were viewed with deep suspicion by several of the other European powers who were quick to see them as a cloak for Russian territorial advance at the expense of the declining Ottoman Turks. Austria-Hungary was bound to see an increase in Russian influence to the south as a threat to its own security and the encouragement of nationalism in the Balkans as a threat to the internal stability of its own multi-national empire. If the Christians of the Balkans were to be set free from the Turks then they should come within the influence of Vienna and not St. Petersburg.

Britain, and sometimes France, were also concerned about Russian expansion at the expense of the Turks which they were quick to see as Russian attempts to gain access to the Mediterranean with all sorts of de-stabilising effects detrimental to their own interests. The threat was real but it was also capable in moments of crisis of being subject to wild exaggeration. This of course made it all the more dangerous and British public opinion in particular was prone to see a vast Russian threat to the British Empire across the globe and particularly pointing at British India. The danger of a Russian presence in the

"British jingoism."

Mediterranean formed a convenient part of this conspiracy theory for the British Prime Minister Disraeli and led to extreme jingoism in the country at large.

In these complex and very dangerous circumstances a critical part of any explanation of why war was avoided arises from outside the Balkans and relates to the role of the Chancellor of the recently united German Empire. Bismarck had by 1871 achieved all his international objectives and wished above all not to have these put at risk in another war. He was also, after the defeat of Austria in 1866, particularly anxious to restore amicable relations between the two German nations and so, although it was in 1878 difficult to see any pressing German interest in the Balkan crisis, Bismarck used his best diplomatic efforts to ensure that it was settled with the minimum fuss. It was Bismarck who, acting the part of 'honest broker', arranged the meeting of the Congress of Berlin and took the initiative in negotiating a crucial series of preliminary agreements. He was able to do this because the unification of Germany had totally altered the balance of continental power in that country's favour. Germany could not be ignored and in 1878 Germany's Chancellor was committed to a peaceful Europe. This is the central part of the answer to this question for, under the shadow of military defeat at Sadowa in 1866, the Austrians were unlikely to take an independent line from the Germans especially if that line posed any risk of war against another major power.

Other factors of course played their part. Most importantly it is advisable not to judge Russian intentions, in declaring war on the Turks in 1877 and in imposing the Treaty of San Stefano on them early in 1878, simply from the view of the jingoistic Britons. They showed little interest in taking Constantinople and the Straits, probably rightly judging that they would never be allowed to keep them. There was a genuine concern for the fate of the Bulgarian Christians and there were limited territorial objectives around the mouth of the Danube. An increase in Russian influence in the region through the creation at San Stefano of the 'Big Bulgaria' was welcome but could be bought at too high a price if the rest of Europe was prepared to resist. In other words, far from having embarked on a well thought out expansionist policy towards the Mediterranean, Russian objectives were limited and negotiable. Still diplomatically isolated after the Crimean defeat it could hardly be otherwise.

> This is a topic in British history papers.

Britain, the country most determinedly opposed to the Russian actions, was represented at the conference by Disraeli who was determined to uphold the integrity of the Ottoman Empire as the best way of guaranteeing British interests in the Mediterranean. On the other hand he was the subject of fierce criticism at home from Gladstone and had to be mindful of British public opinion on which his electoral fortunes depended. This had already swung once from horror at the tales of Turkish massacres to intense anti-Russian feeling as their troops moved towards Constantinople: it could swing again and there was much to be said for a swift diplomatic triumph rather than the danger of a re-run of the messy Crimean War. In short he too was willing to settle at the right price and, in the preliminary dealings with Bismarck, had agreed a substantial part of it. Cyprus was to be surrendered to Britain as a counterweight to Russian advances and as a price the Turks must pay to undo San Stefano.

The Turks themselves were realists, they had to accept what the Powers offered them in the way of restoring lands that they had proved unable to defend against Russian occupation. In return they were prepared to make promises of reform and better treatment of the Christian population which would enable the statesmen at Berlin to re-assure public opinion at home and, in Disraeli's case, provide an argument to counter the moral indignation of Gladstone.

In 1878 there were good reasons for all the protagonists to accept a compromise solution rather than risk the probability of war and it took less than a month at Berlin for this to happen. The most important agreement involved the dismantling of 'Big Bulgaria' with all the perceived threat of a Russian presence in the Mediterranean and in return the Russians settled for the limited gains of territory that they had made at San Stefano, notably around the mouth of the Danube. The Austrians were given virtual control of Bosnia and Herzegovina, as noted Britain obtained Cyprus and even France got a re-declaration of its role as guardian of the Christian shrines in Palestine. Honour was satisfied, Bismarck had emerged as the arbiter of Europe and the real price had been paid by the Turks and, defeated in war, they were in no position to argue. Nor of course did they intend to keep any of their promises of reform towards their Christian subjects whose plight remained as grim as ever. This fact the Christian States preferred to forget rather than risk a major war amongst themselves in the doubtful pursuit of a lasting solution to the Eastern Question.

> 1878: the Eastern Question still unresolved.

USEFUL SOURCES OF INFORMATION

General reading

A Ramm, *Europe in the Nineteenth Century 1789–1905*, Longman 1984
J B Watson, *Success in European History 1815–1941*, John Murray 1981
A Wood, *Europe 1815–1960*, Longman 1984

Further reading

M S Anderson, *The Eastern Question 1774–1923*, Macmillan 1966
L C B Seaman, *From Vienna to Versailles*, Methuen 1972
A J P Taylor, *The Struggle for Mastery in Europe*, Oxford University Press 1971

Linked topic areas

- The Vienna Settlement 1815 and the Congress System (see Chapter 12)
- British foreign policy in the 19th century
- Russian history in the 19th century (see Chapter 14)
- Bismarck's Foreign Policy 1871–1890 (see Chapter 17)
- The causes of the First World War (see Chapter 19)

CHAPTER 16

ITALIAN UNIFICATION

GETTING STARTED

Napoleon's military excursions into Italy in the period following the French Revolution disrupted the traditional patterns of social and political authority: it is argued that in this period the spirit of Italian nationalism was first awakened. This spirit was ignored by the Peace Settlement of 1815 (see Chapter 12). You need to be aware of the arrangements made for Italy, by the Great Powers of Europe, in that year. They rest on restoring to the smaller Italian States the old Bourbon and Habsburg rulers dispossessed in the Napoleonic period and in introducing direct Austrian rule to Lombardy and Venetia. The Papal States, which were also restored in 1815, were to become a particular stumbling block in the unification process. At this point studying a political sketch map to familiarise yourself with the political geography of the region would be of value, as indeed would a reminder of the appearance of the political map of Europe generally, especially note the Austrian Empire.

Maintaining the 1815 arrangements in Italy fell mainly on Austria's leading statesman, Metternich, whose policy in Italy aimed to suppress the slow growing resistance there to the Vienna arrangements. This will in turn illustrate the early growth, to 1848, of Italian nationalism. The terms 'nationalism' and 'liberalism' are much used in this topic area and, at an early stage in your reading and via a good dictionary or a textbook index, you should establish a full understanding of their meaning. The 'Getting Started' section of Chapter 12, on Europe in 1815, offers a preliminary definition.

This topic is also one which is often studied through assessment of the role of individuals in promoting or retarding unification. This can distort the analysis but is, at this early stage, a useful way into the topic. You could look up, in an encyclopaedia, Mazzini, Cavour and Garibaldi, most logically in that order, to gain a preliminary knowledge of their roles.

ESSENTIAL PRINCIPLES

ITALIAN NATIONAL FEELING

ITS DEVELOPMENT 1815–1848

This has links with the Napoleonic period when both political changes imposed by the French and reaction against the French presence greatly enhanced an Italian national feeling which was just emerging in the late eighteenth century.

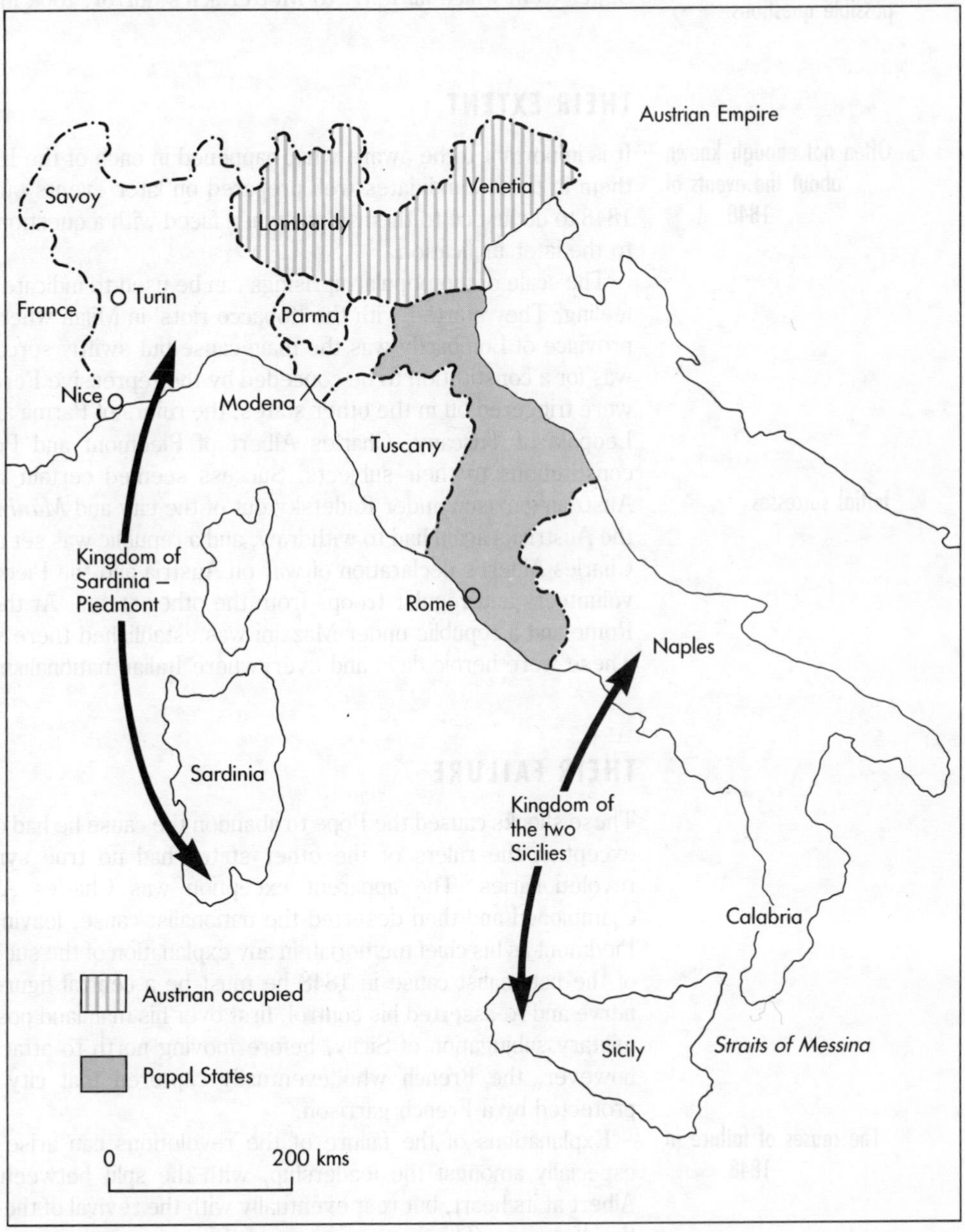

Fig. 16.1 Italy: 1815–1859

THE RISORGIMENTO

The common term for this movement is Risorgimento which means revival; it is as much an intellectual as a political phenomenon located in many of the small Italian states and especially in their towns, it sees national feeling developing via the arts, drama, education and literature. A serious study of Italy in this period should include noting a series of illustrative references to these intellectual aspects of nationalism. Tracing the advance of political nationalism, even just as a background to events in 1848 and after, should include an awareness of:

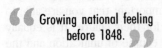

“Growing national feeling before 1848.”

- The growth of secret nationalist societies like **the Carbonari**.
- The hopes pinned, from 1831, on the king of Piedmont, Charles Albert.
- The installation of the apparently sympathetic Pope Pius IX in 1846.

Italy at this point has been described as ripe for revolution. The only real test of the strength of Italian nationalism to this point is by reference to the events of 1848.

THE 1848 REVOLUTIONS

"Widen your range of possible questions."

For examination purposes these should be seen as part of a wider series of revolutionary movements across Europe and revision of what happened in other countries will open up an entirely new range of possible questions. In Italy the unlikely starting point for the study of events in 1848 is with the moderate but enlightened reforms of Pius IX in the Papal States from which all Italy, to Metternich's horror, took inspiration.

THEIR EXTENT

"Often not enough known about the events of 1848."

It is important to be aware what happened in each of the Italian States, as revolutions hit them in turn. Candidates well prepared on later events often lack enough knowledge on 1848 to do justice to themselves when faced with a question requiring them to relate 1848 to the later unification.

The scale of the popular uprisings can be used to indicate the strength of Italian national feeling. They started with the 'tobacco riots' in Milan where anti-Austrian feeling in their province of Lombardy was the main cause but swiftly spread to Sicily where the demand was for a constitution to be conceded by the repressive Ferdinand II. Spontaneous revolts were triggered off in the other states, the rulers of Parma and Modena fled their lands and Leopold of Tuscany, Charles Albert of Piedmont and Pope Pius IX conceded liberal constitutions to their subjects. Success seemed certain when the Milanese drove the Austrian garrison under Radetsky out of the city and *Manin* led a revolt in Venice, where the Austrians again had to withdraw, and a republic was set up. This phase culminated with Charles Albert's declaration of war on Austria and the Piedmontese army being joined by volunteers and regular troops from the other states. At the end of the year Pius IX fled Rome and a republic under Mazzini was established there with Garibaldi as its defender. These were heroic days and everywhere Italian nationalism seemed to have triumphed.

"Initial successes."

THEIR FAILURE

These shocks caused the Pope to abandon the cause he had originally inspired and with one exception the rulers of the other states had no true sympathy with the aims of the revolutionaries. The apparent exception was Charles Albert of Piedmont who first championed and then deserted the nationalist cause, leaving a new liberal constitution in Piedmont as his chief memorial: in any explanation of the successes and the eventual failure of the nationalist cause in 1848 he must be a central figure. Ferdinand II recovered his nerve and re-asserted his control, first over his mainland possession and then with a brutal military subjugation of Sicily, before moving north to attack *Garibaldi* in Rome. It was, however, the French who eventually captured that city and restored Pius IX to it, protected by a French garrison.

"The causes of failure in 1848."

Explanations of the failure of the revolutions can arise in part from Italian disunity, especially amongst the leadership, with the split between the republicans and Charles Albert at its heart, but rest eventually with the revival of the military nerve and strength of the Austrians. This in turn is part of the wider story of events in the Austrian Empire at large.

THE RESULTS

"Lessons to be learned."

The results of 1848 seem entirely negative but arguably the fighting and the deaths re-inforced the feelings of national identity. It was also advantageous that the Austrian military victory, which outside Sicily was chiefly responsible for crushing the nationalist and liberal hopes, meant that the true enemy of any political change in Italy was now clearly visible. From this another conclusion emerged, for it now appeared that only foreign help would be able to remove this Austrian presence from Italy. It is very important that you are able to discuss these 1848 Revolutions and to analyse the reasons for their failure. It is equally important to be able to explain how they affected the future course of unification and the 'Outline Answer' to Question 2 later in this chapter opens up this issue.

THE MODERNISATION OF PIEDMONT

"Cavour a Piedmontese nationalist?"

Victor Emmanuel II became king of Piedmont in 1849 and appointed *Cavour* his Prime Minister in 1852. The latter's contribution to unification, in modernising Piedmont and in the involved diplomacy which he initiated, is one of the most common examination questions. Remember that the Constitution earlier granted by Charles Albert provided an important basis but recognise too the indispensable role of the new king. Cavour's modernisation of the state included a review of its administration, the position and privileges of the Catholic Church and the legal system. He did much to strengthen the economy of Piedmont by encouraging expanding trade through free-trade treaties, railway development and private financial institutions. All of this work made Piedmont seem such an obvious choice, to European liberals at least, to renew the unification process. On the other hand the king, rather than Cavour may have initiated the bid for European recognition with the decision to join Britain and France in fighting the Crimean War. The need for foreign help against Austria is the key to understanding Piedmontese diplomacy in the 1850s.

NORTHERN ITALY

ITS UNIFICATION

"And a realist."

This is probably all Cavour sought. It happened remarkably suddenly from 1858, with the secret pact between Cavour and Napoleon III at Plombières, to 1860, by when Piedmont had obtained Lombardy from Austria and had annexed Parma, Modena, Tuscany and, from the Papal States, the Romagna, and in return had ceded Nice and Savoy to its French ally. You need to read through an account of these exciting events, not to be able to describe them but to be able to use them to illustrate and assess the responsibility of Cavour, the Emperor Napoleon III of France and of Italian Nationalists in Piedmont's neighbouring states for these developments. They, and the motives of those who brought them about, are the heart of the unification story.

SOUTHERN ITALY

ITS UNIFICATION

"The role of Garibaldi."

This, perhaps the single most romantic episode of nineteenth century European history, revolves of course around the achievements of Garibaldi. It started before the territorial changes in northern Italy were complete but has often been treated separately for examination purposes. You must be able to give a balanced assessment of Garibaldi's flamboyant but courageous role but also be ready with some detailed assessment of quite obscure steps taken by Cavour which remain a matter of some debate among historians: did Cavour seek to obstruct Garibaldi or secretly assist him? Careful mastery of the details could be valuable here. Garibaldi's eventual debt to others, especially Cavour, was great but the larger dream of a united Italy including the south might well not have been achieved without his vision and his courage.

CAVOUR, GARIBALDI, MAZZINI

ASSESSING THEIR ROLES

Exam questions

Questions on the factors bringing about the unification of Italy are common and are regularly set in terms of assessing the role of key individuals. The permutations of possible questions, and the stress within them, is almost endless and there is little point in trying to spot specific questions. Revision of the reasons why Italy was unified when it was, and why it took the form it did, will give the frame for more specific questions. You may well be presented with a proposition, often in the form of a quotation, on the contribution of one of these men, or the suggestion that one was more significant in some way than another. Try to offer a balanced assessment, recognising that the unification was a complex story and that no-one deserves all the credit, be able to illustrate this rather than just state it. Questions on great individuals tend to distort what happened so be prepared to argue that there were many more contributors to unification than the question suggests and, again, be able to demonstrate why you believe this: it was for example popular uprisings in the small north Italian states which in 1860 kept the momentum of northern unification going when Napoleon had lost interest and Cavour had resigned in despair.

"Not just a question of some great names."

In assessing the roles of the three principals the least is often known about Mazzini, so he may deserve special revision attention and an encyclopaedia would give you an easily assimilated potted version. Cavour's role is the subject of the 'Tutor's Answer' to Question 1 later in this chapter.

ROLE OF FOREIGN POWERS

This is the other side of the coin of evaluating the role of the Italian leaders, but there is a little more to it than this in that the wider role of Italian nationalism generally tends to be undervalued. The focus is on Napoleon and Austria when it should also take in, for example, the key role played by those who in 1859 rebelled in the northern Duchies and so forced the hand of Napoleon III to reach a general settlement of northern Italy just when he looked to be abandoning his commitments to Piedmont. Italians perhaps did more than has been allowed for towards their own unification and it could be useful to be able to argue this. The Austrian and the later French roles in obstructing and opposing unification are central to the story.

FRANCE'S DUAL ROLE

In assessing France's role remember the French garrison in Rome who had been protectors of the Pope since 1849 and who were to be there until 1870. Also be ready to have at least some comments available on England, generally sympathetic and offering a few naval flourishes but not of the same significance as France. Comments on Prussia should include helping in 1866 to add Venetia to the united Italy, almost without intent to do so, and similarly in 1870 bringing about the French departure from Rome.

POSITION OF THE PAPACY

This involves yet another re-working of the same material! The Papacy, like the rulers of the smaller Italian states, and from 1849 protected by the French garrison in Rome, was seen as an obstacle to unification which others had to overcome. Nationalists found this all the more an affront because of the earlier hopes raised by Pius IX who, in a brief liberal phase from his inauguration to the 1848 revolts, had appeared willing to come to some accommodation with Italian national and liberal aspirations.

Exam questions

Constructing a brief argument in defence or explanation of the Papal position would provide a balance to any assessment of unification. It would enhance the quality of your judgements by revealing a due regard for the position of those who were not enthusiastic about what had happened in Italy. Italian conservatives, for example, saw the unification of 1859–1860 as a piece of aggressive Piedmontese expansionism carried out at the expense of the rest of Italy.

“Aggression by Piedmont?”

Commonly, however, questions on the Papacy are so phrased that your comments have to explain how this obstruction to unification was overcome: the account then needs to go through to the departure of the French in 1870. For related episodes in 1862 and 1867 see the 'Useful Information' section below.

The legacy of ill-feeling between Church and State is one of the most important ingredients in the history of the Kingdom of Italy through to 1929, when Mussolini reached an agreement with the Papacy which resolved the issues still outstanding.

THE KINGDOM OF ITALY

The incorporation of Venetia (1866) and of Rome (1870) are important parts of the unification account but thereafter the new Kingdom of Italy tends to be absent from outline examination papers. It is however a topic which is dealt with quite briefly in most textbooks and would be worth following through to 1914 and to Italy's role, again quite briefly stated, in the First World War. In outline the story is one of political and economic problems and the weaknesses of the new state.

“A less common source of questions . . .”

Exam questions

On occasion a quite difficult question appears inviting comment on the suggestion that these problems arose from the way in which the kingdom was united. You will first need to master the later history and then think back to the intrigues of Cavour and the notion of Piedmontese expansionism. The later paragraphs in the 'Tutor's Answer' to Question 1 should give you some ideas on the connections to be drawn. For the less committed,

“. . . but a useful link with Mussolini's career.”

adding to a thorough study of the Unification some outline knowledge of Italian history through to 1918, is admirable background for another frequent examination topic, the rise of Mussolini.

USEFUL INFORMATION

1796–1814	Italy occupied by French. Nationalist ideas and groups in support begin to emerge; for example, by 1810 the Carbonari.
1815	**The Vienna Settlement**: Italian arrangements were aimed at restoring and strengthening the pre-French balance. ■ Austria received Lombardy and Venetia. ■ Habsburg rulers restored in Tuscany and Modena. ■ Bourbon ruler restored to Kingdom of Naples. ■ Papal States restored. Catholic Church throughout Italy was a reactionary force.
1815–1848	Italy fragmented, states controlled by absolutist rulers, local particularism more marked than national sentiments.
1820–1821	Liberal revolts in Naples and Piedmont crushed, mainly by the use of Austrian troops.
1831	Liberal revolts in Naples, Parma, Modena and the Papal States defeated again mainly by the Austrians. Charles Albert became king of Piedmont. Privately indicated some support for nationalist ideas but ignored a request from Mazzini to lead the nationalist cause.
1833	**'Young Italy' founded by Mazzini**. By 1835 it had 60,000 members and its unsuccessful revolt in Naples in 1844 gave the nationalist cause its martyrs.
1846	**Pius IX became Pope**; political amnesty in the Papal States shocked Metternich and excited liberals and nationalists.
1848	**Revolutions throughout Italy**
1849	Victor Emmanuel became King of Piedmont
1852	**Cavour** became Prime Minister of Piedmont: programme of modernisation of the administration and the economy.
1854–1856	**Crimean War**: Piedmont entered on Anglo-French side in 1855 Pact of Plombières between Napoleon III and Cavour. Napoleon III agreed to join Piedmont in a war against Austria provided that the latter was provoked into declaring war. Territorial agreement to share out lands in northern Italy.
1859	Austria at war with France and Piedmont. Truce of Villafranca. Napoleon ready to accept a compromise on the Plombières arrangements on Austrian lands in northern Italy. Lombardy ceded to Piedmont but Venetia to stay under Austria. Revolts in Duchies (Parma, Modena Tuscany): plebiscites favoured joining Piedmont. Savoy and Nice ceded by Piedmont to France. Garibaldi voyage to Sicily; conquered it and crossed to Naples. Piedmont invasion of the Papal States.
1861	First Italian Parliament proclaimed the establishment of the Kingdom of Italy with Victor Emmanuel as monarch and based on the Piedmont constitution with Turin the capital. **Death of Cavour**
1862	Garibaldi's intended attack on Rome blocked by Italian troops.
1866	Austro-Prussian War: Venetia gained from Austria despite Italian defeat by Austrians at battle of Custozza.
1867	Garibaldi attack on Rome, after French withdrawal defeat of Papal army brought French back to defeat Garibaldi.
1870	Franco-Prussian War: French garrison withdrawn from Rome which was then occupied by the Italian army.

EXAMINATION QUESTIONS

Q1 To what extent was Cavour the architect of Italian unification? (NEAB 1989)

Q2 In what ways did the failure of the Italian Revolutions of 1848–9 affect the later movement for Italian unification? (Oxford 1986)

Q3 How much did the unification of Italy owe to planning, and how much to chance? (London 1990)

Q4 What problems faced the Italian nationalists in 1848, and to what extent had they been overcome by 1861? (Welsh 1989)

Q5 'Unification solved none of the real problems of Italy, as the political experiences of the next fifty years made clear to all.' How far do you agree with this statement? (London 1987)

OUTLINE ANSWERS

Question 1

See the 'Tutor's Answer' below.

Question 2

Answer: rests in how key individuals responded to the reasons for the failure in 1848.

Response:

- *Victor Emmanuel* and *Cavour* drew the lesson that even to lead northern Italian unification (which was their real aim) Piedmont would need to be modernised (describe what they did) and this had an important effect on the course of later events.

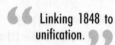

" Linking 1848 to unification. "

- Failure in 1848 also led them to the idea that foreign help was needed to expel the Austrians from northern Italy (explain briefly how Austrians had been key to failure of 1848 and how at Plombières and after they were outmanoeuvred).
- Conversely idealism seen as not enough and so Republicans like Mazzini played little part after 1848.
- 1848 made Papacy reactionary and this complicated and delayed unification, illustrate this.

Conclusion: 1848 failure ensured that it would be a unity imposed by the politicians and not a joining together of the Italian people. This brought about the domination of the rest of Italy by Piedmont and from this stemmed many of the weaknesses of the Italian State in the future.

Question 3

Planning: there was planning; it revolved around Cavour and its nature has been misunderstood.

- Cavour planned to modernise Piedmont and to gain her international recognition and support against Austria (explain his actions to Plombières) but this was intended to bring about Piedmont domination of northern Italy not unification.

" Cavour the opportunist. "

- There was also the quick seizing of opportunities (not the same thing as chance) illustrated by Cavour's backing and manoeuvring of Garibaldi and the seizure of the Papal States – discuss details.

Chance: the best example of pure chance playing a part was the unlikely conversion of Napoleon III to the cause or, later, that it was convenient to Bismarck's plans that the Italians be encouraged to seize Venetia.

Conclusion: a better verdict overall would be that opportunism was more important than planning.

Note: Now read through the 'Tutor's Answer' to a similar question on page 175.

Question 4

See the 'Student's Answer' on page 176.

Question 5

Identify: briefly, the 'real problems of Italy':

- social problems of poverty, public health, the South
- economic, backward economy leading to mass emigration
- the rift with the Church after unification actions
- the dreams of national glory which were beyond its resources

Illustrate: from the *political* experiences of the next 50 years

"Italy after unification."

- Corruption and party intrigues, lack of any reforms, unstable governments, only in 1912 was narrow franchise widened.
- Feud between State and Church, Catholics forbidden by Pope to enter politics until 1905.
- Lack of reform led to growth of strong socialist parties which created another division in society.
- Quest for glory ended in disaster at Adowa and in the defeats in the First World War and the disappointments of the Peace Treaty.

Conclusion: agree with the quotation in the question. Unification had 'solved' the problems of Italians from the past, going back to Napoleon, it could only provide a starting point for solving the future problems, social, economic and political, of the united country. It was not unification but the failure of later Italians to build on it that created the country's difficulties and led, in 1922, to Mussolini coming to power to make a new start.

A TUTOR'S ANSWER TO QUESTION 1

"Defines the role of an architect."

If the title of this question is implying that Cavour had drawn up plans for a united kingdom of Italy and that his political efforts were geared to the implementation of the plan then the answer must be that in this sense Cavour was not the architect of Italian Unification. His plans were less grand. That said, it has to be conceded that Cavour's opportunist schemes and his political skills did a great deal both to create the Italian Kingdom and to establish some of its chief characteristics. To deny that he drew up a blueprint for the unification of Italy is not to claim that his life's work was not of the greatest significance in bringing that unification about.

He became Prime Minister of Piedmont in 1852 and some of his most important work was in modernising that state. This modernisation was derived from an admiration of British economic achievements and acceptance of the liberal principles of the rule of law and parliamentary institutions, which were then in vogue in middle-class Europe. He sought to make Piedmont a more efficient state and to this end worked to reduce the privileged position of the Catholic Church. In this he was acting as a Piedmont nationalist.

"Piedmont and the Crimean War."

It has been argued that Cavour learned, from the defeat of the 1848 revolutions in Italy, the lesson that the Italians alone could not unite their country because this would involve driving out the Austrians from Lombardy and Venetia. To secure foreign help in this he committed Piedmontese troops to the Crimean War. There are two problems in this; first it now seems that the intervention in the war was at King Victor Emmanuel's instigation rather than Cavour's and that it was intended to strengthen Piedmont's international status with France and Britain but not necessarily in pursuit at this stage of any unification of Italy. Piedmont rather had national ambitions to extend its territories in northern Italy and this too would require foreign aid against the Austrians. This was the purpose of the Crimean adventure and also the subsequent intrigues with Napoleon III.

There is no doubt that Cavour was at the heart of the plot through which the French were to assist Piedmont against the Austrian forces, personally meeting with the Emperor at Plombières to work out the arrangements. Piedmont's spoils were to include the provinces of Lombardy and Venetia and some of the northern lands of the Papal States. The Pope was to be compensated by being made President of a new Italian Federation of which the enlarged Piedmont would be one part. From Cavour's point of view it was a scheme purely for the expansion of Piedmontese territory and was limited in this solely to northern Italy. In particular it was unquestioned that the Papal States in central Italy and the Kingdom of the Two Sicilies in the south would continue.

Napoleon's timidity lost Piedmont any chance of securing Venetia and Cavour in despair resigned from office. It was a series of popular uprisings in the northern Italian Duchies which brought them into union with Piedmont. There was no master plan by Cavour in any of this but there was masterly opportunism in snatching what could be gained from the popular risings and the unfulfilled victories of Magenta and Solferino. Cavour's ruthless realism made him able to pay the price in the secession of Savoy and Nice to France. He had greatly enlarged the kingdom of Piedmont though his methods had alienated many idealists and many non-Piedmontese Italians who had seen unity coming through a drawing together of the people and not through the aggrandisement of Piedmont.

"Cavour's important role in uniting the south."

The union of the rest of Italy into the new northern kingdom appears to be largely the responsibility of Garibaldi who first conquered it and then handed his conquests to Victor Emmanuel. This view however undervalues the part played by Cavour at crucial moments in those events. Clearly Cavour was not the architect of a plan to unite southern and central Italy with Piedmont. Indeed at times he feared that Garibaldi's adventures might alienate Napoleon and lose Piedmont some or all of what it had already gained. But the stakes were high and the swift movement of events enabled Cavour to use his opportunist wiles to the full. His role in some episodes is still unclear and we may never know whether he tried to hinder or to help Garibaldi on his way from Genoa to invade Sicily. He certainly and totally unscrupulously took advantage of events, inventing a pretext for Piedmont troops to enter the Papal States and then moved them south to hold in check any extravagant ambitions, that Garibaldi might develop. The King of Piedmont became the king of a united Italy as the people of the newly occupied territories voted by huge majorities for annexation by Victor Emmanuel.

This was all skilful opportunism on Cavour's part: he could be said to have hi-jacked Garibaldi's dream. Equally the intrigues to win local support for Piedmont's expansion, the lies and the bribes, could be said to have tarnished forever the vision of a united Italy based on the free coming together of the Italian people which had been Mazzini's great contribution to unification.

"An attempt at a final conclusion."

Too much should not be made of the fact that, at Cavour's death, Rome and Venetia remained outside the kingdom. So much had been accomplished that the outcome for these territories seemed, even in 1861, quite predictable. Cavour's role in bringing this about was not a glorious one but it was certainly crucial. Others played important parts, Garibaldi and the underestimated Victor Emmanuel, but it was Cavour's opportunism that finally shaped the outcome. It was not an outcome he had planned or even foreseen until events unfolded with dramatic suddeness. Then he exploited them superbly; more an entrepreneur than an architect.

A STUDENT'S ANSWER TO QUESTION 4

"A good attempt to explain who the nationalists were."

In 1848 the only clear cut true Italian nationalists were the Republicans like Mazzini. They wanted a united Italy with a republican constitution which would bring together the people of all Italy into a democratic liberal state. The other group prominent in the movements of 1848 centred on the king of Piedmont Charles Albert. In private he had indicated sympathy for the nationalist cause but did nothing to support it before 1848 where again he soon lost real interest when he saw the recovery of Austrian power. He was truly more interested in promoting Piedmont than in just supporting nationalism. The same is true of his son Victor Emmanuel who became king in 1849 and his Prime Minister Cavour. Both of them were Piedmont patriots rather than Italian nationalists. In this essay however the obstacles facing all of these people in their ambitions will be considered for they were to a large extent the same obstacles. But by 1861 the outcome for the two groups was very different.

"Clarity on the obstacles."

The main obstacle to unification in 1848 was clearly Austria whose army had restored their control over Lombardy and Venetia. Austria

"The essay development is easy to follow."

was completely against any unification of Italy and had acted several times in the past to stop risings in favour of unity. It is true that Metternich was no longer in power in Austria but that did not mean that its policy in Italy was going to change much.

The other obstacles were the lesser rulers of the Italian states who wanted to keep their own status and powers which would be lost in any unification of Italy. The Pope had been sympathetic to nationalist ideas but was so frightened by the revolutions of 1848 that he became an opponent of all reforms. He was protected by a garrison of French troops in Rome and they would be another obstacle to reform.

The final obstacle to reform was the lack of a clear leader for the nationalists and the fact that they could not work together. There was nobody strong enough to stand up to the Austrians as the failure of Charles Albert showed.

"Part 2 of the essay clearly signposted."

By 1861 the situation had greatly changed for Italy had become a united kingdom under Victor Emmanuel of Piedmont. Most of the obstacles had been overcome. The rulers of the smaller states had been swept away and their lands had been joined to Piedmont, the Austrians had been turned out of Lombardy. The north of the Papal States, called the Romagna, had also joined the new kingdom. Garibaldi's expedition had removed the ruler of the Kingdom of Naples and also conquered the rest of the Papal lands. Garibaldi then surrendered these conquests to Victor Emmanuel and they became part of the new Italian kingdom.

Some obstacles remained for the Austrians still kept Venetia and the French troops in Rome still protected the Pope but most of Italy was now joined together. This was because Italy had found a leader to bring about unity. Cavour had modernised Piedmont and had obtained French help to turn the Austrians out of the north. He had not thought of uniting all of Italy but he had by chance overcome the main obstacle.

"An essay which avoids just describing what happened, but one needing more substance."

The formation of the new kingdom of Italy meant that the republicans who had been the true nationalists had lost. They had not had the strength to drive out the Austrians in 1848 and now the wily Cavour had out-manoeuvred them. They were not to get their republic until the twentieth century.

EXAMINER COMMENTS

The best thing about this essay is the attempt to explain who the nationalists were. This prevents any effort, which is far too common in answers on Italian Unification, just to *describe* the sequence of events. The separation of the Republicans and the Monarchists and how their dreams came to very different conclusions is a good point to make. The obstacles are established except that a stronger essay would have mentioned the separatist feelings of many Italian peoples as an obstacle. By 1861 this had been overcome by Garibaldi's adventurism and more by the manoeuvres of Cavour and the force of Piedmontese arms.

The 1861 situation is rather superficially considered in terms of the obstacles remaining. Their strength deserves some analysis, for example, if the Pope had been named as an obstacle it could have been pointed out that his position depended totally on the French presence and that circumstances might well arise which could bring that to an end.

Otherwise the chief criticism is that the ideas lack substantial backing. Some informed comments on Austrian military strength and successes in 1848 and on the failure then of the Italians to work to a common goal would have improved the first part. More precise and more full information on how Cavour and his king worked to overcome some of the obstacles would have given a more substantial answer to the second part of the question. At the very least, having mentioned the Pope, then he could have been named, as could some of the smaller states whose particularism was one of the biggest obstacles that was overcome between 1848 and 1861.

USEFUL SOURCES OF INFORMATION

General reading

A Ramm, *Europe in the Nineteenth Century, 1789–1905*, Longman 1984
J B Watson, *Success in European History 1815–1941*, John Murray 1981
A Wood, *Europe 1815–1960*, Longman 1984

Further reading

A Stiles, *The Unification of Italy 1815–1870*, Arnold 1986
W G Shreeves, *Nation Making in Nineteenth Century Europe*, Nelson 1984

Linked topic areas

- The 1848 Revolutions across Europe
- The Crimean War
- The Austrian Empire 1815–1867
- German Unification (see Chapter 17)
- Napoleon III and the Second French Empire (see Chapter 13)

CHAPTER 17

GERMAN UNIFICATION

GETTING STARTED

Start by looking at two political sketch maps; one of the boundaries of the major European states under the arrangements agreed at the Peace Settlement of 1815 (see Chapter 12), the other the disposition of the states which made up the Germanic Confederation. On both maps particularly note the boundaries of Prussia and the Austrian Empire, both with lands inside and outside the Confederation. The Prussian territories were however overwhelmingly German in culture, language and traditions whereas the Austrian state had vast non-Germanic possessions peopled by numerous different nationalities. For the period to 1848 be aware of the dominance of Austria within the Confederation and of the policies of Metternich to suppress any German liberal or nationalist movements. Be able to illustrate these policies by describing the background to and the nature of the Karlsbad Decrees of 1819. Make sure that you understand what the terms *liberalism* and *nationalism* mean, the 'Getting Started' section of Chapter 12 offers a simple definition.

The only German state powerful enough to challenge Austria was of course Prussia. Prussia however was an autocratic, socially conservative state where both the army and the growing state bureaucracy played key roles. It was distrusted by the largely intellectual German liberals as the home of reactionary politics and it was difficult to envisage them making common cause with the Kingdom of Prussia to dent the control over Germany exercised by Austria.

Prussia's only move was economic – but it was a very important one – the creation of the *Zollverein* (Customs Union) in 1821, abolishing trade duties within Prussia and setting common tariffs at Prussia's frontiers. This in the long term promoted the economic advance of Prussia for it led, in the 1820s, to neighbouring German states applying to come within the tariff zone, often coerced into this by the high taxes imposed on goods in transit across Prussian territory. The Zollverein came into full existence in 1834 with only three German States and the Austrian Empire left outside. The Zollverein became increasingly important after 1848. You need to be able to explain how it promoted Prussia's position in Germany at the expense of Austria's undoubted political pre-eminence.

Consult the entry on Bismarck in a good encyclopaedia and re-read it after you have studied the topic. German Unification is a densely packed tale. It could be advantageous to read up what happened in chronological sequence, in a brief text book account, before considering the more analytical questions which arise and which are favoured by examiners at A-level. A question on some aspect of German history in the second half of the nineteenth century occurs regularly in many examination papers so that it is well worthwhile to make a decision that this is one of the topics you will really master.

ESSENTIAL PRINCIPLES

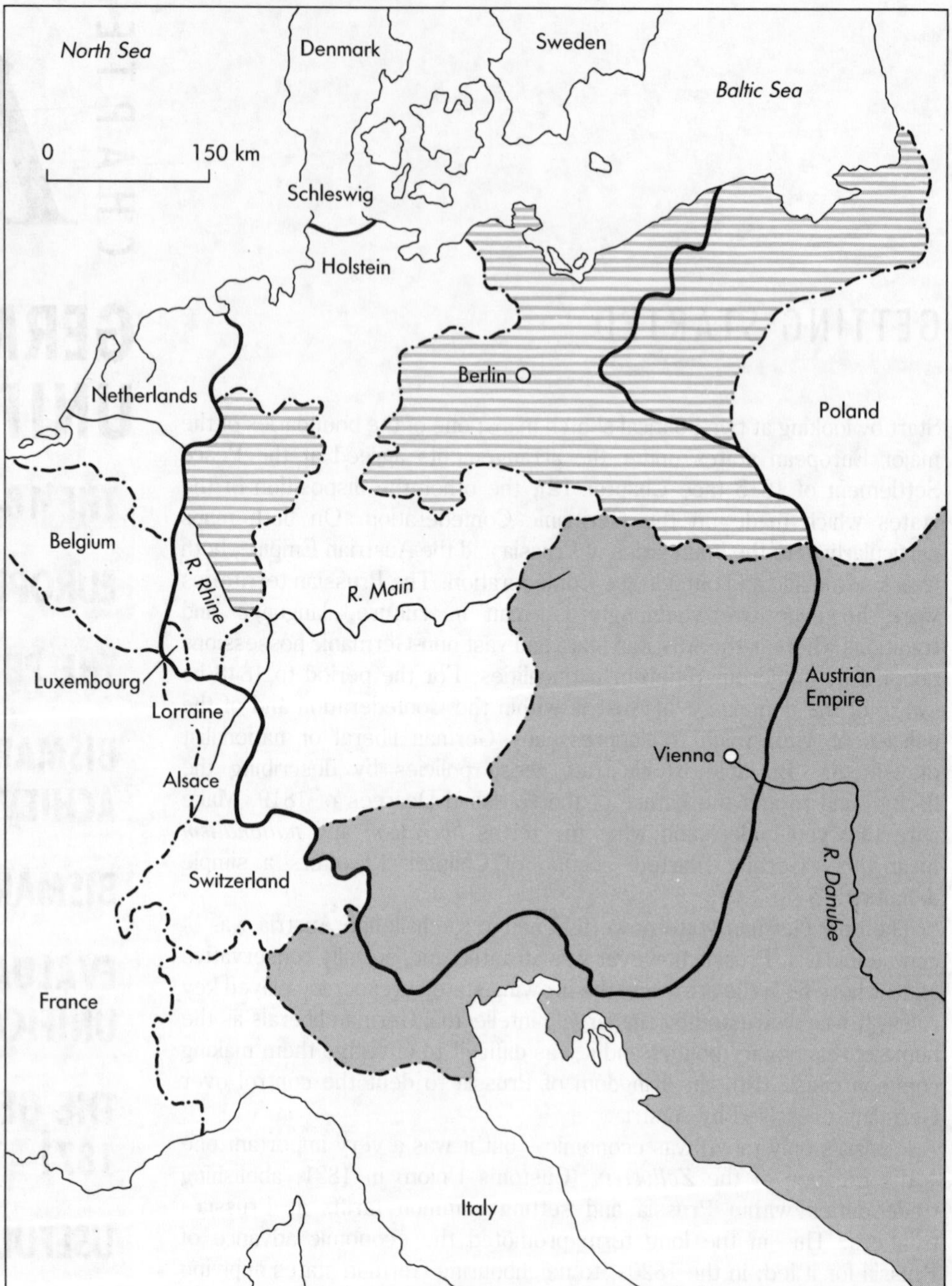

Fig. 17.1 Germany: 1815–1866

THE 1848 REVOLUTIONS

"The 1848 Revolutions across Europe should be studied."

THEIR OUTCOME IN GERMANY

These cannot be studied apart from the revolutions which also occurred throughout the Austrian Empire. This being so it would be sensible to read up what happened in France and in Italy and so be prepared for a general European question on 1848 (consult Chapters 13 and 16).

Causes

The causes of the revolutions in Germany were partly economic, though socialist ideas played a smaller part than in France, and were partly inspired by news from Italy and Paris.

The first outbreak happened in Baden and they soon took on a nationalist form and led to the setting up of an elected German Parliament at Frankfurt. Following riots in Berlin Frederick William IV made rapid concessions, first agreeing to call the Prussian Diet and then announcing that Prussia would be merged into Germany. You need to be able to offer a commentary on the causes of the revolutions but, in establishing these, remember that a loss of nerve amongst the established German rulers and, above all, the overthrow of Metternich and the consequent chaos in Vienna, contributed greatly to the dramatic success of the series of sporadic local risings.

Reasons for failure

Look, even at this stage, for the seeds of future disintegration. The revolts were, for example, almost entirely middle-class and the rulers, by giving in easily, kept control of their administrations and armies. In Prussia the king recovered his nerve, and had by the end of the year once more dismissed the Diet, and this marked a turning point throughout Germany. Events at Frankfurt, where the increasingly divided Parliament lost its way, have also to be understood. The delegates there lacked the support of the working-classes, commanded no military support and indulged in endless debates whilst their opportunities slipped away. Their offer to admit Austria into a new German Empire was rejected as was the offer of the Crown of the Empire to Frederick William of Prussia. Following these refusals both major powers withdrew from Frankfurt. This, linked to the re-establishment of Imperial power at Vienna and the use of Prussian troops to restore order and traditional authority in the smaller states, marked the collapse of the liberal nationalist dream of a more united, more democratic Germany.

The outcome

"National and Liberal aspirations were not identical."

The brief existence of an all German Parliament strengthened the desire for national unity in some form. The failure of the Frankfurt Parliament showed the weakness of liberalism in Germany and it became clear that nationalist developments might now occur without parallel advances towards democracy. There has been much debate on whether the 1848 revolutions in Germany achieved anything worthwhile and, from your reading you need to form a view on this and not just a political view; for example they led to a weakening of feudalism, which may have been more helpful in theory than practice to the peasant, but almost certainly assisted later economic growth. In Berlin and elsewhere in Germany there had also been the first stirrings of socialist ideas and support which were to become a major force in German history only after the country had been unified.

The immediate aftermath of the events of 1848 were the attempts by Frederick William of Prussia first to set up a League of Princes to consolidate Prussian influence in north Germany and then in 1850 the Erfurt Union of states committed to devising some form of German union. Austrian disapproval led the other states to leave the League and, on the brink of war with Austria over a rebellion in Hesse-Cassel, Frederick William abandoned the Erfurt Union and in 1850, at a meeting at Olmutz, he withdrew his support of the rebels at the insistence of the Austrian Chief Minister Schwarzenberg. Both Prussian prestige and prospects of German unification appeared to be at an all-time low.

"1850 Olmutz showed Austria's continued strength in Germany."

EUROPE AFTER 1848

"Crimean War isolated Austria diplomatically."

"Prussia better able to protect German interests?"

This is important background because of its effects on the relative power of Prussia and Austria within Germany. Neither country fought in the Crimean War (1854–1856) but Austria's chiefly non-German interests were clearly revealed and, more importantly, the war's outcome left it diplomatically isolated in Europe, estranged from Russia which had been so helpful in the 1848 revolutions and whose disquiet in 1850 had contributed greatly to Frederick William's climb down at Olmutz.

The Austrian defeat in 1859 by Piedmont and France (see Chapter 16) weakened its military credibility just when growing French strength began to concern rulers of the German states. Prussian troop movements on the Rhine seemed at this point to provide a more likely source of defence against the French than would any reliance on the Austrian Empire. This changing perception should be remembered when studying Bismarck's work in the 1860s.

THE PRUSSIAN STATE

THE ECONOMY AND THE MILITARY

This is not merely background material. A comment much quoted in early examination questions comes from the British economist, Keynes 'The German Empire was built more

Developments inside Prussia are of central importance.

truly on coal and iron than on blood and iron,' which, by picking up a comment of Bismarck's, invites an argument that economic changes were more important than the military victories, with which Bismarck's policies were associated, in bringing about the German Empire.

Economic dominance

The dominant position of the Prussian economy within Germany, and the reasons for it, need to be established:

- the resource advantages
- the good communications by river
- the growth of heavy industry
- the growth of a railway network

This infrastructure was all more notably developed in Prussia by the 1840s than elsewhere in Germany. Be ready to illustrate this. You should also understand the role of the Prussian State in encouraging such economic development and, as noted above, the importance from 1834 of the Zollverein in promoting Prussia's central role in the German economy.

Military expansion

During the 1850s and early 1860s the Prussian army, under the inspiration of the War Minister, Count von Roon and the new king, William I, was greatly increased in size and reorganised. The planning of central strategy was strengthened, taking note of the role to be played in troop movements by the new railway network. The heavy industrial development facilitated rearmament of both the infantry and the artillery. In 1862 military plans, especially that to double the size of the mainly conscript army to 400,000 men, provoked a major constitutional crisis in Prussia between the king and the Prussian Assembly. Only Roon's suggestion that William send for Bismarck prevented the King's abdication.

BISMARCK'S ACHIEVEMENTS

WITHIN PRUSSIA

Have ready a view of Bismarck as a person.

All textbooks on this topic attempt a brief analytical biography of Bismarck: it is well worthwhile to read at least two such accounts quite closely. So many questions on this topic involve assessing the motives, the role or the achievements of Bismarck that a feel for him as a person is of great value. He is much more complex than the picture of an iron Chancellor from a conservative, social, Prussian, Junker background suggests. The perception of him as an automaton relentlessly pursuing a masterplan leading to unification is much less interesting than the more complex personal and political reality. At times he cried, at others he smashed things in rage.

He emerged in the 1850s as a conservative Prussian patriot contemptuous of the parliamentary carryings-on at Frankfurt. He grew to resent the arrogant post-Olmutz re-establishment of Austrian power in Germany and moved, at this time to the idea of a Prussian dominated Germany from which Austria was excluded. (Kleindeutschland – little Germany). When in 1862 the expense involved in the army reforms provoked a crisis between the Prussian King and his Parliament, William I appointed him Prime Minister of Prussia. His work laid the military basis for Prussia's unification of Germany:

His work in Prussia in the 1860s.

- securing the army reforms
- illegally collecting the taxes to finance them
- resisting the opposition
- ruling Prussia for four years in defiance of the majority of the Assembly

It deserves close study but in assessing it do not forget the contribution of von Roon and of William I. The question is often asked whether Bismarck was more anxious to expand Prussia than unite all or part of Germany. Look for ideas on this in the course of your reading on this period of his career; the 'Student's Answer' on page 189 may give you some ideas.

BISMARCK'S STRATEGY

"Bismarck the international diplomatist."

AUSTRIA

1863 to 1866

A period of complex diplomacy during which Bismarck first blocked an Austrian scheme to create a greater German confederation which it would dominate, won Russian gratitude by supporting it over a rebellion of its Polish subjects, and then combined with Austria in a tangled episode to thwart Danish designs on the Duchies of Schleswig and Holstein.

1864 to 1866

Bismarck's diplomacy isolated Austria from Italian and French help and then in 1866 provoked it into war and swift military defeat.

Revision exercises

There are perhaps two ways through this thicket:

- First read through a brief chronological account and note down Bismarck's moves and how they helped strengthen Prussia's position against Austria. This material will be a substantial contribution to an overall assessment of how Bismarckian diplomacy helped to unite Germany.
- Then work out an outline plan of how to explain why Austria fell from its pre-eminence in Germany, restored at Olmutz in 1850, to its humiliating defeat in 1866. (See the 'Outline Answer' to Question 2.)
- Finally ask how Bismarck's lenient treatment of Austria after that defeat fits into your assessment of him.

You need to understand how victory over Austria greatly strengthened Bismarck's position in Prussia, where his one time opponents were now in disarray. It also strengthened Prussia's position in northern Germany where it annexed several states, including Hanover. Prussia now set up and led the North German Confederation, a body where political power was highly centralised.

1866

"Keep above the tangle of detail."

1866 is a good point in time at which to review Bismarck's achievements. This will help you keep above the tangle of detail of the three previous years.

FRANCE

By 1870 Prussia had added total and humiliating defeat of Napoleon III's French Empire to the defeat of Austria.

Revision exercises

"Bismarck the opportunist."

- Start by following a chronological account of events.
- From your reading, form a clear view on how you would examine the extent to which Bismarck planned the events which led to war, and to the diplomatic isolation of France, as opposed to taking advantage of fortunate circumstances as they arose.

The war

The war was the triumphant test of *von Roon's* army reforms and for the strategy of the Commander-in-Chief *von Moltke*. Faced by a prospect of a French attack on their lands the south German states joined with Prussia. The other nations of Europe though expecting a French victory, remained neutral. This outcome constituted the greatest diplomatic achievement of Bismarck's career.

"A turning-point in nineteenth century history."

Prussian victory

The scale of the Prussian victory was more surprising to contemporaries than it is to us with a hindsight view of the economic and military progress made by Prussia in the two previous decades. The outcome could not have been more dramatic with the crowning of William I as German Emperor in the French Palace of Versailles; the glory of victory in their common war led to the ready acquiescence of the till then independent south German states in these arrangements. The defeat of France in 1870 had momentous consequences for that country and for the balance of power amongst the great nations of Europe; with it the arrangement of Europe of 1815 was a dead letter.

EVALUATION OF UNIFICATION

BISMARCK'S ROLE

Inevitably such evaluation centres on an assessment of the motives and the tactics of Bismarck. In such an evaluation remember that he had some good cards dealt to him by:

- the economic and military progress of Prussia
- the support of William I
- the leaders of the Prussian military, von Roon and von Moltke.

Remember that they, not he, won the wars of 1866 and 1870. Equally, however, remember his part in strengthening Prussia and the skill of his diplomacy in isolating Austria and France; it is essential to be able to illustrate this. You might like to consider whether his enemies' mistakes did not at crucial moments also assist.

Advance planning?

"Unlikely that there was a masterplan . . ."

". . . but be ready to discuss the issue."

Much debate amongst historians has revolved around the question of how far German Unification was planned in advance by Bismarck. For long this was held to be the case, apparently confirmed by predictions he made as to what he would do, to the future British Prime Minister Disraeli. In elaboration of this notion the picture was painted of a master politician plotting each move of the diplomatic game in advance as though to an inevitable conclusion. Many decades ago these events were subject to close historical scrutiny by the British historian A J P Taylor, whose popular scholarly reputation it helped to establish. Little of the superman diplomatist survived this investigation and, since Taylor, historians have seen Bismarck as:

- a patriot seeking first to promote the interests of Prussia
- an opportunist who sought to profit from the indecisions and the mistakes of others.

The *central analysis* rests on whether Bismarck deliberately manipulated France into war in 1870 as part of grand design for a German Empire, through his diplomatic intrigues over the Spanish throne or whether he stumbled from crisis to opportunity towards a war he did not really want. For anyone who enjoys reading history that part of the story provides an intriguing if detailed read.

Revision exercises

From your reading across the years from 1848 to 1871 you need to form your own assessment of Bismarck's character, plans and achievements. If you can adapt this to any appropriate examination question set in front of you then you are more likely to impress those who mark your paper than by learning counterpoised quotations from great historians. For most of us these events need to be made more clear rather than more complex.

THE GERMAN EMPIRE 1871–1890

BISMARCK'S DOMESTIC POLICY

"Building a unified state."

Until 1890 Bismarck was Chancellor (i.e. Chief Minister of the Reich). Power in the German Empire was very centralised but the Constitution was based on a federation of States. Bismarck worked, helped by a common language and a common culture, to build a unified nation but on a Prussian model. In the 1870s his relations with the National Liberals in the Reichstag are important especially as they became more strained over his protectionist economic policies. In the 1880s he relied more on the Catholic Centre Party and was faced by a new opposition party, the Social Democrats. Until 1888 he could rely on the total support of the Kaiser, William I.

Exam questions

As well as an assessment of the measures Bismarck took to unify the new Empire there are two great episodes on which examination questions tend to be set:

The Kulturkampf: this involved Bismarck in a full-scale confrontation with the Papacy and with the Catholic Church in Germany. It arose from his desire to unify the country and to ensure its total loyalty to the Emperor in any crisis. The most repressive measures were introduced in 1872 and in Prussia in 1873 by *Falk*, the Prussian Minister of Culture. They were resisted by the Centre Party whose representation was increasing as a result of the persecution. When Bismarck's relations with the National Liberals deteriorated, he had to compromise, blaming and dismissing Falk in order to win Centre Party support.

The Socialists: a Workers Party won a handful of Reichstag seats in 1874 and in 1875 the Social Democrats were founded and in the 1877 election obtained half a million votes. As with the Catholics the international dimensions of socialism concerned Bismarck in his quest for German unity. From 1878 repressive legislation was enacted against the socialists. They provided a useful propaganda weapon for Bismarck in his efforts to keep more right-wing Germans loyal to their Chancellor. The repression was not savage and was accompanied by effort to outbid the socialists for working-class support by concessions to trade unions and by introducing state insurance schemes, in which Germany led the way in Europe. The Social Democrats survived but did not flourish until after Bismarck had departed.

BISMARCK'S FOREIGN POLICY

“Bismarck's aims in foreign policy.”

For the security of the German Empire Bismarck sought peace in Europe. In practice this meant striving to keep France isolated which in turn involved a resolute effort to stay on good terms with both Austria-Hungary (so called after a constitutional struggle in the Austrian Empire in 1867) and Russia (and this despite their potential rivalry in the Balkans). Bismarck's foreign policy should be judged by how far he succeeded in these objectives.

Evaluation

The main episodes to be considered in a judgement include:

- His major role in resolving the major crisis in Eastern Europe in 1878 (on the Congress of Berlin see Chapter 15).
- The defensive alliance with Austria-Hungary in 1879 which was renewed every five years thereafter.
- The Dreikaiserbund (League of the Three Emperors) a secret treaty created in 1881 between Russia, Austria-Hungary and Prussia, balancing agreements in Eastern Europe between the three – a much looser arrangement than that of 1879; it was renewed in 1884 and lapsed in 1887.
- The Re-insurance Treaty with Russia, complete with secret clauses, signed in 1887.
- In 1882 a Triple Alliance was made with Austria and Italy, the main value of which for Bismarck was that it kept the latter away from France.

The alliance system grew ever more complex between 1871–1890. Bismarck's complex series of balancing alliances were already under strain before his dismissal in 1890 despite his signing of the Re-insurance treaty and the Triple Alliance.

It remains just to add that Bismarck was reluctant to build up a colonial empire in Africa because of its potential for arousing British opposition and encouraging it to forge ties with France. Eventually internal pressure forced a change in this policy.

Achievement

Bismarck's achievement in foreign policy was that for twenty years he kept the peace between Russia and Austria-Hungary and so kept the peace in Europe which he was certain the national interests of the German Empire required. In these conditions its likeliest enemy, France, was isolated and quiet. It was a considerable achievement.

“An over-elaborate system?”

There is little point in pretending that this is not a complex topic. In fact that is just the point to bear in mind. Bismarck's alliance policies are open to criticism on the grounds that they created a system that must one day break down under its own complexity and which would encourage those outside it to come together for mutual protection in a rival system of alliances. This is what happened between 1890 and 1914 with catastrophic consequences (see Chapter 19). A balanced judgement, recognising Bismarck's skill in constructing and maintaining the alliances and in keeping peace in Europe, can be set alongside a comment on this potential for future disaster which was fulfilled when German foreign policy came to be directed by the impulsive Kaiser William II. Was the system indeed already crumbling before 1890 with the growing isolation of Russia?

“Do not let the detail put you off.”

You should now read the ‘Tutor's Answer’ to Question 6 below which should at least suggest that the complexities of this topic can be cut through and that, in any event, there will be little time in an examination to use all the detail with which this topic is surrounded.

USEFUL INFORMATION

1815	**The Vienna Settlement**: arrangements ignored national aspirations, for example: – Set up the German Confederation of 39 States, – Prussia made extensive territorial gains; half of Saxony, the prosperous Rhineland, Swedish Pomerania, – Austrian gains were outside Germany.
1815–1848	Metternich used the Confederation as a means of stifling both liberal and nationalist demands.
1819	Carlsbad Decrees proposed by Metternich were approved by the Confederation Diet to quell popular agitation, censorship, ban on political meetings, persecution of intellectuals.
1830	Further repression following on growth of the nationalist Young Germany movement.
1834	Zollverein created; helped Prussian economic pre-eminence.
1848	Revolutions in German States
1848–1849	Frankfurt Parliament
1850	Austrian ascendancy re-established at Olmutz.
1861	William I King of Prussia
1862	Bismarck became Chief Minister of Prussia.
1863–1865	The Schleswig-Holstein Question
1866	Defeat of Austria in the Seven Weeks War. Formation of the North German Confederation.
1870–1871	Franco Prussian War: defeat of France. Germany took Alsace and Lorraine from France.
1871	Establishment of the German Empire; Bismarck Chancellor.
1871–1890	Bismarck in charge of German affairs.
1871–1880	The Kulturkampf
1878	Laws against socialists The Congress of Berlin settled the conflict in Eastern Europe.
1879	Beginning of Protectionism Dual Alliance with Austria-Hungary
1881	The Dreikaiserbund established
1882	Italy joined the Dual Alliance (Triple Alliance).
1883	Beginning of State welfare provision
1887	Re-insurance Treaty with Russia
1888	Death of Kaiser William I
1890	Resignation of Bismarck

EXAMINATION QUESTIONS

Q1 'Unification is the wrong word to describe the process.' Discuss this opinion with reference to the creation of the German Empire. (Oxford 1989)

Q2 'Without the decline of Austria neither the unification of Germany nor the unification of Italy would have been possible.' Comment. (Northern Ireland 1989)

Q3 Why had Austria lost the leadership of Germany to Prussia by 1866? (Cambridge 1989)

Q4 How far did the events of the years 1862 to 1871 support the claim that 'Bismarck steadfastly schemed to bring about the unification of Germany'? (London 1989)

Q5 Critically examine the diplomatic skills displayed by Bismarck in pursuing his objectives as chief minister of Prussia before 1871. (London 1986)

Q6 'The mutual antagonism of others enabled him to develop his own system.' Discuss this verdict on Bismarck's conduct of foreign policy after 1871. (London 1990)

OUTLINE ANSWERS

Question 1

See the 'Student's Answer' on page 189.

Question 2

Explain: how Austria to the 1860s stood in the way of German and also Italian unification (be brief). Stress the events of 1848 and the subsequent failure of nationalist dreams in each case – two paragraphs.

Outline: the Austrian block on the aspirations of Cavour and Bismarck.

Explain:

- How Austrian power was in decline
  - struggle to survive 1848 tumults
  - dependence on Russian help
- How the Crimean War left her diplomatically isolated.
- The range of nationalist aspirations she faced.

Indicate: how Cavour and Bismarck were in turn able to exploit Austria's weakness and isolation diplomatically and militarily.

Conclusion: agree with the quotation.

Question 3

"A second question on the decline of Austria."

Introduction: Start with Prussian capitulation to Austria at Olmutz in 1850 which suggests it was events after that which were responsible.

Explain: how Prussia became stronger internally after Olmutz – the work of von Roon in building up the army, important because in 1866 it was military defeat which lost Austria the leadership.

Explain: the skilful way Bismarck isolated Austria from any potential allies and then manoeuvred it into war – explain how this done and bring effect of Crimean War in separating Austria from Russia. Refer to:

- the internal weaknesses of the Austrian State
- disparate nationalities
- inefficient bureaucracy
- inefficient army – order only restored in 1848 by Russian help
- pre-occupations in Italy

Conclusion: argue that in fact the pre-Olmutz period is also significant because there were also long term factors working against Austria:

- Austria was not a purely German state – explain.
- After the 1848 Revolutions German national feeling was aroused.
- Prussia was in much stronger position to emerge as the leading German state from its purely German gains in 1815 and the economic effects in Germany of the Zollverein – explain these.

Question 4

"Did the masterplan exist?"

Introduction: state that claim ill-founded. Bismarck had plans and schemed effectively but for much of the period this was not towards German unification but Prussian expansion. In the last of these years unification was brought about not because of steadfast planning but brilliant opportunism.

Illustrate: each of the two points argued above. Discuss his plans to strengthen Prussia internally and then his schemes to isolate and defeat Austria in order to leave Prussia unchallenged in northern Germany up to the creation of the North German Confederation. Treatment of Austria to preserve the new balance.

Examine: how he exploited Napoleon's mistakes and how he seized opportunities over these rather than had calculated plans to incorporate the southern German states. Scale of victory over France could not have been planned for but, once achieved, was brilliantly used.

Question 5

Define: Bismarck's objectives – make clear their limited nature at each stage, it was not a masterplan for the unification of Germany.

Stages to consider:

- Attitude to Polish Revolt and Russia, Schleswig-Holstein and how he manoeuvred the Danes and the Austrians.
- The isolating of Austria before the war of 1866 – note the question is on diplomatic skills not on the war or its outcome.
- Relations with France prior to the 1870 war, particularly the provoking of Napoleon over the Spanish Succession issue, but also the efforts to ensure the neutrality of Austria, Britain and Italy.

Note: this is a detailed question purely on diplomatic skills, you would need illustrative detail of Bismarck's schemes and approaches to do it well. It is the sort of question to avoid if your reading has not been sufficiently detailed.

Question 6

See the 'Tutor's Answer' that follows.

A TUTOR'S ANSWER TO QUESTION 6

“ Post–1871 foreign policy objectives. ”

Bismarck's objectives in foreign policy after 1871 are simply stated. He considered that the interests of the German Empire would be best served by the preservation of peace in Europe and strove to this end. Peace would be the best means to his second objective which was the continued isolation of France as the most effective way of discouraging that country from any notion of a war to recover the lost provinces of Alsace and Lorraine. In the period from 1871 to Bismarck's fall from power in 1890 the most likely cause of war in Europe lay in the rival ambitions of Russia and Austria in Central Europe and the most likely ally for France was Russia. Bismarck's 'system' was the system of alliance which he constructed primarily for the purpose of preventing hostilities between Austria and Russia and secondly to prevent any prospect of Russia and France coming together. Its other characteristics were the calling of international conferences to defuse potential threats to peace and a reliance when necessary on the practice of secret diplomacy. In this context the quotation in this question is not particularly helpful in understanding Bismarck's conduct of foreign policy. It has more relevance when related to his policies towards the states of Western Europe but these were never really his central concern.

“ Challenging the question. ”

In 1878, Bismarck called the Congress of Berlin precisely because Russian military successes at the expense of the Ottoman Empire had been so overwhelming that they seemed likely to upset the balance of power in eastern Europe and were therefore likely to provoke Austria into taking action to redress that balance. The Congress did not solve the Eastern Question but it did achieve Bismarck's objective of defusing the immediate antagonism between Austria and Russia. Bismarck now regarded Russia as the greater threat to the stability of the region and the result was the Dual Alliance with Austria, complete with secret defensive clause against attack by Russia. This became the cornerstone of Germany's diplomacy through to defeat in the First World War. It was an attempt to contain national rivalries at a time when the 'mutual antagonisms' of Austria and Russia, far from helping Bismarck, were particularly troublesome to him.

“ Analysing policy in Eastern Europe . . . ”

The key to an understanding of German foreign policy in Eastern Europe from this point until Bismarck's departure from office lies in the necessity to maintain, if at all possible, sufficiently cordial and reassuring relations with Russia that she would not feel the need to look elsewhere for allies. This was the purpose behind the formation in 1881 of the Dreikaiserbund where the three powers agreed to consult each other about any further crises arising from the disintegration of the Ottoman Empire and to maintain at least friendly neutrality if any one of them was attacked by a fourth power. This and its renewal in 1884 gave Bismarck an opportunity for diplomatic intervention at an early stage of any future crisis in relations between his partners. The same purpose lay behind the Re-insurance Treaty with Russia in 1887, relations between Austria and Russia had again reached breaking point and Bismarck's 'system', though first committed to the Austrian alliance, strove to hold Russia within Germany's zone of influence. Throughout all this the 'mutual antagonism' of Austria and Russia was a great source of anxiety to Bismarck and arguably he never succeeded in doing more than papering over the cracks in the relations between the two.

"... and in Western Europe."

In Western Europe there is more evidence that Bismarck found the mutual antagonisms of other states helpful to German interests and that he was quite willing when the opportunity arose to promote such rivalries. He had to accept that, following the harsh peace terms of 1871, and in particular the seizure of the Provinces of Alsace and Lorraine, there was no prospect of cordial relations with France. For the moment France could do nothing but if ever the opportunity arose to wage a successful war of revenge then it would be seized. Everything revolved around that fact.

For this reason the cool relations which existed between France and Britain were very helpful to Bismarck and he strove to maintain good relations with the latter by trying to limit the colonial and naval ambitions of his fellow Germans. Britain, protected by its navy, declined to consider closer relations with Germany but British isolationism served Bismarck almost as well and he was never required to devote as much attention to affairs in Western Europe as he had in Eastern Europe. He had perhaps learned the lesson of his clumsy attempts to bully France in 1875, which had for the moment brought France diplomatic support from Britain, and was now happy to encourage both countries in their imperial ambitions. Their mutual suspicions of each other's ambitions in North Africa are perhaps the issue where the quotation offered in this question is most applicable.

Similar motives underlay Bismarck's actions in expanding the Dual Alliance with Austria into a Triple Alliance which embraced Italy. The alliance kept Italy out of the French orbit, where its national interests might have been better served, and this too could be promoted by encouraging Italian imperial ambitions in North Africa.

"The success of 'the 'system'."

In Bismarck's time the 'system' worked to great effect but not, in its most important aspect, in the way implied in this question. It worked because Bismarck was able to reassure Russia that, despite its mutual antagonism with Austria, its interests were safeguarded by its understandings with Germany. This left France isolated in Europe, not because of any differences of note with Russia, but because Bismarck was able to keep Russia in the German orbit through defusing the tensions between it and Austria.

A STUDENT'S ANSWER TO QUESTION 1

"Explain the significance or leave it out."

The unification of Germany was not so much unification as a Prussian absorption of the Germanic states, a result of the swing of dominance in Germany from Austria to Prussia. Furthermore ultimate unification was not completed until Hitler.

Before Bismarck came onto the scene it was clear that despite Austria's official premier position in Germany (owing to Vienna) the German states were far more dependent on Prussia, politically and economically. Although she gained little benefit before 1848 Prussia had ensured her superiority over the states through the setting up of a customs union (the Zollverein) in 1834 and the abolition of all internal tariffs. Politically the other states were also dependent on Prussia; the Vorparliament at Frankfurt was dependent upon Frederick William's support for survival. In 1848 he had to save it from a working-class coup. Similarly over Schleswig-Holstein when they looked for troops from him. Ultimately when both Franz Joseph and Frederick William rejected union the Vorparliament dissolved. On the other hand had it not been for Austria at Olmutz the Prussian proposed Erfurt Union would have been a success.

"Is this relevant?"

Bismarck too did not see 'unification' as unification. He saw the move in terms of Prussian aggrandisement and the struggle between Austria and Prussia for superiority. What he aimed to achieve was a Prussian Empire but he realised that nationalist forces would prevent this. As a result he harnessed these forces to create a Prussian Empire in everything but name.

In 1863 Bismarck realised that over Schleswig-Holstein there was the perfect opportunity for Prussia to act as the leader of German interests. He also used it to manufacture a quarrel with Austria.

The 1865 Treaty of Gastein only 'papered over the cracks' and thus when the army reforms were effective and the diplomatic ground was prepared the war for dominance could begin. The North German Confederation, upon which the Empire was to be based, was set up; although in appearance liberal it was really an enlarged Prussia.

By now Bismarck realised total unification was inevitable - it was unified socially and economically already. However he was concerned that it be achieved maintaining Prussian dominance and preferably with the agreement of the other states. With the Hohenzollern candidature an opportunity arose once more. France was provoked into war and in 1870 at Sedan defeated as totally as Austria had been at Sadowa. So nationalist fervour enabled Bismarck to declare the German Empire at Versailles.

“This seems important so write at greater length.”

Constitutionally the Empire was Prussian dominated as Bismarck ensured that William became Kaiser with extensive powers (war and peace, choice of ministers, dissolving Parliament); he became Chancellor, the Bundesrat was chosen by William and 18 Prussian votes provided a comfortable Prussian base in the Reichstag. Thus the German Empire was a Prussian Empire for, in addition to her political dominance, Prussia in its own right was the third major economic power in Europe.

“And here too!”

No doubt Germany, had it been left to its own devices without Bismarck, would have been united one day. But thanks to Bismarck, true to his origins as a Prussian Junker, who was able to co-ordinate events to his and to Prussia's advantage, speeding up the process at the same time, Germany was united by the victories of the Prussian army and so the German Empire's Constitution was dictated by Prussia to her own advantage.

EXAMINER COMMENTS

This essay contains plenty of relevant ideas but the written style makes it difficult at times to appreciate fully the points which are being made. If it were any less clear it is probable that an inability to express thoughts effectively would have begun to penalise the candidate.

The reference to Hitler (underlined) either needs explaining to show its relevance in this essay or omitting. More should be said on the effects of the Zollverein – it could be argued that, thanks to the Zollverein, there was genuine and valuable economic unification. It is not at all clear what the reference to Olmutz (underlined) is intended to give to the answer. The idea that it was a Prussian takeover is a perfectly reasonable point to make but the examination of the Constitution is muddled and undeveloped. It should at least acknowledge that the German Empire was a federal State within which each state had its own constitutional rights and institutions. This is a point to balance against the stress on the Prussian takeover.

USEFUL SOURCES OF INFORMATION

General reading

A Ramm, *Europe in the Nineteenth Century 1789–1905*, Longman 1984
J B Watson, *Success in European History 1815–1941*, John Murray 1981
A Wood, *Europe 1815–1960*, Longman 1984

Further reading

W Carr, *A History of Germany 1815-1990*, Arnold 1991
W G Shreeves, *Nation Making in Nineteenth Century Europe*, Nelson 1984
A Stiles, *The Unification of Germany 1815–1890*, Arnold 1986
B Waller, *Bismarck*, Blackwell (for the Historical Association) 1985

Linked topic areas

- Metternich and the Austrian Empire
- The 1848 Revolutions throughout Europe
- Napoleon III and the Second French Empire (see Chapter 13)
- Italian Unification (see Chapter 16)
- The Eastern Question (see Chapter 15)
- German economic history 1871–1914
- The causes of the First World War (see Chapter 19)
- The development of socialism in Europe

CHAPTER 18

FRANCE: THE THIRD REPUBLIC

- DEFEAT BY PRUSSIA
- THE PARIS COMMUNE
- ESTABLISHING THE THIRD REPUBLIC
- RELIGION
- POLITICAL CHANGE
- SURVIVAL OF THE REPUBLIC
- PROGRESS UNDER THE REPUBLIC
- USEFUL INFORMATION

GETTING STARTED

To study any period of French history in the nineteenth century you need to appreciate the deep political, social and religious divisions created by the French Revolution in the last decade of the eighteenth century and fixed in place by a generation of violent war and conquest under Napoleon. The legacy of these years was a deep political split in the French nation between a revolutionary anti-clerical *Left* and a reactionary property-owning *Right* which looked either to the monarchical or to the Napoleonic legacy for its political inspiration. The course of French domestic history for the rest of the century seems to revolve around the clash between the revolutionary and the reactionary traditions implanted almost before the century began but powerfully reinforced by a series of later crises. From the mid-nineteenth century the Left was reinforced by the growth of an industrial working-class and by the ideas of socialism. If your syllabus takes in French history after 1815 you will need to establish some idea of the political and social history of the Revolutionary and Napoleonic periods.

Depending on the period covered by the syllabus decide whether you are going to study French history throughout the century. For the hundred years from 1815 to 1914 equip yourself to attempt a French political question from anywhere in the period. The topics included are very popular with examiners, they tend to be self-contained and less complex than the earlier 1789 to 1815 period. Remember to check the terms of the syllabus and look at past examination papers. The major topics of French history between 1815 and 1870 are considered in Chapter 13, essential background for the material studied here.

In addition remember the important economic and social changes which states in Western Europe experienced during the latter half of the nineteenth century. Some of these transformed the framework for political affairs. The growth of socialism, the emergence of left-wing political parties and of a trade union movement provide one example. The growth of industry and of towns, with all their associated social problems is of course linked to this. These social and economic trends changed people's perception of the role of the state; they began to expect governments to deal with the social problems of the day and the move began from *laissez-faire* to *collectivism*. The development of national railway networks did not just affect the economy or people's everyday lives, it also transformed the basis of military strategy. In many countries there was a dramatic growth in population; France was the exception to this and that fact also brought problems for the nation's rulers.

Be aware too of the international context with which French politicians had to work (parts of Chapters 17 and 19 will help with this), and finally note that in these years Paris had good reason to claim to be the cultural capital of Europe.

ESSENTIAL PRINCIPLES

DEFEAT BY PRUSSIA

“1870 – France humiliated . . .”

“. . . and under the shadow of the German Empire.”

This may well be seen as the last episode in Napoleon III's imperial rule but, in studying the period after 1870, the total nature of the defeat has to be recognised. The humiliation could hardly have been more complete with large tracts of the country occupied, the Emperor a prisoner, Paris besieged and an eventual treaty which included a hefty indemnity to be paid to Germany before the army of occupation would withdraw and, worst of all, the loss of the two provinces of Alsace and Lorraine. All this would impose great internal strains on any new regime but additionally France would have to come to terms with the fact that the defeat of 1870 had, apparently irreversibly, tilted the European balance of power sharply against her. The French after 1870 had to accept that their foreign policy was to be conducted under the shadow of a united German Empire, the central principle of whose foreign policy, under Bismarck, was to keep France isolated in Europe.

THE PARIS COMMUNE

“A very popular source of questions.”

The history of this body, emerging from the wreckage of the defeat by Prussia, is the most closely studied subject in the entire history of the Third Republic. It deserves careful revision.

Explanations of the Commune need to take in the defeat of the central government by the Prussians but must also reflect on the long radical traditions of the French capital; despite all Napoleon III's efforts Paris had remained a republican city. The rising was largely caused by the feeling in Paris that an attempt was to be made to restore the French monarchy but it was also a protest at the surrender to the Germans. A full assessment of the Commune must also take into account the growth of an industrial proletariat and the spread of socialist ideas: knowledge of these is in any case required for the study of French society throughout the Third Republic. The Commune has become the stuff of legend with Marxists seeing it as the first of the proletarian risings which would eventually bring down the bourgeois states. This does not square easily with the facts of the rising for many participants and many of the actions undertaken had origins in the bourgeoisie. Some laws were passed against the employers but they were outweighed by those passed against the privileged position of the Catholic Church. Legends however have a power of their own to influence future events and never more so than in this case.

“Military victory for the Republic.”

A study of the events will give reasons why the Commune was crushed; the continuing loyalty of the French army to its opponents was crucial in this.

ROLE OF THIERS

Familiarise yourself with the role of *Thiers* in bringing about the defeat. He was the most able French politician of the period and committed to ending the Commune at whatever cost in order to preserve national unity and social order. First he withdrew French troops from the city and ordered it to be assaulted from the outside: the bombardment was under the direction of the future president, *MacMahon*, but still the capture of the city took two months to accomplish. The appalling savagery and destruction of property during the fighting, when some 20,000 of the city's inhabitants were killed, and the bitter revenge taken after its conclusion reinforced the deep divisions in French society and made the future Republic's chances of survival all the more precarious.

ESTABLISHING THE THIRD REPUBLIC

“A settlement with Germany.”

The armistice concluded when the German authorities, which had preceded the Commune episode, allowed elections for a new Assembly at which the only issue had been that of peace or continuation of the war. The Assembly met at Bordeaux and had no choice but to accept the terms Thiers brought back from the Germans and, after the defeat of the Commune, peace was signed at Frankfurt. Not the least of Thiers achievements was in his dealings with the victorious Bismarck and later in raising the money required to pay off the indemnity to Germany, which had to be done before the occupation army would withdraw.

REASONS REPUBLIC ESTABLISHED

“The monarchist threat . . .”

The majority of the Assembly shared Thiers monarchist sympathies and fear of its intentions had, as noted above, encouraged the setting up of the Paris Commune. It is important to understand why, despite this monarchist majority, a republic was eventually established. The Commune had been a warning of the divisions a monarchical restoration would cause within the nation and this was perhaps more important than divisions within the monarchist camp in preventing its occurrence. Thiers was in principle in favour of a constitutional monarchy but came to the conclusion that its imposition would create unacceptable tension within French society. The arguments within the monarchist camp over the flag to be adopted are to be seen as a symbol of more significant disagreements as to what type of monarchy was to be restored. The Bourbon claimant, *Henri Comte de Chambord* insisting that the old Bourbon flag must replace the republican tricolour, suggested a full royalist reaction which would certainly have split French society. His Orleanist rival, *Philippe Albert*, grandson of Louis Philippe who had ruled from 1830 to 1848, commanded little support. The *Prince Imperial*, Napoleon III's son and the last Bonapartist contender was a more attractive figure and despite the Empire's defeat of 1870 a Bonapartist group started to emerge. The chief result of this was however to encourage the supporters of a monarchy to move towards a republican solution for fear of something worse. Nevertheless the efforts of the military leader, MacMahon, to restore the monarchy need to be known and the reasons for his failure, and that of the monarchist cause, assessed.

“. . . And why it failed.”

It was 1875, before the Republic's Constitution was agreed (see the 'Useful Information' section at the end of the chapter) and 1877 before the electorate crucially turned down MacMahon's attempt to strengthen the President's power at the expense of the Assembly. This established the central feature of French political life under the Third Republic, namely the weakness of the central executive faced by a powerful Assembly. From this stemmed the fluidity of ministries which persisted through to the end of the Republic in 1940.

“You need to understand the political weaknesses arising from the Republic's constitution.”

Revision exercises

A final revision exercise on this period from 1870 to 1877, the period in which the Third Republic was established, would be to think through what comments you would make on the importance of the roles of Thiers and MacMahon.

RELIGION

The Catholic Church in France was, in this period, politically to the right and its position and privileges, particularly in the field of education were the subject of sharp political controversy. The Commune had passed anti-Catholic edicts and at its end had killed, amongst other hostages, the Archbishop of Paris. At the Bordeaux Assembly the Church was in favour of restoring the monarchy and through to 1914 its hierarchy must be regarded as hostile to the Republic. If you are studying Germany under Bismarck in this period see Chapter 17 and bear in mind the possibility of a question on religion, spanning more than one country. In the 1880s and 1890s in France a series of left-wing governments removed Church privileges and control in education, in health and in charitable work. In the early twentieth century many religious orders were banned until in 1905 the Catholic Church lost its official status, the remaining monasteries were dissolved and the State became entirely secular, ending the Church's influence in French politics. All of this is central to the political life of the Republic for the threat to its existence was more than a matter of some colourful escapades by romantic but hopeless pretenders. The real threat from the Right lay in the disaffection of such a large section of the nation from the Republic; relations between State and Church were at the centre of this.

“The Catholic Church hierarchy generally hostile to the Republic.”

POLITICAL CHANGE

The political life of the republic was more than a series of unstable Ministries and its unlikely survival despite political crises and scandals. The solid progress in several spheres is often forgotten, for example:

“It was not merely survival.”

- In 1880 an amnesty for those involved in the Commune eased one bitter division.
- In 1884 the upper House of the Assembly (the Senate) was made the object of popular election, a decidedly democratic step.
- In 1884 trade unions became legal.

Across the period the State took on a definitely more democratic tone which added to the impression of political stability. You should avoid seeing the Republic's history purely as a series of crises.

SURVIVAL OF THE REPUBLIC

THREATS

The German, the Communard and the Monarchist threats in the early years of the Republic have all to be taken account of in any explanation of the Republic's survival, as have the succession of weak ministries and the crises with the Catholic Church. At least the death in 1879 of the Prince Imperial, leaving the Bonapartist supporters without an acceptable candidate removed one threat, if never a very tangible one. There was a growth of socialism during the Third Republic and towards 1914 more strikes and industrial violence. This threat from the Left was of a different order to that from the Right. The Socialists wished to change the policies of Republican governments and even the character of the Republic but they were not a threat to its continued existence in the same way as its enemies from the Right.

DANGEROUS EPISODES

"Be able to assess the gravity of the threats to the Republic."

There were also a series of dangers to the Republic's existence arising from the Boulanger Affair of the late 1880s, the Panama Scandal at the end of that decade and the Dreyfus Case at the end of the century. The dangers to the State were different in form and gravity, each is self-contained and easily comprehended. You should be able to offer comment on how serious a threat each of the above posed to the Republic's existence, and why; then suggest why the Republic, despite them, still survived. The 'Outline Answer' to Question 2 on page 198 offers one approach.

The Boulanger Affair

General Boulanger was an ex-Minister of War who used the loss of Alsace–Lorraine to whip up right-wing nationalist support including ex-monarchists and Bonapartists. He kept standing in and winning elections; there were many demonstrations in his support. In 1889 he thought of a coup d'état but panicked and fled the country when the Government moved to arrest him. He committed suicide in 1891 and, despite the strength of right-wing opponents of the Republic, he at least lacked the nerve to be a real threat to its existence.

The Panama Canal Scandal

In 1888 the Government gave official backing to the Panama Canal Company for whom *de Lesseps* was constructing the canal. Many thousands of French investors lost their money when the company went bankrupt. Jewish financiers and corrupt politicians were held responsible. No real corruption was established by a commission of inquiry but it aroused great cynicism about those in political life and seemed to many to typify the rather grubby intrigues of public life under the Republic. The Socialists benefitted but Jews suffered because of it.

The Dreyfus Case

This too had anti-semitic overtones for Dreyfus was one of the few Jewish army officers. He was in 1894 convicted of selling army secrets to the Germans and given life imprisonment on Devil's Island. A long fight to prove his innocence followed, led by the eminent novelist *Emile Zola*. A second trial in 1899 found Dreyfus guilty once more but found factors in his favour and he was grudgingly given a pardon. In 1906 the Chamber of Deputies set aside his conviction and restored his army rank. In general those to the Right in French life, including the Army authorities were against Dreyfus and those on the Left fought to clear him. The bitterness with which the issue was accompanied on both sides revealed the deep tensions in French society and also an unhappy streak of virulent anti-semitism.

Revision exercises

A weakness in discussing these three episodes is to fall into the trap of describing what happened rather than meeting the evaluation requested by any question posed at this level. It is for example quite possible to argue that the Dreyfus case helped the Republic by rallying its friends and, ultimately, discrediting its enemies. More serious still is the tendency of some students to assume that the survival of the Republic in these years revolves entirely around these well-known crises and to forget all the underlying factors, political, social and economic, which are equally relevant to any assessment of both the gravity of the threats to the Third Republic and to its survival, not just to 1914, but through to the defeat in war in 1940.

PROGRESS UNDER THE REPUBLIC

ACHIEVEMENTS

Often the history of the Third Republic is offered simply as one of crises survived. You should also be ready to offer a more positive evaluation of the achievements of these years.

The Constitution of 1875

The Constitution of 1875 (see the 'Useful Information' section at the end of this chapter) gradually became more democratic:

- the Assembly moved from Versailles to Paris
- the life Senators were abolished
- freedom of the press was guaranteed
- trade unions made legal

Much of this took place during the 1880s. The 'Tutor's Answer' to Question 1 includes a discussion on these points.

International relations

The German indemnity was quickly paid off and during the rest of the period France moved, albeit slowly, out of diplomatic isolation into alliance with Russia and entente with Britain: this constituted solid achievement, ensuring that France would not again have to fight alone against Germany (see Chapter 19).

Colonial policy

“Note the international setting.”

Colonial policy was a source of political divisions at home and caused friction with other European Powers.

- Tunis was acquired in 1881.
- Madagascar and the French Congo were occupied in the next years.
- French lands in Indochina were extended.

By 1914 France's overseas empire was outdone only by that of Britain. More important was the fact that, after the difficult crisis at Fashoda in 1898, colonial rivalries between the two greatest imperial powers ceased to be a source of tension and distrust and the way became open for the Entente Cordiale of 1904.

The economy

The economy, hampered by the loss of Alsace and Lorraine made unspectacular progress, especially contrasted to that of Germany, with a particular concern being caused by the virtual end of any expansion of the population which rose from 37 million in 1871 to only 39 million in 1911 (the comparable figures for Germany were 41 and 65 million). The strong rural base to the economy and to society encouraged a much needed social stability and this continued to be so despite the flow of emigrants from rural areas to urban centres. After 1900 in particular there was a trickle of social reform in the areas of public health, trade unions, working conditions and insurance schemes.

Cultural growth

The growth of Paris led to a great cultural flowering in the arts and literature and any student hoping to find a suitable question on cultural history is most likely to find it, if asked on this period, in a French setting. Spotting such questions does however continue to be something of a lottery.

USEFUL INFORMATION

1848	Revolution in France: formation of the Second Republic.
1852	Napoleon III established the Second Empire.
1870–1871	Defeat of France by Prussia: Alsace–Lorraine ceded.
1871	The Paris Commune
1871–1873	**Thiers President:** his reluctant acceptance of a republic led the Assembly to pass a vote of no confidence in him and he resigned.
1873	Indemnity to Germany paid off: German troops left France.

1873–1879 **MacMahon President:** his aim was to restore the monarchy but failure of the two monarchist fractions to combine undermined this possibility and they started to lose bye-elections.

1874 First exhibition of the French Impressionists.

1875 Proposal to elect the President of the Republic was carried by one vote in the Assembly.

1875 **Republican Constitution** agreed:

- The President was to be elected by the two Chambers of the Assembly – Chamber of Deputies and the Senate (this was a reaction against the plebiscites which had helped Napoleon III).
- Universal manhood suffrage elected Deputies for three years.
- Senators elected for nine years mainly by delegates of the towns (at first there were life Senators but in 1884 these were abolished).
- Prefects appointed by the State were key administrative figures in the provinces.

1877 MacMahon dismissed his Ministers and when Deputies failed to support new ones he called an election but failed to overturn his opponents' majority. This was the last time a President tried to strengthen the powers of the government against the Assembly. After this the fall of a ministry was not followed by an election but by a re-shuffle of ministers, contributing to the instability of governments.

1879–1885 **Jules Ferry** was the most important politician. He led the attack on Catholic Church's control of education, started the tradition of antagonism between the Church and the Republic. Political life made more democratic in these years.

1880 Assembly moved from Versailles to Paris.

1881 Seizure of Tunis

1882 **Gambetta**, hero of the 1870 war and, after Thiers, the most distinguished political supporter of the Republic, died.

1884–1885 Berlin Conference laid basis of French Empire in Africa.

1886–1889 **The Boulanger Affair**

1892–1893 **Panama Scandal**

1890s Growing power of socialists and Trade Unions. Increased labour unrest, strikes and violence, strength of **syndicalism**.

Syndicalism

> A movement amongst industrial workers to gain control of production, and perhaps also political power, by the trade unions by use of the general strike. From the French '*Syndicat*' – a trade union. Mainly flourished in France.

1893 Franco-Russian Alliance.

1894 **Dreyfus trial**

1898 The Fashoda crisis with Britain over control in the Nile Valley after Marchand had marched from French Equatorial Africa to the Nile.

1899 Dreyfus second trial

1906 Dreyfus restored to full military honours

1900–1914 Increased pace of social reforms

1904 Entente Cordiale with Britain

(For foreign affairs 1904 to 1914 see Chapter 19)

EXAMINATION QUESTIONS

Q1 'Frenchmen accepted weak and unstable governments between 1870 and 1895 as the price they had to pay in order to preserve their liberty.' Do you agree?

(Oxford 1986)

Q2 Why did the many enemies and the many crises faced by the Third French Republic not lead to its downfall in the years to 1914? (London 1990)

Q3 How far had France by the end of the nineteenth century recovered from defeat in 1870–71? (Cambridge 1989)

Q4 'Consolidation rather than spectacular achievement in both domestic and foreign affairs was the dominant characteristic of the Third Republic in the period 1899 to 1914.' Discuss this statement. (NEAB 1989)

Q5 Comment on the view that 'the real strength of the French Third Republic between 1870 and 1914 was that no alternative was possible.' (Northern Ireland 1987)

OUTLINE ANSWERS

Question 1

See the 'Tutor's Answer' on page 199.

Question 2

Indicate: enemies and crises but very briefly; avoid trap of describing them or spending too long on them.

Enemies include:

- Germans, monarchists
- Boulanger
- the Right in general (usually hostile)

Crises include:

- Commune
- Panama Scandals
- Dreyfus affair

Discuss: weaknesses of each of enemies briefly.

Show: how crises went away.

"Why the Third Republic survived."

Develop: the theme that the Republic divided Frenchmen least so that there was a lot of grudging acceptance (at least half of the essay). Stress:

- the social cohesion of rural and small town France
- the economic progress of the nation
- the growth of the political Left which backed the Republic
- the foreign policy gains bringing prestige and recognition i.e. paying off German debt, the establishment of alliances, acquiring colonies

Conclusion: a period of social achievement and peace which won increasing acceptance as it proceeded for much of the record of government instability and did not affect the real progress of the nation.

Question 3

Introduction: after the defeat the French army was discredited, France was without allies, the Second Empire had collapsed and there was therefore no system of government and the defeat also brought deep divisions in French society with the Commune. Each of these issues will be considered in turn to explore what the end of the century position was:

- **Army:** still weak, no match alone for the German forces, refer to population problem. Its loyalty and integrity were questionable as the Dreyfus case indicated, very conservative leadership.
- **Allies:** alliance situation had improved with Russian alliance but in the west, France still vulnerable because Italy allied to Germany. This only improved with 1904 Entente with Britain. In fact Fashoda crisis of 1898 meant Anglo-French relations at end of century were at a low ebb.

Conclusion:

"Evaluating France's recovery."

- Third Republic was secure by 1900 and generally accepted by most French people, its weaknesses are often exaggerated, indicate political progress made, social reforms starting and the steady rather than spectacular economic growth.

- Real problem here was that the obvious enemy, Germany, had made much greater strides.
- Commune was however long forgotten and despite syndicalism later there was little danger of internal left-wing revolution.
- Alsace and Lorraine still lost and this is the most powerful symbol that until national pride was restored after the humiliations of 1870–71 then France could not be said to have totally recovered. This was only to happen, at terrible cost, in 1918.

Question 4

Introduction: agree with the quotation:

The economy: indicate examples of growth in agriculture, industry and trade:

- coal production trebled
- steel production doubled
- the railway network expanded from 20 to 50 thousand kilometres.

} slow + insignificant incomparcuson to others especially Germany.

Population: the exception, two million growth scarcely consolidation from a 1871 base of 37 million: this was the real national worry.

Political stability: include progress towards democracy, give examples, despite the spectacular 'scandals', Republic stable and secure by 1900. The threat from the Right had been survived. Social stability also secure in marked contrast to Commune period. Threat of revolution from the Left was being met by a slowly developing programme of social reforms.

"Republican consolidation."

Internationally: France had come from isolation to alliance with Russia and Britain; in 1914 it would not fight alone. Imperial growth had in fact been quite spectacular, indicate where, and by 1914 only Britain had a larger empire.

Conclusion: the answer may depend on one's definition of spectacular and if you look at Germany as the yardstick, with population up from 41 to 65 million and with a sevenfold increase in coal production and tenfold in steel then the quotation in the question seems even more apt.

Question 5

Introduction: Examining the alternatives may suggest there is much in this quotation.

Examine and criticise:

- the monarchists
- Bonapartists
- Boulanger
- the revolutionary left

None at all credible.

"Do not undervalue the Republic's achievements."

Conclusion: quotation however undervalues the Republic's many assets and strengths: and its judgement of the Republic's position and achievements seems at least ungenerous. There was the solid support of the Centre and moderate Left. The willingness of Republican politicians to make the system, however creaking, work. It provided stability and peace as a basis for social and economic progress (give examples) and slowly became more democratic. These assets became more important the longer it survived. Its stronger international position (explain briefly) over time was also a source of prestige and durability. – colonial empire 2nd only to Britain

Peace with German indemnity paid – Social reforms Ferry + education 70's–80's Millerand 90's – Arms race, car + bicycle production – break from isolation 1893 – 1904

A TUTOR'S ANSWER TO QUESTION 1

– Frenchmen accepted weak + unstable govns bet. 1870 – 1895 as the price they had to pay in order to preserve their liberty. Do you agree?

This period of French history was certainly characterised by weak and unstable governments but whether Frenchmen consciously saw this as a price to be paid for liberty seems more contentious. The majority perhaps never reflected on the matter at all.

"Too many short-lived governments . . ."

The Third Republic was marked by numerous short-lived governments, in part a consequence of the convention that the defeat of the government in the Chamber of Deputies or the Senate did not bring about a general election but simply a search for a new government amongst the existing Deputies. This led to intense party and individual manoeuvring, made all the more complex because politicians had to take into account the local interests that had elected them. No government could survive if it lost the support of the majority of the Deputies. Governments came and went and few managed to carry out important measures or look to the long term interests of the country. The fragmentation of political parties and the complicated system of voting ensured that at no point in the period did any party emerge with enough electoral strength to bring this confusion at the centre to an end.

"... and a weak Presidency."

The President was elected by Deputies and Senators and he in turn appointed ministers to run the country's affairs. In this period only President MacMahon in 1877 appeared to try to exploit his position in order to strengthen the central authority. His real motive was the restoration of the monarchy and when this was thwarted he resigned. Later presidents accepted a less positive role, more probably to keep some semblance of political stability than to preserve anyone's liberty.

Threats to the Republic came from the political Right: from the Monarchists and from Boulanger. If they had been successful stronger government might have emerged and in this it was perhaps memories and myths about the tyranny of past monarchs and more recently of Napoleon III that made those who favoured the Republican Constitution all the more resolute in its defence. The surprising firmness shown by the government in standing up to Boulanger was probably based on fear of what a militarist style government would bring. This is perhaps the episode to which the quotation is most applicable. The threat of a strong government imposed from the Left did not emerge in this period.

"A free and flourishing society?"

France under the Republic enjoyed more individual freedom than the subjects of the other great continental powers. Even the powers of the Catholic Church over education received a decisive check. It was a period of great cultural and intellectual achievements and this owed much to the non-repressive nature of the state as Paris became the cultural capital of the Continent. It is difficult to imagine Bismarck's Berlin or Tsarist St Petersburg filling this role easily.

The problem remains that most French people rarely reflected on the links between their personal freedom and the apparent impotence of much of national political life. Their concerns were more mundane. They put up with the scandals and corruption of political life because there was little they could do about them. The most that can be said is that, when faced with the choice, the majority preferred the Republic to the prospect of more right-wing regimes. They probably sought political and social stability rather than liberty for it was 'the Republic which divides us least'. Certainly these were the motives of the bourgeoisie, the small-town artisans and the peasantry. These groups shared few of the political ideals of Parisian intellectuals. It was the latter who talked largely of liberty but they were not typical of French society as a whole, which after the humiliations and the terrors of 1870–1871, wanted above all a peaceful and stable setting in which to get on with the business of making a living.

"'The Republic divides us least'."

USEFUL SOURCES OF INFORMATION

General reading

J B Watson, *Success in European History 1815–1941*, John Murray 1981
A Ramm, *Europe in the Nineteenth Century 1789–1905*, Longman 1984
A Wood, *Europe 1815–1960*, Longman 1984: recommended reading on other topics in nineteenth century European history, is less full on the Third Republic.

Further reading

A Cobban, *A History of Modern France, Volume 2 1799–1945*, Penguin 1971
K Randell, *France: The Third Republic 1870–1914*, Arnold 1986: in a series devised for A-level students.

Linked topic areas

- French history 1815–1870 (see Chapter 13)
- Bismarck's foreign policy (see Chapter 17)
- The causes of the First World War (see Chapter 19)
- The growth of socialism in Europe
- The State and religion in 19th century Europe
- French cultural life in the 19th century

CHAPTER 19

CAUSES OF THE FIRST WORLD WAR

GERMAN ALLIANCE SYSTEM

RIVAL ALLIANCE SYSTEM

THE ARMS RACE

INTERNATIONAL CRISES

WARLIKE MOOD

POLICIES OF THE GREAT POWERS IN 1914

THE CRISIS

WHY WAR?

USEFUL INFORMATION

GETTING STARTED

To make much sense of this topic you need to study a general political sketch map outlining the boundaries of the major powers of Europe before 1914. As you work through the topic try to have available a more detailed political map of the Balkans. Use the first map to carry out a tour of the major nations so that you are able to offer some political comments on each one. Explanations of why the war occurred have to take into account some aspects of the domestic history of the major powers. Students who have been studying late nineteenth century Europe will almost certainly have enough information already available for the present purpose. Chapters 15 and 17 are particularly relevant.

You will need to be aware of the ramshackle structure of Austria–Hungary; that it was hard pressed by the aspirations of the different nationalities within its own boundaries and fearful of the ambitions of the Slav peoples on its borders as the Ottoman Empire in the Balkans crumbled away. In distinct contrast was the growing industrial and military might of Austro-Hungary's ally, the German Empire, formed in 1871. Its existence was threatening to destroy the international balance of power in central Europe. Increasingly isolated from these two fellow autocracies was Tsarist Russia, a country which might well see a need for foreign adventures to counter imagined slights abroad or all too real problems at home.

Russia was allied from 1893 to the Third French Republic, still smarting from defeat by Germany in 1870 and from the consequent loss of the provinces of Alsace and Lorraine. France lived under the shadow of German military might. Britain, protected by her navy and with great imperial possessions, stood apart in isolation from alliances until after the end of the century but thereafter found her easy supremacy, economic, imperial, and naval, increasingly difficult to sustain.

A survey of the status of each of the Powers on these lines is the very minimum you need. A fuller study of them will make your judgements of their motives and their anxieties much more convincing. An examination question might well focus largely on the responsibility of any one of the Powers for the outbreak of war and you will need to have enough knowledge to provide the right level of detail.

Finally the background to the First World War stretches far back and has many, apparently disconnected, strands. Most textbooks finish this topic with a summary giving the author's assessment of why the war occurred. It could be a good idea to read this first before moving into the background detail. From the general reading referred to at the end of this chapter *Watson* (pages 274–277) has *'Why was there a War?*, *Wood*, (pages 293–304) has an analysis of *'The approach of war 1907–14'*, *Ramm,* (pages 56–59) has a *'Review of the causes of the war in 1914'*. These few pages are well worth reading.

Remember to keep the map in front of you as you move into the detail of the topic.

ESSENTIAL PRINCIPLES

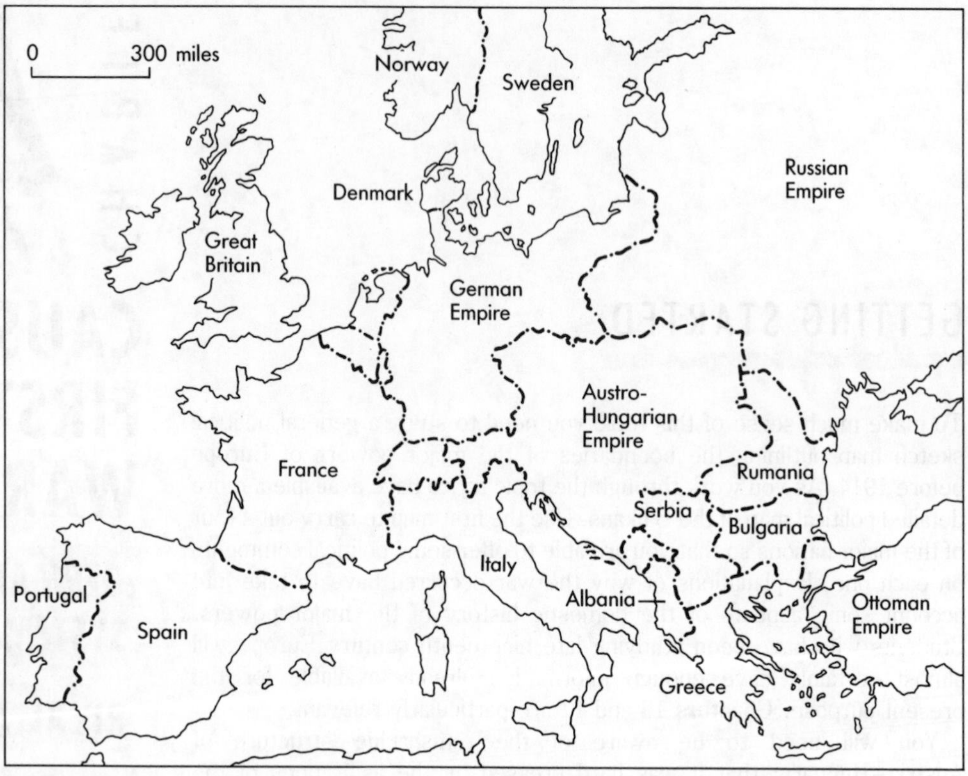

Fig. 19.1 Europe: 1914

GERMAN ALLIANCE SYSTEM

IN 1890

This was a result of the work of the German Chancellor, Bismarck, since the formation of the German Empire in 1871. His achievement is, in its own right, a major topic in late nineteenth century political history and is considered in Chapter 17. The central principle of Bismarck's policy was to prevent a potentially anti-German coalition of the other Powers from being established. In view of the way in which the creation of the German Empire had threatened the political balance across Europe he was remarkably successful in his efforts. In 1890 he handed to his successors a firm alliance with Austria–Hungary but less certain arrangements with Russia; in any event his successors immediately allowed these to lapse. Bismarck's policies had also kept cordial relations with Britain by avoiding challenges to her naval supremacy and, when possible, her imperial position. Such relations kept France isolated.

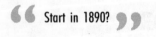

"Start in 1890?"

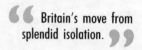

The starting point for a study of the origins of the War is often taken as the fall from power of Bismarck in 1890 and the subsequent disintegration of the arrangements he had made for German security through keeping Europe at peace.

RIVAL ALLIANCE SYSTEM

EMERGENCE

Both the reasons for this development and the stages through which it went are important as questions are often asked on this aspect which do not go on to bring the actual outbreak of the war into the question. A great deal of information can be accumulated and it is important that, in the examination room, this is related directly to the question that has been set. This topic is notorious for students describing what happened, often at great length, but not using this information to give a direct answer to the question set.

You need to:

"Britain's move from splendid isolation."

- Understand why Russia in the 1890s moved into an alliance with France when fear of isolation and continued tensions with Austria–Hungary in the Balkans were looming large.
- Understand what effect defeat by Japan, in 1904–1905, had on Russia.
- Establish the reasons for and the chronology of Britain's emergence from isolation to alliances.

1902 Anglo-Japanese Alliance: if either were attacked by two powers the other would help. This was intended to secure Britain's interests in Asia in the event of it being drawn into a European war.
1904 Entente Cordiale with France: settled outstanding colonial issues between the two, for example, it gave France a free hand in Morocco and Britain one in Egypt.
1907 Entente with Russia: clearing issues between the two in Afghanistan, Persia and Tibet. Russia had been France's ally since 1893.

The precise arrangements with France, and the ways in which they evolved through to the outbreak of war, need to be noted, as does the fact that Britain's arrangements were technically not alliances but understandings – 'ententes'. This topic may appear in British history papers, often in quite detailed form. The 'Document Question' in Chapter 8 will make a useful starting point. The French position on the need for allies might seem more obvious but it would be useful revision of the material to think it through, consulting Chapter 18.

THE ARMS RACE

The arms race was amongst the individual Powers and not between the two alliance systems. It helped to arouse warlike public feelings and heightened the tension in times of crisis, in this way contributing to the crises and sharpening the international divisions. It would be difficult to establish that it actually brought war about (see the 'Outline Answer' to Question 3 later in this chapter). It certainly added to the horrors and perhaps the length of the conflict and those studying the course of the war should familiarise themselves with the 'improvements' in such fields as rapid fire guns, heavy artillery and the new breed of heavy ironclad dreadnought battleships. The conscript armies of all the continental powers, creating vast army reserves also materially affected the nature of the war.

“A topic on British history papers.”

For British history papers this topic is particularly important because the arms race played a large part in bringing Britain into the alliance system. If the pre-1914 climate of opinion is one factor in bringing about the outbreak of war, then the arms race contributed greatly towards this, both at the official level of politicians and military and amongst the general public.

INTERNATIONAL CRISES

BEFORE 1914

“Relate the earlier crises to the outbreak of war.”

It is worth listing these in chronological order but it is even more important to be able to explain how each encouraged the deepening divisions in Europe. The earlier crises did not cause the war: they helped to create the conditions which made a war likely in some future crisis. Nor are all the crises of equal significance in the build-up to 1914. Those between France and Germany over Morocco (**Algeciras Conference, 1906** and **Agadir, 1911**) are important because they drew England and France closer together and made it more probable that Germany would be unlikely to back down on a future occasion. How each crisis may have made a future war more likely needs to be explained. It is not enough simply to be able to recount what happened and assume that everything that happened before 1914 self-evidently led to the outbreak of war in that year.

The crises in the Balkans: these are arguably the most significant, if only because in the event it was a Balkan crisis which brought the war about (for background see Chapter 15). The Austria–Hungary annexation of Bosnia in 1908 is the best case in point: it deeply angered Serbia and, because Russia lost face by not helping Serbia, made it more likely that it would not dare back down again in the event of another Austrian threat to Serbia. In this way it can well be argued that the 1908 crisis contributed significantly to the mad sequence of events in July 1914. It is not, however good enough to assume that the examiner knows that to be the case. If you choose to link 1908 to 1914 then you must clearly indicate, as above but more fully, how you perceive the link to operate.

“Repeated crises did not make war inevitable.”

The surprising thing is that so many potential crises did not lead to war but were sorted out by other means. If historical explanations were subject to some rule of logic and if momentous events, like the 1914–1918 War, always had momentous causes then the deep rivalries over African colonies might well have brought about the war, whereas in practice Africa was carved up with relative ease. Similarly in the Balkans where wars, in 1912 and 1913 between the smaller nations, were fought out and ended without the Great Powers, allegedly always so close to conflict between each other, being drawn in. Early in 1914 the

Balkans seemed to be more settled than for many years. The crises prior to 1914 contributed to the deepening of the divisions and warlike feelings in Europe but they did not make a future major war certain. Diplomatic endeavours had, prior to 1914, succeeded in preventing such an outcome.

WARLIKE MOOD IN EUROPE

"The influence of Social Darwinism."

The crises, the arms race and the imperial rivalries all played their part here. So did popular prejudice and the developing public arena in which the political game was played out with national animosities fanned by a popular press. The ideas of Darwin on the survival of animal species had been translated into a notion of a struggle between human societies with the term 'Social Darwinism' coined to catch the notion of the survival of only the fittest human societies. This bred a frenzy of suspicion in which for example every move of that popular British bogey, the German Kaiser, whether to build battleships or to appear to side with the Boers, was used to support the need for vast British re-armament as a host of British publications raised Germany to the level of the national enemy. Nor was this a purely British phenomenon; such feelings were fully reciprocated in Berlin.

"A general European warlike mood."

In Vienna the Serbs and their potential allies the Russians could be as quickly vilified. The French had never doubted who their national enemy was. Crude popular passions such as had rarely been around in the nineteenth century now created a situation in which, even if they did not lead directly to war, made war only too easy to accept.

This situation became critical, however, precisely because these powerful national prejudices were not just rife amongst mobs fed by sensational journalism but percolated into the highest political and military reaches of the European states. It was this that made them so dangerous as they increasingly became obsessions with the power to dominate policy.

POLICIES OF THE GREAT POWERS IN 1914

Austria–Hungary

Austria was responsible for the war to the extent that it was necessary for her to take extreme steps against Serbia, which had in the crisis tried to be conciliatory, in order to solve the problems of the nationalities inside its own ramshackle empire. Crushing Serbia was an act of deliberate policy to solve this internal problem.

"A will for war in Berlin?"

Germany

In the upper ranks of the military and the government there was a real wish for war. Germany backed Austria against both Serbia and Russia in order to secure space for its imperial ambitions in Central Europe; a victory in war was seen as securing Germany from surrounding enemies and establishing the pre-eminent position in Europe which its economic and military resources deserved. There was a real will for war in Berlin. It was presented to the German people as a defensive war against Russia but in any event the public was also in a mood to welcome an assertion of German strength. It was German supremacy on the continent that was at stake. Some German historians now argue that war was also deliberately brought about to solve domestic problems and in particular to outbid the socialists for the loyalty of the working-class by playing the patriotic card. Such historians also argue that the German government had quite specific plans for territorial acquisitions in Eastern Europe through victory in war.

Russia

The Tsar's government also sought war and victory as the best means of strengthening the regime against its liberal and left-wing critics at home and to restore its prestige after the defeat of 1904–1905. Again there was a real will to go to war which, as the enthusiasm at its declaration revealed, swept up the general public into a very satisfactory loyal hysteria.

France

French diplomacy had struggled for forty years to end the country's diplomatic isolation in Europe. This had now been achieved. The moment to avenge 1870 had arrived and public enthusiasm in Paris ran as high as in the other capitals. The alternative was to renege on the alliance obligations to Russia and return to isolation under the shadow of an even more powerful German Empire. So the French mobilised their forces. In practice the German plan (**the Schlieffen Plan**) for a swift victory in the west as the prelude to a longer war against Russia made France the victim of a German declaration of war.

Britain

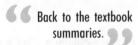

"The invasion of Belgium simplified the issues for Britain."

The British government and public saw Germany as a real menace to national survival. In August 1914, although a few hesitated, to the vast majority it was clear that Britain's survival as a great power depended on France surviving. The German invasion of Belgium simplified the issues. Turn now to the 'Document Question' in Chapter 8 which is directly on this issue. It is worth noting that later it was felt to be unfortunate that Britain had not made its resolution to stand by France clear enough to Germany and this had encouraged the German government to make a fatal miscalculation. Whether this would indeed have influenced events must be considered alongside recent interpretations of German intentions noted above.

THE CRISIS

JULY–AUGUST 1914

"A headlong plunge to war."

This came from nowhere. The Archduke Franz Ferdinand of Austria was assassinated on the 28th June and at midnight on August 4th Britain was at war with Germany. Between those dates the system of alliances had worked with venomous effect to suck all the Great Powers of the continent into a conflict, that was to end in the deaths of tens of millions of Europeans. A history student who is not fascinated by the appalling, close-packed, sequence is almost certainly studying the wrong subject! More coolly you need to be able to explain why in turn the nations were so drawn in: their national obsessions, their commitments, their fears of staying out. An outline knowledge of the five weeks will suffice for you will scarcely have time in an examination to do justice to the sweep of events.

WHY WAR?

A RESUMÉ

You really need to come back to this and to construct an examination length explanation: not to memorise but to satisfy yourself that you think you can see why it happened. You can then adapt your thoughts to the particular form of the question set. Read through again the issues covered above, decide how you would wish to fit them into an explanation for some of the past questions which have been set. Go back once more to the summaries of why there was a war which adorn most textbooks. At this stage you almost certainly need some clear signposts through the forest of background information and interpretation.

"Back to the textbook summaries."

Possible questions

You may well get a question on only one aspect of the topic and so you need a lot of information and ideas on issues like how did Balkan crises or the Arms Race, or Imperial ambitions, or distrust between any two countries, or popular feeling contribute to the final outcome? Was it the result of a breakdown in the hitherto successful practice of international diplomacy or of a deliberate wish for war in too many of Europe's capitals? The list could be extended but it often involves only a re-thinking of the same material, and this is the best form of revision. If, in the examination, you get a general question to answer on why there was a war, then you will quickly find yourself up against the pressure of time: your explanations and their inter-linking will have to be done economically, there will be no time for describing what happened, just time to adapt **ideas** to a direct answer to the form of the question set.

"Work through the content from different angles."

Note: For the last time remember that describing what happened before 1914 does not, in itself, explain why there was a war in 1914!

"A common error."

USEFUL INFORMATION

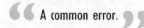

1871–1890	European diplomacy dominated by Bismarck's alliance system, the central principle of which was to prevent Austrian and Russian interests in the Balkans leading to conflict and to keeping both allied to Germany and so keep France isolated.
1890	Dismissal of Bismarck Reinsurance Treaty between Germany and Russia not renewed.

1891	Britain indifferent to Kaiser's efforts to get an alliance.
1893	Franco–Russian Alliance each pledged to use all available forces if attacked by Germany. Bismarck's system at an end.
1895	Kaiser's congratulatory telegram to Kruger at repulsing British incursion to Transvaal (the Jameson Raid) caused annoyance in Britain.
1898	Germany decided to build a heavy battleship fleet.
	Fashoda crisis marked the low point in Anglo-French relations.
1899–1902	**Boer War**
	Britain's difficulties made the first dent in its policy of 'splendid isolation'.
1900	Germany enhanced its naval plans
1901	Failure of Anglo-German alliance negotiations
1902	Anglo-Japanese Alliance ended British isolation, purpose was to secure Far East possessions in event of European war.
1904–1905	**Russo-Japanese War**
	Humiliating defeat of Russia
1904	Anglo-French Entente settled colonial differences.
1905	**First Moroccan Crisis** (Kaiser at Tangier), result was to strengthen the Entente.
	British launched first Dreadnought.
1906	At Algeciras Conference on North Africa firm British support for France.
1907	Anglo-Russian Entente resolving issues in Afghanistan, Persia and Tibet.
1908	Austria, with German support, annexed Bosnia and Herzegovina.
	Russian anger but no action
1911	**Second Moroccan Crisis** (Panther at Agadir) drew Britain and France closer.
1912	First Balkan War
1913	Second Balkan War
1914	
28 June	**Assassination at Sarajevo**
23 July	Austrian ultimatum sent to Serbia
25 July	Serbian reply
27 July	Austria declared war on Serbia
30 July	Russian mobilisation ordered
31 July	German ultimatum to Russia
1 Aug	Germany declared war on Russia
3 Aug	Germany declared war on France
4 Aug	Germany invaded Belgium in implementation of the Schlieffen Plan for a quick victory in the west.
5 Aug	**Britain declared war on Germany**

EXAMINATION QUESTIONS

Q1 How responsible were differences over the Eastern Question for the outbreak of a general European war in 1914? (AEB 1989)

Q2 Should an explanation for the outbreak of the First World War emphasise long-term or short-term factors? (Northern Ireland 1987)

Q3 'Military and naval preparations for war served to heighten tension between the European powers, they did not of themselves occasion the resort to war in August 1914.' Discuss this statement. (NEAB 1989)

Q4 How valid is the view that all the major powers entered the First World War to defend themselves? (Cambridge 1989)

Q5 How much responsibility should Balkan nationalism bear for the outbreak of the First World War? (London 1990)

OUTLINE ANSWERS

Question 1

See the 'Tutor's Answer' at the end of this section.

Question 2

General approach: for an understanding of why a major war occurred it is the long-term factors. For precise form it took, short-term factors are significant.

Long term factors:

- Long standing rivalries and the issues on which they rested, especially Russia and Austria and Franco-German.
- Division of Europe into rival alliance systems.
- The arms race and the incidents which increased tension – Balkans, North Africa.
- Growing war-like mood in the capitals of Europe.

" Long-term and short-term causes. "

These long-term factors created the situation where any small incident had the potential to cause war and for any small war to easily draw in the major powers. Alliance system would mean none would dare stay out. And yet major war was not inevitable, for example, Balkans 1912 and 1913.

Short-term factors: date and precise form of war rested on short-term factors. Outline these, especially the 'trivial' assassination as the spark. Also cite invasion of Belgium as perhaps bringing Britain in. Was this a short or a long-term factor? A bit of both and this may well be true of many of the other causes.

Question 3

Introduction: at first sight this proposition seems reasonable: examine ways in which this had happened with conscript armies, armaments and the Anglo-German naval race. Show how this race had heightened tensions and use Britain and Germany as the example.

Argue: that arms race not the original or only cause of tension, indicate national rivalries and fears as main cause (give examples but very briefly) so the important word is 'heighten'.

" The arms race heightened tensions: it did not cause the war? "

Challenge: it is however possible to challenge the statement in one important respect. The creation of mass armies required a mobilisation period before war could be declared, once one power began mobilising then the move to war could take over and destroy the chances of a diplomatic move to prevent it. In 1914 Russian and then French mobilisation did just this to Germany, just as Austrian mobilisation had worked on Russia. The key moment, when the quotation is most open to challenge, comes with the operation of the German Schlieffen Plan which is certainly part of the military preparations. This spread the war to western Europe and its requirements forced Germany to move for a quick victory in the west and declare war on France. The route taken by the Schlieffen planners, through Belgium, closed down Britain's option of keeping out of the conflict.

" But arguably did extend its scope. "

Conclusion: the quotation is much more open to challenge than at first sight appears. The military preparations had turned an east European conflict into a general European war and must share some responsibility for its outbreak in August 1914.

Question 4

Survey: easy way is to survey powers and consider how true claim is in each case. Consider defensive reasons in turn. Take powers in same order and indicate what other, non-defensive motives they might have had.

Conclusion: France attacked by Germany was,in the event,the most purely defensive; Austria and Russia appear to have had pressing fears about the defence of vital interests. Britain not defensive in the sense that the navy gave it immediate security but had to stand by France to safeguard its long-term position in Europe. Germany the most openly aggressive: perhaps some truth in later 'war guilt' charge? But public mood in many countries welcomed war and there was little thought of defence anywhere but of 'victory by Christmas'.

Question 5

Explain: the nature of Balkan nationalism, especially Serbian, and then propose that it provided the spark in the assassination of the Archduke. Without that spark there would have been no war.

Argue: that earlier outbreaks caused by nationalism in the Balkans had not led to a major European war (cite 1912 and 1913 wars). What turned a difficult regional crisis into a European war was not Balkan nationalism but long-standing rivalry between the great powers (indicate main features) which by 1914 had reached a point where none of the great powers would back down from war. This is the crucial part of any explanation of the outbreak of the First World War.

Note: This question is similar to that dealt with in the 'Tutor's Answer' that follows. It also requires a clear understanding of Balkan nationalism as considered in Chapter 15.

A TUTOR'S ANSWER TO QUESTION 1

The Eastern Question arose from the political instability in the Balkans brought about by the crumbling of the Ottoman Empire. This led to growing national feeling amongst the peoples of the region and a desire by Russia and Austria–Hungary to extend their power there. The situation was sufficiently volatile that it had on several occasions raised the prospect of a war that would spill out from the Balkans across Europe. Yet in 1878 with the Congress of Berlin, in 1908 over Bosnia and in 1912–1913, with wars amongst the small Balkan nations, war had either been avoided, localised or brought to a swift end. In early 1914 the Balkans was more stable than it had been for some years. There was nothing intrinsic to the Balkans situation that made war on a grand scale inevitable.

The madcap race to war in June/July 1914 had its origin in the assassination of the Archduke Franz Ferdinand, heir to the throne of Austria–Hungary, by the young Serbian nationalist Princep. This act was a direct product of the bitter national rivalries of the region with weapons supplied by the Black Hand, a ruthless Serbian secret society committed to the union of all Slavs in one nation by whatever means were necessary. Such ambitions meant at least the partial disintegration of the Austrian Empire and it was the conscious decision of the Austrians, that their status as a Great Power required that a permanent check be placed on Serbian-fostered unrest, and that this brutal act be avenged, which meant that the first step to war had been taken. This was a direct consequence of the conflicting interests in the Balkans of the multi-national Austria–Hungary and the fiercely nationalist ambitions of Serbia.

"Russo-Austrian rivalry made it a major war."

The field of conflict was fatally widened by Russia's vision of itself as the protector of the Slav peoples of the region and the feeling in Moscow that, after the 1908 'humiliation' by the Austrians their own credibility as a Great Power was at stake. At this stage in the widening conflict many factors outside Balkan rivalries begin to influence the course of events. The rivalry of Austria and Russia in the Balkans may have brought them to war at any time but, without the particular set of alliances and national rivalries which had by 1914 come to dominate European politics, this need not have led to the wider total conflict which now occurred.

"German backing for Austria made it a general European war."

The key to explaining this wider context rests with the policies pursued by the German Empire, a power with no direct political ambitions in the Balkans. Bismarck before 1890 had welded together the oldest of the continent's alliances, between Germany and Austria–Hungary and this held firm into the First World War. It is very unlikely that Austria would have acted so aggressively towards Serbia as it did after the assassination unless it had been confident of full German support. It was Bismarck's successors whose ambitions and errors had allowed a rival 'alliance' system to emerge, encompassing Russia, France and eventually Britain. Only the existence of these two rival alliance systems makes the chain of events leading from Sarajevo to total war explicable and even then it is only part of the account.

The support given by Germany to the Austrians reflected a growing militarism in the nation, a confidence in the traditions of Prussian military achievement and growing German industrial might which was not averse to using these assets to re-set the European political map more certainly in Germany's favour. This situation had its origins in the race to build up armaments, conscript armies and heavy ironclad navies, which had dominated the previous decade or more. A warlike mood, perhaps having its origins in the notions of the survival of the fittest which were a central feature of the influential Social Darwinist beliefs of the period, was prevalent throughout Europe. It was fanned by popular newspapers into a general jingoistic sentiment. In countries like Britain and France it had little to do with the Eastern Question as such but it created the volatile atmosphere which could turn that spark into a bonfire. Above all it created a situation where no major power could be seen to back down in a crisis.

The Austrians were always intent on a war to crush Serbian pretensions and so relieve the most pressing of the nationalist problems within their own borders and, despite the Serbians accepting most of their terms and offering the rest to arbitration, duly declared war on July 28th. The Russians ignored German warnings and mobilised their troops, for their status as the largest Slav nation and as protector of the Balkan Slavs meant that, after the humiliation over Austria's annexation of Bosnia in 1908, they could do no less. In any case war fever and visions of easy military glory were as potent in Moscow as in Berlin. Up to this point the Balkans issue is central to the course of events.

" Military imperatives took over. "

The German pre-emptive declaration of war on Russia on 1st August and on France two days later (in response to French mobilisation under their Russian alliance arrangements) widened both the area of conflict and the causes of conflict. The French involvement was only distantly a consequence of any Balkan concerns; it rested on alliance obligations which in turn rested on bitter anti-German feeling and a desire both for revenge for the defeat of 1870–71 and to recover the lost provinces of Alsace and Lorraine. Britain's eventual involvement rested on clear military understandings with France and sentimental obligations of honour towards Belgium with the latter resting in turn on realistic calculations about its own safety if a strong continental power controlled Belgium's coastline. In the end war fever swept Britain too into war for a 'scrap of paper': certainly the Eastern Question played little or no part in the immediate decision.

To sum up – the Balkans provided the spark which Austro-Russian rivalry over the Eastern Question transformed into a war involving major powers. This became a general European war chiefly because of Germany's treaty obligations and because of the warlike mood in Berlin. France and Britain were swept into the war through similar obligations and through old historical interests and grievances far removed from the Balkans. It is true that, in addition to providing the spark for war, Balkan issues had contributed greatly to the build-up of international tension in pre-war Europe. The Eastern Question then is crucial to an understanding of why the war occurred but it cannot, alone, provide the full explanation for its outbreak.

USEFUL SOURCES OF INFORMATION

General reading

A Ramm, *Europe in the Twentieth Century 1905–1970*, Longman 1984: her *Europe in the Nineteenth Century* is recommended for the earlier background.
J B Watson, *Success in European History 1815–1941*, John Murray 1981
A Wood, *Europe 1815–1960*, Longman 1984

Further reading

W Carr, *A History of Germany 1815–1985*, Arnold 1987
J Joll, *Origins of the First World War*, Longman 1984
J Lowe, *Rivalry and Accord: International Relations, 1870–1914,* Arnold 1988

Linked topic areas

- Bismarck's foreign policy (see Chapter 17)
- British foreign policy 1890s to 1914
- The Eastern Question 1878–1914 (see Chapter 15)
- Austria–Hungary 1867–1914
- Russia under Tsar Nicholas II 1894–1917 (see Chapter 14)
- The Third French Republic (see Chapter 18)
- The course of the First World War
- The effects of the War: the Versailles Peace Settlement

CHAPTER 20

USSR 1917–1941

GETTING STARTED

Inevitably students who have followed Russian history in the nineteenth century will have a fuller grasp of the background to the fall of the last Tsar than those whose syllabus starts with this topic. This disadvantage can quickly be overcome. Focus on the reign of Nicholas II (1894–1917) and consider his personal weaknesses and those of his ministers. Politically the defeat by Japan and the 1905 Revolution marked a watershed in his always autocratic reign: the latter lost him much popular support. The constitutional experiments (the Dumas) which followed were half-hearted and provided neither efficient government nor a constitutional basis for Tsardom. You need to be able to illustrate the weaknesses in the Tsar's position by 1914. Much of this preliminary material is touched upon in Chapter 14 – a useful starting point.

Opposition groups grew, some were liberal democratic, others like the Social Democrats inspired by the ideas of Karl Marx wanted fundamental social, economic and political change. *Marxism* is central to the events of 1917 and the creation of the Soviet Union, the world's first state organised on Marxist lines. Marx had published the Communist Manifesto in 1848 and part of *Das Kapital* in 1867. His work was perhaps the most influential in nineteenth century political writing. He observed the growth of the industrial proletariat and predicted a revolutionary struggle between them and the bourgeoisie which would lead to the setting up of a communist society. His work provided a creed for revolutionaries and gave them the self-confidence to conspire against impossible odds. His most important single legacy was that Lenin was converted to his ideas of revolution and at the strategic moment had the courage to apply them, ironically not in the advanced industrial nations of western Europe, which Marx had predicted would be the setting of the proletarian revolution, but in the more backward Russia. See what an encyclopedia or any standard textbook offers on Marx and the influence of Marxism.

In 1903 the Social Democrats split with the majority *Bolsheviks* (majority men) supporting Lenin's idea of a small dedicated party of revolutionaries against the *Mensheviks* (minority men) who favoured a mass socialist party. The 1917 lines were drawn at this point.

Set alongside this darkening pre-war political scene the considerable economic progress made by Imperial Russia in agriculture, industry and transport. Could Russia have emerged from economic backwardness and autocratic inefficiency without revolutionary upheaval? This is historically unanswerable but is a useful learning device in establishing an assessment of the state of Russia in 1914 when, despite the economic progress, enormous social and political problems remain unresolved. Finally you will also need to know enough about the causes and events of the First World War to appreciate what had happened to the Russian forces by 1917.

Note: Some option syllabuses end with the death of Lenin in 1924.

ESSENTIAL PRINCIPLES

THE TSARIST STATE

"A popular examination topic."

IN 1914

Questions on why the Tsarist state collapsed are common. They usually involve the need to assess long term weaknesses and then to take into account the effects of the First World War. If you are not considering answering a question on pre-war Russia then the most economical approach is to prepare an outline note summing up your assessment of the Tsar's position in 1914. This will involve reflecting on the events of war and revolution in 1905, the failure of the Dumas, the Tsar's inability to select and support effective ministers but it need not involve learning a great deal of pre-war narrative history which you will not have time to use in the examination. Consider how you would answer the question 'How close to collapse was Tsardom on the eve of the First World War?' and what information about pre-war Russia you would find useful in providing an examination length answer to the question. Then move on to the war period.

THE FEBRUARY REVOLUTION

EFFECTS OF THE FIRST WORLD WAR

The reasons for Russia being involved in the war need to be assessed. Defeat by Japan had drawn Russia further into the European alliance systems if only because it re-inforced its ambitions in the Balkans. Victory in war could, additionally, solve many pressing internal problems, few expected a long war, and its declaration brought an unaccustomed surge of popularity for the Tsar.

"Russian experience of the war."

There were early advances but for Russia the war had, by 1915, become one of holding the German forces at bay, with superior manpower no compensation for a desperate shortage of war supplies. The Tsar's taking command of the army was a mistake for he was now held directly responsible for the retreats and the high casualties of 1916. In his absence the machinery of central government creaked ever more alarmingly. Food shortages and inflation added to the miseries of the civilian population. Above all there was a growing air of unreality in the Tsarist position, increasingly Nicholas ignored advice whilst the interference of the *Tsarina* and her chief adviser, *Rasputin*, whose excesses and overwhelming influence did much to discredit the system and even the royal family itself, added to the chaos behind the front. The Liberal opposition, hoping to gain political concessions from a weakened Tsar did all they could to undermine the war effort. No-one at the top level of the Tsar's dwindling band of supporters seems to have grasped the depth of misery and war-weariness gripping the soldiers and the civilian population. Their pre-war remoteness from the real Russia denied them an insight into the true depth of the crisis brought about by the war.

Downfall of the Tsarist state

The events of the war on and behind the Russian Front have a dramatic quality which makes them easy to follow. You should be ready to indicate how, in your view, they contributed to the downfall, in February 1917, of the Tsarist state. The collapse of the economy under the strain of providing for the war effort, with shortages of fuel and raw materials and, thanks to conscription and the huge number of war casualties, even of manpower, is as important as the crisis at the front. Your assessment of this needs to acknowledge the personal weaknesses of the Tsar and, depending on the terms of the question, may also need to take into account the fact that the threats to Tsarist autocracy go back before 1914. Early in 1917 there was rioting in Petrograd, with food shortages, strikes and many killed when the police fired on the rioters. When Nicholas dissolved the Duma the decree was ignored and soldiers began to join the rioters. Nicholas, thanks to a strike by railway workers, unable even to move around his country, was driven to abdication.

"Collapse behind the lines."

THE OCTOBER REVOLUTION

"A period well worth revising carefully."

FAILURE OF THE PROVISIONAL GOVERNMENT

Events in Russia in 1917 deserve detailed study and full revision. They constitute a topic in which it is very difficult to bluff one's way to an adequate answer despite gaps in knowledge. They also make up one of the most interesting and significant topics of twentieth-century history. At the heart of the topic is the question of why, following the downfall of the Tsar, the Provisional Government led first by *Prince Lvov* and then *Kerensky*, failed. The government had been founded jointly by some members of the Duma and by the recently established Soviet of workers' and soldiers' deputies in Petrograd and from the start had to share its power with the latter body. Its mistakes and weaknesses, its failure to meet the aspirations of the war-weary Russian population need to be rehearsed as do the events from February to October. In **July** the Bolsheviks failed in an attempt to seize control of Petrograd and Lenin went into hiding. In **August** the reactionary coup, led by General Kornilov, helped to undermine Kerensky's government. It was prevented by the workers blocking his lines of communication and not by the government which had, at first, appeared to welcome it.

"The Provisional Government loses the initiative."

This, the emergence of workers Soviets across Russia and the growing power of the Bolsheviks in the Petrograd Soviet, which now established a Military Revolutionary Committee under Trotsky, indicate that the Provisional Government was losing the initiative. Lenin had been in exile when the Tsar abdicated but, from his dramatic return through to the overthrow of the Provisional Government, his role was of crucial importance. He gave the Bolsheviks the will to keep up the revolutionary momentum.

The background was one of continuing war, food shortages and general misery. The events which led to the Bolshevik overthrow of these experiments in democratic government had a momentum of their own and could, even in detail, scarcely hold more dramatic interest. In **October** the storming of the Winter Palace and the overthrow of the Kerensky Government on the 25th led, on the 26th, to the All-Russian Congress of Soviets setting up a new government led by Lenin. The 'Document Question' at the end of the chapter bears directly on this. The timing of the coup may well have been brought forward in order to impress the All-Russian Congress with the power of the Bolsheviks in Petrograd.

OUTCOME

Within days the Land Decree had handed the land over to the peasants, workers were given control of their factories and both the banks and the property of the Church had been taken over. When elections to the Constituent Assembly left the Bolsheviks in a minority, it was forcibly dispersed and did not meet again.

"A few conspirators or the popular will?"

You need to be able to offer your view on whether the October Revolution, which led on to the setting up of the Bolshevik State, was the product of the mass will of the Russian working-class or a hijacking of the democratic possibilities by a handful of well-organised and ruthless conspirators. It is however an issue where it is all too easy to lapse into unhistorical assertions so try to judge the evidence on its merits.

Exam questions

Often examination questions are asked on the establishment of the Bolshevik State across a wider time span, from the moment of the Revolution through to say 1920/1921. Having read up the events of 1917 it would be advisable to have an outline knowledge of what happened in Russia in the next few years.

Note: The Bolsheviks now abandoned the old Russian calendar and subsequent events in Russia are dated as for the rest of Europe.

CONSOLIDATION

REVOLUTION TO 1921

"The Bolsheviks establish control."

In 1918 the Bolsheviks became the Communists and implemented the decrees carrying out a massive transfer of economic resources, that of land to the peasants being the most significant. Negotations to end the war were begun. The **Cheka**, a separate police force, was set up to defend the Revolution from internal enemies; this establishment of communist power and the early, fundamental changes they introduced should not be forgotten in the more violent events of the Civil War which followed. The clearest focus of study for the Civil War is through considering the reasons why, despite foreign aid for their enemies, the Communists were eventually victorious. This obviously involves a survey of both their strengths, including the policies of Lenin and the work of Trotsky, and the weaknesses of their opponents. It is a question frequently asked by examiners.

WAR COMMUNISM

For this period you need to be able to discuss the purpose behind the economic programme of 'War Communism' which was set up in 1918 to give the government control of all aspects of the economy, in order to meet the disruption of the civil war. It was ruthlessly enforced, particularly on the peasants, by a vast bureaucracy and led the country close to economic collapse, culminating in 1921 in the naval mutiny at Kronstadt.

NEW ECONOMIC POLICY

In 1921 War Communism was abandoned in favour of the New Economic Policy (NEP) which relaxed economic, but not political, controls so that peasants could sell surplus crops and smaller firms were returned to private ownership which meant that some private trade had to be allowed. Major enterprises remained in government ownership. The NEP allowed the emergence of a more prosperous class within the peasantry and also of the *Nepmen*, a class of small capitalists. These concessions ran contrary to strict Marxist principles and were made because the rigours of the Civil War and of War Communism had brought the country close to breakdown. These changes in direction and the workings of the NEP through to its abandonment by Stalin in 1928, are often the subject of examination questions. Finally note that the new federal constitution of 1924 brought the USSR or Soviet Union into official existence.

LENIN'S ROLE

ASSESSMENT

Lenin's role was crucial in 1917: others, including Stalin, would have compromised at that point with the bourgeois state set up under Kerensky. Lenin created the conditions for its overthrow. He thereafter created much of the policy of the new Communist State, particularly in defence of it in the period 1918 to 1921. The dealings over land; the peace with Germany where he was prepared to pay a high price in lost territories in order to secure peace and therefore safeguard the revolution; and the cautious foreign policy, realistically coming to accept that the prospect of a worldwide revolution had receded, all owed much to him.

"Do not assume everything was done by Lenin."

In your reading look out for specific references to Lenin's work which you can use to substantiate an assessment of him. There is a tendency amongst weaker candidates to assume that everything happened because of him and so that a general history of the period will suffice. You should be more precise. In 1921 he was wounded in an assassination attempt and, although still attending to State business, was less effective. He failed to restrict the growth of a vast State bureaucracy and, crucially, failed to make clear arrangements as to who was to succeed him. On the other hand by the time of his death in 1924 the Communist State was secure from its enemies at home and increasingly accepted by foreign powers. You need to be able to give substance to a judgement on these lines.

AFTER LENIN

"Stalin seizes power."

THE POWER STRUGGLE

This topic requires an assessment of the characters and the careers to 1924 of both Stalin and Trotsky. Lenin had misgivings about both men as potential successors. The simplest approach is to follow the steps by which Stalin out-manoeuvred Trotsky and the other potential rivals Zinoviev and Kamenev until, by 1928, his authority was firmly established.

CREATING THE SOCIALIST STATE

"The Five Year Plans . . ."

The economic emphasis from 1928 was on central planning with a series of Five Year Plans started in 1928, 1933 and 1937. You will need to be able to assess the emphasis in each plan and their overall impact on Soviet agriculture and industrial capacity. A high price had to be paid by the Soviet people for the economic dislocation and the ruthless implementation of these plans, particularly those involving the collectivisation of agriculture. There was, in the plans for industry, an emphasis on capital goods production, especially agricultural machinery and the development of electrical power. Taken together the economic plans form a common examination topic but one which cries out for solid evidence to demonstrate the quality and range of your knowledge. It can be argued that Stalin's ruthless programme of industrialisation enabled the USSR to survive the German attack from 1941 through to victory in 1945.

"... and the price to be paid."

Exam questions

Often questions ask that the achievement be set alongside the cost to the Soviet people. Remember that there were accompanying social reform programmes, notably in pension, health and education provision to set against the great shortage of consumer goods which the economic plans did nothing to eradicate. A full assessment of these momentous years involves also the political material in the next section of these notes. It is particularly important in this topic area to read the question carefully and to answer it directly. Questions on Stalin's period of rule seem, inexplicably, to bring out the worst in irrelevance.

STALINISM TO 1941

From 1928 the economy was ruthlessly subjected to central control, opponents were eliminated and even members of the Communist Party were hounded. All possible rivals to Stalin were purged, the great show trials began and personal freedom disappeared. You need to be able to illustrate this with regard to:

- political life
- the national minorities
- the Jews
- cultural activities
- personal liberty

"Consider going to 1953."

It all constituted a tragic betrayal of the hopes of 1917 and can ironically be seen as a more severe form of Tsarist repression. Be prepared to analyse what happened coolly: that will be all the more effective. The most common issues raised are discussions of the centralisation of power in the State and/or how tyrannical Stalin's rule was. If your syllabus continues after the Second World War then it is sensible to take these themes of life in the USSR and the nature of Stalin's rule through to his death in 1953, and indeed to be able to comment briefly on and make use of the attack made on his methods of rule by Khrushchev in 1956.

USEFUL INFORMATION

1894	Accession of Tsar Nicholas II
1903	Social Democrats split between Mensheviks and Bolsheviks.
1904–1905	**Russo-Japanese War:** defeat of Russia
1905	Demonstration outside Winter Palace, St Petersburg fired on, probably hundreds dead. Widespread strikes followed. October Manifesto gave Russia a Constitution. Fundamental Laws issued: Tsar in control of executive and armed forces.
1906	First Duma soon dismissed by Tsar.
1907	Second Duma suffered same fate.
1907–1912	Third Duma (elected on a very narrow franchise).
1912–1916	Fourth Duma (rarely met during the war).
1914	**War with Germany and Austria.** St Petersburg re-named Petrograd.
1915	Nicholas took command of the army at the Front.
1917 Feb	(Old calendar) St Petersburg riots, Duma refused to be dissolved by the Tsar. Abdication of Nicholas II: Provisional Government under Prince Lvov.
Apr	Lenin arrived in Petrograd from exile in Switzerland.
July	Failure of Bolshevik coup; Lenin forced to go into hiding. Kerensky succeeded Lvov
Sept	Kornilov attack on the government blocked by the workers. This and failure to act on land issue or to end the war weakened Kerensky's position.
25 Oct	**Bolshevik Revolution:** key buildings seized. Winter Palace, home of the Provisional Government, stormed and its members arrested.

26 Oct	All-Russian Congress of Soviets set up government under Lenin. Immediate economic revolution; Land Decree distributed land to peasants. National Debt repudiated, banks nationalised, workers to take over factories, Church property confiscated.
Nov	Constituent Assembly elections returned almost twice as many Social Revolutionary members as Bolsheviks (420 to 225).
1918 Jan	Assembly immediately closed by Red troops.
1918 Mar	**Treaty of Brest-Litovsk** with Germany and its allies: Russia lost Baltic Provinces (Estonia, Latvia and Lithuania), Finland, the Ukraine, White Russia, Poland and the Caucasus.
	Bolsheviks adopted name of Communists.
July	Soviet Constitution agreed: power to reside in the Communist Party. By this time Soviet Union a one-party state.
	Murder of Tsar Nicholas II and his family.
1918–1920	**Civil War:** attempts at Allied intervention culminating in the war with Poland. Economic policy of **War Communism**.
1921	The Kronstadt Mutiny
	The **New Economic Policy** introduced.
1924	Union of Soviet Socialist Republics set up with a Federal Constitution.
1924	Death of Lenin
1926–1927	Victory of Stalin over Leftist opposition led by Trotsky.
1928	**Five Year Plans** – swift industrialisation with emphasis on capital goods and power, collectivisation of agriculture – introduced and brutally enforced.
1929	Bukharin and rightist opposition expelled from Party.
	Trotsky expelled from the Soviet Union.
1933	Purge of the members of the Communist Party.
1934	Murder of Kirov launched purges and show trials of many senior Party members.
1936	Zinoviev and Kamenev put on trial.
1939 Aug	Russo-German non-agression Pact. Soviet Union regained lands in eastern Poland and the Baltic Provinces.
1941 June	Germany attacked Soviet Union.

EXAMINATION QUESTIONS

Q1 Evaluate the factors which permitted the Bolsheviks to seize power in Russia in 1917. (Northern Ireland 1987)

Q2 How far was the success of the October Revolution in 1917 due to the determination of a small and largely unpopular party to seize power? (Cambridge 1986)

Q3 'The outside world remained deeply hostile to Russia.' Explain why, in the period 1917 to 1924, this should have been the case. (London 1990)

Q4 'He had the determination, the means of control, and the personal indifference to the lot of the Soviet people to hold on to power whatever his policies involved for Russia.' Discuss this statement with reference to either Lenin in the years 1817–1924 or Stalin in the years 1928–1941. (NEAB 1989)

Q5 How far had Stalin carried out a social and economic transformation in the USSR by 1941? (Cambridge 1989)

Q6 Document question: '*The Establishment of a Bolshevik Government: Proceedings in the Congress of Soviets 25 Oct. 1917*'. (AEB 1989)

I too was convinced that the power of a Bolshevik régime would be ephemeral[1]. A majority of them themselves were at that time convinced of the same thing. I also thought it useful and necessary to *isolate their position* and oppose to it the idea of a united democratic front. But for this why was it necessary to get out? It could be achieved only in the arena of Soviet struggle . . .

Martov asked for the floor on a point of order:

First of all, a pacific settlement of the crisis must be assured. There was blood flowing in the streets of Petersburg. Military activities on both sides must be halted. A pacific settlement of the crisis might be attained by the creation of a régime which would be recognised by the entire democracy.

Martov's motion was voted on: against it – nobody.

If the Mensheviks and SRs left *now*, they would simply write *finis* to themselves and infinitely strengthen their opponents. One would have thought the Right wouldn't do this *immediately*, and that the Congress, though with a wavering majority, would be set on the right road to the formation of a united democratic front.

But the Mensheviks and SRs did do it. These blind counter-revolutionaries not only failed to see that their 'line' was counter-revolutionary, but also failed to realize the complete absurdity and unworthy childishness of their behaviour . . .

In some detail Martov analysed the motives for his resolution. Then he proposed that the Congress pass a decree on the necessity for a peaceable settlement of the crisis by forming a general democratic Government and electing a delegation to negotiate with all Socialist parties . . .

The reply to Martov came from Trotsky. 'A rising of the masses of the people', Trotsky rapped out, 'needs no justification. What has happened is an insurrection, and not a conspiracy. The masses of the people followed our banner and our insurrection was victorious. And now we are told: renounce your victory, make concessions, compromise . . . No, here no compromise is possible. To those who have left and to those who tell us to do this we must say: you are miserable bankrupts, your rôle is played out; go where you ought to be: into the dustbin of history!'

'Then we'll leave,' Martov shouted from the platform amidst stormy applause for Trotsky.

So the thing was done. We had left, not knowing where or why, after breaking with the Soviet, getting ourselves mixed up with counter-revolutionary elements, discrediting and debasing ourselves in the eyes of the masses, and ruining the entire future of our organization and our principles. And that was the least of it: in leaving we completely untied the Bolsheviks' hands, making them masters of the entire situation and yielding to them the whole arena of the revolution.

1. ephemeral – *short lived.*

from: *The Russian Revolution 1917, A Personal Record* 1922 N N Sukhanov

a) Using the document and your own knowledge, explain what Sukhanov meant by a "united democratic front" (lines 4 and 15). *(2)*

b) What was Sukhanov's attitude to the Bolsheviks as revealed in the document? *(4)*

c) In what way is the document helpful in explaining the establishment of a one -party government in October/November 1917? *(6)*

d) Explain how an historian might assess the reliability of Sukhanov's account as evidence about the proceedings of this meeting. *(8)*

(Total 20 marks)

OUTLINE ANSWERS

Question 1

"Put the factors in an order of importance."

Evaluate: this suggests putting in an order of importance; do this at end but point out many linked together. Concentrate entirely on October 1917, nothing needed on fall of Tsar.

- Weaknesses of Provisional Government:
  - no democratic tradition
  - limited authority
  - lack of experience
  - liberalising measures released its enemies to overturn it
  - problems gave enemies means of attacking it
  - economic chaos, especially food shortages
  - the land question where unable to meet peasant expectations
  - continuation of the war
  - loss of support over Kornilov episode
- Existence of an alternative source of political power in the Soviets, especially of Petrograd and Moscow – build up of Bolshevik power there.
  - The organisation and determination of the Bolsheviks
  - key roles of Lenin and Trotsky – their opportunism

Conclusion: classic liberal dilemma of supporters of Provisional Government trying to behave legally and honour obligations (war) in times of upheaval and chaos was the main factor. But this cannot be separated from the fact that this was brilliantly exploited by Lenin. In this Kerensky was singularly unfortunate. (See also the 'Tutor's Answer' at the end of this section.)

Question 2

Again see the 'Tutor's Answer'.

Question 3

See the 'Student's Answer' at the end of this section.

Question 4

Complicated questions need a clear plan.

General approach: take Stalin 1928 to 1941. The quotation is a complicated one to handle so relate to each of its points in turn.

Agree: with the quotation and illustrate Stalin's *determination* by discussing the purges of his enemies and possible critics, mention fate of leading Communists to give emphasis.

Explain: the basis of Stalin's *control* of the state machinery, the Party's key role in the State, his domination of the Party, his use of the Secret Police, censorship etc.

Describe: what his *policies* involved, in particular the Five Year Plans for agriculture and industry. Discuss the suffering they produced, giving examples like the fate of the Kulaks.

Confirm: his total indifference to individual suffering by examples such as the deaths of peasants and the savage persecution of old Bolsheviks in the show trials.

Question 5

Introduction: New Economic Policy meant that in mid-1920s many elements of private enterprise flourished in agriculture and industry, this had social effects, for example, the Kulaks. On the other hand some transformation had already taken place – State very powerful, individual liberties already restricted, Cheka.

Assessing Stalin's impact.

Indicate: great changes that had taken place by 1941 – examples in agriculture, industry and in society. Do not turn it into a descriptive account of changes or stray into political matters. Focus on the social and economic impact overall by 1941.

Conclusion: question is 'how far', so conclusion could be changes underway or predictable before Stalin came to power but still much truth in view that Stalin's ruthlessness (indicate briefly social cost of some of changes) had indeed transformed Russian society and the economy. Some 'old' pockets remained, cite industrial inefficiencies and gaps as an example, but these were trivial compared with the changes which had been brought about.

Tutor's comments on document question 6

a) A coalition of all the groups who had been opposed to the Provisional government, or even wider, all who had once been opposed to Tsardom? Keep it brief for only two marks.

b) He is clearly against them but how many of the four marks you gain will depend on how fully you establish this from evidence in the document.

c) This is an account of a key meeting and it goes in detail through some of the actions and words of important players. It indicates the groups and individuals involved and above all it shows the tactics adopted by the Bolsheviks to hold the initiative, and the mistakes of their opponents. Each of these points will need illustrating from the evidence in the document. With this type of question you must refer to the document to support any points that you make.

d) Again support points made by citing the document whenever possible. It is this account we have to relate to, not the reliability of historical evidence in general. He was an eyewitness to crucial events, but writing five years after the events with his account packed with hindsight judgements, he holds strong views and his evidence may be biased. Do the tone and the vocabulary give any clues here? After five years can we trust his account of the detail of what people said? Presumably an historian would also check on Sukhanov from other sources to set this account against an overall estimate of his reliability.

A TUTOR'S ANSWER TO QUESTION 2

"Bolsheviks an elitist revolutionary group."

The Bolshevik Party, from the moment of its split in 1903 from the Mensheviks, had existed as an elitist revolutionary party committed to the active promotion of class revolution. Lenin and those who had followed him in 1903 had deliberately turned away from the idea of an amorphous mass Socialist party hopefully pursuing vague socialist principles and seeking power by no clearly defined strategy. It is therefore not surprising that in 1917 it did not command mass support. What needs noting is the revolutionary fervour and the tight organisation which Lenin, after his return from exile, had managed to inculcate, especially in the party's two great centres of strength in Moscow and Petrograd.

That the party was largely unpopular in October 1917 is more debatable. It was not as unpopular with the masses as those like the Provisional Government who prolonged the war and all its attendant miseries and who firmly turned their backs on the wishes of the peasantry to gain ownership of the land.

"Acted at the crucial moment."

The Bolsheviks had in fact benefitted from the defeat of Kornilov in August, when they and their working-class allies had stood firm to thwart the reactionary coup at a time when the bourgeois leaders had appeared to approve of it. This had enabled the Bolsheviks to recover from the low point in July when the failure of their own coup against the Provisional Government had led to the arrest of Trotsky and the flight of Lenin. From August Kerensky's government found the Bolsheviks more and more necessary. The Bolsheviks may well, on the other hand, have organised their coup against the Provisional Government at the moment that they did because an All-Russia Congress of Soviets had been called for the next day. Outside Moscow and Petrograd the Bolsheviks were not as strong as the Mensheviks or the Social Revolutionary Party and the timing of the coup probably reflected a desire by the Bolshevik leaders to impress the delegates to the Congress with Bolshevik power in the capital. If the Bolsheviks had had to attend the Congress without this initiative under their belts then they may well have stood out as a minor party within the overall working-class movement. This would have given potential enemies time and courage to organise against them.

More convincing evidence of the limits of popular support for the Bolsheviks in the autumn of 1917 was provided by the results of the November elections to the Constituent Assembly. In these the Social Revolutionaries polled 15 million votes against the Bolsheviks' 10 million. This constitutes the clearest evidence that the Bolsheviks had no popular mandate to seize control of the State, even after their initiative in overthrowing the unpopular Provisional Government.

"There is much truth in the quotation."

The Bolshevik success does come down to that implied in this quotation: it arose from their determination, to which should be added their ruthlessness, decisiveness and their meticulous organisation, much of which was the responsibility of Lenin himself. Prior to the October Revolution Lenin had built up a network of Bolshevik committees in local areas and at places of work and had recruited Red Guards to defend the Bolshevik position; it was these which, after Kerensky's fall, kept the city of Petrograd firmly in Bolshevik control. He had also established the Bolshevik Revolutionary Committee which under

Trotsky actually organised the storming of the Winter Palace and the arrest of the members of the Government. The events of that day were forced through by Lenin despite the opposition of some leading Party members, notably Zinoviev and Kamenev. This provides the clearest evidence that Lenin was determined not to let the opportunity slip away, and this had been his principal contribution to events ever since his return from exile in March.

Lenin went on to organise Bolshevik domination of the All-Russian Congress of Soviets where at first they had less than half the delegates. He won over support from the Social Revolutionaries by abandoning traditional Bolshevik policy on collective farms and passing instead a Land Decree handing the land over to the control of the peasants. He then squeezed both the Social Revolutionaries and the Mensheviks from the Council of Commissars which, with the Provisional Government swept away, formed the government of Russia.

In January 1918 when the long-awaited Constituent Assembly had finally assembled it was disbanded by force by the Red Guards. The election results had gone against the Bolsheviks and this was their reply. They were ready to abandon any pretence of legality or majority support rather than give up power.

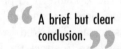

“Ruthless consolidation of the Bolshevik position.”

Lenin stood up to trade union attacks on this emergence of one party rule. Soon workplaces, banks and trade unions were in the hands of the Bolsheviks. Lenin kept up the hectic pace of change so that their opponents were unable to muster support against them. Most significantly an armistice with Germany was agreed in December and savage peace terms accepted in the following March. The war was so deeply unpopular that these actions ensured that for the moment the mass of the Russian people would accept Bolshevik rule. By this stage it would have needed a full scale civil war to oust the Bolsheviks. When that war in fact came the organising zeal of Trotsky (in forging the Red Army into a force capable of defending the Bolshevik state) and the ruthless imposition on the nation of the rigours of War Communism, are further indications of the determination of the Bolsheviks to defend their successful seizure of power in October 1917.

“A brief but clear conclusion.”

In general then it has to be agreed that the quotation in this question offers a convincing explanation of the Bolshevik success.

A STUDENT'S ANSWER TO QUESTION 3

“Is this relevant?”

In October 1917 the Bolsheviks staged a successful socialist revolution. This was helped by the growing dissatisfaction of the population with the Provisional Government and its inability to solve the problems of the war, inflation and the land question.

Lenin's 'Decree on Peace' after the takeover must have caused the allies much concern. They relied on Russia's eastern front to take some of the pressure off their western front as it meant the Central Powers dividing their resources. The Russian army had, in the autumn of 1917, completely disintegrated and Lenin really had no choice except to make peace. An armistice with Germany was signed immediately and the treaty of Brest-Litovsk in March 1918. The Allies however saw it as a betrayal of treaty obligations which would allow the Germans to swing all their forces against them in the west. It also took Russia and her territories out of the war and meant large areas of good agricultural land and industrial production were annexed by the Germans.

This not only meant that they could make a concerted attack on the western front, but they now had increased resources to do it with. Much of the production the Germans annexed was of steel and iron ore which could be used for munition production.

“This needs expanding.”

Many of the Bolsheviks now looked towards a European revolution which they felt was necessary if their's was to survive. With working-class morale obviously low because of the war, the threat of Communism spreading was a real one and may have caused concern and hostility amongst the allied leaders who were trying to win what the Bolsheviks called an Imperialist war.

Many western European countries had floated huge loans in Russia to help with Witte's plans of industrialisation. France had secured the largest loans in its history and England, Germany and Belgium had also lent money. There was widespread anger then when Lenin announced that all foreign debts were to be repudiated. Fiscal solvency was a problem for the whole of Europe at this time, and this coupled with the cease-fire made feelings run high.

There was an allied invasion in 1918 into Russia, it formed part of the White Army which fought to topple the communists. In 1919 the United States joined with other democratic nations and Japan to invade Vladivostock with imperialist views of expanding her territories.

There was much for the outside world to be very hostile about. This alien ideology had cost them dear both in the war and in repudiated loans and openly advocated a revolution spreading across Europe. It is not surprising that they took the actions they did.

"Essay gets the main points, but the points cry out for more development."

EXAMINER COMMENTS

The main points are there: abandoning the Allies, repudiating international debts, fear of the revolution being exported.

Not much is made of some of the later points. The 'outside world' was capitalist, ruled by the bourgeoisie, and so particularly frightened by the confiscations of property and the violence experienced in Russia. Those fears greatly increased by powerful Red revolts in Germany and by growing working-class power and unrest in places like Italy. Communist Russia seemed to challenge their existence and had set up the Comintern to promote worldwide revolution. Whilst Trotsky had influence, Russia was slow to abandon the idea of world revolution and even later the capitalists remained suspicious. The 'Reds' were in any case a convenient scapegoat for right-wing politicians elsewhere to attack the Left in their own countries. This was to go on long after 1924 (e.g. with Hitler).

USEFUL SOURCES OF INFORMATION

General reading

A Ramm, *Europe in the Twentieth Century*, Longman 1984

J B Watson, *Success in European History 1815–1941*, John Murray 1981

A Wood, *Europe 1815–1960*, Longman 1984

Further reading

M Lynch, *Stalin and Khrushchev The USSR 1924–64*, Hodder & Stoughton 1990: in a series for A-level students.

J N Westwood, *Endurance and Endeavour Russian History 1812–1986*, Oxford University Press 1987: probably the best written of all the national histories of modern European states and invaluable on any topic of Russian history in the period covered.

B Williams, *The Russian Revolution 1917–1921*, Blackwell (for The Historical Association) 1987: direct and brief.

Linked topic areas

- Russia under Tsar Nicholas II; political and economic history (see Chapter 14)
- Russian foreign policy from the 1890s to 1914 (see Chapter 14)
- The origins of the First World War (see Chapter 19)
- The growth of socialism in Europe to 1914
- The course of the First World War
- The 1919 Peace Settlement
- The origins of the Second World War (see Chapter 22)
- Events of the Second World War on the Eastern Front to 1945
- The USSR since 1945 (see Chapter 23)

CHAPTER 21

MUSSOLINI AND ITALY

POST-WAR ITALY

MUSSOLINI'S RISE TO POWER

CONSOLIDATION OF POWER

THE CORPORATE STATE

IMPERIAL ADVENTURES

USEFUL INFORMATION

GETTING STARTED

Look at Chapter 16 on Italian unification particularly at the later sections dealing with the Kingdom of Italy's problems after unification. Be aware of the defects in Italian political life before 1914, power was still in the hands of a small elite and the Italian national identity was only superficially established in rural areas, particularly in the backward south. There were huge problems of illiteracy, very little welfare provision, no popular press and a still hostile and powerful Catholic Church. Political life was tainted by intrigue and sometimes the smell of corruption. There were great social and economic differences between town and country and even greater between the north and the south of the country.

Italian disappointments during the First World War and at the terms of the subsequent peace treaties are part of the background to a study of Mussolini's rise to power. The war deeply divided Italian society, both Catholics and socialists opposed it. Its conclusion left a dislocated industrial economy and a new ambitious military class. Italy emerged from the war a divided and an exhausted State. You will need to formulate a working definition of fascism:

Facism was specifically an Italian term in origin but it has often been applied indiscriminately to other extreme right-wing groups in Europe at this time. The 'Fasces' were a bundle of rods which were signs of authority or power in earlier periods in Italy. Mussolini spoke much of Fascism, central to his views was the idea of the all-powerful state. From this state authority was stressed as directing the individual to work for the good of the state as was the idea of the strength and glory of the state in international affairs. It was a right-wing creed, violently anti-communist but it was also radical, wanting sweeping changes in many areas of national life, and this distinguishes it from other right-wing conservative groups.

Look out for elaborations and applications of this in your reading and be ready to note how Fascism's chief features could differ from country to country. It was militantly nationalistic, anti-parliamentarian, preferring totalitarian rule, worshipping strength and leadership, obsessed by uniforms and warlike ceremonial and seeing war as a great test for nations. Its philosophy was superficial, resting on little more than the notion of the survival of the fittest. Its strength was its apparent energy in the face of deeply divisive social and economic problems and its total hostility to the communist threat. Unlike its German equivalent there was little mark of racism in Italian Fascism which looked back nostalgically to the glories of Rome's imperial past whilst Hitler revelled in the German tribal virilities.

ESSENTIAL PRINCIPLES

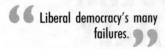

POST-WAR ITALY

“A disappointing peace.”

Italy was on the winning side in the war and obtained Trieste and the South Tyrol at the peace. Its claims to Fiume and Dalmatia were rebuffed by its allies and this loss of what came to be seen as rightful gains was blamed on the liberal politicians. *D'Annunzio* and nationalist supporters, usually ex-soldiers, seized and held Fiume for a year. This episode revealed the weakness of the Italian state which took so long to act against him. The combination of ex-soldiers and popular oratory in an illegal challenge to the despised parliamentary state was a dangerous example for other right-wing activists.

COLLAPSE OF THE LIBERAL REGIME

“Liberal democracy's many failures.”

Internal reasons for the collapse of the liberal regime abound. A major one was the failure to cope with the economic dislocation brought about by the end of the war. There were many industrial firms geared to the demands of war which went bankrupt and, from 1919, unemployment soared to over two million. The lira lost two-thirds of its value in the course of 1919 and many middle-class savings were wiped out. There were strikes, factory occupations and food riots. All this so soon after the ominous events of 1917 in Russia. Economic depression from 1920 added to the mood of bitterness amongst many sections of industrial and urban society. Land seizures by returning soldiers and the rise of peasant unions and co-operatives made the landowning class fearful of social upheaval in the rural areas.

All these pressures proved too serious for the politicians of Liberal Italy to overcome. Entering the war had split the old political leadership, some had been in favour, some against. Catholics and socialists both appeared to threaten the state and the 1919 elections revealed a deep political split between north and south with almost all the socialist deputies from the north and almost all the middle of the road government parties' deputies coming from the south. All this was a disastrous recipe for chaos in central government. The fatal mistake of the centrist Prime Minister *Giolitti* was to treat Mussolini's Fascists as a counterweight to the socialists.

MUSSOLINI'S RISE TO POWER

“Post-war social and economic problems.”

The rise to power of Mussolini was brought about by the lack of a stable political framework within which the democratic politicians could work to solve the many social and economic problems facing Italy after 1918. In explaining Mussolini's rise it is not enough to list the problems and disappointments: you must go on to give reasons why the democratic politicians were unable to provide solutions and how the political breakdown gave Mussolini his opportunity.

THE ISSUES IN 1922

Mussolini's personal career, during and immediately after the war provides the thread of continuity through to 1922 as he went on to build his private army of blackshirted followers, many of whom were ex-soldiers, on hire to protect landowners and industrialists from threats from the unions and the socialists. They took to blackshirts and took the fasces as their symbol; fiercely committed to opposing communism, they called themselves combat groups, ‘fasci di combattimento’. From the start the movement was heavily overlaid with military images.

“Mussolini's supporters.”

Mussolini had in 1914 set up his own newspaper in Milan to promote his right-wing ideas. His support now came from demobilised soldiers from junior officers to other ranks, disgruntled with the anticlimax of peace and unemployment, many genuinely concerned about what was happening to Italy, and from working-men disillusioned with the failure of strikes and unions to get them a better deal, but even more from the lower middle-class self-employed and the professions seeking law and order and protection of their property. These groups were joined by wealthy industrialists, businessmen fearful of the threat of communism and finally by groups of young intellectuals who were valued for their ability to spread the fascist message. In addition to these active supporters of the fascist cause there were many in the army and the Catholic Church and supporters of the monarchy who felt that they had much in common with Mussolini's anti-left stance.

" A fatal miscalculation. "

The liberal governments, over-fearful of a communist revolution, were too slow to curb the blackshirt violence and failed to reach agreements amongst themselves which would have created a broad-based government with some prospect of long-term survival. Giolitti's miscalculation, allowing fascists on to the lists of government candidates in the 1921 elections, gave them 35 seats. It was, however, outside Parliament that the fascists made their real mark, as increasing violence, often ignored by the local civil authorities, was unopposed by a succession of briefly surviving governments. In 1921 they founded the fascist militia and organised their own unions of employers and employees.

" And another, by the king. "

The events of 1922, the fascist bluff of the March on Rome and the fateful mistake of the king, *Victor Emmanuel III* inviting Mussolini to become his Prime Minister, rather than using the army to stop him, have the quality of high drama and reveal the political bankruptcy of the liberal state. With greater courage the king could have resisted Mussolini with the army but he would, of course, still have faced the same political and other problems and with only the old gang of failed liberals to sort them out.

CONSOLIDATION OF POWER

1922 TO 1929

" Steps to dictatorship in the 1920s. "

Most examination questions on Mussolini's gaining power require the story to be pursued beyond 1922 for at that time Mussolini had still much to do. He did not become a dictator in 1922. Indeed he was at first the leader of a coalition government and, when he broke with his partners, for a time lacked a majority in the chamber. The steps, legal and illegal, that he took to consolidate his position need to be known. Deals with the Catholic party and industrialists accompanied the takeover of key administration posts by fascists. The new electoral law, the so-called *Acerbo Law* of 1923, which amazingly some socialists and liberals went along with, allowed the fascist government to nominate two-thirds of the membership of the chamber by decreeing that the party which won most votes in an election would have that fraction of the seats. In the elections of 1924 the fascists did, in fact obtain over 60 per cent of the votes cast. There was a general support at this point for what Mussolini appeared to be doing, particularly in providing effective government.

Moves to dictatorship

The murder of the socialist leader *Matteotti*, the most tenacious and courageous of Mussolini's opponents, who might just have succeeded in winning the moderate fascists from their loyalty to Mussolini, led to the withdrawal from the chamber by the opposition deputies, (an event commonly referred to as the *Aventine Secession*). This was a mistake for Mussolini who was now vulnerable to the charge of murder and, even in the absence of his opponents, it required all his efforts to survive this crisis. By 1925 he felt secure again and indeed admitted his responsibility for terrorism. This admission marked the beginning of the dictatorship, swiftly followed by the banning of opposition parties and the closing of opposition newspapers. These events were, during the mid-1920s, key moments in the consolidation of fascist power. The posturing, the displays of military might and the incessant propaganda which accompanied them also need noting. One matter which tends to be neglected is the skilful and ruthless way in which Mussolini retained his leadership of the fascists by playing off those who favoured direct (i.e. violent) action against the moderates.

" Fascist showmanship. "

At this stage Mussolini was not just the propagandist buffoon that the camera, still or moving, would suggest. Responsible statesmen and the general public of Europe took Mussolini seriously on his own terms. Do not let the benefit of hindsight blind you to this.

The Lateran Treaties

" The most significant achievement. "

The account of Mussolini establishing his position is probably best followed through to the Lateran Treaties of 1929 which secured the regime at least the tacit support of the vastly influential Catholic Church, by recognizing the Vatican as a sovereign state and granting rights and privileges to the Catholic Church in Italy. This momentous healing of old wounds must loom large in any explanation of the durability of the fascist regime.

In 1929 too an all-fascist Parliament was elected, giving some indication of mass popular support for the dictatorship.

THE CORPORATE STATE

THE ECONOMY

A series of questions have been set in examination papers which invite an assessment of the benefits Mussolini's rule brought to Italy and also of the price that had to be paid. A start could be made by working out which groups of Italians gained and which lost, and in what ways, from the development of the fascist state. In any assessment the propaganda element in the fascist achievement, which on occasion loomed large, must be discounted.

In economic policy Mussolini made many concessions to big business interests but the rigidly applied overvaluation of the lira in 1925 was a clear mistake. Propaganda made the most of developments in the railway, hydro-electricity, motorways and, above all the draining of the Pontine Marshes. The battle for grain, the battle for births, the drive for national self-sufficiency (autarchy) and the drive to expand peasant land ownership all need cool assessment. Tourism grew but unemployment, despite the vast labour intensive land reclamation schemes and a doubling in the number of public employees, remained high, and the build up of heavy industry was disappointing. Textbooks can be thin on the nature and the achievements of the Corporate State and a good national history (see the 'Useful Information' section at the end of this chapter) would be a sensible supplement to read on this topic. In any case you will need to balance claims of economic development against the social and political price paid by the Italian people. That Italy was not ready in 1939 (when the Second World War began) to stand alongside Germany, its ally, provides some comment on the reality of Mussolini's achievement in creating a strong national economy.

"On the economy you may need more than a textbook."

SOCIETY AND POLITICS

Again you may need more than just a standard European history textbook. Central to any assessment of this topic is the Italian fascist idea of the Corporate State which was developed in the 1930s. The idea was that all the interests in the state would be represented in institutions which would control production, employment and welfare. All citizens belonged to syndicates of workers, employees or professions: there were 160 such bodies. These were grouped into 22 corporations with a Ministry and a National Council of Corporations at the top of the pyramid. It functioned from the top downwards rather than democratically. You should be able to comment on the effect of this organisation on economic efficiency and on the lives of individuals.

"Be able to explain what the Corporate State was."

Social detail on education, housing, welfare, jobs or other everyday topics, as well as the loss of freedom of speech and of association, should be noted, if only to provide illustrative material on the realities of life in Fascist Italy. Ask which groups benefitted and which suffered becase of the workings of Mussolini's Corporate State.

Politically the regime was authoritarian centred around the increasingly isolated Mussolini who insisted on making decisions down to the most trivial level. The fascist corporations did not really take over the functions of the older state. The monarchy, the Chamber of Deputies, (though all fascists), the army, the police and the local provincial leaders of society all survived. It seemed increasingly unlikely that much of the increasingly inefficient fascist state would last beyond the death of the Duce (Mussolini's popular name) though for a long time the skilful use of propaganda hid this from the Italian people. Foreign commentators and politicians frequently pointed to the apparent energy with which Fascist Italy was tackling its social and economic problems, contrasting this with the inertia displayed by the liberal democracies.

"Increasing isolation and inefficiency."

IMPERIAL ADVENTURES

Fascism's posturing and its emphasis on strength made ambitious foreign policy and military adventures both desirable and likely. Don't forget Mussolini's early adventures at the expense of weak neighbours: seizing Fiume and harassing the Greeks. In the late 1920s and early 1930s Mussolini emerged as a European statesman and an upholder of international order:

- In 1928 Italy committed itself to the *Kellogg-Briand Pact* in which over 60 nations renounced any resort to war to settle differences.
- In 1934 the despatch of Italian troops to the Austrian frontier effectively (and for Mussolini gratifyingly) discouraged Hitler from moving into that country.

- In the early 1930s his role as European statesman and preserver of peace culminated in the formation of the anti-German *Stresa Front* with France and Britain. He was regarded as a major European statesman and Italy was seen as a major factor in the European balance of power and, for an essentially vain man, this was very pleasing.

NATIONAL GLORY

National glory beckoned and in fascist ideology there was no substitute for glory gained through a victorious war. In the mid-1930s Mussolini still sought the great adventure and dreamt of an Italian Mediterranean Empire, in part no doubt to deflect growing disillusion with the regime at home. These ambitions culminated in the war against Abyssinia and the interventions in the Spanish Civil War which are in their own right central topics in European history in the years before the outbreak of the Second World War. These excursions took Italy into alliance with Germany, first as an equal and then, for Mussolini's ambitions greatly outstripped Italian resources, as a decidedly junior partner. The adventures of the thirties brought propaganda glory but no worthwhile extension of Italian power. They led inexorably to defeat and downfall in the Second World War. You need to be able to evaluate the foreign policy achievement and to set it alongside a verdict on achievement within Italy.

Revision exercises

If you are also revising international affairs across Europe in the thirties, do that first and Mussolini can then be fitted into place. You may feel that in the long-term this should be a comparatively humble one but the decision to attack a fellow member of the League of Nations and the coolness this brought between Italy, France and Britain is arguably the key moment in the collapse of collective security in Europe. The military achievements of the Italian forces in the Second World War (see the 'Useful Information' section that follows) could be taken as an indicator of how far Fascist Italy was from living up to its own propaganda or to Mussolini's dreams of glory in war.

USEFUL INFORMATION

1915	Italy entered First World War on Franco–British side.
1917	Defeats of the Italian army – Caporetto campaign.
1919	Mussolini founded the first 'fascio di combattimento'.
	At Versailles Italian territorial claims turned down.
	D'Annunzio seized Fiume
1920	Italian troops re-took Fiume
1921	Growing economic and political violence in the cities.
1922	The **March on Rome**, the King refused to declare martial law as requested by the prime minister, Facta.
	King and Parliament granted Mussolini dictatorial powers within the surviving constitution.
1923	New electoral law (**the Acerbo Law**) gave two-thirds of seats to the largest party.
1924	Under this Fascists obtained 375 seats (earlier less than 40).
	Murder of Matteotti
	Most non-Fascist deputies left the Chamber (**the Aventine Secession**).
	Censorship enforced. Opposition groups not allowed to meet.
1928	New electoral law reduced number of voters from 10 to 3 million.
	Fascist Grand Council to vet all candidates.
1929	**Lateran Treaties** with the Papacy
	System of Corporations evolved based on occupation, supervised by Ministry of Corporations, National Council of Corporations established.
1934	Mussolini blocked Nazi moves against Austria.
1935	**Stresa Front** set up – Italy, France, Britain
	Italian invasion of Abyssinia, League of Nations applied sanctions against Italy but these were ineffective.
1936	Abyssinia annexed by Italy
	Mussolini provided military help for Franco in Spanish Civil War.
	Rome-Berlin axis established.

1937		**Italy left League of Nations**
1938		No Italian objection to Austrian union with Germany.
1939	Apr	Italy conquered Albania
	Sept	Italy declared itself neutral when the Second World War began.
1940	June	Italy declared war on France and Britain after the German troops had broken through into northern France.
	Sept	Three power pact with Germany and Japan.
	Oct	Italy attacked Greece but was repulsed. Greek invasion of Albania. German troops had to assist the Italian forces.
		Italian forces in Libya prepared for attack on Egypt.
1941	Jan	Defeat of Italian forces in Libya.
	Mar	German troops under Rommel sent to recapture Libya.
1943		Allied invasion and conquest of Sicily: invasion of the Italian mainland.
		Collapse of Fascist regime. Armistice between Italy and the Allies.
		Mussolini resigned and arrested, freed by German troops.
1945		Mussolini killed by Italian anti-fascists.

EXAMINATION QUESTIONS

Q1 Why, in 1922, was Mussolini able to become Prime Minister of Italy? (Welsh 1989)

Q2 Account for the establishment of Fascist governments in either Italy or Spain. (London 1990)

Q3 How effectively did fascist rule in Italy solve the problems which had brought Mussolini to power? (London 1988)

Q4 Examine the achievements within their respective countries of either Mussolini or Franco. (London 1989)

Q5 'You believed you had the devotion of the people . . You lost it the day you tied Italy to Germany.' To what extent do you accept Count Grandi's explanation in July 1943 of Mussolini's fall from power? (NEAB 1989)

OUTLINE ANSWERS

Question 1

See the 'Student's Answer' at the end of this section.

Question 2

"A common question."

Develop: the establishment of Fascist government through to 1928–1929.

Account: for the establishment after 1922 by referring to: weakness of opponents, some helping the new electoral law of 1923 which was decisive; the ruthlessness of Mussolini with the murder of his chief opponent Matteotti; the mistake of the opposition walking out just when Mussolini was vulnerable; the subsequent banning of opposition parties; the introduction of censorship and in 1928 the franchise being limited.

Conclusion: Many Italians accepted that as they had the events of 1922, because the fascists offered a new energy, were anti-communist and were making gestures (long before the Lateran Accords of 1929) towards the Catholic Church, for example: over religious education in schools. Proof of this acceptance is that in the 1924 election the fascists gained over 60 per cent of the votes cast.

Note: It would be worth reading the 'Student's Answer' to Question 1 which is quite similar as far as the events of 1922 are concerned.

Question 3

See the 'Tutor's Answer' that follows.

Question 4

“Mussolini's achievements.”

List: the achievements which Mussolini might have claimed for his regime: provided strong government; established a dynamic economy; gave Italians pride in and loyalty to their kingdom; provided Italy with international prestige. Examine each in turn:

- Government: strong in sense of one-party but not efficient, overlapping fascist and state authorities, vast bureaucracy, poor decision making, for example, Mussolini personally involved at trivial levels, much restriction on personal freedoms but not effective in developing the country's interests.
- Economy: question real achievement – grain, births, prestige projects; still too little industrial investment; propaganda made most of everything.
- Social cohesion: here he made his biggest mark, he ended the communist threat which pleased many and, more importantly he ended the rift with the Papacy (explain how) which pleased many in a Catholic nation. The price was paid in the loss of personal freedoms – press, trade union membership.
- National pride (sense of purpose): internally this was flagging in mid-thirties as personal restrictions constrained, inefficiences of fascist state loomed and propaganda was seen through – this was precisely why foreign adventure became so attractive to Mussolini.

Note: the title – *within* the country – so do not waste time developing foreign policy.

Conclusion: few achievements of substance – demonstrated by the speed with which all traces of the fascist state disappeared on his fall.

Note: read the ‘Tutor's Answer’ to Question 3, a similar question.

Question 5

Introduction: quotation is true enough of 1943: explain how German connection had ended in disaster and the fate of Mussolini.

Argue: that the claim made stating the German connection immediately lost him the people's devotion is more doubtful – many people were happy enough with the economic progress and social stability. Explain who benefitted and so who were likely to remain ‘devoted’. Same true of foreign adventures even as the German connection was developed with Mussolini appearing the equal partner and Italian national prestige riding high – only total war and the prospect of defeat undermined this.

Conclusion: raise question of depth of devotion in any case – propaganda? – those who lost under Mussolini (indicate) not likely ever to have been devoted. More a case of cynical self-interest on all sides? Quotation owes much to the benefit of hindsight.

A TUTOR'S ANSWER TO QUESTION 3

The main problem facing Italy in 1922, and one which played the greatest part in bringing Mussolini to power, was the absence of a strong central government capable of preserving internal stability. Office was shared by many groupings who proved incapable of working together for any length of time. This was all the more serious because the country faced grave economic dislocation following the end of the war and this in turn gave rise to serious divisions in society and to a growing threat of violence from both the political left and the right. Many were disenchanted by the corruption and drift in political life. The anti-church traditions of the Liberals, and the Papacy's hostility to the kingdom of Italy had left many of the most respectable Italians outside the nation's political life. The rigours of the war had been succeeded by the disappointments of the peace settlement which had severely dented national pride.

Mussolini exploited the economic and social problems and offered a vision of national regeneration in order to build up fascist support. Those who should have defended the state against him were weak and divided whilst he was ambitious and ruthless.

“Evaluating the fascist political achievement.”

Most of this essay will be concerned with evaluating fascist success in providing Italy with an effective central government but the other problems of the nation, which were present in 1922 will also be considered. In the years after 1922 the fascists had to proceed carefully for the old constitution remained in place and they were not for many years in a majority in the parliament. In 1923 and 1924 Mussolini acted decisively to end this state of affairs. The Acerbo Law of 1923 had guaranteed two-thirds of the seats in the chamber to whichever party polled the largest number of votes in an election. When applied in 1924 it gave the Fascists 375 seats as opposed to the 35 they had held earlier. The chaos of conflicting parties was at an abrupt end and continuity of government was assured. This process was consolidated with the murder of the regime's most feared critic, Matteotti, and by the abolition of opposition parties, which was supported by the imposition of strict press censorship. The final stages of this political transformation took place in 1928 when the number of voters was reduced from 10 to 3 million and the fascist Grand Council was given the duty to vet all parliamentary candidates. In the 1929 election an entirely fascist chamber was elected, Mussolini had by 1929 triumphantly ended the period of weak short-lived governments.

"Mussolini's dictatorship securely established by 1929."

Whether he had succeeded in providing Italy with effective government is a wider and more debatable question. The institutions of the state had fascist institutions placed alongside them as the philosophy of the Corporate State was applied in the 1930s. A system of corporations was introduced with a Ministry to supervise them and a National Council to represent their views. This tended to control many areas of national life and certainly to impede the traditional freedoms of the Italian people. A vast bureaucracy was created parallel to the normal state administration and the equally vast civil service. It is doubtful if the outcome provided a particularly efficient state administration although the full scale of the defects was hidden for a long time by the relentless propaganda to which the fascist state subjected its citizens.

The questionable effectiveness of the fascist regime is illustrated by its limited success in dealing with the other signs of national malaise which had been so valuable in helping Mussolini win support in 1922. Many of the much vaunted economic achievements were less impressive than they appeared. The Pontine Marshes had indeed been drained but the battle for self-sufficiency in grain was only achieved at the expense of other crops. Agricultural productivity and investment remained lamentably low, especially in the poorer southern regions. Mussolini did little to bridge the gap between north and south.

"Limited economic success."

Too much investment went into vast prestige projects such as sports stadia or the autostrada whilst unglamorous investment in basic industries was neglected so that, after almost two decades of fascist rule, Mussolini in 1939 had to admit to his ally Hitler that Italy was not ready to go to war. A view which received ample confirmation in Greece and in Libya when eventually Italy did enter the war.

In terms of social cohesion Mussolini had one great triumph when, in 1929, he reached an accord with the Papacy at the price of granting many privileges to the Catholic Church in Italy. This healed a serious division in the kingdom and ensured the fascist regime the continuing acquiescence of faithful Catholics in its rule. Ending the greatest split in Italian society ranks as the most important fascist contribution to the Italian state. How directly it was one of the problems that had brought Mussolini to power in 1929 is, however, less clear.

"But effective propaganda."

Insofar as the problem of dented national pride assisted Mussolini to power, his propaganda made the best of his efforts to restore national prestige. The impression the regime gave of vast energy in tackling its problems attracted European attention. The impression Mussolini gave of being the great European statesmen worked to the same end. It was when this status was no longer enough and dreams of a Mediterranean Empire, or of colonies and conquest in Africa began to dominate foreign policy that Mussolini over-reached himself. This was quite late in the day and it must be conceded that in terms of national pride Mussolini gave the majority of Italians what they wanted, until that is, he was drawn too closely into the arms of Germany.

"Essay conclusion."

In the end the fascist regime's repressive policies and its disastrous record in war alienated most Italians who had by 1943 forgotten the glories of victory in Abyssinia. The fascist regime then crumbled under its own weight and no-one was left to defend it. Except for the Lateran Accord with the church, all its achievements turned out to be mere propaganda stunts and in 1945 Italy faced much the same range of problems that it had in 1922.

A STUDENT'S ANSWER TO QUESTION 1

The political and economic problems which Italy had faced since unification in 1870 were never satisfactorily solved before 1914, and as a result they were exacerbated by the war. Mussolini was able to benefit from the post-war economic situation, the instability of the Italian governments, and in addition to these factors he used the twin myths of Bolshevism and a mutilated victory to help to bring him to power.

Despite the fact that Italy had been on the winning side in the war she was dissatisfied with the post-war settlements in comparison with the losses she had suffered. Italy had been promised land, which she did not receive by the treaties after the war, however she obtained no colonies, no money and not all the land she had wanted in exchange for the loss of life during the war, and the serious economic problems of the post-war period. Unemployment and a rise in the cost of living were just two of the economic problems in post-war Italy. The outcome of the war i.e. the peace settlements were a blow to national honour. Italian problems were worsened by the fact that the government was not strong enough or efficient enough to take steps to improve the situation. Italian governments were unstable and short-lived relying on corruption to remain in power.

The ineffectiveness of the government can be illustrated by the takeover of Fiume in 1919 by D'Annunzio. The Italians had wanted to control the port of Fiume and hoped to do so through the peace settlements, however Italy was not given Fiume and so D'Annunzio, an ardent nationalist, took the town in 1919. He remained there for two years, the government being unable to make him leave and even unwilling to try in case it should cause a national outcry. The Fiume incident illustrated firstly that the government did not have effective control in Italy, and secondly (a lesson which Mussolini took to heart) that force pays off. Therefore both the economic and political situations aided Mussolini's rise to power.

“This essay is making its points coherently . . .”

Mussolini activated the 'Bolshevik myth' to aid the Fascists. The Italian Socialist Party was the largest party in Italy and in post-war Italy many workers turned to the Socialists in the hope that they would alleviate the economic problems. However men of property – landowners shopowners etc. feared Socialism and especially Bolshevism; they feared that they would lose their property and wealth to the masses. Therefore they turned to Mussolini and the Fascists who were regarded as the only viable alternative to Bolshevism by many people. The Church also favoured the Fascists to the Socialists since they feared 1) loss of land and wealth and 2) that religion would play a less important role. Likewise the government who were unable to control the sit-ins in factories and violence in the country (esp. Summer 1921) regarded the fascists as the cheapest way to curb socialist power since there were constant running battles between the two groups. Even the police tended to favour the Fascists when there were clashes between them and the socialists, even in some cases giving them assistance.

“. . . and has an effective paragraph structure.”

Mussolini and the Fascists won popularity by appealing to various classes and ages. They promised jobs for the workers, to uphold laws of private property for the middle-classes, to prevent Bolshevism taking control, and a reversal of the mutilated victory through an active foreign policy. Mussolini promised a return to the days when Italy was a great power i.e. Roman Empire, and intended to restore national pride. Finally Mussolini was invited to become Prime Minister by the King when he threatened to 'March to Rome', his victory was due to negotiation rather than violence.

“Needs more detail on the 1922 takeover.”

Therefore Mussolini was able to become Prime Minister in 1922 due to various factors. The economic situation and the government's weakness were extremely important: 'Feebleness in foreign and domestic policy left a power vacuum at the heart of Italian politics that gave Mussolini his opportunity.' Mussolini appealed

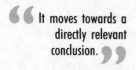

“It moves towards a directly relevant conclusion.”

to many different groups, for different reasons, and he appeared to be a strong figure in comparison with the weak government. He played on people's fears and on the national humiliation after the war. Finally the organisation of the Fascist Party, the use of violence and propaganda all contributed to Mussolini and the fascists rise to power.

EXAMINER COMMENTS

The great virtue is that it tries to offer a direct answer, note for example the conclusion. The best point made is the stress laid on the lesson Mussolini learned from the Fiume incident. It needs a little more on fascist tactics and a reference to the Russian Revolution would have emphasised middle-class fears for their own future. The chief weakness however is that there is not enough said about events in 1922 and how Mussolini exploited them to the point where the invitation came from the king. Consider what, in one short paragraph, you would add to account for this crucial moment. In summary the essay is rather too general but it is coherently written and directly relevant.

USEFUL SOURCES OF INFORMATION

General reading

A Ramm, *Europe in the Twentieth Century*, Longman 1984
J B Watson, *Success in European History 1815–1941*, John Murray 1981
A Wood, *Europe 1815–1960*, Longman 1984

Further reading

M Clark, *Modern Italy 1871–1982*, Longman 1984: an excellent national history which expands the outline accounts of the traditional textbooks in a clear and informative way.
D Forgacs (ed) *Rethinking Italian Fascism*, Lawrence and Wishart 1986: essays on differents aspects of life and culture in Mussolini's Italy, not for the already confused student.
M Gallo, *Mussolini's Italy*, Abelard–Schuman 1974: well worth seeing if the Public Library can raise a copy even if only to dip into to bring some key moments to life, not a revision book.

Linked topic areas

- Italian history 1870–1914 (see Chapter 16)
- The Versailles Peace Settlement 1919
- The rise to power of Hitler (see Chapter 22)
- The Spanish Civil War
- The League of Nations
- The origins of the Second World War

CHAPTER 22

GERMANY 1918–1939

GETTING STARTED

Chapters 17 and 19 contain useful background information and ideas on the German Empire before 1914 and on the causes of the First World War. You will need to understand the outcome of the war, not only as it affected Germany but also the consequences for Germany's neighbours on all frontiers. The disappearance of the Austrian Empire in particular and its replacement by numerous small states created a totally new context for international relations in Central Europe. Familiarising yourself with a map of European national boundaries, subsequent to the treaties which ended the war, will be a valuable use of your time for this topic and for all other European history topics in this period.

An appreciation of the total nature of Germany's defeat in the First World War, and how it came about, will later help you to have a more perceptive understanding of many post-war issues in German domestic and foreign policy. In 1916–1917 German forces had defeated and destroyed Tsarist Russia and gone on to impose harsh terms on the new Bolshevik state at the Treaty of Brest-Litovsk. Germany was then free to turn all its resources to the war against Britain and France, for the dream of dominating eastern Europe, which now seemed so close, could only be confirmed by victory in the west. The spring offensive of 1918 seemed to turn dreams into reality but the exhaustion of German military resources turned tactical victories into headlong retreat which in turn led to attempts at a negotiated peace and finally in November 1918 to acceptance of an armistice which would leave Germany powerless to do other than accept whatever terms were imposed upon her. You then need to understand what happened at the Treaty of Versailles, 1919, and the terms imposed on Germany following its surrender.

It will also be helpful to be aware of the Bolshevik government which had since 1917 been established in the USSR and which had set that country apart from the rest of Europe, raising the fear in Germany and elsewhere that Bolshevism might be exported to them (see Chapter 20). European fears of communist Russia also affected their relations with Germany. The post-war withdrawal of the United States from any commitment to Europe should also be noted, together with the dilemmas this created for France and Britain. Finally the creation of the League of Nations and its growing inability to meet the dreams of its creators affected international relations in the 1930s.

Knowledge of economics may be of some help in studying German history between the wars but is not essential except that the causes and effects of the galloping inflation, which afflicted Germany in the early 1920s, and the effect on the German economy of the reverberations from the Wall Street Crash in 1929, do need to be understood.

In outline papers where Germany is only one topic amongst a vast range of subjects the period prior to 1930 may be studied quite briefly simply to provide an adequate background to the rise of Hitler after 1930.

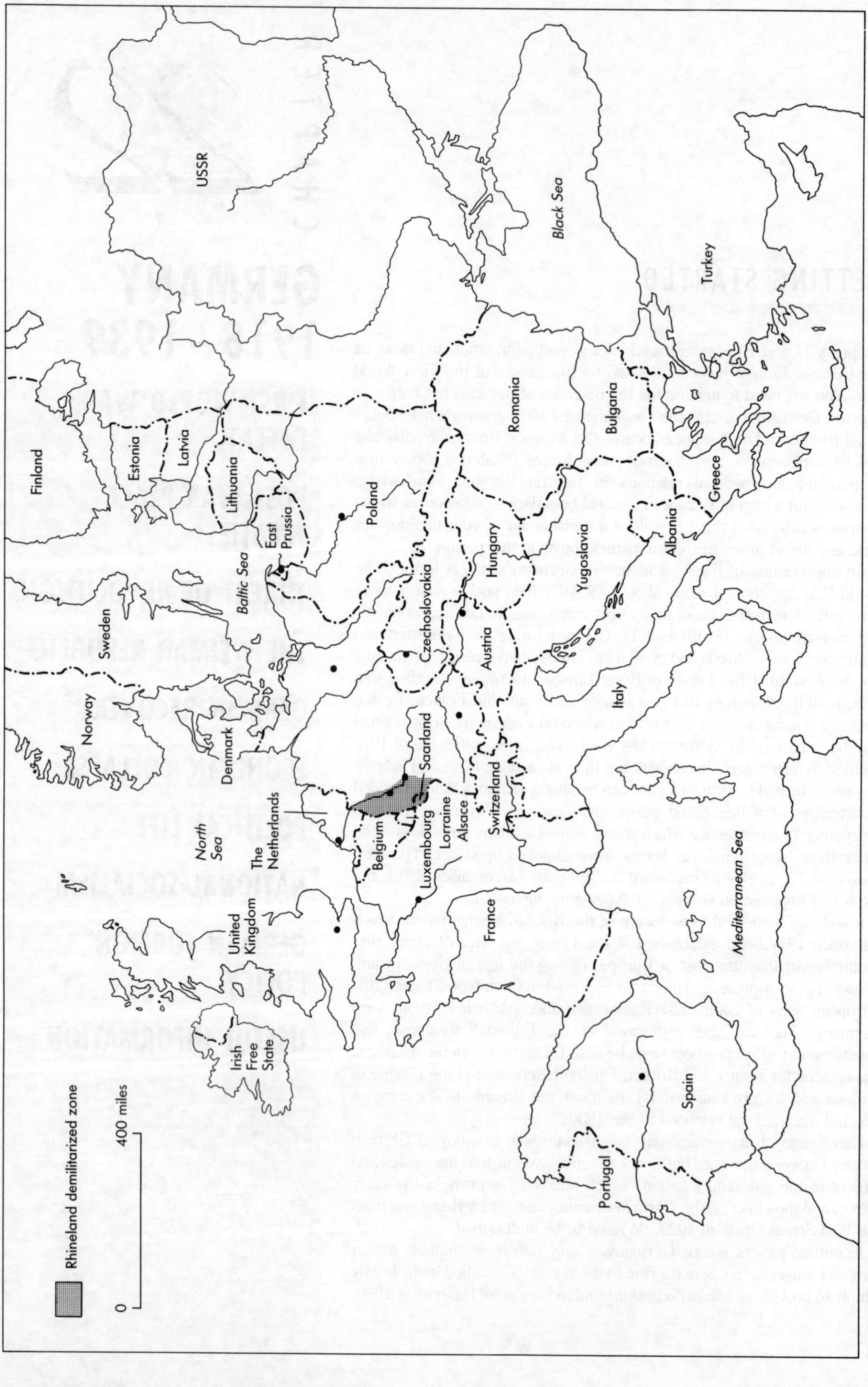

Fig. 22.1 Europe in the 1920s

ESSENTIAL PRINCIPLES

FIRST WORLD WAR DEFEAT

IMPACT ON GERMANY

Germany lost the war because of lack of manpower to face the newly arrived American forces but also because of an almost total collapse of the economy and food shortages at home, largely brought about by the British naval blockade. Food riots in German cities and mutiny in the Germany navy indicated that German society was on the point of collapse. The military collapse of Austria-Hungary and Turkey simply underlined the impossibility of continuing the war. When the German offensives in the west came to a halt there were no plans to hold the line and once the counter-push came the German retreat became a headlong rout as they were driven from France. Germany itself was never invaded and at the end of the war German troops still occupied most of Belgium.

> "Collapse in Germany a major factor behind the Armistice."

You need to understand how this led Germany to the brink of revolution so that the Kaiser had to abdicate and flee the country, after a handful of democratic gestures had proved too little to silence public outrage at what his war had done to the country. When the Armistice came, on November 11, Germany was on the brink of revolution.

> "'The army was betrayed . . .'"

From this debacle emerged the potent myth that, with Germany still not invaded, the Germany army had been betrayed by the politicians and civilians at home. The bitterness of total defeat became a heavy burden for the new state which was to be painfully established and which had no choice, following the armistice but to accept the terms of peace imposed by the Allies. The armistice terms had included the surrender by Germany of much of its military equipment and after it there was no prospect of rejecting any peace terms that were imposed or of resuming the fight. Your reading should lead you to a view of the important part this legacy of defeat was to play in German history during the next twenty years.

POST-WAR PEACE TREATIES

THEIR EFFECT ON GERMANY

The terms imposed upon Germany at Versailles were, in German eyes, harsh and added to the bitterness of the defeat and the collapse of the Empire at the end of the war.

Terms of the Treaty of Versailles

- Germany had to accept responsibility for all the losses of the war which had been brought about by German aggression – the War Guilt clause.
- Germany was to pay reparations for these losses – the amount was only worked out in 1921.
- Germany lost territories:
  - Alsace-Lorraine to France.
  - West Prussia and other lands in the east to Poland.
  - Some border lands to Belgium and to Denmark.
  - Danzig became a free city under the League of Nations.
  - Memel was placed under the League (later taken by Lithuania).
  - The Saar Basin was to be run by the League for 15 years when a plebiscite would decide its future status. The profits from the valuable coalfields would until then go to France.
  - All its colonial territories, taken over by various Allies (especially Britain) were to be run as mandated territories of the League of Nations.
- The Rhineland was demilitarised.
- German armed forces were strictly limited.

> "War Guilt and reparations"

The most controversial of these clauses was the *War Guilt clause* because it justified the demand for reparations. The war had been fought and caused great destruction in Belgium and France, they were certain of the justice of the demand (in 1870 France had had to make heavy payments to Germany following its defeat in war). Payment was intended to be in the form of goods but it was difficult to see how this could be done without disrupting the economies of the receiving nations. Reparations, which were subject to much haggling, created a German sense of grievance and were much exploited by Hitler to arouse national passions which he could then exploit to his own advantage. They were another difficult burden for the newly formed *Weimar Republic* to carry.

Revision exercises

"Defeat had a great impact on political life in the 1920s."

Be prepared to discuss the impact of defeat and of the imposed peace on German political life in the period to 1933. This is more important than the mere memorising of the details of the Peace Settlement. It would help to work through the peace terms as they related to Germany and develop some idea of how each one might impact on German sensitivities and so become a political issue later, for example that Germany's new boundaries left many people who, linguistically and culturally were German, outside the frontiers of the new Germany, and this despite an avowed Allied commitment to self-determination in such crucial matters.

THREAT OF REVOLUTION

1919–1920

"Fears of a communist uprising."

The prospect of a left-wing revolutionary takeover of the German state arose from the defeat in war, the harsh peace and the end of the Imperial constitution, all with the Russian example of 1917 to be borne in mind. The revolution is often, unfairly, dismissed as purely negative and is not used in examinations as frequently as many of the other issues listed in this chapter. For students taking detailed option papers on Germany it is however still essential. You will need to be able to discuss the causes of the revolutions in their post-war setting, to analyse the intentions, the support and weaknesses of the Spartacists who attempted to seize power in 1919 and be aware of the savage right-wing reaction which they provoked with the Freikorps trying to seize Berlin in 1920 in the Kapp Putsch. The latter was blocked when the government called a general strike against it. All students should reflect on what these disorders, to left and right, reveal about the prospects for the survival of the new German Republic. Most of Kapp's supporters, many of whom were ex-servicemen, went unpunished and the courts, the police and many in the army and civil service openly sympathised with them. This gives an indication of the vulnerability of the Weimar Republic to extremist attacks and plots from the right.

THE WEIMAR REPUBLIC

TO 1924

The name comes from the small provincial town where the Assembly met for the first time in 1919. The Constitution was very democratic with universal suffrage and a secret ballot and, unlike the earlier Empire, a government which was to be formed from the majority in the parliament (*Reichstag*). The defects in the Weimar Constitution revealed by hindsight are notorious but still need noting. Take note in particular of the problems perceived to have arisen because of the introduction of proportional representation, these lead to unstable governments, much intrigue by politicians of the centre, and the special emergency powers given to the President, which were increasingly used and were later to assist Hitler to take control.

"1923: Hitler's putsch failed."

Instability plagued the early years of the Republic with short-lived administrations, right-wing inspired disturbances and political assassinations. In 1923 the Franco-Belgian occupation of the Ruhr (carried out in order to enforce the payment of reparations) helped to provoke a series of internal crises, the best remembered of which was Hitler's attempted coup in Munich. The occupation also led to the collapse of the mark and the appalling inflation of 1923 which struck at the savings and consequently the loyalty of the middle-classes who should have been Weimar's staunchest supporters. You should be prepared to assess the consequences of this during the economic crisis of the early 1930s.

GERMAN RECOVERY

PROSPERITY AND STABILITY IN THE LATE 1920s

This period of internal stability and achievement in foreign policy is linked closely to the period in office of *Gustav Stresemann*, German Chancellor from August 1923 to his sudden death in 1929. It followed the conquest of inflation by a revaluation of the mark and the receipt of American aid, under the Dawes Plan, with reparations payments. It was a period of economic boom based largely on industrial rationalisation and concentration. This may have led to the decline in support for extremist political parties which became evident. The

"1925–1929: a new stability."

1928 election results and the decline in political violence hinted at a newly developed political stability. Internationally Germany gained a new acceptance and re-negotiated the heavy reparations payments imposed on her in 1919. The German army was quietly re-organised. It is important to evaluate Stresemann's achievement against the other factors, internal and international, which promoted this apparent golden age. It is also necessary to have a view on how deep-seated this political stability was: there was still cynicism about politicians and parties which reflected their apparently endless fluidity and also the absence of a firm democratic tradition. An important symptom of this was the growing hostility of the Nationalists, led by *Hugenburg*, to the Weimar consitution. Were the late 1920s a golden age only because of what followed and were the seeds of future collapse already sown?

ECONOMIC COLLAPSE

SOCIAL AND POLITICAL CONSEQUENCES

"Destroyed by world depression."

The effects of the world depression which followed from the 1929 Wall Street crash hit Germany very hard for much of the economic recovery of the previous years had been on the basis of United States loans for which repayment demands were now frequently made. A series of banking crises occurred, almost bringing down the State Bank, and business confidence and investment collapsed. At the same time the slump in international trade undermined German exports. Unemployment rose sharply, from 3 million in March 1931 to over 5½ million a year later and then to over 6 million in 1932. These economic calamities undermined faith in the fragile democracy of Weimar and increased the appeal of the extremist parties amongst all sections of society.

POLITICAL LIFE

1930–1933

"A very popular topic for questions."

For examination purposes this is the most important aspect of this topic area. Before entering into the detail it would be wise to pause and briefly list the factors which you have already noted that would, in a crisis, assist the development of right-wing extremism in Germany:

- Lack of a long-standing democratic tradition – the German Empire had been authoritarian.
- Stigma of both defeat and the Peace Treaty had alienated many on the right from the Weimar Republic – make a list of these groups and be ready to comment on each one.
- Distrust of politicians and the weak governments made worse by the losses of 1923 inflation.
- Fear of a communist revolution in Germany.

Be ready with the basis for a paragraph on each of these factors which led to the end of Weimar. Reflect on whether there are other points to make and whether some of the factors are more important than others. The appeal of National Socialism is considered in the next section of these notes. You now need to make a quite systematic study of the period from 1930 to 1933. The detail may at first seem quite daunting but the central theme for taking notes, is clear – 'How and why did Hitler come to power?' The sub-themes are however numerous and need noting. They include the responsibility of other politicians, groups and institutions in the State for the outcome, whether it could, at any stage after 1930, have been avoided and to what extent it arose from the weaknesses of the Weimar Republic already noted. Hitler's tactics and how they changed once he had, by January 1933, control of the apparatus of the State are one important part of the story. For these years the political detail needs to be mastered. The 'Useful Information' section at the end of this chapter will point up some of the important stages and the 'Tutor's Answer' is also directly relevant. All the general books recommended at the end of this chapter have brief but direct accounts.

NATIONAL SOCIALISM

ITS APPEAL

This is more important than some biographical details on Hitler's early career. His limited successes prior to 1930 are one way into an analysis of this important topic. Why did success elude the National Socialists in the Stresemann years? The strength of the personal appeal and the effective presentation of the National Socialist message – what they offered and the type of people whom it would attract are all important. They need to be considered in the setting of changing times for the Weimar Republic with 1929 as the pivotal year.

"The appeal of Nazi virility."

The swastika badge, the uniforms, songs, marches and swagger all date from the failed coup of 1923 but Hitler had since then developed a more compelling style. His nationalist message, the democratic betrayal of Germany, the eager search for scapegoats to explain the defeat in war, the stress on the menace of Red revolution were repeated again and again; exaggerations and half-truths merged into one powerful propaganda message. He was a master of propaganda who exploited both people's idealism and their fears. His National Socialist vision was viciously anti-semitic in a country where such notions had flourished in the nineteenth century and expanded just before 1914; it was also vigorously anti-Marxist and it cleverly drew these two strands together into one conspiracy theory which was being acted out at the expense of the German nation. His autobiography '*Mein Kampf*' was published in 1924.

The appeal of National Socialism was to a vision of national pride and regeneration and it was widespread but its greatest attraction was to the middle and the lower-middle class who became the core of Hitler's support.

ITS ESTABLISHMENT

Hitler's *Third Reich* was an autocracy but an administratively chaotic one with party institutions and personnel duplicating the normal state offices. At the top Hitler's views were dominant and erratic and the central principle of the state was that the Fuhrer's word was law; this was handed down through district *Gauleiters*. After the death of President Hindenburg in 1934 the offices of the President and the Chancellor were joined together.

NATIONAL SOCIALIST POWER 1933–1939

"Establishing autocratic power."

The steps taken by the Nazis, in 1933–1934, to secure their total power is an important topic where detailed knowledge in the correct sequence is important to any assessment of why they succeeded. The key moments were when Hitler persuaded Hindenburg that a further election was needed, Hitler then openly campaigned for the suspension of parliamentary government so that he could have full authority to resolve Germany's problems. This election was different for now the Nazis controlled the machinery of the state and used it ruthlessly to harry and to silence their opponents, employing the burning down of the Reichstag building as an excuse for Hitler to immediately take emergency powers. The election of March 1933 can in no sense be regarded as free or fair. The Nazis alone still could not command the two-thirds majority needed to pass the *Enabling Bill* which would give Hitler total power. However, the arrest of the communist deputies and the fearful co-operation of the Catholic Party provided the votes to end democracy in Germany. In 1934 Hitler, in order to gain the full support of the army, (the one body which could at this stage have ousted him) and the backing of the great industrialists, carried out a coup against his own SA (Brownshirt) supporters. They had been invaluable as streetfighters against the communists but were now a crude embarrassment to an established government. They expected a social revolution to follow Hitler's seizure of power when that would have been quite contrary to the desires of those Hitler now wished to have on his side. In one night in June 1934 perhaps as many as 400 of their leaders died. In explaining Hitler's rise to power never forget to stress his utter ruthlessness.

"The end of the Brownshirts."

The basis of Nazi power for the rest of the decade is a logical, more general extension of these events, involving Nazi relations with the army, the civil service, local government, education, Trade Unions, the Press, the Catholic and Protestant Churches and their own often conflicting and chaotic internal organisation. All writers on this subject stress the conflicting and overlapping nature of the administration and the inefficient chaos which could frequently ensue.

THE NATIONAL SOCIALIST PROGRAMME: 1933–1939

This topic centres on an assessment of how successful the Nazis were in solving the problems which had helped to bring them to power. The price the German people had to pay for strong government, and the reaction of the German nation to the Nazi achievement are important related issues. Where a syllabus goes beyond 1939 it is important to be able to comment upon Nazi domestic policies in peace and war separately if the need should arise. Topics to consider should include the treatment of the Jews before the war, particularly the savagery of *Kristallnacht* in November 1938, and the persecution of left-wing elements and trade unionists. Contrary to earlier promises large-scale industry was supported rather than dismantled, a vast programme of public works, especially road-building, was undertaken and of course the armaments industry and industries like synthetic rubber, which could provide economic self-sufficiency, expanded greatly. Protection of the interests of the small farmers meant that the expansion of agricultural production was limited. Unemployment figures fell dramatically, and were almost non-existent by 1938, but workers' living standards also fell. From 1935 the economy was increasingly geared to preparing Germany to be ready for war by 1940 and this produced considerable financial strains. Youth movements, sports and recreational facilities and subsidised holidays promoted enthusiasm for the Nazis but education was strictly controlled with both science and history pressed into the service of promoting Nazi ideology. The material benefits to the German people deserve assessment but so does the price they paid in terms of loss of freedom. The 'Student's Answer' and accompanying comments later in this chapter cover this topic.

“ Nazi policies and the price. ”

GERMAN FOREIGN POLICY

1933–1939

The 'Outline Answer' to Question 6 opens up some of the issues on this topic. It is best studied as part of the wider range of questions asked about the causes of the Second World War. By far the most efficient way of studying German foreign policy is within this wider European context where it can also provide useful background for questions on foreign policy in British history papers. To understand Nazi foreign policy you will need to go back to the Versailles Treaty of 1919 and look again at the map of Europe. This will provide a basis for answering many other questions on European affairs between the wars so be ready, when your syllabus allows it, to take advantage of this fact.

“ Valuable background for British history. ”

Reaction within Germany to successes in foreign policy is of course more specifically within the scope of German history and is certainly worth studying as an extension of any assessment of the Nazi domestic achievement. You will then be equipped to answer questions on the extent to which, prior to the outbreak of war in 1939, Hitler and the Nazis met the aspirations of the German people. Questions on the war period will require outline knowledge of the course of the war and German domestic history through to 1945 can only be studied satisfactorily in that context.

“ Meeting the aspirations of the German people? ”

USEFUL INFORMATION

1918 Nov	Armistice ended the First World War. Abdication of Kaiser William and a Republic set up.
1919	Extreme Left Spartacist Revolt crushed by the army. Germany accepted terms of Versailles Treaty. Weimar Republic Constitution established.
1920	The right-wing Kapp Putsch failed because of the general strike called by trade unions.
1923	French occupation of the Ruhr to enforce reparations payments. Galloping inflation Hitler's Beer Hall Putsch. Hitler imprisoned, wrote '*Mein Kampf*'.
1923–1929	**Stresemann the dominant political figure**
1924	Dawes Plan helped stabilise Weimar economy.
1925	Field Marshall Von Hindenburg became President.
1926	Germany joined the League of Nations.
1928	In Reichstag Elections the National Socialists gained only 12 seats.
1929	Wall Street Crash
1930 Sept	National Socialists gained 107 seats in Reichstag elections.
1931	Financial collapse in much of central Europe.
1932 Jan	6 million Germans unemployed
July	National Socialists gained 230 seats in Reichstag elections.
1932	Year of manoeuvres amongst right-wing politicians. Hitler refused to serve except as Chancellor.

1933	Jan	**Hitler became Chancellor** – appointed by Hindenburg.
	Feb	Reichstag fire; emergency decrees suspended parts of the Constitution.
	Mar	Nazi terror at the Reichstag elections.
		Passage of the Enabling Act suspended the Weimar Constitution and established the Nazi dictatorship.
	July	Nazi Party declared the only legal party.
1934		**'Night of the Long Knives'** purge of the more radical Nazis.
		Posts of President and Chancellor combined. Hitler took all executive power after death of Hindenberg. Plebiscite approved
1935		**Nuremburg Laws** – State repression of Jews began.
1936		Germany planned for economic self-sufficiency by 1940.

Foreign Affairs 1933–1939

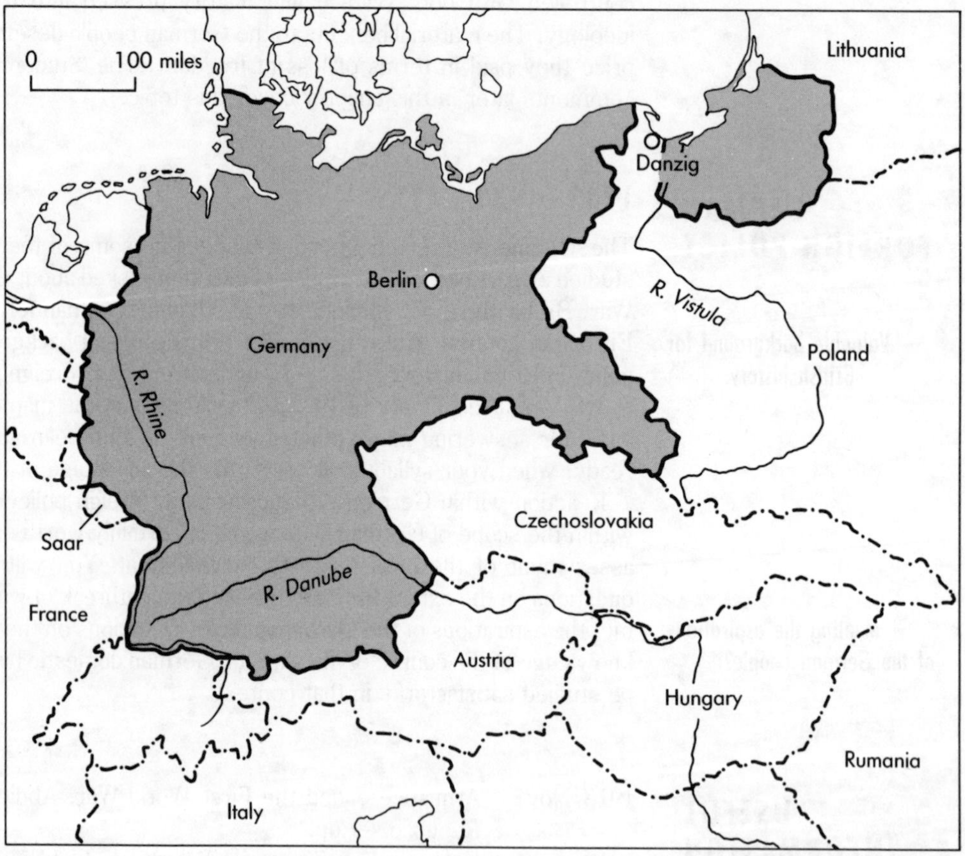

Fig. 22.2 Germany and its neighbours in the 1930s

1933	Oct	Germany walked out of disarmament talks.
		Left League of Nations
1934		Attempted Nazi takeover in Austria thwarted by Mussolini.
1935		Conscription introduced. Began to build an air force.
		Naval agreement with Britain.
1936		Moral and material support for Mussolini over Abyssinia.
		Reoccupied the Rhineland
		Assistance to Franco in the Spanish Civil War.
1938	Mar	German annexation of Austria (the Anschluss).
	Sept	The Munich Agreement on the Sudetenland.
	Mar	Germany occupied much of the rest of Czechoslovakia.
	May	'Pact of Steel' with Mussolini.
	Aug 23	Russo-German 'Non-aggression Pact' signed.
	Sept 1	German invasion of Poland.
	Sept 3	France and Britain declared war on Germany.
1941	June	Germany attacked the USSR (Operation Barbarossa).

EXAMINATION QUESTIONS

Q1 'Hitler and the Nazis used the democratic system which tolerated them to destroy German democracy.' Examine the truth of this statement with reference to the years 1928 to 1934. (London 1989)

Q2 'Economic collapse; outraged nationalism; anti Marxism.' Which of these factors most aided the rise of the Nazis in Germany? (Cambridge 1986)

Q3 'The regime, after all, gave most Germans what they wanted.' Consider this view of Nazi Germany in the years 1933 to 1939. (London 1990)

Q4 Why was Hitler able to score so many successes in foreign policy without going to war? (Welsh 1989)

Q5 Hitler's foreign policy successes between 1933 and 1941 rested on his remarkable tactical skills and ability to exploit his opponent's weaknesses.' Discuss. (Oxford 1989)

OUTLINE ANSWERS

Question 1

See the 'Tutor's Answer' later in this section.

Question 2

Consider: take each topic in turn and indicate how it is relevant to the rise of the Nazis

- Outraged nationalism: explain how the Versailles terms annoyed the German people and how Hitler was able to exploit it. Comment also on the idea that the German army had been betrayed and how Hitler also used this. It gave the Nazis the sympathy of conservative forces in German society.
- Anti-Marxism: explain why fear of communism was so strong amongst many groups in Germany and again link it to the Nazi exploitation of the issue and their very effective propaganda. Their street-fighters gave the impression that they were the only force standing up to the Marxist threat. Appealed especially to the middle-class (the industrialists) who provided funds for the Nazis as a result.
- Economic collapse: explain its impact from 1929. Argue that it was this which most aided the Nazi rise. Justify this by reference to their weak support before 1929 and how this rose dramatically after the economic collapse. It made people more receptive to the nationalist and the anti-Marxist propaganda, especially the latter as fears of a communist resurgence revived.

Question 3

Define: 'wants of most Germans' – economic stability, national pride, end of communist threat. All arising from situation which allowed Hitler to come to power.

Examine: achievement of Hitler in meeting these wants and illustrate each one. Seems likely some truth in claim but no free elections so cannot assess accurately, brilliant use of propaganda also a complication.

Analyse: which groups would be particularly happy with what being done. Identify those who would not approve.

Conclusion: Satisfaction perhaps particularly at international improvement in German position and at regaining of lost lands. Undesirable features could be ignored, many quite skilfully hidden. One certainty is that for those who did not approve there was little incentive to show their feelings.

Note: Now look at the 'Student's Answer' to this question at the end of this section.

Question 4

Introduction: briefly establish the foreign policy successes – do not describe what happened, just indicate the nature of the successes.

Reasons for success: deal with the factors generally and illustrate each factor rather than going through episodes chronologically:

- Weaknesses of victims – Germany often had a good case so gave possible opponents an excuse not to act.
- Failure of other European powers to act or work together – refer to roles of France, Britain and the Soviet Union.
- Hitler's skill and opportunism – gaining Italy's support, clever tactics against Czechs; general fear of another war which he exploited; dealings with Chamberlain.

“Foreign affairs.”

Conclusion: seems so obvious with hindsight that he had to be stopped but at time honest European statesmen thought legitimate German grievances could all be dealt with reasonably. Above all Hitler exploited this feeling with great skill and utter ruthlessness.

Question 5

This question is very similar to Question 4 although it tries to lead the student in a particular direction. You are of course entitled to argue that factors come into the explanation of the successes other than the quotation suggests. But do pay attention to the quotation first! Notice the end date of 1941. If your syllabus does not come to a final stop in 1939 then 1941, with the attack on Russia, is a more logical date at which to end your study of Nazi foreign policy.

“Take foreign policy to the 1941 attack on the USSR.”

A TUTOR'S ANSWER TO QUESTION 1

“The theme of the answer laid out at the start.”

There is arguably a great deal of truth in this assertion but it scarcely constitutes a full explanation of the Nazi success in subverting the Weimar Republic.

By 1928 a series of extra-legal violent attempts to overthrow Weimar had clearly failed and at the same time a new affluence had undermined the appeal of extremist political parties. In the 1928 Reichstag election the Nazis won only 12 seats on the basis of a mere 810,000 votes whereas in 1924 they had held 32 seats. The Nazi appeal seemed to be an irrelevance so the ban on Hitler speaking in public in Prussia was lifted – surely a good example of the tolerance extended to him at this time. In the main Hitler now set out to follow constitutional paths but with a few instances of physical political bullying of weak opponents by his well-organised supporters which were intended to impress the general public with the dynamism of the Nazi movement.

In 1929 Hitler joined in the quite constitutional campaign of the Nationalists under Hugenburg against the foreign policy of the democratic coalition government. He gained great publicity in Hugenburg's newspapers which re-established him as a major respectable politician in the main stream of national politics. On the basis of his restored reputation, having ditched his links with Hugenburg, he continued to pursue the democratic path and in the 1930 election the Nazis obtained 6½ million votes and 107 Reichstag seats. In the troubled aftermath of the effects of the Wall Street Crash Hitler appealed to right-wing fears of the communist threat so much more dynamically than the more traditional right-wing parties, that he made great electoral gains in small towns and rural areas.

Hitler proved a skilled exploiter of the democratic electoral system, a brilliant propagandist and a compelling orator. Pursuing the democratic path was however based on cynical calculation that it offered the best hope of political power. Even this election triumph was marked by the street violence practised against Marxist opponents who had few friends amongst the middle-classes and who had by now begun to see Hitler as their own best protector from the 'Red menace'.

In 1930 the proportional representation system of voting produced a political deadlock within which the democratic parties found it more and more difficult to provide effective government, except through use of the constitutional but hardly democratic emergency power of the President to enforce laws by decree. Major economic and social problems appeared to be being ignored and it was easy for Hitler to attack the weakness of the democratic parties and of the State itself. He had no need to stray blatantly from the constitutional path but was happy for the growing street violence of his followers to continue to promote the vigorous image of National Socialism. By the end of 1931 street violence had become a potent factor in politics and it was a fatal mistake by the Weimar authorities to take no action to curb it.

“Many Weimar weaknesses to be exploited . . .”

“. . . but violence still useful to the Nazis.”

Whether the constitutional or the violent tactics were more important in the continuing momentum of the Nazi campaign is difficult to determine but in any case the Presidential election of 1932 gave Hitler over 13 million votes, making him the most powerful politician in Germany. His progress since 1928 owed more to the weakness and the blindness, rather than the tolerance, of the German democratic parties. Their willingness to pursue their own petty quarrels even at the cost of not providing effective government, had played a large part in Hitler's success. With mass popular support secured there now began a new stage in the Nazi rise to total power.

During 1932 leading right-wing politicians, such as Schleicher and Von Papen intrigued amongst themselves either to provide effective government or to advance their own ambitions. The Centre and the Left, unable to work together, or like Chancellor Bruning unable to command the confidence of the right-wing President Hindenburg and so dismissed, became helpless spectators. All of them greatly underestimated Hitler and the Nazis. Both Schleicher and Von Papen were convinced that he was their natural ally and one who could easily be manipulated to their advantage. Hitler continued to play the constitutional game even when the Nazi vote slumped in the Reichstag elections.

"The intrigues of right-wing politicians."

With Hindenberg falling out with even the right-wing politicians time was on Hitler's side and he carefully refused to be drawn into coalition governments until in January 1933 the President, fearing Schleicher would impose a military dictatorship, appointed him Chancellor.

Hitler had reached the most powerful position in Germany by an entirely constitutional path and had indeed insisted on elections to confirm his appointment. Nothing could seem less revolutionary. The reality was very different. Hitler had always sought absolute power but after the failures of the 1920s had realised that the only route to this was within the constitution. Now he had succeeded and the State was in his control. He proceeded ruthlessly to use the elections he had insisted upon to destroy potential enemies and to establish his own position regardless of the wishes of the politicians with whom he had been forced to intrigue until now.

"By 1933 he no longer needed the democratic system."

In 1933 and 1934 it was less and less true to say that Hitler used the democratic system for he no longer needed to. It is certainly true that in these two years he succeeded in destroying it. The police force was purged and largely replaced by Nazi thugs drawn from the SA and the SS and where the Nazis were in control their electoral opponents were subject to a reign of terror. This was backed up by an unscrupulous use of the radio to promote little else than Nazi propaganda. Just before polling day the burning down of the Reichstag gave Hitler the chance to persuade Hindenburg to issue an emergency decree which suspended most civil liberties. This was Hitler's last 'democratic' step and now, under his new powers his political opponents were arrested, their meetings broken up and their papers closed down. The Nazis obtained 17 million votes and on the strength of the mass support pushed through an Enabling Bill giving total powers to the government for four years. Democracy was at an end.

"Offers a balanced conclusion to the question posed."

The quotation on which this question is based gives only part of the story of the reasons for Hitler's rise to power. It is true that he found it convenient to appear to be just one right-wing politician amongst many and then to work, apparently democratically, to win mass support. But in this he was, even before 1933, always ready to use illegalities like his street fighting bullies if this were tactically helpful. His backstairs political intrigues in 1932 were strictly legal but he was always determined to have absolute power. Again only the tactics were 'democratic'. Once he had power his contempt for the spirit of democracy took over and the Weimar Constitution with its democratic safeguards was swiftly dismantled. It was, in any case, not so much that democratic politicians 'tolerated' him as that they grossly underestimated him and thought that they could use him for their own ends. In this way too the quotation needs amending.

A STUDENT'S ANSWER TO QUESTION 3

"Is this at all relevant?"

```
Following his rise to power as Chancellor in 1933 in Germany, Adolf
Hitler went on to establish one of the most controversial
dictatorships Europe has ever experienced.
  Between the years 1933–39 he led Germany from the economic and
political collapse, following on from the Wall Street Crash and the
death of Stresemann in 1929, to a situation in 1939 where Germany was
able to embark into a major world war and by mid-1940 occupy most of
```

Western Europe. In assessing the phrase 'The regime, after all gave most Germans what they wanted' one must first of all figure out what exactly the people of Germany did want.

In 1933 the Nazis won a substantial number of votes in the elections thus proving that the Nazi Party was what the people wanted but what did they have to offer?

The first thing was the leadership and character of the Nazi Party chairman, Adolf Hitler. He presented a strong yet respectable image which the German people could admire. They needed and wanted a strong personality to appear who would be able to lead Germany in the fight against communism. Hitler also promised to remove Germany from the shackles of the hated Versailles treaty. Nobody in Germany liked the settlement which followed the First World War and Hitler achieved his aim of removing the treaty from Germany by not paying any further reparations from the day he got in power and in 1938 and '39 regaining some of the land, i.e. Memel, which was lost. Hitler also annexed Austria to Germany which was a very popular move since it contained many German speaking people who wanted to be re-united with their Motherland.

" Muddled use of information. "

Unemployment was one of the major problems of Hitler's Germany and in 1933 Hitler passed a law to reduce unemployment which was very successful. In his campaign to become Chancellor Hitler had promised 'Bread and Work' to the 6 million people who were unemployed and starving at the time. By 1935 the numbers of unemployed were only 1½ million and the success of this was due to the immense increase of government spending on public works. Economically Hitler was rather ignorant but with the help of some of his economic ministers he devised some four year plans which put some much needed stability into the German economy and even managed to reduce the rate of inflation.

Another way in which Hitler gave the people of Germany the stability they wanted was when he banned strikes in 1934 and made people join the German Labour Front. This removed the threat of strikes although the workers also lost the right to bargain for wage rises.

" Returns again to foreign affairs. "

One of the most important things to the Germans was when they regained their international prestige as a powerful nation again. Hitler not only re-organised and re-armed the army but also led an active foreign policy and regained the Rhineland in 1936, took over Czechoslovakia in 1939 and made powerful allies with Italy and Japan.

One aspect of this policy the Germans may not have wanted was that of the almost inevitable outbreak of war. Germany suffered so heavily from the First World War that they were worried that history may have repeated itself.

" Probably true but too vaguely expressed. "

However, not all Germans were happy with the way that Hitler had arranged Germany and numerous opposition groups appeared. Hitler however had very well organised methods of dealing through the SS and the Gestapo with any group who went against his regime.

It can therefore be concluded that the Nazi regime did supply many Germans with the stability, sense of belonging and work that they so desperately required. It must be noted that all of this was at a loss of civil rights like censorship of the press and a ban on all other political parties except the Nazi Party. The fact that there was any opposition to Hitler's mighty regime proves that not all Germans were given what they wanted.

" More on this please! "

" This essay needs a clearer structure. "

EXAMINER COMMENTS

This essay would probably obtain a pass mark but with little to spare. It avoids the danger of merely describing what Hitler did and offers an attempt at a directly relevant conclusion. Like many essays on Germany after 1933 knowledge is very thin. The second paragraph would have been an effective opening and, crucially, in the third paragraph the student acknowledges the need to define what the Germans wanted in order to answer the question. This is however not followed through.

A good answer would at some point have identified those groups who perhaps got what they wanted and those who did not and said why.

Note: this could be a useful revision exercise at this point. Because this is not done the conclusions are too vague. The final point about opposition groups is difficult to credit for none are named.

It is not a well-organised or well-written essay. How would you improve it in these respects? Grouping all the foreign achievements together would be a start. Very unusually this essay suffers from having too many short, undeveloped paragraphs. It at least observes the finishing date for the period and does not carry on, irrelevantly, into the war period.

It is an example of an essay where the historical comments have been undermined by a weak essay plan which turns into a list of points rather than presenting an argued case.

USEFUL SOURCES OF INFORMATION

General reading

A Ramm, *Europe in the Twentieth Century*, Longman 1984
J B Watson, *Success in European History 1815–1941*, John Murray 1981
A Wood, *Europe 1815–1960*, Longman 1984

Further reading

A Bullock, *Hitler: a Study in Tyranny*, Penguin 1968
W Carr, *A History of Germany 1815-1990*, Arnold 1991
G Layton, *Germany: The Third Reich 1933-1945*, Hodder and Stoughton 1992

E Wiskemann, *Europe of the Dictators*, Fontana 1973

Linked topic areas

- The impact of the First World War on Europe
- The Versailles Peace Settlement 1919
- Italy under Mussolini (see Chapter 21)
- The origins of the Second World War
- The course of the Second World War in Europe

CHAPTER 23

THE USSR SINCE 1945

STALIN

KHRUSHCHEV

BREZHNEV

POST-BREZHNEV

SOVIET SOCIETY

ECONOMIC ISSUES

FOREIGN POLICY

USEFUL INFORMATION

GETTING STARTED

Look at a map showing the extent of the USSR at the end of the Second World War. Your curiosity may then encourage you to look at some larger scale sectional maps. If you have not studied earlier periods of Soviet history you need to be aware of the Communist takeover of the State in the revolution of 1917 and, in brief, outline what happened to the economy and society from then until 1941. Look through Chapter 20 and note that Stalin had gained total power by 1928. The pre-war Five Year Plans laid the basis for the build-up of heavy industry and armaments as well as the ruthless collectivisation of agriculture. Stalin's purges of all suspected opponents culminated in the great show trials of the late 1930s and by then the machinery of oppression for all dissent was firmly in place.

Any judgement on the internal affairs of the Soviet Union in the thirty or so years after 1945 is likely to have to take into account the country's experiences during the Second World War. You should be able to indicate the colossal damage suffered with something towards 20 million dead and the total destruction of the industrial and agricultural heartland in European Russia. The mass-movement eastwards of large ethnic minority groups, under way before 1941, was greatly accelerated by the war. The victories gained by the Red Army in 1944–45 brought it to the centre of Berlin and laid the basis for the creation of communist satellite states in Eastern Europe. Victory brought the integration of the Baltic States, former Russian provinces, into the USSR, and also the movement of the Russo-Polish border hundreds of miles westwards. Very quickly, at the end of the war the anti-Nazi alliance crumbled and within four years the USSR and its former allies were on opposite sides in the Cold War.

Questions may come in tidy chronological packages – the Stalin years; the Khrushchev years; the Brezhnev years: the years since Brezhnev, but be ready also for more narrowly focussed questions stretching across a longer period – on economic problems, dissidents, relations with the USA, China or eastern Europe. The same material needs revising in different forms – which is probably the best form of revision! The political ferment of the late 1980s, the end of Soviet domination of the smaller states of Eastern Europe and the apparent disintegration of the USSR itself in the early 1990s will provide a great range of history exam questions for many years ahead.

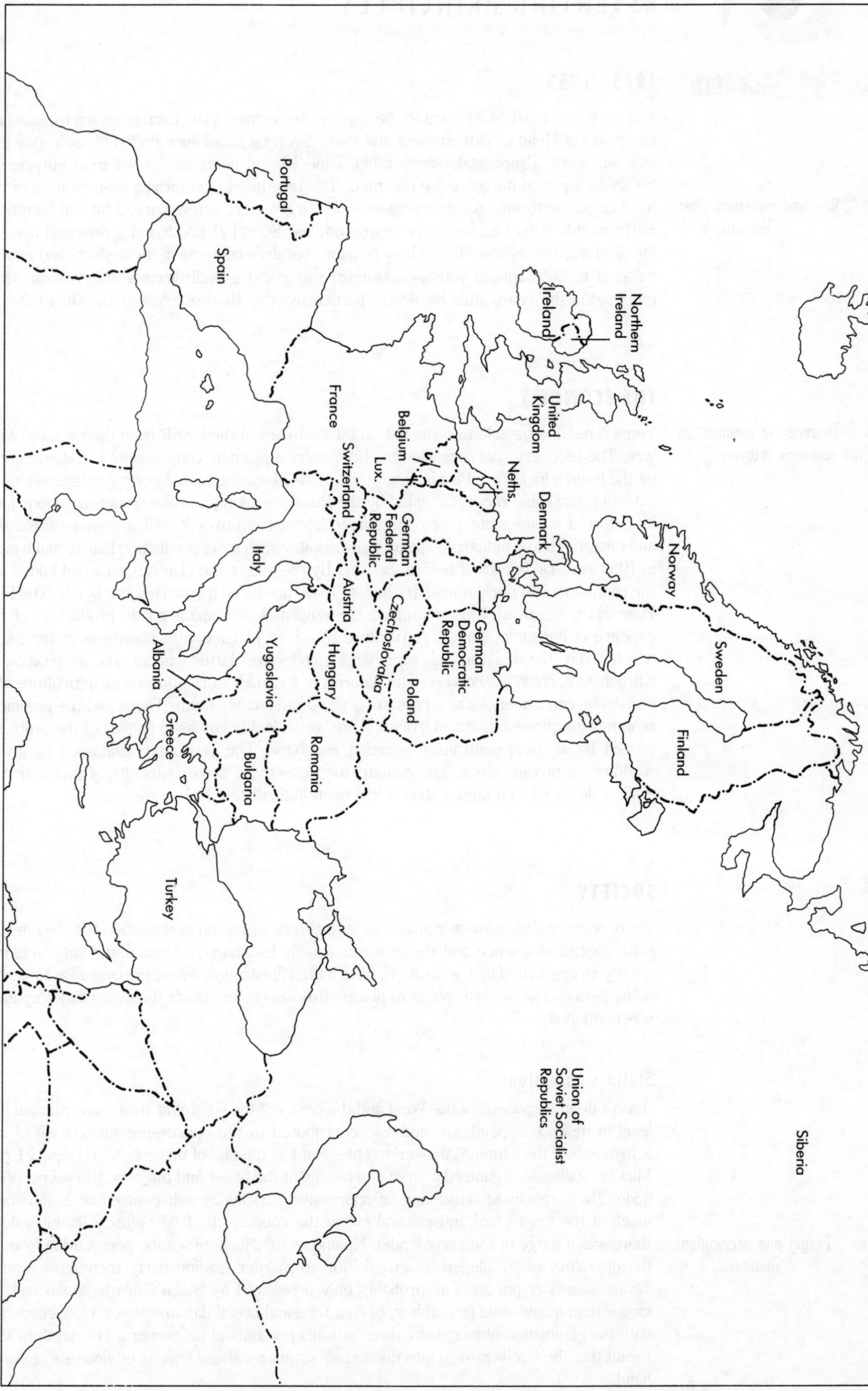

Fig. 23.1 Europe: post-1945

ESSENTIAL PRINCIPLES

STALIN

1945–1953

Victory in war marked a return to the oppressive regime of the thirties. Stalin retained the key posts of Head of Government and Party Secretary and surrounded himself with pre-war ministers. Propaganda, censorship, especially of news and views from outside the Soviet Union, and purges were resumed. The treatment of returning ex-prisoners of war has become notorious for its savagery; the purges were often marked by anti-semitism. Party membership became more restricted, the Secret Police found a renewed lease of life. You need an assessment of how tyrannical Stalin's rule was in these years and enough material to substantiate your assessment, this could usefully include information which emerged in the years after his death, particularly the 1956 revelations by Khrushchev.

"Renewed repression after the war."

THE ECONOMY

"Be ready to comment on the economic recovery."

You will need to be able to comment on the recovery of the USSR from the ravages of the war. The recovery was organised by the country's planning commission, *Gosplan*, initially by the Fourth Five Year Plan inaugurated in 1946. Despite acute labour shortages industry made a remarkable recovery, aided by the Russians taking machinery as reparations from its defeated enemies and employing forced labour from over 3 million prisoners, Russian and foreign. Heavy industry expanded remarkably with steel production half as much again in 1953 as it had been just before the war. By the end of the plan rationing had ended and the newly founded nuclear industry had, in 1949, produced its own nuclear bomb. The Fifth Plan which began in 1951 continued the emphasis on capital goods production at the expense of consumer goods. Agriculture remained plagued with enormous inefficiencies which even the build-up of ever larger collective farms, under the inspiration of Khrushchev, could not correct. The theories of Lysenko were imposed on agriculture with disastrous consequences as a result of Stalin's patronage of him. These and the grandiose schemes for afforestation and irrigation are worth looking up as examples of the problems caused by an over-centralised agrarian economy. The peasantry continued to prefer working on private plots and, despite the collectivist drive, agricultural production at Stalin's death was no higher than it had been immediately before the war.

SOCIETY

There were notable post-war advances in health facilities and in education but the effect of state control of science and the arts was usually less happy. Again comments would be greatly strengthened by the ability to offer a brief illustration within the overall assessment of the period. The pre-war policy of placing Russians in key posts throughout the republics was continued.

Stalin's obsessions

Stalin's deep suspicions of the West and the crises of the Cold War meant a continued high level of defence expenditure and also contributed to the oppressive supervision of civil activities (see the 'Outline Answer' to Question 1 at the end of this chapter). Deputy Prime Minister *Zdhanov* organised a strict censorship of the press and the arts, the secret police under *Beria* remained active and an oppressive personality cult centred on Stalin stifled much of the intellectual and cultural life of the country. In 1948, after Zdhanov's death there was a purge of the party leadership and in 1952 an anti-semitic persecution followed the discovery of an alleged 'Doctors' Plot' to murder leading party members. A more savage series of purges was probably only prevented by Stalin's death. Stalin had, for longer than many could remember, been a total and brutal dictator obsessively concerned with the elimination of imaginary threats to his person and his powers. His death in 1953 meant that the USSR moved into uncharted waters for there was no obvious successor to hand.

"Purges and persecutions continued."

KHRUSHCHEV

1953 – 1964

The leadership struggle following Stalin's death involved:
– *Malenkov*, who became chairman of the Council of Ministers.
– *Beria*, the sinister and apparently very powerful leader of the secret police.
– *Khrushchev*, who became secretary of the Communist party, a post from which he imposed ideas of collective leadership.

"The leadership struggle."

An immediate effort was made to relax the Stalinist tyranny with some political prisoners being released. Beria was arrested and shot and then blamed for all that was wrong in the USSR. Khrushchev used his post as secretary to put his nominees in key positions and asserted the control of the party over the state administration; by early 1955 he was able to force Malenkov's resignation and to replace him with the easily dominated *Bulganin*. By 1958 he had out-manoeuvred the other Soviet leaders and taken over the prime minister's post. He became the key figure until his fall in 1964; this was the result of a cleverly engineered coup by other party leaders.

"The remarkable frankness of 1956."

At the Twentieth Party Conference in 1956 he had attacked Stalinism, especially the personality cult and the repression. In the totally enclosed Soviet society this had a devastating impact. Khrushchev never established his position with total security nor did he advance solutions to the many problems to which he had in 1956 drawn attention; although he appeared to have recognised the need to reduce central direction and to encourage local initiatives especially in economic matters. His leadership was erratic and a full verdict will require notice of social and economic (especially agrarian) affairs and foreign policy in the period 1956 to his downfall in 1964.

SOCIETY

In this period political terror disappeared, the authorities' stranglehold on the arts was relaxed and education at all levels was expanded, with a great increase in part-time and correspondence courses and some evidence of greater academic freedom. Wages increased and social security provision improved.

THE ECONOMY

"Khrushchev's ambitious agrarian schemes."

Khrushchev's great concern was with agriculture, he saw himself as an expert and did not spare himself to bring about greater productivity. Control at the centre was relaxed but the process of farm amalgamation went on. The peasants however, remained attached to their own plots so productivity was slow to rise. After initial successes the 'Virgin Lands' schemes were pushed too far and they led to soil erosion and disaster. The 1963 food shortages, following grain crop failures in both the Virgin Lands and the Ukraine, led to imports from the USA and this undoubtedly helped bring about Khrushchev's fall.

More generally there was an increased emphasis on the production of consumer goods and a massive drive to build more houses. The chemical industry expanded and some of the railway system was modernised. The launching of the first earth satellite in 1957 suggested that the USSR was the equal in some respects of the United States but the heavy spending on arms and space was already proving to be a brake on economic growth. That Khrushchev was allowed to go into private retirement until his death in 1971 suggests that some of the uncompromising Stalinist rigour (of which until 1953 he had been an effective exponent) was being softened.

BREZHNEV

1964 – 1982

As with Stalin and with Khrushchev you need an assessment of Brezhnev's personal role and of the policies that were pursued in the years of his dominance in social, economic and especially foreign policy matters. Within the USSR he continues to suffer from unhistorical analysis of alleged defects which seem intended to put his successors in a favourable light. Questions comparing him to Khrushchev are gradually giving way to questions setting him against the developments in the Soviet Union since his death in 1982.

"Changing style of questions on Brezhnev."

After Khrushchev's fall a collective leadership emerged with power shared between Brezhnev as Party Secretary, *Kosygin* as Prime Minister and *Podgorny* as President; their rule was dull and cautious and by its end it appeared a government of rather static old men.

The provision of stability had begun to look close to stagnation. On Podgorny's retirement in 1977 Brezhnev took his office as well as continuing as Party Secretary. Kosygin retired in 1980. Something of a Brezhnev personality cult developed in these last years.

THE ECONOMY

“Economic disappointments.”

Brezhnev's efforts to bring about a relaxation of international tensions were prompted by the heavy burden that the arms budget placed on the economy but powerful interests in the USSR worked to maintain military spending which continued to impose strains on the industrial economy. In agriculture the great plans of the previous era were played down in favour of administrative efficiency and continuity; peasants were encouraged to produce more by being offered higher prices and bonus payments on the collective farms but despite this labour productivity and crop yields remained poor. In industry more consumer goods were produced but economic growth rates overall began to stagnate. The increased complexity of the economy with new industries made the planning systems more bureaucratic and resources were not being used efficiently; initiative was too often discouraged. On the other hand contracts for capital goods were negotiated with western companies and in aircraft design, space technology and nuclear energy the USSR appeared to be well advanced.

Note: Soviet foreign policy in the Brezhnev era is considered below.

POST-BREZHNEV

“New directions under Gorbachev.”

The period since 1982 is much more difficult to compartmentalise than the earlier decades. *Andropov* and *Chernenko* are its unjustly forgotten figures and it is dominated by *Gorbachev* whose problems and ideas are both packed with interest and, for the historian, invaluable in illuminating the legacy left by his predecessors. In the sense that the outcome of his policies is far from clear any historical verdict on him, and on his period in power, must be very tentative. The newspapers rather than the textbooks seem likely to provide the more important information and commentary on him. When the time comes for a historian's judgement on him it is quite clear that his period in power will be acknowledged as one of the key turning-points in both the domestic and the external history of his country. He survived the 1991 reactionary coup but this event placed the future of the U.S.S.R. in doubt as the demands of democrats and nationalists became more sweeping and in 1992 the country disintegrated into separate independent states facing an uncertain economic and political future.

SOVIET SOCIETY

LIFE IN THE USSR POST-STALIN

“How repressive was Soviet society after Stalin?”

Knowledge of trends in Soviet society might well be needed in aid of a judgement on any one of the major Soviet statesmen of the period. The repression of the Stalinist period was succeeded, under Khrushchev, by limited measures of liberalisation, for example over visits by foreigners and foreign cultural visits by Soviet citizens. The Brezhnev period saw a growth of both financial corruption and crime. Throughout, the laws remained, by Western standards, repressive and the privileges of members of the Communist Party intact. Problems of civil liberty centred on the treatment of the dissidents in society and this issue in particular deserves close attention throughout the period. It involves the activities of the secret police, the Gulags and the mental hospitals used to imprison undesirables. In many ways the Brezhnev period saw a tightening of these repressive practices. It is essential that in relation to these matters your reading enables you to comment on the characteristic features of each of the periods identified in the sections above.

ECONOMIC ISSUES

“Questions on economic problems are common.”

Questions on the Soviet economy usually relate to the problems it faced and on the efforts and relative lack of success individuals had when attempting to promote greater efficiency and growth in the economy. The problems span the period since 1945 but the policies and their success or otherwise need to be revised also in terms of the Stalin years, the Khrushchev period, under Brezhnev and since 1982. If invited to assess say Brezhnev's economic achievements you will need to have a general grasp of Soviet economic history both before and after his period in office. It is simply a case of being flexible enough in your approach to be able to use the same material and ideas to answer questions set in different ways.

Note: The 'Tutor's Answer' later in this chapter examines the Soviet economic performance since 1970.

FOREIGN POLICY

"Check that foreign policy questions have appeared in past papers."

This also should be studied and revised by both theme and period. Look at past papers to ensure that questions on Soviet foreign policy figure sufficiently frequently to make its revision a worthwhile undertaking. Foreign policy under Stalin attracts particular attention. Cross-check with the syllabus if necessary. The themes likely to be covered are quite obvious:

- The re-disposition of territories in eastern Europe at the end of the Second World War. The origins of the Cold War.
- Relations with the communist nations of eastern Europe.
- Relations with China.

Use of appropriate maps will be of great assistance in organising your knowledge. Remember that questions on periods of Soviet history or individual leaders should be read very carefully to establish whether you are expected to comment just on internal matters or also on the foreign relations and policies of the Soviet Union.

"Revise the big crises."

Note: Revise all the well-known international crises thoroughly. They can often be used to illustrate general themes, for example:

- The Berlin Blockade 1948 ■ Hungary 1956 ■ The Cuban Missile Crisis 1962
- Czechoslovakia 1968

The dismantling of the communist East European bloc in 1989–1990 could mark the end of an era in Soviet international relations which began with the advance of the Red Army across eastern Europe in 1944 and 1945.

USEFUL INFORMATION

1941–1945	The Great Patriotic War: devastation inside USSR.
1943 Feb	Surrender of German forces at Stalingrad.
1945	Red Army fought its way into Berlin.
1945	Meetings of Allied leaders at Yalta and at Potsdam.
1946	Fourth Soviet Five Year Plan inaugurated.
1948	Death of Zdhanov followed by purge.
1951	Fifth Soviet Five Year Plan.
1952	Nineteenth Congress of the Communist party (first since 1939). Alleged 'Doctors' Plot' followed by purge.
1953	**Death of Stalin**
1953–1958	**Leadership struggle**
1955	Malenkov forced to resign.
1956	Twentieth Congress of the Communist Party: Khrushchev attacked Stalin in secret session, speech leaked.
1956 on	Cooler relations with Communist China.
1958	Khrushchev established as Party Secretary and Prime Minister.
1958–1964	**The Khrushchev years**
1962	Cuban missiles crisis
1964	Khrushchev forced from office; replaced by Brezhnev.
1964–1982	**Brezhnev in power**, at first with Kosygin and Podgorny.
1968	'Brezhnev Doctrine' used to justify action against Czechoslovakia.
1979	Invasion of Afghanistan
1982	Brezhnev died
1982–1984	**Andropov the key political figure** – General Secretary of the Communist Party: died 1984
1984–1985	**Chernenko General Secretary:** died 1985
1985	**Gorbachev emerged as leader** Policies of *perestroika* (restructuring) and *glasnost* (openness).
1989	Uprisings against communist regimes in eastern European states not resisted by the USSR. Growth of communal violence and demands for national separation in many Soviet Republics. Economic problems mounting.
1990	The privileges and the role of the Communist Party as the only political party successfully challenged. Growing discontent with the economic performance of Gorbachev.
1991	Attempted reactionary coup thwarted primarily by Yeltsin.
1992–3	Division of the former USSR into independent states faced with worsening economic problems and social and political tensions.

EXAMINATION QUESTIONS

Q1 How tyrannical was the rule of Stalin in post-war Russia? (London 1989)

Q2 Why, and with what results, did the USSR embark on a policy of de-Stalinisation after 1953? (Cambridge 1989)

Q3 Why did the Soviet Union seek to extend its control over Eastern and Central Europe between 1945 and 1955? (AEB 1988)

Q4 Account for the growing hostility between the Soviet Union and the Chinese People's Republic from 1956 to 1962. (AEB 1988)

Q5 Why has the Soviet Union found it difficult since 1970 to achieve high rates of economic growth? (London 1989)

OUTLINE ANSWERS

Question 1

"A popular question."

Introduction: it was less tyrannical than in the pre-war period in two important respects, – the mass deaths caused by the collectivisation of agriculture and the purges of leading party members were not repeated.

Repressions: it was a very repressive regime, give examples from work of Secret Police under Beria; fate of returning prisoners of war; Gulags; purge of the party in Leningrad after death of Zhdanov; the 'Doctors' Plot' of 1952 which looked as though it was to be the beginning of a full-scale purge but Stalin died before it got under way. All of these could create a climate of personal insecurity, for example, after the 'Doctor's Plot' many ordinary doctors, especially if Jewish, were denounced by discontented patients.

Tyrannies: tyrannical controls were imposed on the press and all information, no intellectual or artistic freedom, use imposition of Lysenko's scientific ideas as the example, authorised versions of Soviet history, e.g. all references to Trotsky excluded. Restrictions on movement around the country remained and those who had been in earlier mass deportations were not allowed to return.

Paranoia: Stalin's personal paranoia grew in these years and it was dangerous to be near the top in politics and administration. The sinister Beria carried out many quiet persecutions, as often in his own interests as that of his master. Illustrate from Khrushchev's 1956 attack on Stalin.

Conclusion: the tyranny had been relaxed during the war but, largely thanks to Stalin's suspicion of the West and of rivals to his own position from within the USSR it was to a great extent restored after the war and relaxation only came after his death.

Question 2

Reasons: argue that the reason for de-Stalinisation was because the leading members of the Politburo wanted it. Cult of personality had reached absurd proportions and it, and the machinery to enforce it (Secret Police etc.) were dangerous to the surviving leaders. Repression of any dissenting voice was having harmful economic effects.

"De-Stalinisation a product of fear."

Results: the results in the period to 1964 (end of Khrushchev) were mixed: idea of collective leadership overtaken by Khrushchev but he was never as free to act as Stalin had been, was eventually overturned peacefully, his retirement rather than execution suggesting things had changed. The 1956 attack on Stalin was a great psychological shock to many people who had been brought up to accept him as the saviour of the nation. Terror machinery swept away.

Then discuss efforts to extend civil liberties where it was again a mixed record, e.g. emptying prisons but repressing religion, blocking Pasternak but allowing Solzhenitsyn to be published. More contacts allowed with the West. Too much depended on Khrushchev's own erratic tastes but more intellectual freedom than later under Brezhnev.

There was a greater willingness to consider the people's interests, consumer goods, great house-building programme.

"A cautious verdict is needed on its results."

Conclusion: significant changes in style of government and end of state terror were irreversible but in 1964 civil liberty was still fragile and something of a reaction was about to occur under Brezhnev. Khrushchev's commitment to a free society had been too erratic and fitful to affect the basic framework of the lives of Soviet citizens. They were less fearful but only a little more free than in the last days of Stalin.

Question 3

See the 'Student's Answer' at the end of this section.

Question 4

Note: The answer to this lies as much in Chinese history as in Russian history. To prepare for this essay you could usefully consult the appropriate sections of Chapter 25.

General theme: since the communists took over in China in 1949 they had received aid from the USSR but after Khrushchev's coming to power this declined. In 1960 Khrushchev withdrew all Russian technical assistance. Mao Tse-tung saw the USSR as ideologically unsound on issues like Yugoslavia and in turn supported Albania which remained wedded to Stalinism and which was increasingly hostile to the Soviet Union. De-Stalinisation was opposed by the Chinese. The USSR's failure to persist in a tough line with the West was another issue with an ideological base in different interpretations of the world role of communism. Personal dislike and personal abuse between Khrushchev and Mao played its part. The long frontier between the two countries with a history of border disputes was another source of tension. Even racial tensions were involved. It was more than just a much publicised personal quarrel because matters got worse later in the 1960s, after the fall of Khrushchev.

A TUTOR'S ANSWER TO QUESTION 5

In the 1970s and 1980s, even by optimistic estimates the Soviet economy grew only by about 2 per cent per annum. A rising population meant that growth per head of population was less than this. This was in contrast to annual growth rates in the 1960s of around 5 per cent. The causes of these declining rates of growth have been and are still much debated.

“Agriculture the major element in the economy.”

Agriculture is more important to the Soviet economy than is the case in western capitalist states and the very disappointing performance of the agrarian sector became proportionally that much more important. In part this poor performance was a consequence of over-ambitious plans in the Khrushchev era. There has been a strong emphasis in agrarian planning on total production figures and too little attention paid to food distribution including transport facilities, storage and refrigeration. Agriculture remains riddled with too many ambitious large-scale plans and targets and too many bureaucrats. The series of ecological disasters in Central Asia alone, with the drying up of the Aral Sea and the over-use of nitrates to promote cotton production which lead to an alarming increase in human genetic birth defects are just two of the most sensational consequences. Large-scale planning mistakes did not end with the departure of Khrushchev. Since 1970 Soviet agrarian growth has lagged markedly behind that in industry perhaps most importantly because the large collective farms, despite efforts to introduce incentive schemes, remain inefficient in their use of both men and machinery, particularly the latter.

Industrial growth has been more impressive and arguably, from a lower base, has compared quite well with that in western countries; often it has been disappointing, because initial targets have been set unrealistically high.

“Planning defects at the heart of the economic problems.”

Planning defects were at the heart of many problems but the efforts of Brezhnev to encourage more local management initiative had only limited success. The market system has been a very inefficient guide to developing production for artificially based prices have produced bottlenecks and shortages with equal profusion. Breaking away from a centrally planned economy has been difficult to achieve. The many defects of the State Planning Commission (Gosplan) made the effort necessary for it came to lack any flexibility in responding to changing economic needs. Central planning had served the Soviet economy well at earlier times and in regard to large-scale heavy industrial and power developments but since 1970 has proved very inefficient in providing more varied production of lighter capital goods, such as computers, and of consumer goods and in the promotion of smaller units of production. This planning inertia and the absence of an effective market stimulus to innovation have done much to slow down even industrial growth.

“The size of the country itself creates economic difficulties.”

There are other technical and economic reasons for the slow overall rate of economic growth. The sheer size of the USSR is a formidable obstacle to the efficient operation of either plans or markets, and one often forgotten in western capitalist explanations of

Soviet problems. One result is the heavy Soviet dependence, for the movement of goods, on its rail network. It has been of crucial importance that investment here has failed to keep pace with the growth in traffic, especially on the main arterial lines. This has in turn created inefficiencies everywhere in the economy. Railways and many other forms of productive investment have suffered from the priority given to defence investment and development and, with less excuse, through the preference for investment in large-scale prestige projects of doubtful economic worth. Heavy investment in the nuclear power industry at first produced impressive results but a series of management failures led to serious accidents which culminated at Chernobyl and the future progress of this industry is now less certain. Other examples could be cited, the technical, investment and transport delays to the development of the oil and gas resources in Siberia or the bureaucracy and antiquated monetary controls still crippling the potential for tourism.

“Non-economic reasons for sluggish economic growth.”

Western critics of the failures in Soviet planning and the lack of individual initiatives to overcome these would argue that they are necessary consequences of a totalitarian communist society. The causes of economic sluggishness require non-economic explanations.

Such thinking appears to lie behind the reforms initiated in the Gorbachev era though earlier Andropov had launched a severe attack on such problems as the alleged laziness of Soviet labour and the linked disease of chronic over-manning. Gorbachev introduced Draconian measures to eliminate alcoholism which he saw as a major cause of inefficiency. Whether this will be more successful than earlier attempts, by Andropov, to stamp out the black economy, which merely resulted in a decline in the level of economic activity, remains to be seen.

Economic growth, in the industrial and commercial sectors at least, will depend on an educated workforce and the free flow of information to encourage innovation. These may in turn depend on a free society and the development of a market economy. This appears to be the philosophy driving Gorbachev; whether it can, in the Russian context, come to fruition remains unproven.

A STUDENT'S ANSWER TO QUESTION 3

“The terrible legacy of the war.”

In 1941 and 1942 the German armies had driven deep into the Soviet Union, reaching the outskirts of Moscow, besieging Leningrad and reaching the banks of the Volga at the battle of Stalingrad. They were then pushed back in 1943 and 1944 and the Red Army broke out of the Soviet Union to cross Poland and invade Germany reaching Berlin in early 1945. In the war forced on the Soviet Union by Germany probably 20 million Russians died and the towns, industry and agriculture of western Russia were devastated.

The first reason why the Soviet Union wanted to control eastern and central Europe was that they were determined never again to leave themselves open to invasion from aggressors in the west. The Poles had not proved to be an effective obstacle in the past and were in any case unreliable allies for there was a strong anti-Russian tradition and since 1917 also a strong anti-communist tradition in Poland. The Poles, it was felt in 1945 must be made reliable and subservient allies of the USSR, so that they would automatically provide a defensive barrier. The only reliable barrier would be an ideologically sound communist one. It was for this reason that the Russian massacred the Polish officers at Katyn and deliberately allowed the destruction of Warsaw rather than moving their forces to help the uprising there, they wanted Poland to lack leaders and to be beaten into the ground so that they could impose their own will on her without opposition.

“The desire for a defensive buffer.”

The same is true of other countries of eastern Europe which became part of the Soviet bloc, governments friendly to the USSR were installed in these countries in order to provide a territorial barrier between Russia and any possible enemy in the West. To make the barrier more certain the Soviet Union had earlier taken land from Finland after the war took hundreds of square miles of land from Poland and also re-took the independent nations of Estonia, Latvia and Lithuania, giving itself control of the east Baltic coastline. Pushing the Polish western frontier deep into German territory worked to the same end. The allied occupation of Germany and the Russians taking reparations from her would keep Germany too weak ever to disturb the peace of eastern Europe again.

"Ideological differences with the West . . ."

Partly because of these moves by the Soviet Union relations with the western allies went sour and by 1948 the Cold War had come into existence. Stalin convinced himself that the USSR was in danger of either direct attack or subversion from the capitalist countries, especially the United States. Because he did not want US economic domination he refused Marshall Aid and refused to allow the countries under Russian domination to accept it either. A bloc of communist countries tied economically to the Soviet Union would provide mutual economic strength against capitalist threats and a market for Russian goods and a source of raw materials.

"... or was it old-fashioned Russian imperialism?"

The old allies of the USSR, especially Britain and the United States were convinced that these moves in eastern Europe were to build up an even greater Soviet Empire. This was linked to the idea that the Soviet Union was in the business of exporting communism, a godless creed which de-humanised people in order to glorify the communist state. Churchill's speech in 1946 at Fulton illustrated these suspicions of Soviet imperialism. The British Labour Government shared them and with the Berlin Airlift and the formation of NATO prepared to resist the red menace. The stage-managed communist takeover of Czechoslovakia in 1948 had confirmed all these western anxieties.

Stalin was a very nasty dictator with deep suspicions of the west. For example he made sure that Russian prisoners who had had wartime contacts with the west were sent into Siberian camps where they could not contaminate the rest of the country with any subversive ideas they had picked up. A barrier of subject states would help in this process. Whether he really dreamed of dominating all of Europe as the West feared is less likely. The best example is in Greece where Stalin honoured his agreements that this should be a British zone of influence and so he gave no help to the strong communist movement there. Following the appalling Russian losses of the Second World War his motives were largely defensive, first to secure protection of Russia's frontiers from further attack and later to build up a block of communist states to protect the Soviet economy against a capitalist onslaught.

"'Bloc' not 'Block'."

"An effective direct answer but there are some further points to consider."

EXAMINER COMMENTS

This is a good direct answer. The way in which it shows that the motives changed as circumstances changed is very impressive.

It needs some more concrete information on the experiences of some of the countries of eastern Europe, especially East Germany where Soviet motives were perhaps different from elsewhere and more deliberately intended to provide an advance base in the west. The Berlin blockade suggests that Soviet intentions might have been more ambitious than the final conclusion here suggests. It deserves more discussion. There is no mention of Soviet anxieties being aroused by the US atomic bomb to which they had no riposte until 1949.

This is still a good essay. Are there ways in which you would improve it, given the time constraints of the examination?

USEFUL SOURCES OF INFORMATION

General reading

A Ramm, *Europe in the Twentieth Century 1905–1970*, Longman 1984
J B Watson, *Success in World History since 1945*, John Murray 1989: the textbook which comes closest to the present.

Further reading

P Calvocoressi, *World Politics since 1945*, Longman (3rd Edition) 1977
G Hosking, *A History of the Soviet Union*, Fontana 1985
P Kennedy *The Rise and Fall of the Great Powers*, Fontana 1988: for the ambitious student, the last two chapters of this exciting work are well worth reading.
J Laver *The USSR 1945–1990*, Hodder and Stoughton 1991
M Lynch, *Stalin and Khrushchev: The USSR, 1924–1964*, Hodder & Stoughton 1990: one of a series designed for A-level students.
M McCauley, *The Soviet Union since 1917*, Longman 1981
J N Westwood, *Endurance and Endeavour: Russian History 1812–1986*, Oxford University Press (3rd Edition) 1987: a very readable national history with an extensive bibliography.

Linked topic areas

- The USSR 1917–1941 (see Chapter 20)
- Eastern Europe since 1945
- The Cold War
- Soviet-American relations since 1945 (see Chapter 24)
- Soviet-Chinese relations since 1949 (see Chapter 25)
- Western Europe since 1945 (see Chapter 26)
- Soviet relations with the Third World since 1945
- Great Power relations and status in the 1990s
- The disintegration of the Soviet Union in the 1990s

CHAPTER 24

THE USA SINCE 1945

GETTING STARTED

You will need to understand the workings of the United States Constitution and the electoral system. The president as the chief executive; the Congress, made up of the Senate and the House of Representatives, as the law-making body; and the Supreme Court as interpreter of what was allowed under the Constitution. It is a system of checks and balances which has proved quite resistant to amendment. The president is elected every four years in November, taking up office early in the following January. Two senators from each state sit for six years, and representatives in proportion to the population of each state sit for two years. This has frequently created a situation in which the president has to work with a congress where power has swung to the opposing party in the mid-term elections. The separate powers reserved for the individual states have also frequently inhibited the freedom of action of both president and congress. Any judgement of policies or the achievements of individual presidents should bear in mind these constitutional and electoral constraints.

The US economy after 1945 was the strongest in the world. You need an outline understanding of the basis of the economy, both agrarian and industrial, and also an appreciation of how this strength could affect the economies of other nations.

There were deep divisions within US society; the origins of these, and of the equally significant regional differences, need to be borne in mind. From the pre-war period, you need to remember the isolationist tradition which had been so powerful a constraint on foreign policy. Equally important was the effect on the United States of being plunged into and becoming the key player in the Second World War with the dawning realisation that retreat into isolation was not this time an available option. Victory over Germany and Japan was quickly followed by the onset of the Cold War with the USSR.

The post-war administrations had also inherited, some more happily than others, the tradition of more active internal government fostered during the 1930s by President F D Roosevelt in the 'New Deal'. The issue of the proper role of the state in relation to its citizens and to the separate states of the union, and the limits of their legitimate expectations upon the state, was to be a recurring theme in these years.

Finally a few minutes spent browsing over an atlas of the country and its neighbours would give a more solid basis to your historical comments. Given a map of the boundaries of the nations of the world could you also confidently identify Korea and Vietnam?

ESSENTIAL PRINCIPLES

THE TRUMAN PERIOD

1945–1953

Domestic issues

His achievements in bringing the US from war to a peace-footing and his further development of Roosevelt's social reforming tradition both need assessing. The latter has been seen as half-hearted and it was soon allowed to fall away when the post-war mood began to change.

1946: the mid-term elections saw the Republicans exploiting the anti-communist, anti-Russian feelings generated by the onset of the Cold War to capture control of both Houses of Congress; Nixon entered the House of Representatives after a particularly unscrupulous campaign in California. They used this control to push through legislation preventing anyone after Truman from serving three terms as president; this was generally seen as a slur on the memory of *F D Roosevelt*. They also pushed through the Taft–Hartley Act which sharply restricted the powers of the unions. Truman was unable to block these measures. One clause required union leaders to swear that they were not communists and empowered the President to forbid any strike for 80 days. It was a product of the bitter labour relations of the years after the war. The Republicans at this stage made permanent the House Committee on Un-American activities and stepped up its public hearings. They bear some responsibility for the growing intolerance which became such a prominent feature of American life in the next few years.

“The Republicans promoted intolerance.”

1948 and after: with a democratic majority in Congress after 1948 the Fair Deal social and economic programme was promoted but little was achieved. Truman's responsibility and that of his opponents, Republican and right-wing Democrats from the southern states, need to be evaluated. The civil rights movement became effective only in the 1950s and Truman's moves against discrimination were again limited by his southern Democrat and Republican opponents. He did, however, set up a committee on Civil Rights and tried to help blacks to progress in the civil service as well as bringing to an end colour segregation in the army. The real campaign against discrimination started in the Eisenhower period.

“An unexpected personal triumph.”

Truman's re-election in 1948 was a great personal triumph against all predictions. It was the last election before such events were taken over by television. His second term was dominated by *McCarthyism* and this deserves the closest study as a subject in its own right and as the best single example of intolerance in US society. Again Truman's role has been seen as ambiguous and you need to be able to comment on this; the 'Tutor's Answer' later in this chapter will give you a starting point. The impact of anti-communist feeling on the conduct of US foreign policy in this period is also a common examination topic.

Foreign policy

Controversy, much of it non-historical, continues around Truman's early decision to use nuclear weapons against Japan. A useful exercise would be to think through the strategic reasons which may have influenced him in this, the final episode of the Second World War. The arrival of the nuclear age had, of course, the most profound effects on military strategic thinking and on diplomacy.

“Truman – the Cold War warrior.”

The Cold War: Truman's foreign policy comes down largely to the US role in the Cold War. Truman as the unknown domestic politician who stood up to Stalin deserves examination. Certainly Soviet actions in eastern Europe caused great alarm and indignation in the United States and saving the states of western Europe from the danger of communist takeover was the main motive behind the introduction of the largely successful Marshall Plan. In his years as president the US role was decisive in determining the political shape of post-war Europe and the United States was largely responsible for the creation in 1949 of the North Atlantic Treaty Organisation. The Truman Doctrine, on the need to 'contain' the Soviets, promulgated in 1947, was central to US foreign policy for long after his presidency.

“McCarthyism – a major examination topic.”

The Far East: the re-shaping of Japan after its defeat was entirely an American enterprise with an army of occupation under General MacArthur in the country until 1951. From the view of the United States their policy there was a total success. Truman's failure to give total support to Chiang Kai-Shek on mainland China was much used by McCarthyite opponents, especially as the Republicans prepared for the next presidential election, to claim that he was soft on communism. This may well have led to his much sharper stance on Korea which is in its own right a major topic in the international history of the period.

EISENHOWER'S ACHIEVEMENT

1953–1961

Eisenhower's large majority in the 1952 election owed much to his attractive personality, as conveyed via the television, and to his military reputation, for the chief issue was the conduct, or rather the ending of the Korean War. You should be ready to offer a full explanation of the outcome of the election.

Domestic issues

In domestic politics there is an impression of calm, indeed of lethargy about his administrations. He did little to bring McCarthy to heel (the latter's attempt to investigate communist subversion in the army led to his downfall in 1954). He blocked some small but useful social reforms proposed by the Democrats and many in his governments had too close ties with big business. He was efficient and both wrote and spoke well. Feeling strongly on the issue of race relations he acted resolutely when sending federal troops into little Rock, Alabama, to enforce the Supreme Court decision against educational segregation. *Martin Luther King* came to national prominence in the associated black protests.

race relations

1957: Eisenhower agreed to the *Civil Rights Act* which set up a Commission on Civil Rights to safeguard minority rights.

1960: Eisenhower agreed to a second such act which tried to protect the voting rights of blacks in the South.

Revision exercises

"Questions on Eisenhower less common."

There is not as much to bite on in judging Eisenhower's achievement as there is in the case of Truman, and indeed examination questions on Eisenhower are less common. If you have already studied the 1945–1953 period it would be wise to widen your period of study to at least 1961 and to have enough ideas and information available for a saving question. Look up the role of the vice-president, *Richard Nixon*, and in foreign affairs, the hawkish *John Foster Dulles*.

Foreign policy

Foreign policy saw the end of the Korean War, maintenance of US defences, dubious intervention in Guatemala and in Iran, a resolute and effective resistance to the Israelis, British and French in their 1956 Suez adventure and a limited success in easing relations with the Soviet Union. All this is best seen as useful knowledge for a question on US foreign policy across a wider time span.

THE KENNEDY PRESIDENCY

1961–1963

Often the challenge in questions on Kennedy is to debate whether there was substance behind the image and the rhetoric. Examinations apart he represents an heroic and absorbing moment in US history and one well worth studying for its own sake. There is much truth in the claim that everyone of suitable age in November 1963 can still remember exactly the circumstances in which they heard the news of Kennedy's assassination, a remarkable tribute to the hold he exerted on the popular imagination across the world.

Domestic issues

"Comparative questions very popular."

Questions frequently invite comparison of his actual achievement with that of his successor Lyndon Johnson. For Kennedy the main issues of substance at home were the new Frontier policy; welfare and public works spending; the civil rights issue; using troops to ensure the admittance of a black student, James Meredith, to the University of Mississippi and again, a year later, to secure black access to the University of Alabama. In this presidency the black issue became central to American politics. His civil rights legislative proposals were, at the time of his assassination, blocked in Congress by the Republicans working with the southern Democrats. It has been argued that, whilst sympathetic to black aspirations, Kennedy failed to treat them as a matter of urgency. The record of his brother Robert working as Attorney General to enforce civil rights upon reluctant citizens and state officials through the law courts struck a more positive note.

civil rights

Foreign policy

“A crisis worth studying.”

The dramatic inaugural speech, the equally dramatic visit to Berlin, the formation of the Peace Corps to do good deeds abroad, and, pre-eminently, Kennedy's handling of the Cuban missiles crisis, where he outfaced the Soviet leader Khrushchev and his ally Castro, were the main matters in foreign affairs.

JOHNSON'S ACHIEVEMENT

1963–1969

“Johnson's record on reform.”

Examiners frequently imply that Johnson, unlike Kennedy, had real political achievements to his credit, and then invite you to comment. When this happens it is worth insisting that Kennedy's idealism, public image and martyr's death all greatly assisted Johnson's early achievements and were indeed deliberately exploited to this end by the latter.

Domestic issues

Evaluate the substance of Johnson's 'Great Society' programme and his success in pushing controversial legislation through Congress, where he had had vast experience. Two Civil Rights Acts were passed, 1964 and 1968, a Public Voting Act in 1965 and, in the same year, an Equal Opportunities Act. In 1966 the Development Act set a basis for the restoration of decayed city centres. The Job Corps to assist unemployment and the extension of Medicare and Medicaid added to an impressive list of social initiatives for which you need to learn some illustrative details as the basis for a solid and measured assessment of how far Johnson went towards resolving the nation's social problems. Do not get swept away; be able to indicate some shortcomings if only by pointing to the unrest at the end of his presidency for not all of this was made up of anti-war demonstrations.

Foreign policy

“A major foreign policy topic.”

Against all Johnson's domestic activity must be set the entanglement of the United States in the Vietnam War, which stands as an examination topic in its own right. It provided the most disastrous foreign engagement for the USA in the period and only many years later, when wounds in the United States had begun to heal, was it immortalised in many poor and a handful of really great films. It is best studied in the context of foreign policy since the Second World War. The eventual disruptive effect it had within the US was profound and formed the main reason why, in 1968, Johnson was unwilling to seek re-election.

NIXON, FORD AND CARTER

1969–1981

Even when syllabuses reach forward to very recent times, Presidents Nixon, Ford and Carter have proved less popular than their predecessors with those who set examination papers. The social problems and the foreign policy problems and achievements of the period from 1969 to 1981, however, do seem increasingly likely to figure in questions on such matters across a wider time span. Nixon's efforts in bringing the US troops out of Vietnam, and in bringing about closer relations with China, and Carter's problems with Iran provide important insights for anyone working-up US foreign policy. Both, for very different reasons, also provide unhappy illustration of defects in the use of presidential power at home. Carter could still be due a re-evaluation of an unlucky presidency. Ford seems destined to remain the unknown and indeed never-elected president.

REAGAN AND BUSH

THE REPUBLICAN REVIVAL FROM 1981

“Reagan and Gorbachev.”

The period since 1980 has a unity, in terms of the presidency, that the earlier period did not have. Both the dramatic changes in foreign policy, linked to changing perceptions of the status of the world's superpowers, and the much sharper policies at home, in the fields of economic policy and social programmes, are likely topics for future examination questions. A start could be made by revising the ideas and the information you would use to 'Assess how effectively the policies pursued by President Reagan in the period from 1981 to 1988 promoted the interests of the United States at home and abroad'. Eventually there will no doubt be invitations to compare the record of Bush with that of his Republican predecessor.

DOMESTIC THEMES

As well as revising the period chronologically by presidencies much of the same material, and certainly the same contexts, can be used to prepare for thematic questions across longer periods. Three obvious themes are:

"Obvious themes for examination questions."

- Racial issues and racial legislation.
- Poverty and deprivation – including the inner-cities.
- Racial and political intolerance in American society.

Do not fall into the trap of just recording what the governments did or failed to do. Be ready to write about these subjects in their own right; the causes, the nature, what the subject tells us about US society. Then be ready to adapt this in-depth knowledge, briefly and efficiently, to any question on what a specific president did about the matter. Truman and intolerance; Kennedy/Johnson and poverty/race are particularly popular with examiners. Chapter 25 of H Brogan's *'Pelican History of the United States'* gives greater depth than the textbooks on these matters in an easily accessible and adaptable form. There is of course a wealth of visual news material on these topics.

FOREIGN POLICY THEMES

Much depends here on the precise terms of the syllabus and, more importantly, the pattern of questions in recent past papers. Check these first. Some obvious themes are:

"Foreign policy issues."

- Relations with the Soviet Union and with western Europe, especially in the first decades after 1945.
- Relations with Chiang Kai-Shek 1945–1949.
- The Korean War.
- Relations with communist China.
- Policy in South East Asia from the Korean to the Vietnam War.
- Relations with Latin America as a general topic, inviting an overall judgement of the motives behind policy and the effects of the region generally and in respect to Central America separately.
- More specific questions occur quite frequently on US relations with Cuba, Nicaragua, Panama and Colombia – they may well appear in future papers.
- Relations with Israel and with the Islamic States of the Middle East.

USEFUL INFORMATION

1945	Death of President Roosevelt, Truman took over.
1945–1953	**Truman – President**
	US played a leading role in founding the United Nations.
	Truman social programme (21 points) announced.
1946	Republicans gained control of Congress in the mid-term elections.
	Taft–Hartley labour legislation pushed through by Republicans.
1947	**The Truman Doctrine** formulated: policy of the US must be to support free peoples against attempts at subjugation.
	Marshall Aid for Western Europe.
1948	Truman re-elected President, a personal triumph.
1949	New social programme introduced, the Fair Deal, a partial success.
1949	Chiang Kai-Shek and the Nationalists driven from mainland China.
	US leading role in founding of NATO.
1950	McCarthyism – a national issue.
1950–1953	Korean War
1953–1961	**Eisenhower – President** (re-elected 1956)
	Watchful of communism abroad and socially conservative at home.
1957	Civil Rights Act (also use of federal troops to enforce school desegregation in the South). Start of the Civil Rights movement.
1959	Castro came to power in Cuba.
	First US technicians sent to help South Vietnamese Government.
1960	Kennedy narrowly defeated Nixon to become president.
1961–1963	**Kennedy – President**
	New Frontier social and economic programme.
	Increased number of American 'advisers' in Vietnam.

1961	Kennedy founded the Peace Corps.
1962	Cuban missiles crisis
1963	Kennedy assassinated, Johnson became President.
1963–1969	**Johnson – President**
	Great Society social programme.
1964	Congress passed the Kennedy Civil Rights Act.
1965	Public Voting Act and an Equal Opportunities Act passed.
1965	Bombing of North Vietnam began. Further escalation of American aid until half a million troops committed there.
1968	A further Civil Rights Act.
	Civil disturbances in the US: civil rights, students, war protesters. Johnson did not seek re-election.
	Nixon elected President; war and domestic unrest main issues.
1969–1974	**Nixon – President:** re-elected 1972
	Nixon and Secretary of State, Kissinger, pursued active foreign policies, especially re China and the Soviet Union. Great triumph was to get US troops out of Vietnam.
1974	Nixon resigned after Watergate scandal. Ford became President.
1974–1977	**Ford – President**
1976	Carter elected President
1977–1981	**Carter – President**
1979	Bad relations with Russia over Afghanistan and Iran over American hostages.
1980	Reagan elected President (re-elected 1984).
1981–1989	**Reagan – President**
	Hard economic policies introduced – Reaganomics; socially very conservative. Foreign policy at first fiercely anti-communist but with arrival of Gorbachev mood slowly changed.
	Libya and Nicaragua policies also controversial.
1988	**Bush – President**
1990	Major crisis caused by Iraqi occupation of Kuwait. Bush committed US forces to the defence of Saudi Arabia.
1992	**Clinton – President**
1992	Election of President Clinton ended the years of Republican domination of the presidency.

EXAMINATION QUESTIONS

Q1 Assess the relative importance of the issues which led the United States from 1945 to 1950 to move from alliance to confrontation with the USSR. (London 1989)

Q2 How effectively, as President, did Harry S. Truman resist the forces of intolerance in United States society? (London 1988)

Q3 With what validity can it be argued that Lyndon Johnson did more than John Kennedy to meet the aspirations of black citizens of the United States? (London 1989)

Q4 Why did the 'massive resistance' threatened by the South fail to halt the process of de-segregation after 1954? (AEB 1988)

OUTLINE ANSWERS

Question 1

Introduction: list the issues without any elaboration.

Comment: on each in turn saying how it soured relations:

- Perceived Soviet expansionism in East and Central Europe with Poland, Berlin and Czechoslovakia the flash points.
- Fear as to where Soviet expansion would lead next led to decision to help Western Europe (Truman Doctrine and Marshall Aid) and to push for NATO.

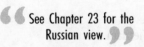

“See Chapter 23 for the Russian view.”

- Fear of Russian communist subversion of democratic states, including communist activity in the US.
- Growing US belief in a world-wide conspiracy including China: greatly sharpened when in 1949 USSR built an atom bomb.

Conclusion: consider relative importance of these issues, acknowledge all were linked together but argue that in the end it was the notion of a godless communist conspiracy, however unjustified, which created the climate established by 1950 in which to most Americans the Soviets threatened everything they believed central to their way of life.

Question 2

See the 'Tutor's Answer' at the end of this section.

Question 3

Introduction: start by briefly indicating likely aspirations of black citizens as an end to racial discrimination and as an escape from the poverty trap in which so many were, whether in the deep south or in northern city ghettos. Agree that in practical terms there is much validity in this claim.

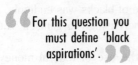

> For this question you must define 'black aspirations'.

Kennedy: explore what John Kennedy and Robert Kennedy did but make central point the stalling of Civil Rights law in Congress.

Johnson: establish Johnson's more impressive legislation on both civil rights and poverty.

Conclusion: two qualifications are needed however. Many black aspirations not met by Johnson, for example, the unrest in 1968; and Johnson legislation owed much to climate created by the Kennedy rhetoric and 'martyrdom'.

Question 4

Introduction: central part of the answer lies in the growing self-confidence of the black community, this was linked to the war years and to the relative freedom enjoyed by blacks in northern cities. An economic, social and political leadership emerged which meant that the poor blacks of the south did not fight alone, the freedom riders, for example.

Other factors:

- The media, especially television, meant that the black cause and the manifest unreasonableness of the white bigots was sharply and regularly exposed. The 'Black Cause' then caught the imagination of white liberal Americans and it became a national fight.
- The political power of the old south was in decline. Truman had won the 1948 presidential election despite a segregationist candidate, Thurmond, standing and this had begun to set the Democrat Party free from the control of its southern wing. Kennedy was ultra-cautious but came to realise that he had to support Civil Rights if he was to hold the northern liberal vote. Johnson came to the same conclusion. Both eventually were prepared to use the full power of the state to end segregation.
- The rulings of the Supreme Court made it difficult for politicians to continue to support segregation. The international reputation of the USA pointed to the same message.
- There were then a lot of decent people who had come to see that segregation was intolerable in a united democratic society. Some showed great courage in asserting this: a few, black and white, gave their lives for the cause.

Conclusion: in the end there was no 'massive resistance' just some unattractive demagogues and hoodlums. The respectable white citizens of the south, especially the business community did not want de-segregation but also did not want trouble on the scale which was developing, preferring to accept the inevitable imposed upon them by a mixture of black pressure, northern Liberal conviction and the liberal rulings of the Supreme Court.

A TUTOR'S ANSWER TO QUESTION 2

In the period from 1945 to 1952 intolerance in United States society had three major aspects. There was the deep seated intolerance of many whites to black aspirations for a

> "And in this question explain your understanding of 'the forces of intolerance'."

decent life and some form of equality with the whites. Then there was the class-based intolerance of some important elements of American 'Big Business' to the aspirations of the working-class wishing to organise themselves into effective Trade Unions which could defend them against exploitation and raise their standard of living in the free-wheeling capitalist society where little legal protection existed. Finally, and most sharply, there was the fierce intolerance by right-wing Americans for anyone of a liberal disposition who could conveniently be labelled a communist and therefore a potential traitor at least. Truman's response to each of these forms of intolerance will be considered in turn.

Intolerance of the blacks in the United States was deep seated especially in the southern states where it was often given a legalised basis. Riots during the war had also demonstrated popular intolerance of blacks immigrating to the cities of the north to take industrial jobs. It has to be conceded however that acts of intolerance did not achieve the high profile that they were to have in and beyond the Eisenhower period. In this area Truman did not have to confront a crisis of intolerance. In consequence he did only a little to combat it. Truman came from Missouri, where intolerance of blacks was endemic, but he realised how important to the Democratic Party the increasingly organised voting strength of the black vote was becoming.

> "Truman's record is limited."

His actions were modest. There was action to restrict the use of federal money in racially segregated housing projects, he ordered the desegregation of the armed forces and opened the civil service more widely to black employees. He considered, but did not pursue, civil rights legislation and appointed, in Dr Bunche, a black American to be US Ambassador at the United Nations. The deep seated popular intolerance by whites remained largely untouched in this period, as did the institutionalised discrimination of the south. In the 1948 presidential election southern Democrats, annoyed at the increasingly liberal stance on racial issues being taken by northern leaders of the party, though not particularly by Truman himself, fielded an independent presidential candidate in Strom Thurmond. Truman nevertheless won re-election and so, perhaps accidentally, helped to free the most likely party of reform from the southern veto on progressive race legislation. But that was for the future.

In the field of labour relations the Taft Hartley Act, pushed through by the Republican majority in Congress, is legitimately described as an instance of tolerance. The closed shop was banned, unions could be sued for breach of contract in the event of a strike and their leaders had to swear that they were not communists. The Republicans sought to restrict the powers and the influence of the big labour unions, not least because of their links with the Democrat Party. Public opinion was often anti-union, a result of the numerous strikes of the 1946–1947 period, and, faced by the hostile majority in Congress, Truman made little effort to resist the measure by which the Republican Party paid part of their debt to the 'big business' interests which backed them. The sufferers were the host of unprotected workers who were even less protected from exploitation than before.

The clause in the Taft Hartley Act requiring denial of communist affiliations reflected the growing political intolerance in United States society which reached its climax between 1950 and 1953 in the increasingly manic persecutions of suspected 'Reds' orchestrated by Senator Joe McCarthy. The bullying tactics, the pursuit of the undoubtedly innocent, the assumption of guilt by association or by silence of anyone in the centre or allegedly to the left of centre in American political life make this the most serious instance of active and deliberate intolerance in the Truman period.

> "No clear stand against McCarthy."

Truman's record in resisting the unattractive Senator and his persecuting bandwagon is at best an ambiguous one. The lies and the bluster at the heart of McCarthyism destroyed the credibility of the State Department and the charge of being soft on communism, even treasonably soft, lapped at the doors of the presidency itself. Privately Truman disdained McCarthy but the public frenzy was such that he could do nothing to undermine the force of the Senator's increasingly wild attacks. The international climate, the fate of Chiang Kai-Shek and the exploding of the first Russian atomic bomb, had made the American public too fearful of the 'Red Menace' for reason to prevail. The Republican Party rode the new mood on the way to the 1952 presidential election. Truman feared to resist it, he merely failed to endorse the Senator and the evil intolerance of McCarthyism rolled on into the Eisenhower Presidency.

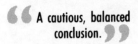

“A cautious, balanced conclusion.”

Truman was fundamentally a decent and an intelligent man; he was also an astute politician and politics is the art of the possible. He mounted no aggressive campaigns to fight intolerance on any front. On the other hand, unlike many in the Republican Party and within the southern ranks of his own party he never stooped to promoting intolerance of fellow Americans for either personal or political advantage. His social reforms, in the New Deal tradition, may have helped a little to make the United States a more kindly and tolerant society but their effectiveness should not be over-stated.

USEFUL SOURCES OF INFORMATION

General reading

H Brogan, *The Pelican History of the United States*, Penguin 1986: the last 90 pages of this highly readable general history provide a wealth of information and ideas in an easily accessible form.

J R Brooks, *The United States of America 1919–1980*, Harrap 1982

J B Watson, *Success in World History since 1945*, John Murray 1989: the USA is part of a wider canvas but the relevant chapters are packed with information on both domestic and foreign policy matters.

Further reading

S E Ambrose, *Rise to Globalism: American Foreign Policy 1938–1980*, Penguin 1980.

P Calvocoressi, *World Politics since 1945*, Longman (3rd edition) 1977: for foreign affairs in the period 1945 to 1975.

P Kennedy *The Rise and Fall of the Great Powers*. Fontana 1988: an ambitious student should consider reading the last two chapters of this exciting work.

Linked topic areas

Since 1945 United States foreign policy and its economy might have had a great impact on social, economic and political events and trends throughout the World. A small minority of students allow pro- or anti-US feelings to get in the way of historical analysis and explanation. Avoid this. Topics which might well be opened up very quickly from a study of US foreign policy include:

- The Cold War (see Chapters 23, 25 and 26)
- The Korean War
- The Vietnam War
- Central and South American politics

CHAPTER 25

COMMUNISM IN CHINA

GETTING STARTED

To be able to judge why, by 1949, the Communists had succeeded in gaining power in mainland China you need an outline knowledge of the chaotic political and archaic social conditions that existed there prior to the Second World War. Japanese aggression against China, both in 1931 and from 1937 to 1945, is particularly important and, like many other aspects of this topic, is best understood in association with a reasonable sized map of the country in its regional setting. Chinese names can be difficult to remember and a secure grasp of the geography could help make the topic as a whole much more concrete.

The roles, in the war against Japan, of the Kuomintang under Chiang Kai-Shek and of the communists under Mao Tse Tung, and also their own mutual rivalry, are important for an appreciation of the confused state of affairs in China when the Second World War came to its abrupt end.

The Chinese government in 1979 asked that the spelling of Chinese names should be standardised but, more than a decade later, the new forms are only slowly becoming more widely used. Beijing for Peking is the most common example. Mao Tse Tung becomes Mao Zedong and is used in this form below. Chiang Kai-Shek is unchanged, though there are variations in use, and only time will reveal how common Zhou-Enlai (Chou En-lai) or Xianggang (Hong Kong) will be in the future. Learn one form and stick to it: displays of knowledge through quoting both traditional and standardised versions are not likely to impress. In practice the only real difficulty will arise in the possible additional problems created in remembering the names of a handful of political figures below the highest rank.

It seems likely that events in China will remain headline news in British newspapers if only because of its developing links with Hong Kong. An intelligent interest in reports from modern China should do a great deal to develop your overall grasp of the country's history, especially if you remember to use that map when appropriate.

ESSENTIAL PRINCIPLES

NATIONALISTS AND COMMUNISTS

1945–1949

"A very common examination topic."

The reasons why Nationalist (Kuomintang) control of mainland China collapsed and the main events of the Civil War between 1945 and 1949 are linked topics of major importance. They can be approached through a study of the numerous weaknesses in the Nationalist position, including political, economic and military matters, and also through study of the strengths – political, social and economic – of the communists. The roles of the USA and the USSR in these years are important to the outcome. The main issues involved are contained in the 'Tutor's Answer' at the end of this chapter. The survival and varied fortunes of the Nationalists in Taiwan, previously Formosa, across subsequent decades are then a less important theme in most syllabuses, though Taiwan's relations with the mainland regime remains important for a study of Communist Chinese foreign policy. This is exactly the sort of topic which, if it is ever to make much sense, needs the use of a map.

THE COMMUNIST STATE

1949–1956

"Communist political control."

A 1949 conference, in which non-communists took part, drew up a common programme which included the end of all foreign privileges and property; the confiscation of nationalist assets; land and marriage reform. Leadership of the country was in the hands of the Chinese Communist Party (CCP) which in the next few years set up a highly centralised administration which took over from the military and which was supervised at each stage by party committees. The CCP Politburo had control over the central administration of the state and Mao as Chairman of the Party was the key figure in the power structure. The Constitution, establishing a one-party state, was not in operation until 1954.

Reforms

"Early social and economic reforms."

The most urgent business was to carry out land reform throughout China, confiscating the holdings of the landlords and handing them to the poorer peasants. This alone produced a social revolution in the rural areas, wiping out the previous social leadership. This process, under the Agrarian Reform Law of 1950, and accompanied by much violence and some attacks on the holdings of wealthier peasants, was completed by 1952. The Marriage Law reform, allowing both sexes free choice of partners took much longer to be accepted. Anti-corruption drives in the cities saw the end of gambling and prostitution but not, at first, of private businesses, though by 1956 almost all had been nationalised. The First Five Year Plan started in 1953 and was largely devoted to the development of heavy industry but included a programme of bringing together peasant land holdings to be farmed collectively which had by 1956 successfully swept away the individual ownership of land.

In 1950 an alliance was signed with the Soviet Union which gave the Chinese communists some shelter from the growing hostility of the United States and also some economic aid, though from the start there were deep Chinese suspicions of the Russians.

SOCIAL RE-ORGANISATION

1956–1960s

Fundamental changes had been achieved by 1956 but Mao became increasingly fearful of their direction; alarmed by Khrushchev's criticism of Stalin's excesses, and generally concerned by the direction in which the USSR had been led, he increasingly developed his ideas of the need for continuous revolution. In 1956 he inaugurated the '*Hundred Flowers Campaign*' to encourage self-criticism. Party support was lukewarm but student criticism of the system took off in 1957 and reached such proportions that it had, with difficulty, to be controlled. Party opposition brought the campaign to an abrupt end and many who had joined in the criticism were now punished, being dismissed from their posts and sent into rural exile. Mao had lost the argument.

"The 'Great Leap Forward'."

At the end of 1957 he promoted the '*Great Leap Forward*' which was the second Five Year Plan, industrial output was to double and agricultural output rise by a third. The economy was to be organised into communes which would promote industry as well as agricultural growth.

All this caused much economic dislocation and even food shortages and it was, in the early 1960s, much toned down and with central control restored (communes were for example greatly reduced in size so that their number trebled from the 25,000 of 1958; private plots were permitted and a free market in some foodstuffs allowed). It is important to understand what was attempted in the 'Great Leap Forward', if only to be able to illustrate Mao's ideas and evaluate his contribution to China's development.

THE CULTURAL REVOLUTION

"Mao's ideal of the 'continuing revolution'."

"The Cultural Revolution ended in chaos."

By 1962 Mao was again fearful of reaction and in 1963–1964 pushed through the *'Four Clean-ups Campaign'* of purges of those holding suspect ideas. This was overtaken in 1966 by the greatest of the upheavals he imposed on China – the *'Cultural Revolution'* – which was linked to an attack on Soviet revisionist ideas. It was anti-bureaucratic, opposed to intellectuals and experts and against allegedly 'Russian' ideas which favoured more consumer goods and better relations with the west. Rivals of Mao in the CCP were removed, and for Mao this may have been one of the main purposes. Since the 1950s Mao had increasingly stood above the CCP and the Cultural Revolution which he launched can be seen as an attack on the party in the cause of continuous revolution which he held so dear. Attention has, however, mainly focused on the revolutionary ferment in the country at large with gangs of youthful *'Red Guards'* roaming the country carrying little red books containing the *'Thoughts of Chairman Mao'* and for two years bringing chaos and disruption in their wake. There grew up a cult portraying Mao as a superhuman saviour of his country. Many intellectuals and people in positions of authority, very broadly defined, were forced from their jobs and made to do physical labour on the land. The Cultural Revolution came close to wrecking the economy and the revolutionary fervour proved difficult to control. Even though Mao in 1967 called on the army to restore order it was 1970 before calm was achieved. The episode provides evidence and ideas central to any attempt to judge Mao's achievements and is a common examination topic in its own right.

THE DEATH OF MAO

"Assess China's progress from 1949 to 1976."

CHINA TO 1976

From the end of the Cultural Revolution to Mao's death in 1976 there was a series of sharp struggles involving jockeying to secure the succession after his death but also to influence the direction to be taken by the communist state. The ideological quarrels did not end in 1970. A new Constitution was published in 1975: the CCP remained at the centre of power and Mao was not only its Chairman but also Head of State and Commander of the Armed Forces.

1976 is an obvious point at which to attempt an assessment of what had been achieved in China since 1949 and the 'Student's Answer' at the end of this chapter (together with the examiner comments on it) should provide some ideas.

POST-MAO

"Post-1976 patterns are more difficult to trace."

This has proved too confusing a period to provide easy study themes. Mao's work has been re-evaluated, especially his promotion of the Cultural Revolution but in the context that his earlier achievements far outweighed what have become known as the *'ten bad years'*. His successors have worked to open up relations with the West, have pursued a policy of trying to control population growth, of which Mao would not have approved, and appeared to be encouraging a policy of liberalisation of Chinese life. Then, in 1989, the leadership felt that this move was getting out of control and crushed the rising expectations of many young Chinese in the Tiananmen Square massacres.

The direction in which China will move from this point will provide endless interest for anyone who has studied its history since 1949. It will, however, for the moment, be quite difficult to predict what form examination questions on the period after 1976 are likely to take.

FOREIGN RELATIONS

Foreign relations and policy: the changing pattern of relations with the USA and the USSR are central and their interaction with domestic developments need to be noted, especially in the case of the USSR. The issue of China's membership of the UN; the Korean War and the Vietnam question are best considered as extensions of the uneasy relations with the USA.

A map survey of China's frontiers throws up a list of other topics:

- The offshore islands of Quemoy and Matsu link to the continuing nationalist presence in Taiwan.
- The frontier disputes with the USSR and over Mongolia.
- The control of Tibet.
- The frontier disputes with India.
- Relations with Pakistan.
- Concern over Afghanistan.
- The negotiation with Britain over the future of Hong Kong.

CHINA UNDER COMMUNISM

AN EVALUATION

After 1949 the various directions taken by the communist regime within China are best studied chronologically, though an overall assessment of the communist achievement needs to be made at certain key points and, as noted above, particularly on the death of Mao in 1976. One theme worth bearing in mind throughout is that of changes in the organisation of the economy, particularly changes related to land ownership and agriculture. From this you could comment on the improvements in the material and social conditions of the mass of both rural and urban Chinese. In terms of education, housing, clothing, pensions and health facilities Chinese provision even after 40 years of communist rule would seem rudimentary by western standards but in none of these fields could China be compared with vast areas of the Third World. The lives and prospects of women have been transformed. Education and health services have been greatly expanded. Consumer goods remain in short supply but many families have bicycles and sewing machines. Freedom, and intellectuals, have not fared well. Communist China is a highly centralised authoritarian state with a constant emphasis on serving the community and obeying the Party; there is a vast bureaucracy and much inefficiency. Immediately prior to the 1989 clampdown there was evidence of growing dissatisfaction amongst the young with the regimentation of their lives.

“Evaluating life in Communist China.”

Exam questions

For examination purposes you need to have an idea of the main points you will make if you are invited to assess the progress made by China since 1949. In presenting your assessment remember to set it against the chaotic state of the country when the communists gained power and also that at that time there were some 500 million inhabitants, a number that was to double in the course of the next 25 years.

USEFUL INFORMATION

1931		Japanese attacked Manchuria
1934–1935		Communist 'Long March' north to Yenan to avoid attack by the Nationalists (the Kuomintang) under Chiang Kai-Shek.
1937		Japanese at war against China
1937–1945		Uneasy alliance between Communists and the Nationalists.
1945		Japanese forces in China surrendered.
1945–1949		Struggle for supremacy between the Communists and Nationalists.
1949		Chiang Kai-Shek and Nationalists driven from mainland to Formosa (Taiwan).
	Oct	People's Republic of China (PRC) proclaimed.
		US blocked membership of United Nations.
1950–1951		China took over Tibet
1950–1953		**The Korean War**
1950		Under the Agrarian Law land re-distribution to peasants began.
		Sino-Soviet Treaty of Friendship signed.
1953–1957		**First Five Year Plan**
1954		People's Republic of China (PRC) constitution established.
		Organisation of farming co-operatives.
1956		After death of Stalin relations with Soviet Union worsened.
1957		**Hundred Flowers Bloom** (and censorship soon re-imposed).

1958	Collectives began to be merged into Communes.
	The Great Leap Forward – Second Five Year Plan.
1959	Tibetan rebellion – Dalai Lama fled to India.
1960	Khrushchev withdrew Soviet aid.
1962	Border war with India in Assam.
1963–1964	**Purges** 'The Four Clean-ups'
1964	China became a nuclear power.
1966	Start of the **Cultural Revolution**.
1967	Army began to restore order.
1968	Mao ended the Cultural Revolution but order took two further years to be totally restored.
1968–1976	Jockeying for position in succession to Mao.
1972	US President Nixon visited Beijing; sign of improving relations.
1975	New Constitution. Central role of Chinese Communist Party (CCP) continued. Mao Head of State and Commander of the Armed Forces.
1976	Deaths of Chou En-lai and Mao.
1981	Trial and conviction of the 'Gang of Four' and their supporters.
	Emergence of Deng Xiaoping as the leading political figure.
1984	Agreement with Britain on the future of Hong Kong.
1986	Growing student protests for a more liberal regime.
1989	Student protests crushed in Tiananmen Square. The regime continued to pursue repressive policies.
1992–1993	Tensions between Britain and China, over the 1997 handover of Hong Kong.

EXAMINATION QUESTIONS

Q1 'The Chinese Nationalist debacle in 1947–1949 was a failure less of arms than of aims.' Discuss. (London 1989)

Q2 Examine the reasons for the triumph of the Chinese communists in 1949. (Cambridge 1986)

Q3 Why and with what results did China form communes from the farming cooperatives in 1958? (Cambridge 1986)

Q4 'He was more concerned with ideological purity than with the practical results of the policies he advocated.' Discuss the validity of this verdict on Mao Zedong in the period 1949 to 1976. (London 1990)

Q5 Compare and contrast the Great Leap Forward (1958–60) with the Great Proletarian Cultural Revolution (1966–76). (Cambridge 1989)

OUTLINE ANSWERS

Question 1

Note: First read the 'Tutor's Answer' to the very similar Question 2; this question requires the focus to be more on the Nationalists.

Introduction: In many ways the Nationalists were militarily stronger than the communists in 1945, in numbers and equipment and controlled the cities. Communists won because they captured peasant support and also because of the unattractive image of their opponents.

Consider: reasons so many Chinese abandoned the Nationalists – corruption; represented the old privileged classes.

Conclusion: military mistakes played their part in the Nationalist debacle, for example, getting trapped in northern cities and reduced US support, but in the end driven from mainland because the bulk of the Chinese population preferred the communist message.

Question 2

See the 'Tutor's Answer' later in this section.

Question 3

Reasons: Why communes were first formed:

- The collective farms developed in the early 1950s were too small to organise the rural economy, particularly to organise urgent water conservation and flood protection schemes.
- Ideology played a part – the communes would be the new social unit which would replace the bourgeois state, for example it had its own military units.

Results: closely tied to the outcome of the Great Leap Forward because the new communes were the instrument used to impose the Leap. In this process the idea of the communes being self-governing and replacing the State got lost: they became agents of the central state and so the dream of de-centralisation never came about. The Leap and its agents the communes, ended in economic disaster with terrible harvests in 1960 and 1961, some estimates say that as many as 20 million people died of starvation and it was lack of food which ended the experiment of the Leap. There was a return to private peasant plots and more of a free market in food.

Conclusion: for a time in 1963–1964 it looked as though the collective organisation of farming would collapse but enough of the commune ideal survived for it to become central to the later Cultural Revolution and to hold a permanent place in the Chinese economy. Its chief economic achievement had been to provide the economic organisation for dealing with the very important problem of water control. This was the permanent economic legacy of the founding of the communes in 1958.

Question 4

See the 'Student's Answer' later in this section.

Question 5

Compare: argue first that the two had much in common:

"Comparing the Great Leap Forward and the Cultural Revolution."

- Both originated with Mao and arose from his fear that the communist revolution was stagnating.
- Both were part of his insistence on the continuing revolution.
- Both were opposed by senior party members.
- Both ended in a high level of economic, social and organisational chaos – give examples from both.

Contrast: show the ways they were very different:

- The Great Leap Forward – two major themes were the need for economic reorganisation and an anti-Soviet theme. The structuring of the economy around the commune was at the heart of the Leap: it was a genuine attempt at radical economic reorganisation.
- The Cultural Revolution – ideology rather than economics, explain the main ideological features. It was also pushed to greater extremes and the results were far more serious than the Leap.

Conclusion: because both came from Mao's ideas of revolution it must be agreed that the Cultural Revolution was a logical consequence of the failure of the Great Leap to achieve his objectives. In Mao's mind at least they shared a common purpose.

Note: Now read through the 'Student's Answer' with its examiner comments at the end of this section.

A TUTOR'S ANSWER TO QUESTION 2

"This question needs more than just a military explanation."

The triumph of the Chinese communists in driving their opponents, the Kuomintang, from the mainland to ignominious sanctuary on Formosa was essentially a military achievement which four years earlier had seemed unthinkable to the leaders of both the USA and the USSR. It rested on the initially unrecognised strengths of the communist forces and on the more evident ineffectiveness of the Nationalists. The triumph however requires more than a purely military explanation and had its origins in the warfare which had ravaged China in the period 1937 to 1945. It involved a battle for the hearts and minds of the Chinese people as much as a quest for military victory.

In 1945 the communists controlled areas of north China with a population of one hundred million. Mao Zedong had by then created an effective honest administration based on the Communist Party. His own position as leader was secure and, through speeches and pamphlets he had begun to impose his vision on the entire communist cause. Morale amongst Mao's followers was high and he commanded perhaps as many as three million armed men, experienced fighters against the Japanese and particularly adept at guerrilla warfare. Large scale fighting had begun in 1946 mainly because of the intransigence of Mao's opponents and the early victories went to them, with the communists forced to evacuate some areas.

The Nationalist forces under Chiang Kai-Shek outnumbered the communists and, as the chief beneficiaries of American aid, were much better equipped than their opponents. Their armies however suffered from serious weaknesses which, at this early stage of the war, were to be more damaging to their cause than the strengths of the communists. Chiang himself was a remote leader who surrounded himself with puppets rather than effective military advisers; he even ceased to listen to his American allies. He made major strategic mistakes, the most serious being to commit many of his best troops to the occupation of Manchuria where they became trapped as isolated garrisons holding desperately on to a shrinking number of towns, unable even to keep open the rail links between them. Chiang then compounded this initial error for, when the military situation deteriorated he refused to pull back these Manchurian troops to help strengthen the new crucial southern front. Towards the end of the civil war the best forces of the Nationalists were irrelevant to its outcome and this was almost entirely the fault of Chiang Kai-Shek.

“Mistakes by Chiang Kai-Shek.”

The command structure under Chiang was badly co-ordinated and ill-led by its officers, who were often appointed because of their connections and more interested in making a personal profit than fighting an arduous campaign. Many of the ordinary soldiers were unwilling conscripts from the civilian population of the areas still under Nationalist control. Provisions and conditions of life for these men were totally unsatisfactory and this led to a high desertion rate despite a brutal disciplinary sytem. Many deserters moved immediately across to the ranks of their former enemies. The Nationalist record in fighting the Japanese had been unimpressive, their troop movements had been slow and cumbersome and they had been reluctant to act in a co-ordinated effort, preferring their own security to assisting beleaguered colleagues: these weaknesses were to be cruelly exposed by the increasingly confident mobile guerrilla tactics employed by the communists.

“Poor Nationalist military record.”

In the autumn of 1948 and the first weeks of 1949 the Nationalist army was harried and routed, first in Manchuria and then on the North China Plain, losing almost one million men and leaving south China open to the virtually unscathed communist forces.

The scale of the Nationalist collapse requires more than just a military explanation for it rests in no small measure on their losing the support and goodwill of the Chinese population in the areas that they had controlled. The corruption, the lawlessness of the troops, the brutality of the administration all played a part. It was not only that the Nationalists appeared increasingly as the party of the rich and privileged, of war profiteering middle-class businessmen and exploiting landlords but that they could not even run the free market economy efficiently. Accelerating inflation led to the collapse of the currency which, with high taxation, destroyed the savings of even their supporters so that, within the cities which they still controlled, they lost the support of the students and even of the middle-class. Their own corrupt practices undermined any effort at economic reform and by 1948 Chiang Kai-Shek himself came to recognise how ‘decrepit and degenerate’ his Kuomintang had become.

“A crucial loss of popular support.”

The other side of this explanation demands parallel recognition of the strengths which the communists brought to their cause. Their fight against the Japanese had enabled the communists to build themselves into a mass movement through an appeal to national sentiment against the foreign enemy. They increasingly captured the support of the peasants by reducing rents and loan interest rates and from 1947 they embarked, in the areas they controlled, on a policy of land redistribution in favour of the poorer peasants which brought them invaluable support. The sympathy and the support of the peasants was of course particularly important in helping their countryside-based guerrilla campaign against the Nationalist-held cities, not least in denying the latter essential food supplies.

“The basis of communist popularity.”

In military terms the communists benefited from the errors and weaknesses of their opponents. The hardened core of veterans who had gained military experience in fighting the Japanese may, initially, have been less well equipped than the Kuomintang forces but their morale, mobility and clear command structures compensated for this. Soon they were joined by deserters from their enemy and became the recipients of captured supplies, often

American in origin. The first stages of the communist victory came from their ability to command the rural areas of north China and Manchuria and in explaining this it is difficult to decide whether to lay stress on their own military mobility and flexibility or on the support of the rural population. The two seemed to go hand in hand. Once the early victories had isolated many of the best Nationalist troops in the cities of the north then the victory came from its own momentum. The disastrous miscalculations of Chiang had left the south open to occupation with virtually no opposition to the headlong progress of the communists.

> "Superior communist strategy."

The communist victory owed nothing to outside help. Immediately after the defeat of the Japanese the USSR had appeared to favour the Kuomintang and certainly failed to hand over Manchuria, which it had occupied, to the communists, so that it became possible for the Nationalists to take it over. Even at a late stage Stalin had little faith that this peasant army could gain control and, as late as 1949, with south China wide open he was urging caution and compromise on Mao. The significance of what had by that stage happened in the North was lost also on the West which was by then helpless to stop the communist sweep south. Later the US Government was accused of betraying Chiang through providing inadequate financial and military aid. However such foreign aid could be a double-edged sword by strengthening the national appeal of the communists, and there was in any case no evidence that it would be used to fight the communists rather than go to line the pockets of Chiang's more corrupt followers. If Chiang could only hope to win through foreign aid then, in a country the size of China, he had already almost certainly lost. The only difficult issue is whether Nationalist weaknesses and errors or the high morale and military skill of his opponents contributed more to the outcome.

> "Foreign aid irrelevant to the outcome."

A STUDENT'S ANSWER TO QUESTION 4

> "Explain what sort of a country Mao wished China to be."
>
> "A longer opening section needed."

Before starting to answer this question it is first necessary to define what is meant by ideological purity. This relates to Mao's views on how the country should apply Marxism to the governing of China. He wanted to keep the revolutionary spirit alive in China and was worried that an elite would be established who would become privileged and corrupt as in the Soviet Union.

In the first years after the Communists came to power in 1949 the Chinese pursued practical policies, re-distributing the land to the peasants and allowing private businesses to continue in the towns. The USSR helped the Chinese to build up heavy industries like railways and electricity in the 1950s and at the same time the peasant lands were put into collectives. During this period Chinese production increased sharply.

> "Good: it is concentrating on Mao as the question expects."

Mao became concerned about how the revolution was developing after he had encouraged the Chinese people to give their opinions of communist rule during the Hundred Flowers Campaign in 1957. The answers showed a great lack of sympathy with what was happening and Mao became very alarmed and re-imposed censorship. In any case Stalin had died and Mao had begun to distrust the heavy industry development that the Russians had encouraged. He was determined that the revolution should continue.

This led to the Great Leap Forward which aimed to bring back the enthusiasm for the Revolution. The aim was to set up communes all over the country which would group together the collective farms and also include industry, even small iron and steel furnaces. In the communes private family life and private possessions were discouraged and a great propaganda campaign was mounted to promote the Great Leap. But it all ended in disaster as famine struck and millions died from lack of food. Mao was blamed for all of this and lost a lot of his political power and his successors tried to restore the economy.

In 1966 came the Cultural Revolution which was Mao's biggest attempt to impose ideological purity. Gangs of young Red Guards went round the country to 'encourage' people to follow the teachings of

Mao who had come back into the limelight by doing his great swim in the River Yangtse. During the Cultural Revolution a great personality campaign made him out to be an almost god-like figure was to be worshipped. Mao attacked the other Communist leaders and ordered a purge of the communist party. His ideas were put in a little Red Book and distributed everywhere. The campaign concentrated on young people and tried to bring them back to revolutionary ideals. Mao was afraid that the young people who had never been involved in the communist conquest of China would turn their backs on socialism. He was also afraid that party members were becoming privileged bureaucrats and corrupt. After the death of Stalin he had begun to feel that this is what had happened in Russia and he was determined not to let China go the same way. It all ended in political chaos as the Red Guards got out of hand. Skilled workers and professional people were forced out of their jobs and made to go and work in farming. This was disastrous for the economy and for education. Many millions of 'enemies' of the Cultural Revolution finished up in jail or in concentration camps. In the end it all went too far even for Mao and the army was brought in to restore order and bring the revolution to an end.

Mao was by now an old man and played only a small part in politics after the Cultural Revolution. Mao died in 1976 and a fierce political struggle to decide his successor followed.

“Too much packed into one paragraph.”

“Relate this to the question of 'practical results'.”

“No real conclusion relevant to the question set.”

EXAMINER COMMENTS

An examiner might well feel that this essay covers the right ground (for example it avoids the trap of a long introduction on Mao prior to 1949) but could have done it more effectively. You could usefully skim through a textbook account on China from 1949 to 1976 and identify the references to Mao (using the index to the same end could be more efficient) and then consider in what ways you would try to strengthen this essay in terms both of additional information and further comments. This commentary will make only a few suggestions.

We do need (Paragraph 1) to understand Mao's view of what constituted ideological purity and the reference to Marxism is essential but it does need drawing out in terms of where political power was to lie (with the Communist Party), what social and economic structures were needed and the relationships between the State and the individual. What sort of a country was China to be, according to Mao's Marxist vision? This is hinted at later but would have been more effectively set out at the start. All this means a longer opening section but this is a brief essay and time should be available for such expansion.

The second paragraph's great virtue is that it deals directly with Mao, who elsewhere in the essay tends to get lost in the general account. Here, and in the next paragraph on the Great Leap Forward, the distinction between practical and theoretical developments needs to be pointed out quite specifically. Show the examiner that you are aware of the terms of the question.

The student is right to see the central importance of the Cultural Revolution in an assessment of Mao's intentions and the first part of the paragraph is effective in bringing this out. It all deserves elaboration but instead the paragraph (which is in any case far too long) drifts into a commentary on the results of the Cultural Revolution. Is this at all relevant in an essay on Mao's motives?

The ending of the essay is weak and far too abrupt. It looks very like a final essay on the paper where either ideas or time have run out! At the least it needs some recognition that by the time of Mao's death he had immense practical achievements to his credit. It also needs to offer a final conclusion on where the writer stands in relation to the two views of Mao which the title has set in opposition to each other. Where does this student wish to strike the balance?

The examiner would probably see this as a promising skeleton of an answer but would also feel that the student, writing to this title, has failed to stay close enough to Mao. An example of this is that the essay does not make the telling point that, as first the Great

Leap Forward and then the Cultural Revolution brought chaos to China, it was Mao's lieutenants who had to initiate the necessary retrenchment and drag him along reluctantly with them. This point could indeed be made central to the answer to this question.

USEFUL SOURCES OF INFORMATION

General reading

P J Bailey, *China in the Twentieth Century*, Blackwell 1988: the last twenty-five pages contain an invaluable commentary, including reference to the conflicting interpretations of other historians.

J B Watson, *Success in World History since 1945*, John Murray 1989: this work, as its title indicates, has a much wider brief than China alone. It has one chapter packed with useful information relevant to this topic and it offers a valuable introduction to China in the period.

Further reading

J Gray, *Rebellions and Revolutions: China from the 1800s to the 1980s*, Oxford University Press 1990: readable and up-to-date, this is the obvious step up after textbook reading.

E E Moise, *Modern China: A History*, Longman 1986: the later chapters vividly bring this topic to life and provide a first class source of information and ideas.

P Calvocoressi, *World Politics since 1945*, Longman 1977: especially for the international dimension.

Linked topic areas

- China, Japan, the USA and the League of Nations in the 1930s
- The course of the Second World War in the Pacific Region
- The Far East (including Japan) since 1945
- Sino-Russian relations since 1949
- Sino-American relations since 1949
- The Korean War

CHAPTER 26

WESTERN EUROPE SINCE 1945

GETTING STARTED

You need a map of Europe at the end of the Second World War (see page 245). Contrast it to the inter-war map and note in particular the loss of territory by Germany and its division into separate military zones of occupation. That occupied by the Soviets became East Germany and that occupied by the troops of the United States, Britain and France became West Germany. Be aware that the outcome of the war was decided largely by Soviet manpower and United States technology.

The period when world politics had been centred on London, Paris, and Berlin, was coming to an abrupt end. Look at a world political map at any time between 1900 and 1939 and note the vast imperial possessions of the European States; those Empires too were about to come crumbling down. On the European map plot the line of the new divide between east and west which Churchill in 1946 labelled 'an Iron Curtain'. These realities and the appalling destruction and bloodshed created by national rivalries and political extremism provided the context in which west Europeans had to learn to survive and to thrive. Internally Western Europe recovered from the destruction of its national economies in the war with remarkable speed. The division of Europe into two opposing zones remained in place until the opening of the last decade of the century. The changed relationship with the rest of the world, which had emerged quite rapidly after 1945, is almost certainly a permanent one.

The most common questions in a vast area of study relate to the origins of the Cold War (where it would be advisable to say something about the Soviet view of events which is touched on in Chapter 23), German recovery and political life to circa 1970, France under the Fourth and Fifth Republics, and the emergence of the European Community. Students seem particularly to welcome questions on Adenauer and on de Gaulle.

Note that, whilst a few history syllabuses come through to the present (London Syllabus D for example) most have a clearly stated end date and it would obviously be a waste of precious revision time to take any topic beyond this date in anything except the most outline form.

ESSENTIAL PRINCIPLES

THE COLD WAR

ORIGINS IN EUROPE

This a dramatic and oft told story. In world history syllabuses it is best studied as one important part of the emerging rivalry of the superpowers. Start with the successes of the Red Army across Eastern Europe, find out what happened at the meeting of the allied leaders at Potsdam and be ready to outline the matters, such as the future of Poland and Germany, and the terms on which United States aid to Europe was to be provided (on hich the quite artificial wartime alliance drifted apart). Beware of propaganda from all sides. So far as the states of Western Europe were concerned the issues which loomed large were the Berlin Blockade; the division of Germany into increasingly hostile zones; the communist coup in Czechoslovakia; the formation of NATO, and the Warsaw Pact. Throughout these years the United States umbrella loomed large. The existence of a hostile, potentially dangerous, ideologically different, Eastern Bloc is from 1949 a constant pre-occupation for Western European statesmen. As you read of the developments within Western Europe bear in mind the importance of the Cold War in influencing events, particularly in encouraging moves towards mutual co-operation in a variety of spheres.

> “Origins of the Cold War – frequently a source of questions.”

GERMAN RECOVERY

Start with the post-war devastation, the unconditional surrender, and the division of the country into four occupied zones. The Federal Republic of Germany (FRG) was set up in 1949; and the politics of its early years centre around its first Chancellor, *Konrad Adenauer*. Assessment of his political achievement both in building up the West German State and in his increasingly controversial role in later years has become one of the most common questions on this topic. You need to develop a view of the credit he and his government deserve for the dramatic recovery of the economy. His relations with his economics minister, *Erhard*, with the chief opposition party, the SPD, and his attitude towards the communists, are all important. His external work, in securing international recognition and respect for the new state, should be noted, as indeed should his fiercely pro-western stance in all foreign policy matters.

> “Questions on Adenauer figure prominently . . .”

The Federal Republic's recovery from the devastation of the war until, by the 1960s, it had the strongest economy in Western Europe, has been labelled the West German '*economic miracle*'. The causes of this form the basis of another commonly set question. The effect of the economic policies of Ludwig Erhard need to be assessed, as indeed does the contribution made by political stability and by American aid. You need to be able to comment on the economic aspects, especially an abundant labour supply, an enterprise culture with low taxation and public spending and capital available for long-term investment. Prepared material for an Adenauer question alone is not an adequate basis for the equally common economic miracle question. If you revise one, revise both. In the 1970s and 1980s the pace of economic growth slowed but the German economy, with low inflation, a strong currency and high labour productivity, remained the envy of the rest of Western Europe.

> “. . . but revise the causes of the German economic miracle as well.”

A third popular topic for examination questions is the rise to power in the 1960s of the Social Democrats (SPD) which is closely related to the policies and appeal of their leader *Willi Brandt*; the 'Outline Answer' to examination Question 4 later in this chapter considers this topic. From the 1969 election the SPD held office until 1982 but towards the end of the period were troubled by economic recession; they split on how to deal with it. The Christian Democrats formed a government in 1982 and under Chancellor *Kohl* were still in office when the 1989 political revolutions in East Germany provided a totally new, and quite unexpected, framework for the conduct of German politics. These dramatic developments brought to an end a distinctive period in German history which had begun in the defeats of the Second World War.

> “A third German topic.”

POST-WAR FRANCE

The most popular question with students is one on *de Gaulle* whose contribution to the French political life must be revised: do not forget the early days after the liberation of France for they set the scene for his later career. Be warned that examiners seem to struggle to avoid asking too straightforward questions on de Gaulle. On the other hand thorough revision material on him is likely to be of value in many other French questions, providing only that you are able to adapt to the question as set.

> “Questions on de Gaulle are popular.”

THE FOURTH REPUBLIC

“Constitutional weaknesses of the Fourth Republic.”

The weaknesses of the Fourth French Republic is the other standard topic on France in the 1950s and a survey of these should start with the main features of the constitution of 1946, with a system of voting based on proportional representation, elections only possible every five years and a figure-head president chosen by the Assembly. All this de Gaulle saw as a recipe for feeble short-lived coalition governments which prompted his voluntary retirement from political life. In twelve years only one government survived for more than a year.

Its collapse

The difficulties experienced by the Fourth Republic included some arising from France's imperial past: French military disasters in, and the 1954 withdrawal from, Indo-China and, in 1956, the far from successful Suez adventure. Most important of all there was the difficult situation in Algeria where French settlers, the Colons, had since 1954 faced an increasingly aggressive nationalist movement. Events in Algeria in 1958 and their repercussions in France, as the Colons and the French Army lost confidence in the succession of Paris governments, led to fears that the French army in Algeria might stage a coup and even invade France itself. It was to prevent this possibility and to solve the Algerian crisis that de Gaulle was recalled to political life.

Accounting for the collapse of the Fourth Republic often has added to it an invitation to consider any positive achievements of the period; the economic progress; the expanded social provisions (especially family allowances) to encourage population growth; and credit for pushing along the wider vision of European co-operation, are the most obvious points to make. The 'Student's Answer' at the end of this section opens up many of the relevant issues.

THE FIFTH REPUBLIC

The Algerian Crisis, which spanned the last years of the Fourth and the early years of the Fifth Republic, is relevant to many issues and is worth understanding in detail. It could be of value in general questions on the decline of European power in the wider world.

New constitution

“Evaluating the Fifth Republic.”

De Gaulle insisted that a new constitution be drawn up and after its approval in a referendum it became in January 1959 the basis of the Fifth Republic. The most important feature of the constitution of the Fifth Republic in contrast to that of the Fourth Republic was the establishment of a much stronger presidency. The president nominated the prime minister and if the latter lost assembly support then the president could call an election to break the deadlock and make the politicians accountable to the voters. De Gaulle became the first president and in 1962 used his presidential right to put an issue to the people directly by referendum. It was to force through the direct election of future presidents by the people, rather than by the Assembly. In 1965 he went on to win the first such election. You can hardly assess de Gaulle's political achievements without commenting on the consitution he imposed on the state. This and the granting of independence first, in 1962, to Algeria and then to the rest of the French colonies in Africa, must rank as his main political achievements.

Foreign policy

De Gaulle's characteristically independent foreign policy as president of the Fifth Republic forms an interesting and easily appreciated aspect of any wider assessment of the man. Relations with the United States and with Britain were usually prickly. He spoke much of French honour and greatness but he was far-sighted enough to see that the days of vast overseas empires were over and this stands as a great contribution to his country's history. If your syllabus comes up to the present day be prepared to comment, however briefly, on the style and the achievements of de Gaulle's successors as presidents of the Fifth Republic. Start with the list of names and dates contained in the 'Useful Information' section later in this chapter.

“Know something about de Gaulle's successors.”

THE EUROPEAN COMMUNITY

ITS ESTABLISHMENT AND EXPANSION

This is not as exciting a topic as it might appear. There is a lot of factual information to be organised on the chronology and the different stages of the development. Unless you are prepared to master this it may be a topic to avoid: equally once the facts are known you will have to resist merely listing developments instead of answering the question as set! The most interesting questions on this topic are on the motives of those who strove for Western European co-operation and on why, both initially and later, states sought to join the European Community. The reluctance of other states to commit themselves needs noting and commenting on. British relations with de Gaulle on the issue could well be a question in its own right but do not twist a general question on the overall attractions of membership to European states into an answer purely on Britain or you will pay heavily for it.

“Motives for creating the European Community.”

“It needs more than just some British information.”

Another range of questions can arise from an assessment of the effect the Community has had on the economy of the region and on the lives of inhabitants of the member countries. You will need to be able to comment on the work of Community institutions which will involve an understanding of their respective roles. You should also be ready to offer illustrations of economic benefits and economic problems. Many of these remain the object of current media coverage. It will still be necessary for you to provide the historical dimension and the 'Outline Answer' to Question 2 at the end of this section will give you some of the main relevant points.

BRITAIN'S RELATIONS WITH THE EUROPEAN COMMUNITY

“One aspect of Britain's post-war search for a role.”

This could well be expanded, in a British paper, into British attitudes since 1945 towards continental Europe, which is in turn one aspect of Britain losing an empire and seeking a role in the post-war world. From the Community's point of view it is only one aspect of an overall development. Resist the temptation to turn Community questions into British questions. If your only knowledge of the development of the European Community, its policies and institutions, comes from the continuing debates in the British media on British relations and attitudes towards the wider community, then it could well be advisable to look elsewhere for an examination question.

OTHER STATES OF WESTERN EUROPE

GREECE, ITALY, PORTUGAL AND SPAIN

There is an element of lottery about revising for questions on the internal affairs of these nations. Only do so after checking your strategy against the offerings in past papers and only then if you find particular interest in the country. There are worse reasons for studying a country's history than the fact that you had an enjoyable holiday there but in terms of examination effort do keep a sense of proportion regarding the amount of time you are prepared to invest in the necessary historical study. The precarious survival of democracy in Greece from 1945 to its joining the EEC is one possible theme: the moves from autocracy to democracy in both Portugal and Spain are others. Italian questions, except perhaps on the economy, often seem to cause difficulties.

“Greece: Portugal: Spain?”

THE NINETIES

THEMES AND ISSUES

Trying to predict what questions the examiners will set either because of anniversaries of notable events or, as here, because of current social and political trends, can be a hit or miss business. It might however be a very good revision device, making you think about your history instead of just learning it. Relations between Western Europe and its eastern neighbours, including the USSR, might well spark off examination questions in the future. Remember though that they will be historical questions looking back in time and will need revising in that form. Current affairs knowledge may enable you to bluff your way through one such question but it remains a poor strategy for examination revision. A-level economics study could give some students a more secure base for answering very modern questions. Remember too that some examination boards are setting papers over two years ahead of the examination date.

USEFUL INFORMATION

1945	Defeat of Germany: end of the Second World War.
1947	Beginning of Marshall Aid to Europe.
1948	Blockade of Berlin and the western airlift.
1949	NATO formed (North Atlantic Treaty Organisation).

1953	European Coal and Steel Community (ECSC) set up by the 'Six' – France, FRG, Italy, Belgium, Holland, Luxembourg.
1955	The 'Six' start to plan further co-operation.
1957 Mar	Rome Treaties set up European Economic Community (EEC) and Euratom.
1958 Jan	EEC and Euratom came into existence.
1959	European Free Trade Association (EFTA) formed.
1963	De Gaulle vetoed British application to join EEC.
1967	ECSC, EEC and Euratom merged to form the European Community (EC).
1973	Britain, Eire and Denmark joined the EC.
1981	Greece joined the EC.
1986	Portugal and Spain joined the EC.
1992	The Maastricht Treaty agreed between the member states.

France

1944	Allies recognised de Gaulle as head of the provisional French government.
1946	Fourth Republic established: de Gaulle stepped aside.
1946–1958	Political instability but economic progress.
1954	Defeat in Indo-China at Dien Bien Phu: French withdrew.
1954	Beginning of Algerian Nationalist struggle for independence.
1956	The Suez affair
1958	Algerian crisis reached its climax.
	De Gaulle became chief minister with emergency powers.
	Formation of Fifth Republic.
1959	De Gaulle President of the Republic.
1962	Algeria granted independence.
	Constitution changed so that president elected directly.
1965	De Gaulle elected President
1966	De Gaulle withdrew France from NATO: developed French nuclear deterrent.
1968	Year of student agitations.
1969	De Gaulle resigned after losing a referendum.
1970	Death of de Gaulle
1969–1974	Pompidou President
1974–1981	Giscard d'Estaing President
1981	Mitterand (Socialist) President
1986	Chirac (Gaullist) became Prime Minister
1988	Mitterand defeated Chirac in presidential election

West Germany

An era ending?

1949	Federal Republic of Germany (West Germany) founded.
	Konrad Adenauer of Christian Democrats (CDU) Chancellor.
1961	Building of the Berlin Wall
1963	Adenauer resigned as Chancellor of West Germany.
1963–1966	Erhard (CDU) Chancellor
1964	Willi Brandt elected leader of Social Democrats (SPD).
1966–1969	Kiesinger (CDU) Chancellor Brandt in Coalition Government.
1969	SPD win election
1973	West Germany joined United Nations.
1969–1974	Brandt Chancellor until forced to resign over spy scandal.
1974–1982	Helmut Schmidt (SPD) Chancellor
1982	Helmut Kohl (CDU) Chancellor in Coalition Government.
1983	Election: swing to right, Kohl Chancellor in CDU government.
1989	The Berlin Wall came down.
1989–1990	Moves to re-unite West (FRG) and East Germany (the GDR).
1990	Union of the two countries completed, but leading to further internal political tensions and an increase in violent attacks on foreign immigrants.

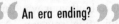

EXAMINATION QUESTIONS

Q1 How far was US assistance responsible for the recovery and prosperity of Europe after 1945? (Oxford 1989)

Q2 Evaluate the political and economic consequences, to 1973, of the formation of the European Economic Community. (AEB 1989)

Q3 Why and how, during the 1960s, did the West German Christian Democrats lose power to the Social Democrats? (London 1988)

Q4 Assess the validity of the assertion that 'by 1958 the Fourth Republic had failed the people of France'. (London 1989)

Q5 'In the fifteen years or so after 1945 West Germany proved politically stable while France was politically unstable.' How do you account for this? (Northern Ireland 1989)

Q6 Assess the relative importance of the forces promoting greater unity amongst the nations of Western Europe since 1945. (London 1989)

OUTLINE ANSWERS

Question 1

Introduction: indicate devastated state of Europe after the war. Indicate also the main spheres of US assistance:

- Bretton Woods conference
- GATT
- the IMF
- US loans to Britain
- 1947 Marshall Aid programme – the cornerstone

All leaned heavily on US initiatives and finance.

Effect of US aid: West European states owed much to this – aid came to 12,500 million dollars by 1951 under the European Recovery Programme, it encouraged a broad measure of economic co-operation under the OECD and led also to currency agreements. Argue that it was US initiatives that created the climate for continental European countries to come together later in the EEC also enabling their economies to prosper in the 1950s; difficult to see how they could have replaced their lost capital equipment without US help in this time span.

Conclusion: the big qualification is that none of this assisted the eastern European countries at all. Indeed argue it had a negative effect by driving the USSR and its satellites into an economic isolation that was to distort their economies for the next forty years.

Question 2

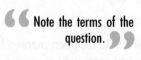

"Note the terms of the question."

Note: Period is 1958–73 only: both political and economic needed.

Economic: agriculture main area affected, guaranteed prices and food mountains. Fishing affected more slowly. Internal customs removed, external protectionism, currency exchange rates regulated. Heavy industry planned on international scale (also power industry). Investment in projects promoted. Results can be seen in economic growth rates which outstripped other countries of western Europe, especially Britain.

Political: was it just a rich man's club, dividing Europe into rich and poor? One political consequence was more countries wanting to join – Britain from 1960s. New prosperity helped political stability in western Europe but had little effect on East-West relations where continuing Cold War meant Nato took lead. Nationalism continued (cite de Gaulle) but France and Germany at last forgot their bitter rivalry.

Conclusion: still a half finished story in 1973 but economically by then the world's third largest market; political consequences, in and outside Europe were, in 1973, incalculable because it was impossible then to envisage the final political arrangements within the EEC.

Question 3

How: explain first:

- Retirement of Adenauer as Chancellor 1963.
- Erhard less able.

- 1966 Kiesinger succeeded him – forced into coalition with Social Democrats 1966.
- 1964 Brandt became leader of Social Democrats.
- 1966 coalition with Christian Democrats gave experience of office.
- 1969 election won 22 seats, and formed coalition government with Free Democrats – Brandt Chancellor.

Why:

- A mixture of CDU 'mistakes' and growing appeal of SPD where Brandt leadership appeal crucial – explain this.
- 1969 Election is central point of explanation.
  - CDU suffered from loss of the economic momentum in Germany and from its image of uncaring social policies
  - SPD captured middle ground votes as it lost its Marxist image
- Brandt Ostpolitik and possibility of better relations with the East helped greatly.

Conclusion: German 'economic miracle' increasingly taken for granted, Brandt 'charisma' and promise of more active social and positive foreign policies better represented German mood in 1960s as memories of wartime faded.

Question 4

See the 'Student's Answer' later in this chapter.

Question 5

General theme: this is really two separate topics but at some point it will need some comparative comments. Analyse reasons for French instability, then analyse reasons for German stability. This makes up bulk of answer but a general conclusion is still needed.

Conclusion: for example German defeat total, radical economic action therefore essential, totally new constitution under shadow of communist threat. Adenauer able to impose tough political and economic measures, these made palatable by US aid. France intact at the end of the war, all the old political divisions re-asserted themselves and prevented an authoritarian constitution. France was still living with its pre-war political weaknesses whilst, paradoxically, total German defeat enabled it to make a new start.

Note: Ideally comparative style questions are best answered point by point – 'in Germany this applied . . . whereas in France . . .' and so on. In the case of this particular question it would be a very good student who, in examination conditions, could rise to such heights!

Question 6

See the 'Tutor's Answer' that follows.

A TUTOR'S ANSWER TO QUESTION 6

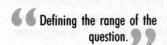

"Defining the range of the question."

The two areas in which the history of Western Europe has, since 1945, been marked by greater unity are in terms of defence against external enemies and in respect of economic co-operation or at least through the establishment of common economic markets leading to attempts at economic rationalisation. This move to economic unity has in turn brought about moves towards political unity.

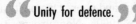

"Unity for defence."

The main vehicle for co-operation in defence has been the North Atlantic Treaty Organisation founded in 1949. It is not all-embracing, since the early 1960s France has been the most notable absentee. There is no doubt that the overwhelming force that created NATO was fear of perceived Soviet expansionism in Eastern and Central Europe which might well in turn become a threat to the integrity of the nations of Western Europe. The Berlin Blockade and the communist coup in Czechoslovakia were central moments in this. It was easy in the late 1940s to see Western Europe as open to conquest by the vast and victorious Red Army. Both distrust of Russian expansionism and ideological fears of communism had a part to play in this. Russia was increasingly seen as an enemy to be guarded against by West European political leaders ranging from the emerging strong man of West Germany's right-wing Christian Democrats, Konrad Adenauer, to the Prime Minister and Foreign Secretary in the British Labour government, Attlee and Bevin. Another factor contributing to a unified defence structure for Western Europe was the anxiety of the United States not to have to continue shouldering all the burden of western defence so that far from discouraging the development of a common approach to military strategy the US did all it could to promote it.

These defence considerations remained valid during the next 45 years and of such force that, with the exception of France, the European members of NATO were happy to maintain their common military umbrella.

"Moving the answer on to economic unity."

The other area in which there were remarkable developments towards unity in the 1950s and 1960s was in relation to economic matters. From the Coal and Steel Community and Euratom developed the European Economic Community which in 1967 became the European Community. The original driving force behind these bodies was undoubtedly a move to economic efficiency in industries that required vast amounts of capital either for re-organisation or to establish initially. In both cases a rationalisation of competition and markets was seen as an additional benefit; with larger markets both industrial and agrarian production would be conducted more efficiently to the benefit of both producers and consumers. The formation of the Benelux customs area had been a first step in 1947 but now the pace was being set by a new-found co-operation between France and Germany.

The vast destruction of national economies during the Second World War had spurred on these efforts at unity but as well as economic forces there were good political reasons behind these moves. The emergence of those enormously strong powers, the United States and the Soviet Union, lent support to the idea that the relatively small nations of Western Europe must co-operate with each other or be dominated by one of the superpowers.

"Now the political motives."

Political idealism also played an important part in both the economic arrangements and the political developments towards unity which followed. The statesmen of the 1940s and 1950s had the memory of the bitter national quarrels of earlier decades still close to them; these had led Europe close to destruction and it seemed that a conscious move to unity was the best means of preventing their repetition. This was certainly a factor which greatly influenced the French and German statesmen in their early moves. The European Parliament set up in these early days was another product of this idealism as was the Council of Europe set up to promote international discussions between parliamentarians and ministers.

The later political moves, which after 1967 began to be debated within the Economic Community had a more pragmatic force behind them. The economic power of the European Community over its members became greater and affected people's lives more and more. It became necessary to ensure that it functioned rationally and was controlled to the common good. So in 1967 a strong executive was created in the Commission. This in turn led to only partially successful efforts to breathe life into the European Parliament through European elections. Idealism ran high in this but the results have been meagre.

The forces promoting all these moves towards unity have been so varied that proposing a rank order of importance seems artificial. Fear, idealism and greed were all present and often closely inter-linked. The economic advantages of unity were those usually paraded but it can well be argued that the prime motive behind all the steps to unity was that which lay directly behind the formation of NATO for in a world dominated by hostile superpowers the nations of Western Europe were too small to stand safely alone.

"Attempts an overall conclusion on the 'forces'."

A STUDENT'S ANSWER TO QUESTION 4

The Fourth Republic lasted from 1946 to 1958. Throughout these years it was dogged by political instability to such an extent that it can well be claimed that by 1958 it had failed the French people.

In the twelve years it existed there were twenty one different governments. There were two reasons for this. Firstly the republic's constitution laid down a fixed period between elections for the Parliament (Chamber of Deputies) which even the President could not alter. When a government was defeated in the Chamber then the Deputies had to look among themselves for someone who had enough support to form a new government. There was no way of having an election and getting a more stable government according to the votes of the people. Secondly there were too many parties in France and

"A clear account."

under the proportional representation system of voting most of them had seats in the Chamber of Deputies. Any government had to be a coalition of parties which could easily fall out over an issue and have to resign. This was made worse because the Communist Party of the Left and the RPF (Gaullists) of the Right were at different times quite strong. If a Coalition annoyed them then they would vote together to overthrow it but then there was no way they would work together to form a new coalition. Under this system it was easier to destroy governments than it was to make them. Another reason for instability was the creation of a neo-Fascist party led by Pierre Poujade which towards the end of the Republic gained over 50 deputies. They despised the other parties and were happy to wreck governments but could never build one themselves.

Once a government was beaten it could take weeks of negotiation to form a new one.

All this political weakness meant that the country's problems were not being dealt with, especially inflation and industrial strikes by miners and the Renault car workers. When some Prime Ministers like Mendes France tried to be tough and deal with these matters they lost the support of the other parties in the Coalition because no party wanted to be unpopular with the people.

"Too limited a discussion of the Republic's achievements."

Some things did improve under the Fourth Republic. Farming became more prosperous and France helped to form the European Coal and Steel Community on the way to forming the Common Market. Socially the main improvement was with the introduction of family allowances so that the birth rate, always a problem in France, began to rise.

The most important failure of the Fourth Republic was its failure to solve the crisis in Algeria. There had also been defeats in Vietnam and the fiasco at Suez. But the Algerian crisis was much more serious and it looked as though the French army there was going to invade France in order to force the government to defend the French settlers against the Algerian nationalists. A strong leader was needed to deal with this and the only man was de Gaulle who was allowed to become Chief Minister, but he had already said he would not work under the constitution and so he was given emergency powers to run the country and to set up a new constitution. This was the end of the Fourth Republic.

"The argument needs pulling together at the end."

EXAMINER COMMENTS

This essay has many strong points, it tries to answer directly and argues both for and against the quotation. It could well gain a C mark.

Its main weakness is that it forgets about the French people. Some, like the shopkeepers who voted for Poujade, or the white settlers in Algeria, felt that they had been failed. The peasants with the guaranteed farm prices, which are not mentioned, were quite prosperous; even the discontented started to desert Poujade before the end of the Republic. So a brief survey of different categories of French people would have been directly relevant.

The essay needs more substance at some points, especially in the paragraph that argues that there were some things going quite well and perhaps also on foreign policy where you could develop a strong argument that in Vietnam, Suez and Algeria the Republic failed France badly. The writer of this essay avoids the trap of describing at length all that happened in the Algerian crisis.

A final brief conclusion is needed to pull the argument together. Could you now write one in ten lines? A reference to the fact that, in a referendum in 1962, de Gaulle's destruction of the Fourth Republic was overwhelmingly approved by the French people, suggesting that they then felt that it had failed, might form an effective last sentence.

USEFUL SOURCES OF INFORMATION

General reading

A Ramm, *Europe in the Twentieth Century 1905–1970*, Longman 1984

J B Watson, *Success in World History since 1945*, John Murray 1989

Further reading

P Calvocoressi, *World Politics Since 1945*, Longman (6th edition) 1991

W Carr, *A History of Germany 1815 –1990*, Arnold (4th Edition) 1991

M E Chamberlain, *Decolonization: The Fall of the European Empires*, Blackwell (for the Historical Association) 1985

A Cobban, *A History of Modern France 1871–1962*, Penguin 1965

P Neville, *France 1914 –1969: The Three Republics*, Hodder and Stoughton 1993

J R Wegs, *Europe Since 1945*, Macmillan (3rd edition) 1991

Linked topic areas

- The outcome and effects of the Second World War
- Britain since 1945 (see Chapters 10 and 11)
- The Cold War
- United States relations with Europe since 1945
- Eastern Europe since 1945
- The end of European Empires since the Second World War
- The history of individual countries of Western Europe in the second half of the twentieth century

INDEX